Dennis O'Harrow: Plan Talk and Plain Talk

Dennis O'Harrow, 1961

DENNIS O'HARROW:

Plan Talk and Plain Talk

Marjorie S. Berger, Editor

Planners Press
American Planning Association
Washington, D.C.   Chicago, Illinois

Contents

Foreword

It is staggering to take a Dennisean revel through the variety of subjects on which he wrote and spoke with brevity, with authority, and with rare and wonderful levity over a 20-year period.

He developed to a fine art the skill of patient and pungent persuasion. And this, after all, is still the heart of planning in a democratic society.

His monthly voice from the heartland came to personify democratic planning in our times. One suspects it was rather by choice than by accident that he maintained that mid-American position, that Midwestern stance as interpreter, translator, mediator, and critic of the practice of city planning in the U.S. and abroad. O'Harrow stayed "out there." And it was from "out there" that he chose his targets, found his mark, and spread his words.

As an editor O'Harrow had a superb collection of native gifts and developed talents. His legacies include hundreds of speeches to a miscellany of audiences, and some 14 years of monthly editorials in the *ASPO Newsletter*.

His 20 years with ASPO were spent in a position of great trust although not immediate power; his was leverage with which to move men's minds, but not power to shift their position of the moment. His was often a voice of reason in a world where the raw exercise of political and economic bribery and/or power to promote speculative profit has been and remains commonplace.

The power to plan is the power to advise and—increasingly—to decide that one man shall profit from his access to scarce resources, and that the next man shall not.

Lacking such direct, personal power, Dennis O'Harrow used his writing as a pervasive educational force. He attacked the buying and selling of zoning rights long before national magazines did so and, although he never had that independence which came from owning his own journal, he substituted independence of intelligence and of judgment in what he wrote and in what he spoke. He was that rare person—the conscience of his profession.

Simple were his weapons: a penchant for clear thought, a zest for precise and varied language in many forms, a capacity for phrase making, a dislike of stuffed shirts and their windbaggery; and a capacity to play many roles, from court jester to outraged father, from waggish raconteur to nagging Dutch uncle.

Had he been more brutish, personal, and vituperative—in a profession which was attracting more than its share of paper tigers, witch doctors, and barkers of dubious remedies—he would have enjoyed great controversy—and survived only a couple of years.

As it was, he chose to outlast his enemies—up to the moment in August 1967 when the choice was no longer his—and to operate in the belief that ASPO was a medium of communication rather than a vehicle of personal power.

Now, it was to mundane tasks of training others to think and write clearly, of inspiring and advising uncounted men and women on wiser courses, sounder policies, that he concentrated many effective energies.

Rather than in magic, he believed in logic, in organization of language, lucidity of image, the persuasive power of the small and the concrete. He was concerned with conversational street furniture—things that ordinary people bump up against in daily life, and know in their bones and viscera.

Most of his writing was straightforward exposition, packed with metaphors, analogy, and illusions. But those editorials! Here you could expect a change of pace—blockbusters, fables on mink-covered beer can openers, scripts for not-so-fictional zoning hearings, and those To-Whom-It-May-Concern letters. His phrases were pervasive, spreading through the literature like trace elements in the body politic.

Master he was of the final clincher. The solution to certain air pollution problems, he wrote in November 1966, is quite simple: "No federal assistance unless the completed project meets strict standards on the emission of air pollutants: no tax relief unless the new plant is clean." Time and again his colons were warnings: here comes that final punchline. What was operating all this time was a highly developed capacity to look back dispassionately—even at what he himself had just written. He practiced the second look, the double take.

Analogies flowed easily to his mind, and such a skill made his speeches unforgettable. It was an analogy of his—a delightful word picture of a man piling sand up higher and higher, past the angle of repose, until it slipped and sprawled down again—that first caught my ear and inner eye as a reporter covering an O'Harrow speech in 1949.

That old literary coin trick of reverse imagery was another, as when he wrote an essay on "The Ten Worst Cities." He made definitions work for him, instead of the other way around, beginning his review of Jane Jacobs' book with the headline, "Jacobin Revival," followed by a damning definition of the word *Jacobin*.

Occasionally he grew cynical or even sounded hopeless—even as the rest of us. I think he may often have been unhappy, for his editorials show an extraordinary capacity to see both sides of controversies. He knew how often responsible men in public positions are "damned if you do, and damned if you don't."

There was about him a touch of the old-fashioned, cranky moralist that resisted oleagenous public relations gestures, and those lingo-jingoists, the superpatriots of the obvious.

He was ahead of his time, but not too far ahead of his readers. He praised performance standards for industrial zoning early in the game, and he—quite early—questioned imposing huge public housing sites on poor people.

And this brings me in closing to his "Prayer for Perspective," in 1959, which he called the confession of "a middle-class American with a Middle-Western rural background:"

> "Let me, oh Lord, offer my neighbor a free choice, the same thing that I reserve for myself....
> "Let me not say to him 'Take my culture, do as I do, think as I think....'
> "Let me, oh Lord, be not precipitate, but make me go out and walk around the block and consider the diversity of Thy creatures."

Grady Clay, Editor
Landscape Architecture

Preface

"Mr. Planning" was one of the titles given to Dennis O'Harrow. "Widely recognized as the official voice of the city planning movement in the United States" was the way it was stated in the program notes for the first North Carolina Planning Conference in 1958; "the center of and advisor to the planning profession in this country" was the way he was identified by the financial editor of the *Cincinnati Enquirer* in 1962.

His own description of his role is exemplified in his letter to his Martinsville (Indiana) High School class in response to a request to "send an account of yourself" for a class reunion:

> I am Executive Director of the American Society of Planning Officials. My job is to worry about what is happening to cities. From time to time I hop around the country so I can worry about a city while actually looking at it.

How much he hoped and worried, and how well he earned the title of "Mr. Planning," or as "Papa ASPO" (as he sometimes referred to himself) to the many people who turned to him and counted on him, or as "the conscience of the planning profession," as he was characterized in Memorial Tributes, the following pages reveal. But it is not just for a recapture—it is for a continuance of his extraordinary ability to counsel and to open the minds and consciences of others—that this book is intended. The guiding test in preparing it has been that this legacy of his innovative and knowledgeable opinions, no-nonsense idealism, hard-hitting and humane advocacy, and delightful verbal artistry have as important a meaning for audiences today as during the 20 years of his writings.

The number and diversity of his audiences are astonishing. The frequency of his fresh ideas on specific assigned subjects is even more amazing. He never used a speech twice, although, a speech was sometimes the basis for an editorial, and many were reprinted. Occasionally, a DOH "law" or "prophecy" reappeared a year or so later in another speech or article—further refined. And a number of his beliefs and worries kept cropping up: the vital role of public officials and citizens; the achievement of mutual understanding between planners and those affected by their plans; the full significance of the impact of population growth; the inattention to the basic resources of air, water, and land; the questions of ethics; the dilemmas, the tools, the trends and the future of planners, planning, and of cities. Underlying all was a worry, and a belief, expressed in one of his admonitions: "Refuse to compromise with any proposals that threaten to violate human rights and human dignity."

Among his most memorable habits were humor, word pictures, and his crusade against jargon. ("Anything that can be said in planning can also be said in English.")

The titles he gave to speeches and editorials are also memorable—some becoming a means of communicating an entire message: for example, "Have you had your melon pinched?" from his 1953 editorial protesting certain recruiting practices, which he titled "Lady, *Please* Don't Pinch the Melons!"

He also had a habit of dropping bombs: "A visiting city planner from Chicago startled a conference of traffic experts . . . Dennis O'Harrow . . . punctured virtually all the conventional approaches to solution of New York's traffic congestion problem." (*New York Herald Tribune*); "Dennis O'Harrow . . . dropped a bomb on the 2,200 planners at ASPO's convention in Toronto. Said he: 'It is time that we recognize publicly that a small—but still much, much too large— group of public officials are engaged in selling zoning favors for a price!' " (*House and Home Magazine*).

Some insight to the quantity, variety and reach of his product is provided by the Bibliography, in which editorials, speeches, articles, research reports, and miscellaneous material not excerpted for this book have also been included. The quantity, variety, and reach of his correspondence—much of which also included nuggets of advice, explanation, warnings, reflections—is incalculable, and unretrievable except in certain special instances. An invaluable source of background material has been some large envelopes of newspaper clippings on his speeches. Notebooks and card files with ideas he was developing for editorials and speeches were, unhappily, cryptic jottings—with an occasional teasing title such as "Duck in the Puddle" and the indication that this was to be another DOH "law." (He also had a habit of diagramming the wiring for his greenhouse, or including notes for his Sunday school class or a meeting of the mathematics committee of the Flossmoor High School, in amongst his notes on planning!)

Another dimension to consider is that in addition to his writings, he was an itinerant—as speech maker, conference goer, and conscientious worker on numerous committees and boards (and as an adviser wherever he was); he was a constant contributor to ASPO's research publications and answers to inquiries as well as a more-than-full-time ASPO executive director; and he was a public official in his home town.

Editing a brilliant and prolific writer is not an easy task, and when practically everything has a message, an approach and turn of phrase, and a careful bit of research, the weeding and cutting demand many hard decisions. Priority has been given to the currency for today and for the future. Many pages of facts on localities or then current statistics and situations, carefully assembled to back up his thesis for that day, have had to be omitted under this guiding rule, with inevitable injustice to his raconteur-researcher combination and his skilled imagery *cum* logical development of thought. The material has, of course, been considerably condensed, and lightly edited. Documentation of this with ellipses and brackets has been omitted as too intrusive and disruptive of the text. Some major works that exist in published form have been omitted entirely, but are noted in the Bibliography.

Various alternatives were proposed initially on ways to organize the subject matter: for example, in accordance with the ideals he worked for, his basic objectives; for example, in accordance with the changing scene in planning and how he illuminated different facets at different times; for example, in accordance with the principle of maximum utility to a great variety of people, such as his original audiences. The organization that developed from the subsequent reading of the varied types of material—from the range of subject matter and the time span of 20 years—classifies the papers in nine chapters, each with its own internal principle of organization, rather than all conforming to one overall system. There are numerous cases where a particular paper could have been placed in another chapter with equal validity, and the decision on which section would be most appropriate had to be equally arbitrary.

Many of his titles, albeit intriguing, are cryptic. In some instances a phrase from a paper has been used, or added as an introduction to a series of extracts. In fact, the title of this book is borrowed from one of his speeches.

The headings include identification of dates and audiences. Commentaries contain some additional explanatory data. This eliminated footnotes. (In commenting on a manuscript submitted to him for review, DOH once said, "I disparage the use of substantial footnotes at the bottom of the page, in the back of the book, or anywhere else. Either put it in the text or forget it.")

Frank So, deputy executive director of the American Planning Association and an ASPO staff member during the last half-dozen O'Harrow years, reviewed the entire manuscript. Fred Bair, Jr., assisted with an initial selection of editorials and together with Israel Stollman and Grady Clay, served in an advisory capacity. The enormous task of typing the manuscript was done by Shirley Mallace— who had also transcribed many of the papers as secretary to DOH since 1961. Frank So and Sylvia Lewis supervised the publishing; Sandi Schroeder prepared the manuscript for printing.

One of the hundreds of comments DOH received over the years from his audiences was "Please continue exposing the sacred cows." Another said, "It is good to be able to laugh at our weakness and you are to be commended for leading the laughter and for the thoughtfulness of your humor. Your thinking obviously delves deeply into these matters." One of the messages received after his death said, "His keen sense of responsibility . . . places a responsibility on us all to try to maintain the intellectual and ethical standards for which he stood." He was called "a friend and a help . . . and the results of his help will be felt in many ways for years to come."

To encourage the continuing exposure of sacred cows, continuing laughter, continuing thoughtful and deep delving into matters, and a continuing sense of responsibility to maintain intellecutal and ethical standards—this is what Dennis O'Harrow would want this volume of his papers to accomplish. Above all, he would want to continue to be a friend and a help, and this is the prime objective of this publication.

Marjorie S. Berger, Editor

Introduction to the DOH Perspectives

A Prayer for Perspective

The ASPO Newsletter editorial, November 1959.

Dear Lord:

I have a monstrous problem and I need help. I do not like slums and I want to sweep them from my land. Help me to clear the scales from my eyes. Help me to see the people of the slums as clearly as I see the buildings that surround them.

I would not live in a slum. Nor do I believe that anyone else should be forced to live in a slum.

But help me to remember that I am a middle-class American with a middle western rural background. And I hope my friends remember that they too are like me, perhaps from a New England village or a small city or a large city with two or three or ten generations of American ancestors. Or maybe they are just first- or second-generation Americans but persons who adapted themselves quickly and easily to my middle-class American culture, like ducks to water.

So when I look at a slum and get incensed and roll up my sleeves and start to do something about it, let me, Oh Lord, be not precipitate, but make me go out and walk around the block and consider the diversity of Thy creatures.

I know that I like my own kind. They speak my language. It is no worse, but let me remember it is no better than any other language. I have my gods, which are likewise no worse and no better than other folks' gods.

Because my strength when I set out to destroy a slum is as the strength of one hundred million men and a thousand billion dollars, I can so easily destroy gods and language and customs and a thousand other values that are strange to me. Caution me to make haste slowly.

Often, Oh Lord, I find myself thinking "strange" and "foreign" and "different" are the same as "inferior" and "dangerous." I am moved to

1

attack instantly, as a small boy hurls a stone at each snake he finds. Or in my magnanimity I try to shove my own brand, my middle-class American culture, on others. Because, unthinking, I mistakenly feel it must be the best or else I would not maintain it.

My intentions are good, Oh Lord, but we both remember what paves the road to hell.

I do not like murder and robbery or any crime and I am apt to equate them with slums. Yet I must confess that my culture glorifies and produces violence in Gargantuan quantity for cinema and television and exports it for the education of the entire world. Someday I must have a talk with You about this.

I have thought a lot about segregation, Oh Lord, and I have concluded that I do not like forced segregation. I do not believe that just because a man's language or religion or skin color is not the same as mine I should quarantine him until he learns my language, bows to my gods, or changes the color of his skin. This does not jibe with my own culture because I have an axiom on the diginity of the individual human being.

But I have also concluded, Oh Lord, that in my zeal to help, to erase that slum that my different neighbor lives in, I may be just as cruel to scatter his group as I was when I put a barbed wire fence around him. I use the word "ghetto" to describe the area in which my different neighbor and his fellows live. I have made it an unpleasant word, because it reminded me of my guilt in imprisoning strange and foreign persons, isolating them until they forsook their strange and foreign ways and adopted mine. Because to divide is to make conquest easy, I am not sure—I may be only using a new method to make him over in my image.

Let me, Oh Lord, offer my neighbor a free choice, the same that I reserve for myself. If I am yet unable to strike down the economic barrier that encloses the slum dweller when I strike down the buildings, still let me help him to preserve his cultural heritage and to resume his way of life with his own kind if he so chooses. Let me not say to him, "Take my culture, do as I do, think as I think, or forever be an outcast."

Help me to understand and offer wise aid in my own land; help me to go beyond the oceans and to understand and to offer wise aid to my different brothers in other lands.

So be it.

A Preview of Plain Talk

Refuse to compromise with any proposal that threatens to violate human rights and human dignity (page 16).

If plans are not possible of accomplishment—then they are not plans, they are doodles (page 16).

I propose a change in our public philosophy to make it just as socially unacceptable—criminally culpable—to injure someone living 20, 30, or 40 years in the future as we have made it anti-social and culpable to injure someone living today. We can no longer plead innocence. It is perfectly clear that because of the things today we do to the land and to the water and to the air we are laying up a store of troubles, a store of expenses, a store of injury and an abundance of shortages for future generations (page 39).

So long as we live in a democracy the people must be heard. Their case is entitled to the best presentation we can give it. We, as planners, must act as their advocates (page 284).

We are clearly heading for a troika in which on an equal basis with land use planning (or physical planning) we shall have social planning and economic planning (page 295).

One of the most dangerous diseases in the world today is xenophobia—the fear of strangers, of foreigners, of persons who differ from you in language, in clothing, in religion, in food, in race. Xenophobia is a disease that can be fatal for the entire world. The only lasting cure is for us to meet and see and talk to each other, to understand that we, as human beings, have the same hopes and desires, the same questions and problems—we are more alike than we are different (pages 328–29).

1

What Planning Is . . . and Is Not

Editor's Commentary

Almost everything Dennis O'Harrow wrote had to do with what planning is—and is not. The basics of his beliefs, observations, and counsel are collected in this chapter. These principles in his philosophy of planning are indicated by 'the headings used in organizing the material—all of them either quotes or titles from the papers selected:

Unless we make common cause . . .
The basic principle: planning for human beings
Planning must come from the people
By plan or by chance?
Realism in community development
Planning must be a part of government
Let's get the record straight
Trends . . . and the urban future

These speeches and articles reached leagues of municipalities, city managers, public administrators, county officials, and the League of Women Voters—as well as statewide planning associations, regional planning agencies, citizen planning groups, an ASPO conference, and the readership of the *ASPO Newsletter*. And they reached also audiences such as a chamber of commerce, a conference of representatives of national business firms, the readers of *Kiwanis Magazine*, and members of the Railway Systems and Management Association and of the National Sand and Gravel Association—reflecting what his successor as ASPO Executive Director, Israel Stollman, identified as his interest in getting close to people that other planners "shunned as the 'enemy,' because he knew that there is plenty of overlapping territory among competing and enlightened self-interests. His work with sand and gravel operators, railroads, utilities, home builders, the petroleum industry—all had the common element of showing how *their* legitimate interests can be integrated with community interests."

At least a third of the papers included in this chapter reached beyond their initial audience in reprints. And the principles extended to and influenced much of ASPO's research.

Those who were then practicing planning, and knew ASPO, will remember some of the editorials on what planning and planners should and should not be. But the many unpublished speeches and articles and their additional, varied observations and insights—in this chapter and throughout this volume—will be a surprise.

Throughout the two decades of his writings, Dennis O'Harrow focused on examining, questioning, and changing planning. Throughout, tenets such as those described in this chapter were basic to his beliefs and arguments on what planning is—and is not.

Unless We Make Common Cause

Quoted from "Planning Your Community for Tommorrow," the dinner address at the Annual Meeting of the Warren Chamber of Commerce, Warren, Ohio, November 27, 1956.

In the course of about 25 years spent professionally working with and observing and worrying about cities, I have come to an unorthodox view about planning, which differs a great deal from the conventional view.

I believe that planning is best described as an attitude. It is recognition and acceptance of change. It is faith in the future, not starry-eyed worship, but belief based on a realistic appraisal.

It is faith in the ability of men working through democracy to meet and solve the problems of the future. It is willingness to try and to keep trying to work out common problems as honestly, as efficiently, as sympathetically as we possibly can.

Above all, it is a shared attitude, a shared faith in the city, a shared belief in democracy—shared alike by citizens and officials. Unless we make common cause, we are lost.

Sometimes we think that only such spectacular forces as those released by war or by violent natural catastrophe are strong enough to bring cooperation such as this. I tell you that economic, social, and political forces are just as powerful as war and flood in their ability to maim and destroy a city. They are more deadly, because they are more subtle and more easily ignored until too late.

The Basic Principle:
Planning for Human Beings

**Extracted from "Planning," a speech to the
League of Women Voters, Evanston,
Illinois, September 22, 1949.**

Sometimes we are so bent on questioning some of the minor axioms of
our craft that we forget the many major axioms which remain unquestioned.

The basic principle in planning a city is that it should be designed
for human beings. The city is an agglomeration of physical objects
whose only proper use is to provide facilities for people to live, to
work and to play. In every way in which the city falls short in providing those facilities, there lies the need for planning, for redesign,
rebuilding.

That sounds elementary. It is. But it's an idea we forget too easily:

One of our solutions was the erection of Stuyvesant Town and
Peter Cooper Village in New York City. Ostensibly those were built to
provide places for people to live. People? Better termites! The unfortunate truth is that Stuyvesant Town and Peter Cooper Village were
built not to provide a place for people to live, but to provide an investment for insurance company funds. The city exists to provide a place
to live, but, to quote Porgy, "Who calls that livin?"

The city is to provide a place to work. I know a man (and we all
know many like him) who lives on the east side of his city and works
on the west side. Two hours he spends in the morning riding to work,
two hours he spends in the evening riding home. And if you've ever
ridden street cars, "Who calls that riding?" If he were to keep that up
for years, he would have spent two and one third years of his life on
street cars. The city provided him a place to work—all he had to do
was spend something more than 10 percent of his time going to and
coming from that place.

I don't have to illustrate the failure of cities to provide a place to
play. I merely say that I don't believe a street is a place to play, nor is
ten square feet of the Lake Michigan shore, nor is an asphalt-surfaced
school yard.

The truth is that cities and the way we have built them in the past are not built for people. On the contrary people were being forced into a mold which permits them to maintain life, of a sort, in cities. People are being made for cities—not cities for people.

Last summer, the deputy commissioner of Bombay, India, visited our office. His job corresponds roughly to that of a city manager. I mentioned to him that there seemed to be some correlation between our increasing urbanism and our insanity rates. He said, "I can believe that, I can even add to it. My people are the Parsees. We are the most urbanized group in the world, over 95 percent of us live in cities. Also we have the highest insanity rate in the world." I haven't checked lately, but the last figures I saw indicated that one out of 20 Americans would spend some time in a mental hospital. We don't come into the world crazy—we have it thrust upon us. But I don't want to infer that city planning is a substitute for mental hygiene or that planners are going to throw all the psychiatrists out of work. There must be a lot of other things besides cities that drive people crazy.

Of course, if a planner is real honest he may admit that there is not a great deal he can do about cities. In fact he sees several forces at work which are taking matters away from him and away from the people.

Back in 1945 a bomb was dropped on Hiroshima—and on all mankind. We know that the echo of that bomb is still bouncing around the world.

Another very potent force is sniping away at our cities—and my commuting acquaintance is an example. He will never be happy and will never be an efficient employee until he stops devoting one day out of every ten to riding the street car. Probably his mildest protest against his environment would be to quit his job. And that is expensive for the employer, labor turnover is very costly. His more explosive reaction would come through wage and pension demands, strikes, even violence. I am not making a categorical implication on the justification or lack of justification, in labor disputes. I merely point out that labor unrest has as one of its sources the intolerable living conditions in our great cities. They are conditions which the employer and employee cannot remedy—at least over the bargaining table, or through a president's fact-finding committee.

The city planner can do a great deal to make the city a good place to live and a good place for a manufacturer to bring or hire his employees. But he must have those two ingredients without which he might as well quit—good government and active citizen interest.

The days are gone in which people could sit back and let George build their cities. George no longer puts up houses one at a time, he builds by the thousand. He isn't afraid to build an entire city almost overnight. He isn't afraid to stack families in layers 20 deep. He conceives highways to disgorge automobiles and trucks at mile-a-minute speeds. He makes rivers flow up hills.

And unless George is watched and held in check, he is going to reshape people to fit cities—not reshape cities to fit people.

Extracted from "Planning and Zoning," an address to the North Dakota League of Municipalities, Valley City, North Dakota, September 11, 1950.

The greatest natural resource of your state and your cities is human beings. Compared with this, your lignite, your Red River Valley, your irrigated lands, your Glauber's salt, your possible petroleum and gas—are nothing.

For most natural resources, a measure of the quantity that we export is a measure of our prosperity. But with human beings, the opposite is true. On a dollars and cents basis, every boy and every girl that leaves your city and your state to seek his fortune elsewhere takes with him as a gift from his parents and the state an education worth many thousands of dollars. You have carried him through the unproductive years; the benefit from his productive years will go to another state.

You lose your most valuable resource, human beings, just about the same way that you lose topsoil by wind and water erosion. Once gone, both topsoil and people are hard to get back. If you would conserve these human resources, which are so easily shown to be economic resources, you must persuade your children that your state is a good place to live in and work in. No amount of visiting experts, and no amount of federal grants will accomplish the job. Your only method of combating this loss is to make your state and your cities so attractive that no one will want to leave.

Planning Must Come from
the People

**Quoted from "Cities Don't Need to be
Ugly," an article written for** *Kiwanis
Magazine,* **June 1958.**

Planning in a democracy is not handed down from above. It must
come from the people, or it just doesn't come.

**Quoted from "Public Planning and Private
Plans," an address at the Second Company
Planning Conference for representatives of
national firms, sponsored by Roosevelt
University's College of Business Administra-
tion, June 11, 1959.**

The citizens, and in particular the civic leaders of the nation, if for no
other reason than numbers alone, are the most important segment of
public planning. The professional planners work out the technical
details. The administrators' job is primarily to see that those plans, if
acceptable, are carried out. But the group that really calls the shots are
the citizen leaders of the nation. They are the ones who must decide
what they want in their neighborhood, in their village, in their city,
their county, their state, and in their nation.

Civic leaders and citizens do public planning in one of two ways.
They do public planning by being interested in and understanding
public affairs; by supporting intelligent policies and plans and schemes
by their public administrators or by criticizing unintelligent schemes
and policies; by demanding that their public administrators use the
best technical help they can get, base their plans and policies on
research data, shape their plans to the needs and desires of the people.

Civic leaders do their planning in this way—or they do it in the
other way: by complete neglect.

The civic leaders of today and tomorrow have a duty toward public
planning. It is not optional. It is not something you can take or leave,
because by leaving it alone you are planning by neglect, by default.
This is a negative method of planning and the results are just as
positive as those of the other approach.

Quoted from "Simplicity in Planning," a
speech at the Third Annual Meeting of the
Stark County Regional Planning Commission, Canton, Ohio, January 14, 1959.

The problems that planning can solve arise always, change always,
and are likely to be always with us in one form or another. The city or
village that does not have any community development and growth
problems is a ghost town. The very fact that there are community
problems means that there is life and vitality and growth in the community. Planning is a process—the process of continually watching
and trying to work out solutions for those problems in a vital community. Those problems have never in the past been solved by the
dead hand of a pompous report, nor will they ever be solved in the
future by that method. They will be solved only by the live hands and
the live heads and the live hearts of the people of the community.

By Plan or By Chance?

Extracted from the speech "Chicago
Grows—By Plan or By Chance?" given at
the Annual Meeting of the South Side Planning Board, Chicago, May 2, 1957.

There is a basic law of civilization implied in the words "by plan or by
chance." Nature left to herself seeks a random distribution, or in other
words, a distribution by chance. Physicists have a word for this: "entropy," which signifies a completely mixed-up, helterskelter, planless
state of affairs. Many scientists believe that the law which expresses
this relentless drive to randomness is the strongest and most
widespread of all natural laws.

The history of the slow ascent of human beings from jungle
savagery to the world of today is a history of the growth of man's
knowledge of how to overcome randomness. It is the story of how he
learned to corral and domesticate animals rather than stalk and kill

them where he could find them—or die himself because he could not find them. It is the story of how man learned to gather the seeds of food plants and sow them in ordered rows. It is the story of the carefully controlled reduction of metals to use for making tools. It is the story of dikes to hold back rivers, of boats to cross rivers. It is the story of mathematics instead of counting stones and finger tally. It is the story of the division of labor and the building of cities. It is the story of orderly government instead of anarchy.

In short, the story of the advance of man will be found in the growth of his ability to substitute plans and control for chance.

I could spend a lot of time developing this idea all the way to city planning, zoning, thoroughfare planning, or what have you. I will just point out that planning is a basic key to man's control of his environment, a key to civilization itself.

Obviously, nothing as complex as city planning comes into existence in full perfection. It is feeble at birth, it requires constant watching and adjustment, it may fall on evil days and nearly die. But if it is inherently good, it evolves and becomes stronger and stronger, until at last it becomes so integrated that we accept it without question.

During the 50 years of development of planning in the United States, we have had to do a lot of self-examination to try to find out just what "city planning" is and what it can do for the people and their cities and how best it can do it. There are many and varied answers to these questions, but they amount to this: Planning consists of bringing to bear on the problems of city development the best objective judgment we can find. The standard by which we judge is the welfare of the *entire* city. No significant development in a city can be isolated from the remainder of the city development. We use a "comprehensive plan," for effective guidance of future city growth, although it does not necessarily have to be in the form of maps and graphs; it may even be unwritten—like the constitution of Great Britain. But we cannot have effective planning unless and until planning is accepted routinely as part of the process of arriving at administrative and legislative decisions. To consult planning must be just as automatic as to examine financial ability.

I believe that planning, and growth by plan, is inevitable in every large city and in most small ones. I believe it is the only way in which a city can survive the flood of population and technology that is going to sweep over the land between now and the year 2000. Survive the cities will, so plan they must.

It then becomes only a question of when do we start.

Extracted from the ASPO Newsletter editorial "Why Plan? Why Not!" May 1959.

There are a number of good reasons why you should do planning consciously and systematically and as far in advance as possible. Some of
these may be hard to understand, others hard to believe. But one simple reason for formal planning of community development is that it
saves money. For example:

A master plan for fire stations in Wichita was responsible for eliminating one station at the original cost of $60,000 and an annual oper-
ating cost of $40,000.

A master school plan for Tacoma made it possible to pick up seven
school sites from county tax-title lands at a savings of $150,000.

Fairfax County, Virginia, showed a savings of $834,000 by use of a
thoroughfare plan and the reservation of 127 acres of right-of-way for
a major circumferential expressway.

An analysis of a park plan for Oak Park, Michigan, shows that advance planning and purchase of park and greenbelt land has saved
$1.3 million in seven years.

The city of Cincinnati has calculated an average annual savings of
$325,000 a year through its continuing application of a master thor-
oughfare plan, an average savings of $11,200 per acre on park sites
because of a master park plan, and an average of $16,400 per acre on
school sites because of a master school plan.

Quoted from the ASPO Newsletter editorial "Small Talk or Prejudices," August 1955.

Money talks. At least it seems to be an effective way of calling attention to the need for planning. Take the replacement value of a city, of
the houses, stores, factories, of the schools, hospitals, churches, of the
streets, railroads, sewers, utilities, and so on. For a city of 100,000
population, this would be on the order of $500 million. If by good
planning we were able to make only a 1 percent improvement over
conditions resulting from no planning (which is really bad planning),

we should have made a $5 million contribution—enough to finance a liberal planning budget for many years.

Realism in Community Development

Extracted from "Realism in Community Development," the keynote address at the Second Annual Community Development Conference, Columbus, Ohio, November 4, 1960.

Perhaps the greatest deviation from reality affecting community development efforts is in the image the citizens have of their present city, and of their future city, if they honestly want to improve it. They are apt to aim too low and to aim at the wrong things. This can be illustrated by the quite common worship of low taxes.

If your image of the city you want is one that is cheap to live in, then be realistic about it. You will get just that—a cheap city, in the worst sense of the word.

Parallel to the rising line of governmental expenditures is a rising line in the standard of demands—and ability to pay—of America's people. There is also a rising line in the education and skills and taste of Americans. The vanishing American of today is the unskilled, uneducated worker. Tomorrow's worker will demand the best living environment that can be produced, and the community that fails to give it to him is the community he doesn't want any part of.

The community that plans only for today is the community that has already started backwards. If your ideals are too high, certainly they will not be accepted and nothing will happen; maybe you can try again in five years or so. But if your ideals are too low, while they are quite likely to be reached, you will find yourself in five years or so completely out of date and entombed in a community pattern that you can't get out of.

Realism in community development means recognizing that this is an age of change: change in technology, change in human beings, and change in living standards. The business axiom that says "If you want to succeed, you must give the customer what she wants" also applies to community development. It is most unrealistic to ignore it.

Design your community for change, growth, improvement. Design your community for tomorrow, because the only thing deader than yesterday's newspaper is yesterday's city. That is what I call being realistic in developing your community.

Extracted from "Planning and Public Economics," a paper given at the Annual Meeting of the Pennsylvania Planning Association, Pittsburgh, November 11, 1954.

Community planning operates much of the time in a situation governed by the common or garden variety of economics—the science that measures things in terms of money. But in the case of cities, instead of "cost" and "selling price," we work with "cost" and "benefits." Or sometimes "costs" and "bonding power." I believe in community planning operating in an atmosphere of economics measured in dollars and cents, wherever it is possible to take that sort of a measurement. City planning would certainly be a lot easier if we could always translate everything into money amounts, into costs and benefits. But it doesn't always work, and I think we are being hypocrites in many cases when we try it.

Actuaries—insurance mathematicians—calculate the money value of a human life by figuring the present value of future net earnings—how much money you would need to invest now to bring in the same income the average person would probably get for the rest of his life, minus the food he would eat. But think about trying to apply such a figure in public economics.

It has been done. For example: you have a dangerous railroad crossing. For the past several years the average has been three persons killed at this crossing each year. Can you afford to put in a grade separation? You look at the table and you find that the average net worth of a human life is $20,000. Save three of them each year and you have saved $60,000 each year. Now compare this $60,000 worth of human beings with the cost of building an underpass or an overpass. If you can build and maintain it for only $50,000 a year, you can afford to go ahead. But if it costs you $70,000 a year to save $60,000 in human lives, it isn't an economic undertaking.

How many people do you think would really buy that kind of "economic" reasoning? Precious few!

This and many other things are not to be computed by ordinary economics. They are in the domain of public economics. When we try to justify an attack on slums by citing fire costs, welfare costs, health costs, and the ever-present crime costs, or by recourse to figures on assessed values—we're trying to solve a problem in calculus with fifth grade arithmetic methods.

It is all well and good to say that many of the problems of cities must be studied in the light of values that we can't measure, but how do you bring these into planning? I don't know of any rules that are infallible, but there is one impression I have gained. The more I see of cities and city problems, the more I feel that the intangible is more important than the tangible. A simplified illustration:

A lot line is an intangible thing, an imaginary line defined by two short pieces of iron pipe driven in the ground. When you come to build, you erect a structure—a very real object made of brick and mortar, wood and steel—on a bit of land defined by four imaginary lot lines. Which is going to last longest, which is going to be there 100 years from now? The answer is, of course, that 99 times out of 100 the lot lines will long outlast the building, the intangible will outlast the tangible.

For lot lines, the idea is clear and easily demonstrated. But there are many ideas that we must deal with in public economics that are more general, much harder to demonstrate, and much harder to measure or pin down on a cost and benefit balance sheet. Among these I would include such things as neighborhood well-being and community well-being. I would include clean air and public safety. I would include the right of children to play and to get a decent education. On an even larger scale I would include freedom and democracy and the bill of rights and peace. I will admit that to many people these ideas are fine words with little substance. Some people will never understand, but I believe they are a minority.

In public economics it is necessary, at times, to compromise. When do you compromise and when do you stand firm? I have no pat answer for that. If I had to give any rule for the operation of planning in the field of public economics, it would be this: Compromise if you must, on the tangible things, on the comparatively few proposals that can be truly and completely analyzed in terms of costs and benefits, in terms of common economics. But beware of the balance sheet! The best embezzler is not the man who takes the most money. It is the man who best conceals the theft by his manipulation of the accounting records.

Hold firm on the intangibles, and particularly, refuse to compromise with any proposals that threaten to violate human rights and human dignity.

Some operations partake of the nature of farming, a little over-cultivation one year can be counteracted by cover crops and fertilizer the next year. But other operations resemble mining, after which there is no turning back.

**Extracted from "Why Planning and
Financing Must be Related," a paper given
at a conference of the Railway Systems and
Management Association, Chicago,
April 14, 1961.**

The professional planner takes the inseparable relationship between plans and finances so for granted that he does not bother to discuss it in those terms.

The closest relative to planning is—believe it or not—politics. The definition of politics is "the art of the possible." This means getting things done through government that you *can* get done, tilting at windmills almost never. To paraphrase: planning is the *science* of the possible—through government. I will not debate anyone who challenges me on just how scientific our "science" is at present—but I will maintain that we use as much science as we possibly can and that we are doing everything within our power to increase our use of scientific tools.

The key word in this definition, however, is "possible." The object of planning—city, metropolitan, county, regional—is to determine the future needs and problems of the area, to propose actions or projects to meet the needs and solve the problems—*actions that can be carried out.* The actions or projects must be ones that can be accomplished. They must be *possible.* If plans are not possible of accomplishment—then they are not plans, they are doodles.

What are the limits of possibility in government activity—what divides the possible from the impossible? Basically, the boundary line is financial. The limit is determined by the amount of money available to the government: through taxes; through bonds, which are deferred taxes; through grants-in-aid, which are taxes collected by another governmental unit. I do not overlook private investment. This is also a very important part of urban development, and the planner takes it into consideration. In an urban renewal project, for example, a government investment of $10,000 can be parlayed into a total investment of $50,000,000—$40,000,000 of which comes from private funds. But there is always a limit to government funds.

Planning is more than just *related* to financing. Financing is a *part* of the planning process. Unless they are inextricably integrated—you do not even have planning, you have hot air.

**Extracted from the ASPO Newsletter
editorial "Magic and Master Plans,"
February 1959.**

There is a little store on Chicago's south side that, according to the sign on the window, sells religious articles. Behind the show window, merchandise is displayed: icons, gaudy plaques, candlesticks, and candles. But there are also on display a series of pasteboard containers that are bottle cartons for varieties of liquid bath salts.

These are not ordinary bath salts, not even Hollywood inspired, glamorizing type, bubble bath salts. These are *magical* potions, as their names clearly show. There is one for success: *bano exito;* one for conditioning (whatever that might be), *bano condicion.* If you would be lucky in love, you are advised to try *bano de amor;* lucky at the races, *bano de dinero.* Finally, the most costly is *bano conquistador,* which, according to the merchant's translation, means "High Conquering."

Magic is not a thing of the past nor is it a quaint custom, surviving only in the beliefs of the uneducated. In a careful study of the advertising industry, Martin Mayer advanced the theory that what advertising actually did was to *add* something of value to the product that was being touted. He wrote:

> Take the case of a soda pill, a placebo, which is advertised as a headache cure. (Carefully advertised, so as not to run afoul of Federal

Trade Commission regulations.) The pill may have virtually no medical value, but it will actually cure the headaches of a number of people who take it. The suggestive power of the advertising has created a value for an otherwise worthless product.

This is pure magic!

Social scientists have thought a lot about magic, trying to assess its value and to differentiate it from religion and to determine its function. In fact, there is a quite respectable theory (not universally accepted, however) that magic actually *works.* This agrees with Mayer's theory on advertising. Whether it works or not, we do know that magic always shows up in those instances where human knowledge falls short of explanation, where human understanding fails to solve problems.

Why doesn't my dream boy fall in love with me, asks the teenage girl. It surpasses understanding—maybe—maybe—maybe the magic *bano de amor* will turn the trick!

It now appears that there is abroad in our land another elixir with magical properties: the Master Plan. Harried mayors, overanxious chamber of commerce executives, frustrated industrial development promoters—all face supernatural forces causing supernormal problems in supersaturated urban centers. Situations like this that we cannot understand call for magic, and what better magic than the comprehensive look, the overall and once-and-for-all scheme, the Master Plan? The master magician is the long-range planner, the comprehensive planner, the Master Planner!

If anyone thinks that the Master Plan is not seen as a truly magical document, he need only talk to a mayor or civic leader in the city that is buying or has just bought one. Their faith in the omnipotence of the Master Plan is touching, just like the savage's faith in the incantations of the witch doctor.

But this unquestioning faith is also disturbing. The danger in accepting the "functional" theory of magic—the theory that magic actually works—is that too easily you forget the dysfunctional aspects. Too easily you overlook the fact that so long as you use a magical remedy, so long do you postpone the use of nonmagical remedies.

In the case of the magical treatment of disease, postponement may mean death to the patient. In the case of the magical treatment of urban ills, reliance on the magic of a Master Plan instead of on planning, with a small p, may not spell death, but it certainly means that later, successful treatment, if it is ever possible, will be more difficult and more expensive.

**Extracted from the ASPO Newsletter
editorial "The Mink-Trimmed Beer Wrench:
A Sort of Christmas Fable," December 1964.**

Someday a budding social historian will study the ads in the Sunday supplements and write his doctoral dissertation on the rise of the diamond-studded cigarette holder, the stuffed bird with the tape recorder in his craw, the musical cuff links, the floppy clock.

The only one I ever had a brush with was a beer wrench trimmed with real mink fur. (For those youngsters who may not know the term, a beer wrench is a gadget for removing bottle caps on one end and punching holes in beer cans on the other end.) This was only half a beer wrench, the hole-punching half, but it had a lovely mink fur handle. I don't know how much my mink-trimmed beer wrench cost, because it was a gift. It wouldn't punch a hole in a dixie cup, let alone a beer can, but it sure was pretty.

I thought of the many expensive, beautiful, and completely worthless city planning reports that are accumulating throughout the land. And I felt sad. I claim I have a good eye for beauty in planning reports, a whole-hearted appreciation of a real professional job of drafting, charting, illustrating, and printing. But I am getting suspicious of beautiful reports. So very many of them are so very thin and watery and pompously platitudinous.

The loveliest beer wrench in the world is no damn good it if won't open a beer can. And the most beautiful planning report, if it doesn't have anything in it to plan with, is also no damn good.

But maybe these beautiful and watery plans aren't really meant to plan with. No more than my mink-trimmed beer wrench was meant to open beer cans with. Maybe the plans are for the city that has everything. All it needs the plan for is to use it as a conversation piece—just the way I use my mink-trimmed beer wrench.

Planning Must Be a Part of Government

**Condensed from "Meeting the Planning
Needs of Metropolitan Areas," an address to
the American Society for Public Administration, Pittsburgh, May 22, 1956.**

The office of the American Society of Planning Officials receives a steady flow of questions on planning and organization for planning. One type of question frequently goes like this: "Dear Sir: Will you please send me a list of the cities in our population class which you feel are doing the best job of planning in the United States?" Since there are no accepted standards for judgment, there is no way to make an objective appraisal of a planning operation.

You might take the budget for planning, reduced to a per capita figure. You might use the relative size of the staff compared to the total city population. You might check on the dates of the legal tools that are the principal weapons in the arsenal of planning: zoning, sub-division regulation, housing code, thoroughfare plan—on the theory that the more recent, the better. It doesn't take much experience in the field of public administration to recognize that criteria such as these are weak reeds on which to lean.

From time to time, budgets are blown up out of all proportion by big consulting contracts. Again, they may be small to the point of mis-representation because of the use of volunteer citizen effort or the cooperative assistance of friendly municipal departments. Recently, the director of one metropolitan planning staff estimated that cooper-ating technical committees had furnished more than a half-million dollars in free work during the past half-dozen years.

Staff size may also be deceptive. The directors of large agencies fre-quently tell me that they have one or two or a half-dozen political appointees that they must harbor. I know one city which reports a planning staff of six full-time employees. I also know that there isn't a planner on the staff in this city and that there has not been a single legitimate planning move made in the city for at least 20 years.

So it goes with almost any criterion that you pick. A recent date on the zoning ordinance may mean that the city is on its toes, keeping abreast of the rapid change in technical knowledge in the field of zon-ing. Or it may mean that the old zoning ordinance had been garrotted and ripped with such ruthlessness that they have merely sutured all of the bleeding pieces together again and are starting out on another course of mayhem.

However, I *do* believe that some planning operations are more successful than others; I *do* believe there is a rational basis for such successful operations; I *do* believe that within certain limits we can differentiate among operations.

Any argument worthy of the name always gets back to a definition. There are hundreds of definitions of "planning." They generally boil down to three parts: First, a study and analysis of the past and present of the area—economic, social, physical; second, a prediction of the economic, sociological and physical future; and third, documents, methods and tools to guide future development along the course that seems to be in the best interests of all citizens.

You get a tripartite idea like this and there is quite a temptation to compare it to a three-legged stool, to say: "Which is the most important leg, analysis, prediction, or plans to guide development?" However, it seems to me that the figure of speech is not quite correct. The comparison should be to a fence post with guys in two directions. Your post won't be as strong without the guys, but it will stand up nevertheless.

I put the third part—the methods and tools to guide decisions—in the role of the post, with the analyses and predictions in the role of supporting guys. For the truth is that decisions are going to be made, and that the city or metropolitan area will continue to develop, whether or not there is something we call "planning." The decision makers are going to be "guided" by some considerations, be they holy or be they venal.

As simple examples of successful planning, I cite two areas of urban development in which there has been a great deal of success, as I define it. These areas are traditionally within the jurisdiction of the planning agency. They are also, I fear, traditionally looked upon as burdens under which the planning purist frets; tasks from which he would like to be relieved. These two examples of successful planning are the control and regulation of subdivisions and the administration of the zoning ordinance.

When a subdivision plat is presented for consideration to the city, this means that the city government is asked to take on certain added responsibilities: to add more miles of streets that will require maintenance; to permit the construction of additional residences, which means more pupils to be educated in the local schools; to furnish fire and police protection; to permit the passage of additional sewage through its treatment plant; to furnish more water. The executive branch of the local government must decide whether or not it will assume these added duties and expenditures. Through subdivision regulation, there is automatic consultation with the planning agency before the decision is made. This is planning for the extension of urban development. The quality of this planning varies widely, but in general, it means no extensions unless and until standards of street construction, standards for residential density, and standards for sewage and water are all met.

The operation of a zoning ordinance is similarly an executive decision made on the basis of planning considerations. On the advice of a planning commission, the city has established rules for the development of private land uses inside the city limits. Thereafter, the city decides to permit the construction of a building only after it has consulted the land-use plan as expressed through the zoning ordinance. We are apt to think of the zoning ordinance as a law which often gets in our way by prohibiting us from doing the things that we would like to do. I think it is more appropriate to view the zoning ordinance as a guide for the city's development.

We have formalized and institutionalized subdivision control and zoning until it is difficult to recognize that there has been an executive decision made only after consultation with the planning agency. Also, non-, mis-, or mal-administration, particularly of the zoning ordinance, frequently make it difficult to recognize that any rational or intelligent planning has been used anywhere in the procedure. Nevertheless, these represent the pattern toward which we must work if we are to have successful planning. It is only successful when it is used in making executive decisions.

Throughout the United States, there are two general ways of putting the planning process into the local government organization chart. One of these sets up a citizen planning commission which supervises a paid staff of technical planners. It is removed, aloof from the regular city government, although it usually does have the two functions of subdivision control and zoning administration. On the whole, however, its proponents consciously would take it out of the crass world of politics and municipal administration and let it operate in the clean, pure, outer air.

The other spot for the planning agency is integrated in the municipal family, where the technical staff is a regular department. There may be, and usually is, a citizen planning commission which advises on policy, but this commission in no way supervises the planning operation. In this second form of organization, planning is a staff operation, directly assisting the mayor or city manager. The "best" cities in planning, are, without exception, cities in which planning is a staff prop for the chief executive.

Extracted from the ASPO Newsletter editorial "Planning: In or Out?" March 1957.

For a number of years there has been a gradual change from the original planning board idea to the planning department, a part of the official family reporting to the chief executive. There have been charter revisions, reorganizations, new ordinances. There have also been many planning staffs pulled into the city government with no formal action—merely because the chief executive and the planning director have discovered close cooperation to be more effective than an apartheid policy.

There is now integration of planning into administration at a stepped-up rate. A major cause has been urban renewal. Basically it is the same as ordinary urban development, with one changed dimension. The change is in the dimension of *time*. In urban renewal, all the natural urban processes are speeded up. The long needed utility improvements are made. Obsolescent schools are replaced. Street changes and traffic rerouting that might have taken several years are all accomplished within a brief period. Inspection and law enforcement that were going along at an ordinary pace are telescoped into a rapid concentrated effort. Even the forces of natural decay are accelerated with wrecking bar and steel ball.

Before urban renewal it was possible for city administrators to adapt urban change without worrying too much about planning. The rate at which plans were produced was slow, but so were the processes of growth and decay. In spite of gloomy predictions, very few cities became ghost towns because they failed to plan. But when the urban processes are condensed in time, the cross-relationships, the ramifications and implications, the pop up there when you push down here— all these show up clearly. The executive and legislature are asked to make decisions in one year that formerly could have been stalled for 20 years. The need is urgent for all the technical help you can muster.

If to this pressure of urban renewal we add the pressure of suburban growth—another natural process now happening at an accelerated rate—we see what is behind the move to bring planning closer to administrative action.

Planners also are having to learn to adjust to the new pattern. No longer can they afford to wait "until the master plan is completed," the master plan that has been five years in the making will take at least five years more. Today is Friday. Council meets Tuesday night. The mayor has to have the answer before council meeting. If you need more basic data, more analysis, more correlation, more research, you had better arrange to get it all done between now and Tuesday.

It may be more difficult to advise sound decisions when we are under pressure, more difficult than we thought it would be under the scriptural authority we attributed to the master plan we were making. But I am not convinced of this. I think planning is at last finding its proper place.

Extracted from "Planning and the Future," a speech at the First Annual North Carolina Planning Conference, Chapel Hill, May 2, 1958.

Whether a local government is modern is an important question. From the viewpoint of planning and the planner, it can be just about the most important consideration in the whole local picture.

It is hard to pin down modernness, or lack thereof, in a local government, but partly it is a professional attitude on the part of the governing officials toward the job of running the city or county. There is an expressed and clearly apparent desire to operate efficiently. Department heads and supervisors are on the lookout for methods to give the same service for less cost, or to give more service for the same cost. When you have adopted the calling, as I have, of a carpetbagging municipal commentator, you learn quickly to size up a city and its government in rapid-fire order. You do it by little things; by what must be called circumstantial evidence.

I plead guilty to some bias in the matter, but I judge the situation *first* by finding out where planning sits in local government, how it is used, what is its place. Planning must be in and part of local government. It must be of, by, and for local government. It cannot be an extramural operation. Another thing I look for is most quickly apparent in attitudes—an attitude toward planning that indicates planning is accepted and used by the city's chief executive or administrator, that it is respected and listened to by the local legislative body, that there is an automatic and instinctive referral of appropriate questions to the planning body. There is also an attitude of the plan commission members and of the planning staff that tells a lot: they show that they feel themselves part of the group of city officials who are working on the city's problems.

Planning is as much a part of good, modern local government as finance administration or personnel administration. It shares with those two tools of management the distinction of being a function which applies in every part of municipal government operation. As such, planning, along with personnel administration and financial policy, is a function for which the chief executive must be directly responsible.

I believe that good government and only good government is up-to-date government. I think that bad government is out of date, declasse, old hat. And, by good government, I do not mean to imply that only one or two forms of organization can qualify as good government. You can have good government with a strong mayor system, with a council-manager, with a weak mayor system, with a village government, with a town-meeting government, with a government by county supervisors. You can likewise have bad government under any of these forms.

But just as good government does recognize and use planning, you cannot have good planning without good government. It is a contradiction in terms to say that you have poor government in a city or a county but that you do have good planning, because planning is not something that can be isolated from governmental operation and talked about as though it had a life and existence and meaning all its own.

**Quoted from "Getting the Job Done," an
address at the Arizona City-County Planning and Zoning Conference, Tucson,
October 2, 1959.**

A requirement for successful planning is this: You must build up
throughout your community the *habit* of planning, the *habit* of coordinating activities, the *habit* of checking community policies and community goals before anything affecting communiy development is
undertaken. You build up this habit just as you build up good habits
in children. The child's habit of brushing his teeth, the habit of
washing his face—it becomes part of him by constant repetition. In
community development it is the same. We do it by being sure that
every activity is checked, by being sure that people *know* that every
project is checked, by letting people know that planning schemes are
carried out, by letting people know that planning and zoning ordinances are enforced. When you get this good habit ingrained in your
community, you are over the hump.

**Condensed from "Who Plans?" an address
at the 52nd Annual Conference of the Texas
Municipal League, October 4–6, 1964.**

Planning cannot be packaged in a report, a map, or a local law. Planning is the total of all the information on which the city officials base
the decisions that affect the future of the city. It is the goals that they
are seeking when they make those decisions. It is the way they choose
the goals when they are contradictory—as they often are.

They plan the city when they decide to widen X Street instead of Y
Avenue. They plan the city when they decide to build a new fire station instead of adding a wing to the hospital. They plan the city when
they say to a department head: cut your budget request, we are not
raising taxes this year. They plan the city when they appoint one person rather than another on the board of zoning appeals.

Time is a one-way street. There is no trick by which you can now
do something that would actually change the past or make something
happen in the past. Therefore, all decisions will affect the future. Of
course, many of these decisions have relatively little long-run consequences. Not every act of a city council is planning, nor is every act

particularly significant to the future of the community. Nevertheless, every city council does plan, by my definition, whether the city has all of the machinery, the reports, the maps, the ordinances, the board and commissions, the staff that are associated with planning—or none of these trappings. The council is making the decisions that will determine what the community will be like tomorrow, next year, a decade and a century hence.

In listing what I have observed about the conduct of planning by governing bodies—some of the problems, some of the mistakes that are made—my first caution to mayors and councils would be: *Make up your minds!* There are few things less conducive to rational development than a council that blows hot one meeting and cold the next, a council that is consistent only in its inconsistency. And the second caution, which relates to a major cause of inconsistency, is: *Don't let yourself be stampeded into doing things or into being the victim of a false compromise.*

My third observation is that *city councils are too damned apologetic* about some of the decisions that they make. When some councils turn down a rezoning request, the councilmen apologize to the property owner. If they grant the rezoning request, then they apologize to the rest of the citizens, to all the neighbors who came in to protest. There is one simple idea about zoning that I would like to implant in the minds of councilmen everywhere. Whenever they are faced with a request to rezone property, they should hold this thought: *When we zoned this city, we did the best job we knew how. We believed that we were as fair and accurate in drawing the boundaries and designating the use districts as it was possible to be. Anyone who wants to change this zoning map has to prove that we were wrong. If he does not prove it to our satisfaction, we do not have to apologize in any way for turning him down.*

There are two important questions that probe deep into the quality of decisions that are made in relation to planning for the best development of a city. These are:

1. Is there a set of clearly understood policies that guide the council (and for that matter, the planning commission and the board of zoning appeals, if you have those bodies) when it makes its decisions?

2. Do the policies, and the decisions based on the policies, advance the community toward well-defined community objectives?

If you can answer both of these questions with a clear, ringing "Yes," you have little need of my preaching. If your answers are "No," then I advise self-analysis. These questions are designed to bring out the reasons for inconsistency, for the apologetic manner, for the risk of being stampeded or taken for a sucker. The citizens of your city have asked their city officials to operate it. That includes guiding its progress into the future. They expect you to do a good job, or they wouldn't have elected you. And if you do not do a good job, they would be perfectly justified in throwing you out.

The mayor and council will take the final planning decision, but they should demand that the best possible information be furnished before they make their decision. This is where the planning machinery comes into play. There are three aspects of the planning machinery that each mayor and councilman should examine: money, personnel, and recognition.

First, money. Are you spending enough money on planning in your community? The future of your city is your responsibility. You are being remiss if you shortchange yourself here. Some city councils are inclined to cut the budget, saying that they do not want to "waste money" on planning. In my opinion, too little spent on planning is much more likely to be wasteful than too much; if you do not spend enough to carry on a respectable research-analysis-administrative job in planning, you are quite likely to be wasting all of the money you spend.

The need for professional personnel with adequate training and experience is obvious. In addition, there are other people who are most important to the proper functioning of a planning operation: the citizen members of the planning commission and of the board of zoning appeals. You want the best persons you can get in these positions. You want the civic leaders, the persons you could not possibly hire to do the work, but who can be interested enough to serve their community in these positions and who can be depended on to serve unselfishly. This is no place to pay political debts!

The third aspect that you should examine is what use you make of the planning assistance that is given you. What recognition do you give to it? Certainly if because of an inadequate budget, a low salary scale, or inferior appointments, the planning help you get is poor, you are well advised to ignore it. But if the quality is so low that you ignore it, then you should either throw the planning organization out and forget the whole thing, or you should do what is necessary to make it useful to you.

A workable plan is one that states in general terms the objectives you seek in development of the city and sets forth the policies to guide decisions so that you can attain those objectives. It is not a precise blueprint. When the council does adopt it, the council is also fully authorized to amend it whenever necessary. And we certainly can expect amendments, because no one is gifted with enough clairvoyance to see very far into the future. Nevertheless, if the plan, the policies, the objectives need to be amended, they should be amended openly, not by whittling away or by ignoring them.

There is a strong advantage to a plan that councilmen will appreciate: the stated policies can be used to back up and give sufficient reasons for a council decision. There is no need for further explanation or justification if the decision is made "in accordance with the adopted plan."

The mayor and council have a heavy responsibility in preparing their cities to accommodate to the future. They will be penny-wise and pound-foolish if they do not get the best possible help to meet that responsibility. Then they must use it, use it in the planning that they, and only they, can do.

Let's Get the Record Straight

**Extracted from the ASPO Newsletter
editorial, September 1958.**

A man who should know better (he is a professional in public administration) said to me, "I'd like to know what you planners mean, locating schools the way you do! Why, the other day, I saw a new high school going up at the most congested traffic corner in the whole area! Why. . . ."

Let's get the record straight.

In 1957 there were 50,457 school districts in the United States. I should be astonished if as much as 1 percent of those school districts paid any heed whatsoever to the commonsense principles of comprehensive planning or employed the services of a qualified technical city planner. Over the nation as a whole, city planners and plan commissions are conspicuously absent from school planning. My purpose is not to snipe at school districts nor to pretend that all planners and planning are ignoring and being ignored by school districts. What I am getting at is a growing tendency to point at planners (once you have admitted they exist) as the villains behind every stupid public urban development project.

Perhaps the most conspicuous bonehead projects being blamed on planners are some of the peculiarly placed thoroughfares and interchanges that we are getting and will continue to get under the speeded-up highway program. In a number of places planners have been able to work with highway engineers to get some consideration of the countryside to accompany decisions on road or interchange locations. If the people still do not like it, they can snipe at the planners in these instances. But in any given case of citizen unhappiness with thoroughfare location, it is ten to one that a city planner or plan commission had nothing to do with it.

Planners get blamed for all sorts of monstrosities: misplaced convention halls, air pollution, mass-produced shotgun residences, crowded private swimming pools, bad public housing, juvenile delinquency, garbage dumps, bankrupt shopping centers.

Maybe we should be thrilled. Maybe this means we have arrived. I think, however, that we will make enough mistakes of our own on which we can be justifiably called. We have no need to shoulder the blame for the mistakes of others. We should state in loud, clear voices that a large number of boo-boos—avoidable ones, at that—are the doings of outfits that cannot be bothered to use planners or plan commissions.

We should get the record straight.

Extracted from the ASPO Newsletter editorial "Jacobin Revival," February 1962.

Jac´-o-bin, n. [F.] 1. Eccl. Hist. A Dominican friar. 2. One of a society or club of radical democrats in France during the revolution of 1789; hence a plotter against an existing government; a violent radical or turbulent demagogue. 3. [not cap.] A breed of fancy pigeons having the neck feathers reversed, forming a fluffy hood. —Webster's New Collegiate Dictionary

Within the past few months, planners have been transformed from relatively harmless people who really didn't bother anyone very much to a group of arch villains who are callously and systematically destroying civilization in this country. The transformation has been wrought by Jane Jacobs through her book, *The Death and Life of Great American Cities*.

Using a well-proven technique of demagogy, Mrs. Jacobs has selected the planner as the public whipping boy from the first sentence in the introduction—"This book is an attack on current city planning and rebuilding"—to the last chapter where she finds that, at best, planning is really stagnation, and usually planning is retrogression.

Mrs. Jacobs' book hit the market shortly after the appearance of another book that also takes a dim view of city development: Lewis Mumford's *The City in History*. But in popular appeal Mumford is way, way back. Which leads us to try to figure out why.

Although Mumford has been *the* critic of cities and their development for a number of years, still some of his best friends—many of his best friends—are planners. In fact, planners are pretty fond of Mumford in spite of his barbed commentary on some of their actions. However, Mumford talks to planners and he speaks their language.

But Mrs. Jacobs clearly knows so little about planning that she continually (or intentionally) confuses it with architecture and, especially, with public housing and site design.

Death and Life is lively and gossipy, whereas Mumford is involved, turgid, impossibly heavy going. He has made a subject that is normally somewhat dull (in the eyes of the public) even more tedious. Mrs. Jacobs has managed to make it reasonably readable. Jane Jacobs' book reads like a series of case histories. She appeals to the reader through his emotions, and she is very good at this technique. Mumford's book, on the other hand, is the epitome of scholarly dullness.

Mrs. Jacobs has managed to incur the enmity of planners on nearly every page, but perhaps her most unkind cuts are her jibes at "orthodox" or "conventional" planning or planning as a "pseudoscience." Only Mrs. Jacobs seems to know what "orthodox" or "conventional" planning is. As for a "pseudoscience," this is an obvious strawman since no planner that we know has ever claimed that planning was a science—which would justify Mrs. Jacobs belittling it with the term "pseudoscience." It is also exasperating for planners to hear Mrs. Jacobs hailed as having discovered something new. Every valid criticism of urban development that she makes has been made by

planners for years. If she had bothered to seek out real planners, she
would have known this.

Whether or not Mrs. Jacobs gets planners all riled up is not important. No, what is important is that Mrs. Jacobs has presented the
world with a document which will be grabbed by screwballs and reac-
tionaries and used to fight civic improvement and urban renewal projects for years to come.

Say something, say it firmly and loudly and positively enough, and
it makes no difference whether or not it is true. Enough people will
believe it so that you achieve your point. Refutation of these untruths
will always be ineffective. For example, Mrs. Jacobs spends a great
many words lambasting the planners of Boston because they are going
to clear out the North End. This is in the book. What is not in the
book is a letter from Edward J. Logue, Development Administrator
for Boston, which appeared in the *Saturday Evening Post* in answer to
Jane's contention. Logue says: "Just to keep the record very straight,
we have no plans whatsoever for clearance in the North End. . . ."
But Jacobs' book will go on through the years, while Logue's letter to
the editor in last year's issue of the *Saturday Evening Post* is dead as
mackerel.

The Jane Jacobs book is going to do a lot of harm, throw a lot of
monkey wrenches in the machinery. But we are going to have to live
with it. So batten down the hatches boys, we are in for a big blow!

Trends—and the Urban Future

**Extracted from "Trends in Planning," a
paper given at the 41st Annual Conference
of the International City Managers Association, Bretton Woods, New Hampshire,
October 5–8, 1955.**

It would be reasonable, after reading a few books on the subject, to
say that the main concern of city planning is with the future. The planner will use his skills to guide our city ever upwards to a perfect

tomorrow. But if you watch a planning staff in action, or if you read the endless stream of reports that issues from planning offices, you quickly get a different slant. You conclude that most of the time and effort is spent either on cleaning up yesterday's mess or fighting a last ditch stand to hold today's amenities, unsatisfactory though they may be.

This is a trend in planning—this preoccupation with correcting yesterday's mistakes and solving today's problems. In many ways it has been good for the cause. It has shown city planning to be a practical art. It has given city councils courage to back the planning staffs with substantial appropriations. Nevertheless, if these pressing, immediate problems are all that we assign to planning, we are doing our cities a great disservice. In the long run, the most important duty of planning is to prepare for the city of tomorrow which is going to be vastly different from a tidied-up version of the city of today.

You do not hear so often nowadays that planners are dreamers. Maybe this also is a trend and planners have lost their vision and can no longer dream. If it is so, it is a grievous fault. It is a loss we cannot afford.

I believe the urban problems 20 years from now will make those of today look like kindergarten stuff. If we are to handle those problems when they come, we must give planners time to work on them now— today.

We must ask them, nay *order* them, to dream and to have vision.

**Extracted from the ASPO Newsletter
editorial "Cooperation with the Inevitable,"
October 1955.**

[In an editorial on "Small Talk or Prejudices," DOH made a brief statement on the inevitable doubling of metropolitan population by the year 2000 and quoted a definition of planning as "intelligent cooperation with the inevitable." Following a reader's complaint that this definition is "meat for downgraders, two-bulldozer highwaymen, build-and-run developers and redevelopers, and all other professional cynics," he wrote a full editorial on the subject.]

Planning is intelligent cooperation with the inevitable.

The definition requires drawing the line between the evitable and the inevitable. For example, I believe it to be inevitable that the population of our metropolitan areas will continue to increase and that at some stage in the plannable future—perhaps 25 to 40 years from now—the population will double. It is also inevitable that these persons will be housed in some manner. However, the particular manner of housing is not inevitably to be a slum, either vertical or horizontal. What we must try to cooperate with is a doubled number of human beings. We try to use our intelligence by choosing only those alternatives which produce the best, most efficient, most liveable, etc., urban environment.

Or to take another example of inevitability, we can talk about automobiles. I believe it to be inevitable that total automobile travel will increase and will increase more rapidly than the population. This is the result of a continuing increase in automobiles per capita and in total miles traveled per automobile. At the same time I do not think it inevitable that we should continue to have, and cater to, all of the debilitating effects of automobile travel. I do not think it is inevitable that parks should be ripped to pieces by expressways.

To put it on a statistical basis, some events will have a probability of 1.0. These are inevitable. Other events have a probability of 0.999. These latter events are avoidable. True, if they are unpleasant developments that should be forestalled, it will take a hell of a fight because you have only one chance in a thousand of avoiding them. In the first case you cooperate, in the second case you offer and fight for alternatives.

I fear also that it is inevitable that we will make mistakes, that we will not be persuasive or forceful enough always to put over the intelligent one-in-a-thousand alternative. The fact that we are going to get licked occasionally doesn't discourage me because it seems to me that in some cases honor will accrue to us as prophets only after the people see a couple of our dire prophecies come true. This has been our experience.

There are some other things that I think are inevitable. Among these I would put automation, shorter workweeks, and an increased proportion of older persons in the population. I even put world peace among the inevitables.

Another attribute of an inevitable occurrence is that it belongs nowhere on any scale of moral values. This does not mean that there is no *emotional* content in the public attitude toward such an event. There undoubtedly is an emotional reaction to practically everything I have listed as being inevitable. There is, for example, plenty of emotional reaction to the idea of a doubled population; there is no shortage of people who think that there are enough—if not already too many—people in the world.

Probably I like the definition of planning as cooperation with the inevitable because I feel in many cases when I talk to people that either (a) they sit apathetically and blindly while these forces are bearing down upon them; or (b) they hustle around and try to cast magical spells to scare away the demons of population, automobile traffic, aging persons, and automation. And in doing so they lay themselves wide open for some unpleasant things.

Condensed from "The Shape of Plans to Come," a dinner address at the 40th Anniversary Meeting of the Ohio Planning Conference, Columbus, February 16, 1959.

As the title for this talk, I chose "The Shape of Plans to Come." I think the shape of *things* to come is getting more apparent each day. And I lean to the belief that it is the shape of *things* to come that will determine the shape of *plans* that we make. This is heresy, as any planner will tell you.

I lump all things that planning is interested in under the general term *urban growth*. This includes population growth, population migration, industrial development, housing, family formation, public works, hospitals, schools, increased leisure, and so on. It is a miscellaneous and formless collection of ideas, problems, statistics, and social actions. To generalize: we will have continued urban growth with only occasional and relative respite, growth eventually at a rate beyond that we have seen since the end of World War II. I am assuming—this we must assume—that there will be no all-out World War III during the rest of the 20th century; that somehow, someday, China will solve its own problem of population explosion. How shall we plan for and during the coming years of urban growth? What will our plans look like? What will our cities look like?

Grand plans will be carried out in the future neither more nor less than they have in the past. Past experience will in no way slow down the preparation of grand plans, of even grandiose plans. We shall probably have even more of them because there will be more people to make them. But there is a relativity about grand plans. The grand plan of the past for a city of 100,000, when applied to the future and to a city of a million, becomes merely a moderate-size project. So we can expect to see more project developments of limited area, such as Pittsburgh's Golden Triangle, Philadelphia's Penn Center, Chicago's South Side, New York City's Columbus Circle and Lower Manhattan developments.

It seems certain that the downtown pedestrian plaza will come to be the rule in most cities, although in 1959 there is not one such plaza in full operation. But the return of the central business district to the pedestrian will be strictly on a limited scale; I don't see any magic transformation of our cities to the kind of things you see in science fiction magazines—at least during this century.

Years ago, planners talked about the problems of railroads, what we were going to do with them as our cities grew and the number of passenger trains inevitably increased, and the number of grade crossings multiplied. At the 1920 National Planning Conference, a Cincinnati speaker talked about the deficiencies in his city's public transportation and told about the plans they had for rapid transit, plans that would certainly be implemented within the next few years. When you look at 40-year-old predictions, you must admire the prophetic abilities that some planners showed some of the time. But all of them were out in left field some of the time; and some of them were clear out of the ball park all of the time!

Most planners know and own up to their deficiencies as fortune tellers. And most mayors and city councils do also. Which means that most of our planning efforts will go into the improvement of our tools and the invention of new tools, because both planners and administrators are modest about their powers on guessing what is coming tomorrow. We shall be improving zoning, subdivision regulations, capital budgeting, and the more basic research tools of economics, sociological and population analysis.

There is not much glamour to this prospect. Nevertheless, we know that these tools are deficient, we know that in the past they represented the most effective and workable aspects of planning, we know that we have never been able to predict what sort of dragons will come snorting out of the forests of tomorrow, and that the best chance we have for conquering any dragons that show up is to have an armory full of sharp and lethal weapons.

Another important change to come in planning has also been foreshadowed during the past. This is the shift in the definition of public interest—the enlargement of that field in which we, the people, find it proper to exert governmental control. This is a delicate subject. Well-advised angels keep out of it, but I make no angelic claims. We would certainly be ostriches if we tried to pretend that the public attitude on governmental control is the same as it was in 1919. You need only to go down the line in matters not even relating to planning. Tick them off: unions, the stock exchange, deposit insurance, mortgage insurance, unemployment insurance, stream pollution, child labor, restrictive covenants, public housing—even compulsory military service and agricultural production. We have found in each of these justification for governmental interest. Can you have any doubt that by 1999 we shall have found more and more reasons for more and more controls?

We now find much to regulate in public transit. In the future we shall quite surely find that the whole question of mass transit can be answered only when all parts of every aspect of urban mass transit is in the hands of government. We shall also find the continued life of our cities will be possible only if we subsidize this same mass transit.

Another area of expanded governmental controls will be in middle-income housing. This is the forgotten land of housing, although we have played around with a few ideas. Over the next decades we can expect governmental interest in middle-income housing every bit as thorough as we now have in public housing, even to the extent of subsidy.

The most significant development related to planning has been the evolution from slum clearance through urban redevelopment to urban renewal. In the way in which I describe planning, urban renewal is both an improved tool for solving urban growth problems and also a broadening of the field that we find appropriate for governmental action. During the next decades we can expect to see the use of the urban renewal project increased until it becomes the dominant method of city replacement, to the nearly complete exclusion of the old hit-or-miss private replacement. But I believe that this also means a switch to more and more governmental financing in all phases, less private financing in any part of the urban renewal project. It also means that we will continue to have a project approach to solving urban problems in contrast to the comprehensive approach that planners feel to be so important. You can expect an increasing orientation of development and renewal projects centered around an institution of some kind: a college or university, a hospital or medical center, a governmental center, a church, even around a large industry or an industrial park functioning as an institution.

As urban growth increases, as development comes under more guidance and control by government, there will be a corresponding heightened interest in planning and urban development among special interest groups, organizations of specialties within our economy: organizations for power boat manufacturers, bowling alley proprietors, the petroleum industry, billboards, trailer manufacturing, swimming pool sales—even organizations of planners and planning officials. In the past, many of these groups concentrated on lobbying, both in Washington and in the state capitals. But they now see that the fate of their industry is not decided entirely at these high governmental levels; much is in the hands of county, city, town, and village government. More and more persons with special interests will be showing up at public hearings, at council meetings, at plan commission meetings, in community study groups.

To be certain you get your money's worth in this hocus-pocus business of future peering, I will say a word about the beginning of the 21st century, A.D. This will be a period of shortage planning. In fact (and this is the reason I mention it), shortage planning will be necessary, and started, during the final decades of the 20th century. "Shortage planning" is that type of planning which becomes necessary when there is clearly a shortage of some necessary commodity. It is about midway between conservation and rationing. You indulge in conservation when the wiser heads among you foresee that there will be shortages someday if you don't take care of what you've got. But the wiser heads don't prevail in most cases, so that sooner or later there is just not enough to go around, and then you have to go into rationing.

I don't believe there will be shortages of food, however, I foresee shortages of prime urban land and of small crop agricultural land. There will be shortages of water, probably a shortage of breathing air, and there will long have been a shortage of air for the use of airplanes. I am sure there will be shortages of many mineral resources. There will be shortages of skilled and trained human beings for the technical and managerial jobs of the day.

I do not like the idea of shortage planning, but I like even less the idea of rationing. There are many things that we can do to avoid either shortage planning or rationing. We have in our collective grasp—or will have during the coming years—the intelligence, the knowledge, and the tools to prevent shortages in land and to prevent shortages in water and breathing air. As of this moment, however, I am not convinced that we will use that intelligence or perfect those tools in time to preserve some of our irreplaceable resources.

It seems to me that we need a basic revision in our public philosophy. We recognize that a large part of the urban growth problem of today is a result of things that were done incorrectly by the past two or three or four generations. We are inclined to excuse our predecessors on the basis that they didn't know any better. I propose a change in our public philosophy. I propose that it should be just as socially unacceptable and criminally culpable to injure someone living 20, 30, or 40 years in the future as we have made it antisocial and culpable to injure someone living today. We certainly can no longer plead innocence. We can no longer say that we do not foresee the consequence of our actions. It is perfectly clear that because of the things that today we do to the land and to the water and to the air around us, we are laying up a store of troubles, a store of expenses, a store of injury and an abundance of shortages for future generations. Yet our public philosophy does nothing much more than click its tongue at the offenders.

This is a philosophy which needs changing. We have no right to saddle future generations with problems we could avoid now; our descendants will have more than enough trouble with those problems we cannot help them with today.

Quoted from "Planning: A New Look," an address at the Annual Meeting of the Philadelphia Citizens Council on City Planning, June 1, 1965.

There are events, there are forces, we must know about and think about. The first force is the complex mixture of the civil rights struggle, the equal opportunity program, the war on poverty, the crime and delinquency program, and the revolution in education.

We see the poverty program, the war against delinquency, the revolution in education as operations in the *social* field, as part of a strong move of government into *social* planning and *social* development. In the same complex of activities and programs, we also recognize an *economic* flavor—economics overtly present in the Appalachia program, but also inescapably a part of the equal opportunity program and the surge in education. For if you train a man for a new skill or a first skill, you must be there with a job in which he can use that skill.

The federal government predominantly, but also state and city governments, will be pouring enormous sums of money into this complex of socioeconomic programs. Most of this money will go into cities— probably 90 percent or more of the social problems that we attack are urban based, and 95 percent or more of the money that will be spent to solve these problems will be spent in urban areas. We must not be surprised nor too impatient if much of the money spent on these programs in the early years is wasted. An undertaking of the magnitude of this multiheaded attack on socioeconomic problems is bound to be inefficient and is bound to make many false starts before it settles down into an effective operation.

The second force with which we must reckon in the immediate future is the new press for *quality*. You will recall a description our parents had for the sort of hypocritical family, which seemed to be found in nearly every neighborhood, that had a Queen Anne Front and a Mary Ann Behind. I fear this description applies to all of our larger cities. Quality and beauty do not extend to the entire city. We have a tremendous job ahead of us.

These are the two forces that I see as dominating the coming urban future—social and economic change, and recognition of the right, yea, the necessity, for quality and beauty in the environment.

Citizens should take a new look at what they are doing in their city, what they should be doing for the next decade or so. Make a reappraisal. Recognize the new forces. Become aware of the impact of the socioeconomic revolution, become aware of the impact of the new demand for quality in the urban environment. And they should look over their planning tools, and try out some of the new tools. An arsenal of tools, properly employed, can create miracles.

2

Scylla, the Bathwater and Other Pitfalls

Editor's Commentary

In writing on dilemmas and pitfalls in the practice of planning, Dennis O'Harrow drew on both the constant flow of information he received from around the country, and his own years of experience as a planning commissioner and as the first president of the new town of Park Forest, Illinois. His approach was a mingling of the roles described by Grady Clay—interpreter, mediator, critic, waggish raconteur, nagging Dutch uncle. His method was frequently analogy—with a range from the rules and findings of science to the differing skills needed for shooting ducks, quails and jacksnipes. His medium was usually an ASPO Newsletter editorial.

The editorials and the one speech selected for this chapter deal with the baker's dozen of dilemmas and pitfalls explicit in the titles—situations, problems, responsibilities, attitudes that befall and confuse the planner, the planning agency, the mayor and council, and the public. They contain a dash of laws and prophecies and of what this county needs (the focus of another chapter), and the spice of DOH as the conscience of the planning profession.

Although all the editorials evoked comments from Newsletter readers and three were reprinted in other journals, the 1957 speech on "Planning for a Workable Program for Community Development," delivered to a special session of the New Jersey League of Municipalities, brought a letter to the ASPO President saying: "His paper . . . was outstanding. It is my belief that it should be put in the hands of every municipal official and planner in the country, if that were possible. The staff of the New Jersey League of Municipalities tells me that they have never had so many enthusiastic comments about a speaker and his paper." The paper was subsequently reprinted for distribution, and widely circulated. The first part, which documented with "some archeological research" the history of "how an idea that started as part of a scheme to get rid of blight and to prevent additional blight came to be a formula and a ritual prerequisite to federal government aid," has been omitted. The second part, a classic in the pitfall category, is reproduced here.

Scylla and Charybdis

**Extracted from the ASPO Newsletter
editorial, December 1962.**

The English language (and probably most other languages) is loaded
with colorful figures of speech that refer to the problem of choice between contradictory alternatives. To walk a tight rope. The straight
and narrow. Between the devil and the deep blue sea. The frying pan
or the fire. Between cliff and canyon. Between hell and high water.
The pit and the pendulum. Damned if you do and damned if you
don't.

Public planning is an activity in which the practitioner must always
operate in a state of delicate balance, must always walk a narrow
path. There may be a priority problem—shall the money be used for a
park or a fire station? But the choice between such alternatives is not
the important one. The real devil-deep sea choice pertains to carrying
out the plans, to enforcing planning decisions. How far should the city
go in insisting that plans be followed?

The philosophy of most planners is that planning is an advisory
process, giving counsel to a rational citizenry. But nowadays the rationality of the citizenry clearly does not differentiate between plans
and actions. What gets itself built must first have been planned. If
what gets built is not pleasing to the public, then the planner is to
blame—he could have planned it better.

And all the signs point toward less differentiation in the future.
Therefore the planning agency—and its confreres: the mayor, the
council, the city manager, the urban renewal agency—must become
more and more conscious of this hell-and-high-water aspect of its
operations.

The most effective planners are those who walk skillfully on their
path and are fully aware that it is more than likely that the path is
changing, widening at one side, pulling in at the other.

In the past, planning could be more aloof because there was generally little or no connection between the published plan for a city and
the way the city actually developed. Therefore, the public could not
blame the planner for things that went wrong because no one paid attention to plans anyway. But today, plans have a greater likelihood of
being carried out. The hiatus between plans and action gets smaller.

Those responsible for planning must face up to assuming more and more responsibility for what actually happens. They will find some of their most sacred cliches must go by the board. Especially, they must survey the situation on the authority of their plans.

The decision-makers are sure to be damned if they insist on plans being taken seriously, and just as sure to be damned if they don't.

Ideas-Ahead-of-Their-Time

Extracted from the ASPO Newsletter editorial, April 1958.

The timing of the appearance of ideas is the source of a lot of the trouble we have in planning. It is quite likely that much of the outcry against long hair, ivory towers, and dreamers in planning has been caused by planners championing ideas-ahead-of-their-time. Yet the very nature of planning is such that proposals must be acted upon ahead of time.

Take the chronology of a simple undertaking—say, the first public artificial ice skating rink in a middle-latitude city. The planner sees a need for the rink because he knows the popularity of ice skating for all age groups and he foresees the growing demand for recreation facilities. The public will resist because: (1) local winters are not reliable producers of natural ice skating; (2) it looks like a frill and costs money; and (3) it is now April—spring—and who is interested in ice skating anyway when the dogwood is in blossom?

Now figure the timetable. The best the planner should hope for is to convince the city council of the need for the ice rink within a year after he starts talking about it. It will take another year to get authorization and the rink constructed. Because it is bad to underdesign, the planner should calculate a rink that would at least have capacity enough to meet the neighborhood demand for five years. All this adds up to seven years. Today the planner must start advocating a project that will not hit peak efficiency and use for seven years.

With a seven-year lead for a small project, the planner is not taking much risk of pushing an idea-ahead-of-its-time. But the illustration is an exceedingly mild one of the advance calculations the planner has to make. Most of his plans by their very nature must be for much longer advance periods. They are just that much more likely to be considered ideas-ahead-of-their-time and to be rejected.

This also may explain why plan commissions and staffs that spend all their energy on repairing current municipal maladjustments and doing nothing to prepare for the future are likely to be best accepted by the public. In solving only current problems, you are less likely to come up with ideas-ahead-of-their-time. You are also less likely to make any lasting contribution to the good health of your city.

At the same time, it is foolish to come up with nothing but fine advance schemes, no matter how good and right and logical they might be. Neither you nor your ideas will be accepted, and you don't even have the saving grace of having cleaned up any of yesterday's mistakes.

The really successful planning operation is one in which it is possible to time proposals so that they see the light of day at precisely the earliest moment at which they can be accepted by the public. Knowing what this moment is requires a high order of intelligence and probably a higher order of luck.

Explanation and Prediction

An ASPO Newsletter editorial,
October 1959.

It has been claimed that there is a peck order among sciences. The mathematician looks down on the physicist, who in turn looks down on the chemist. In descending order from that point are biology, psychology, sociology. Casual observation on the behavior of scientists in their natural state seems to verify the claim.

Whether a science is high or low in the peck order appears to have some correlation with its ability for accurate prediction. The mathematician predicts unhesitatingly that each and every time he multiplies two by two, the result will be four. The physicist is almost as certain about the outcome of his experiments, like dropping a weight in a vacuum, although he is having some trouble in predicting the antics of subatomic particles. But when you get down to the sciences of human behavior, at the bottom of the peck order, the record for accuracy in prediction is abominable—or it would be if the behavioral scientists were foolish enough to stick their necks out.

The shadow of shame has also fallen on Darwin and evolution because the theory has no value for accurate prediction. Michael Scriven, writing in *Science* (August 28, 1959) examines the case against Darwin and evolution and the survival of the fittest. His analysis of a tricky problem in the philosophy of science may have pertinence to some underlying contradictions in the practice of the science or art of planning.

Scriven demonstrates that a science functions as well when it explains cause as when it discovers a law that allows future prediction of events. He points out also that knowledge of cause does not automatically make a scientist a competent prophet.

From time to time a man will fall asleep at the wheel of his auto, run into a culvert, somersault into a ditch and get killed. The immediate cause of death—the accident—is quite clear. It may also be possible to back up one step to show why he dozed off: less than eight hours of sleep the night before, a heavy meal, a long straight road. It was too much for the driver and he fell asleep. This is a causal explanation of a particular accident. Yet if you were given a driver under the same prior conditions, you would not predict the accident. Why? Because this accident will happen only once in 10,000 times and the probability of 0.0001 is a weak reed for prediction.

Explanation without prediction does not leave us helpless. We can advise drivers not to drive too many hours in a single day, not to drive when they are tired; we can urge them to pull off to the side of the road at the first sign of sleepiness, to keep the car windows open, etc. Whether they follow our advice or not, we still would not predict a fatal accident—there are still too many unknowns.

Explanation links present events with past events. Prediction links present events to future events. The two are similar enough so that it would seem the only thing needed was a slight shift in tense to make them interchangeable. But the difference is more than one of time. We explain an event by showing a causal connection between the prior condition and the event. To predict a future event, we do not need to know the cause at all, we need only to have a symptom and a highly

probable *if*—*if* the barometer drops suddenly to below 29 inches, we
are in for a big blow. The brass instrument we call a barometer has no
causal connection whatsoever with the storm. Our predictive accuracy for hurricanes has increased with our increased density of
weather observations and speed in communication and analysis. But
our hope for tempering the storm's fury rests not on increasing our
ability to predict the storm, but on increasing our ability to explain
and remove the causes.

It seems to me that in planning and guiding urban development, we
are inclined to confuse explanation with prediction. Or if we don't
confuse it ourselves, our constituents confuse it. Or we are forced into
making predictions when we know we should stick to explanations.

Our past reports are littered with the corpses of our bad predictions—bum guesses about population, automobiles, roads, mass transit, airplanes, unemployment, residential habits, income, parks,
schools. Our guess on a city's future population and its composition
will be made on the projection trends, which are in no sense causes,
although the result may be reasonably accurate. But we can take a
current census and by working with past counts and other studies we
can begin to know actually what happened, what were the causes in
the change in number and composition during the intercensal period.

A planner prepared a master plan for a city during the late 1920s.
He predicted that the daily traffic count over a certain bridge would
reach 20,000 vehicles in 20 years. Just 20 years after his report appeared, a count of traffic on the bridge showed the prediction to have
been miraculously accurate. But although the actual and predicted
figures coincided, it was purely accidental. In the intervening years
there had been our worst depression and our greatest military involvement. The auto traffic curve had undergone violent and completely
unforeseen gyrations and, by coincidence, had arrived at the magic
figure of 20,000 at the date of planner had said it would. By his
method, however, he would not have been even remotely close to predicting the traffic five years earlier during gasoline rationing; nor five
years later when the postwar boom got into high gear.

Explanations offered as predictions probably do most damage to the
cause of urban planning in land use. We explain that among the causes
of blight are nonconforming uses, residences in industrial districts, filling stations in residential areas. We explain it and prove it by showing
where it has happened in the past. But if we predict that it will happen
in the future at any particular point where there is presently an

offbeat use and no blight, or where an overgenerous board of zoning appeals might grant permission for an offbeat use—then we are in trouble. Because the explanation is neither a law nor a highly probable correlation by which we can make predictions. The advocates of leaving the nonconforming use where it is and the pleaders for special privilege from the hands of the board of appeals will be only too happy to demonstrate our fallibility to us. This clearly weakens our effectiveness in our work. We have to make some predictions and we should do so when we have a law or a highly probable correlation. We may be forced into making predictions by extending the line on the graph in a certain direction only because it is already going in that direction.

At the same time we should also spend more and more of our effort to seek explanations and ferret out causes. Sometimes it seems that a lot of planning is like trying to prevent hurricanes by holding the barometer needle in place with the forefinger.

We must also try our best to understand the difference between explanation and prediction and to convey that difference clearly. We must take special precautions not to be tempted into predicting where we can only explain.

Indeterminacy and Planning

An ASPO Newsletter editorial, June 1960.

A capital budget, prepared by the planning staff, approved by the plan commission, and adopted by the city council—this is probably the most satisfactory accomplishment in planning. The adopted capital budget is concrete, the projects become tangible streets, buildings, parks, schools. The capital budget is immediate, no delay once the city council has said yes, no endless evening speeches before civic clubs trying to sell an idea. No waiting until you are old and hard-of-hearing to find out if you will be accepted or rejected.

But there is apt to be a feeling of desperate urgency about getting a capital budget adopted that is more than just the urgency of the need for the scheduled projects. There is apt to be a feeling (not conscious, to be sure) that if we don't get these projects built soon, we may not need them.

During the first years of the '40s when it was clear that the United States was not going to be able to act as the arsenal for the Western Allies and at the same time keep its urban physical plant up to date, there was a big push to store up a batch of public works plans. This was a shelf of projects. When the war was finished and the inevitable depression occurred, you had only to reach up on the shelf and you were ready to put all the unemployed soldiers and munitions makers to work on useful public projects. Cities were encouraged to prepare projects that were needed to carry out the objectives of a master plan, and most of those that were prepared did follow from planning studies.

The campaign for a shelf of projects was not overwhelmingly successful. This was partly because the engineers and architects who would have designed the projects were so involved in the immediate demands for war-oriented construction there was nohing left for peacetime planning. But this did not turn out nearly so unfortunate as we guessed it would. In the first place, there was no devastating depression after the war, so the made-work aspect was unnecessary. But the war years did create a backlog of public needs, and public construction eventually got underway on a large scale.

In the second place, it was the experience in those cities that did have a shelf of sorts, that the more detailed and precise was the planning of the project, the more out-of-date and inadequate was that planning. In 1940 we would have built it this way, in 1950 it was a good thing that we weren't permitted to build it that way.

This is a fundamental problem in planning: trying to do something that is valid today and will still be valid in 10 or 20 years. The capital budget gets it done quick, before we change our minds because the situation, when tomorrow comes, is different from what, yesterday, we thought it would be.

The dilemma shows up another way in zoning, where it is making conscientious planners have nightmares. A planner tries to design the zoning regulations so that they foresee all situations and forestall all sniping. This takes a terrific amount of verbal gymnastics, even to the point where pictures and diagrams become necessary because syntax is so involved and tortuous. The zoning ordinance becomes thicker and thicker, ever more detailed and precise, ever more inflexible and authoritarian.

The law is an immediate instrument also, like a public building under construction. A completed building, however, is relatively difficult to amend so you adjust your life as best you can to live with it. The 1955 zoning ordinance, on the other hand, is easy to amend or tamper with in 1960, so you can adjust it to fit 1960 conditions— maybe legally, or probably illegally or at least improperly. Then the best laid zoning plans start eroding away.

Rigid rules are self defeating. When, as in some modern zoning ordinances, they go to extremes to be perfectly clear and definite, they leave no room for change. But change is inevitable. The greater the accuracy of words in giving the idea, the less margin for interpretation to accommodate unforeseen changes in the future. And if the words provide accurately for the future, they will have fallen short in meeting the needs of the present.

This is not intended to be a criticism of capital budgeting or zoning—useful, if imperfect tools. Instead it is meant to point out the dilemma that we face in all planning efforts. It is just that there is need for something, some rule or creed or idea that we can fall back on. This idea or set of ideas must be simple. It cannot be too specific, and it should rarely if ever be directly applicable to a particular problem. But it must be of such nature and power that it may be interpreted to answer many questions. The example of the constitutional phrases *general welfare* and *interstate commerce* come to mind.

It is hard for us to admit that the usefulness of a plan may increase with its generality, even with its ambiguity—like the Delphic Oracle. It is hard to admit that even a little part of the softness of the zoning board of appeals may be justified to correct the too carefully engineered strait jacket of the modern zoning regulations. We also like to favor the rule by law rather than by men—but honesty makes us recognize that we live under a rule of men's interpretation of law. This we shall have in planning as well—an interpretation by men of laws, or rules, or goals. We need improvements in the laws and goals, but we will not get improvement by being more detailed and picayunish in our plans.

A New Technique

Condensed from the ASPO Newsletter
editorial "For Planning and Development: A
New Technique," May 1962.

I have identified a new technique in the urban development field. Perhaps it should not be labeled *new*, it has been around a long time. But the use of this technique has increased to the point that it must be reckoned with, whereas it was once insignificant.

I received two hurry-up calls for help in one day, both urgent enough to warrant telephoning. One came from a planner in a small city. He, his plan commission and the city council were under great pressure to downgrade the zoning in a certain commercial district adjacent to a new million square foot regional shopping center.

The regional shopping center had been in operation about three years. But the property on which the zoning change was sought, quite a large parcel, was still undeveloped. The owner was screaming. How much longer could he hang onto this property? It was costing him money to hold it—interest, taxes—every year! He had bought it for about $40 a front foot just before the shopping center was announced, but he could not sell it, at his price, for any use permitted in his zoning district, which was a restricted business classification. Now here he had a chance to sell it for an auto agency plus a used car lot and he would get his asking price, about $400 a front foot. The city owed it to him! They had to relax the zoning ordinance!

The auto dealer was also screaming. He needed to expand, and he could not do this at his old site. The auto dealer submitted a letter that he had received from the giant Detroit company that made the cars he sold. The writer of the letter was of the opinion that the land opposite the shopping center was a real hot spot and the dealer could sell lots of cars from it. This letter from the auto gods of Detroit was *the* imprimatur—what was the city waiting for?

The planner who called was desperate. As he saw it, the proposal meant the beginning of a commercial slum, a used-car row. But the council was shaking its collective head—a man has a right to make a living. The planning commission was weakening—three years, no development, maybe they were wrong in the first place. Only the mayor was standing pat, but the heat on him was getting intense, and he was pushing the planner for protective insulation.

The second telephone call was from a planner in a much larger city. The city has a long-standing height limit in the zoning ordinance, primarily to protect a favorite local landmark. The maximum height would permit a 20-story building. Local businessmen with local capital had erected a number of buildings since the war, all following the height regulation without question. Now a super-developer of super-apartments, from out of town, had picked up an option on a property near downtown.

But he was yelling: he could not possibly build under the height restriction. He had to have 30 or maybe 40 stories. The land was so expensive (he still had only an option to purchase, not the title to the land) that he had to get more apartments per square foot. The city was unreasonable, arbitrary, discriminatory, and cruel. (The local businessmen had not found it so, but then they were local yokels, not hep to big city ways.)

Finally, if the city didn't give in and let him go up as high as he wanted, he would pick up his marbles and go build his apartments in another city. And how would they like that?

Local businessmen, even the ones who themselves had obeyed the rules, were restless, talking privately to the mayor and council. This was a big name from out of town. He had put up those real fancy buildings in New York and Chicago. Maybe they had better listen to him. They couldn't afford to let sentiment for the old landmark interfere with business. They couldn't afford to let him go somewhere else with his money. Maybe just this once they could let the building go up as high as he wanted. Anyway, it would sort of put them in the class of skyscraper cities along with New York and Chicago.

I have christened this "planning by stampede." I have studied Western drama on television and recognize the technique. By shouting loudly enough or shooting a six-gun in the right spot, the noise can be amplified psychologically until there is panic. No one by himself is wholly convinced of the imminence of disaster, but each one is a little uneasy. The individual uneasinesses bounce back and forth until they add up to one big scare, and then *wham!* all the cattle go thundering down the range and over the edge of the canyon into the gorge below.

If these two illustrations were isolated cases, I wouldn't worry. Just in the natural course of events, I could expect a stampede now and then. But I checked back through questions I have been getting, and I find evidences of panic and stampede in city after city, in question after question. I believe that planning by stampede is fast becoming an important force in urban development. I also believe it is an undesirable force.

While I am not yet ready to write the definitive work on how to prevent planning panic, I think it may be useful to list a few of the earmarks of the induced stampede:

1. The property owner threatens to leave town if he doesn't get his way.

2. The property owner claims that he stands to lose great sums of money—while really he only stands to make less profit under the existing system than if it were changed to suit him.

3. Outside experts come in to testify to the justice of the claim and the injustice of the city. Occasionally these experts are planners, but usually they are architects, management consultants and real estate type persons.

4. The proposed development will, according to the promoter, be of great economic benefit to the city.

5. The promoter has already given in to the city, compromised. He asks for permission to build only 10 stories above the height limit—he might have asked for 20!

6. The local regulations are claimed to be obsolete, arbitrary, and unfair.

Of course some of these, especially the last, are likely to be correct and applicable in a true case of hardship. But the planner, the planning commission, the city fathers—yea, the citizens themselves—should be wary of the proposal if there is more than a couple of these signs. Trying to outrun a stampede is not the same as being in the forefront of progress.

Too Much and Too Soon

**Extracted from the ASPO Newsletter
editorial, April 1964.**

The push for sensationalism, drama, and speed in news has built up a
public attitude of perpetual impatience about nearly everything. Problems must be solved neatly, completely, and promptly. If the solution
we are now trying seems to be somewhat messy, less than complete,
or a little slow, then we must try a new one. Everything should fit into
a half-hour program, with time out for commercials.

You can see this impatience in the current attitude toward urban
development problems.

What's the latest parking ratio for blacksmith's shops?

We hear that Podunk has three-dimensional zoning, we want it, too.

All our troubles will vanish if we can get a defense industry.

Why wait until it has been tested? Like the cancer drug, try every new
gimmick as quickly as you learn about it: performance standard zoning, transit subsidy, pedestrian malls, cluster subdivisions, condo-
miniums, data banks, new towns.

Certainly we should not be a stick-in-the-mud, scared to try anything new. Certainly someone must experiment, and at times make
mistakes, if we are ever to have progress.

And it will never be possible to say precisely how far ahead of the
crowd one should walk, or how long one should wait before following. But today everything seems to require emergency action. Everything new is better just because it is newer. And we have no patience
with an improvement that is just that—an improvement. It should be,
or appear to be radically different from that which went before.

Thoreau said the mass of men lead lives of quiet desperation. Today, they lead lives of noisy desperation. *That* can hardly be called an
improvement.

The Moving Target

**Extracted from the ASPO Newsletter
editorial, September 1964.**

Before World War II and automatic fire control (and since then to a great extent), the skill of a successful antiaircraft gunner was in his ability to follow the target, *at the target's own apparent speed.* This meant training the sights of a gun exactly on the target, then staying on target and moving smoothly with it as the target moved across the line of vision. Auxiliary gunners cranked into the gun adjustments for distance and speed until the projectiles came around to the right spot and collided with the enemy plane.

A similar system holds for the successful clay pigeon shot or the successful wild fowl hunter. He does not pull up, hold the gun steady, then fire. He moves the sights of his gun until he is matching the apparent speed of his target (with the proper lead because he must do his own calculation for target speed and distance) and then fires.

A game bird with a reputation for being a difficult target is the quail. This is because the quail is flushed from the ground, ordinarily is visible for only a short time before disappearing in the underbrush, and, during this short period, is accelerating rather than flying at a constant speed—as a duck or goose would fly. It is unusually difficult to keep the gun sight moving with the target.

Antiaircraft gunnery and wing shooting parallel community planning. The too general approach—by planners, by public officials, by citizens—is to refuse to recognize that the target will always be moving, will never be fixed. You cannot pull up, bang away with a static plan, and expect to hit anything.

In the world of hunting, to make the point-blank system work, you are not a sportsman. Your act is variously called the "pot shot" or shooting a "sitting duck" or "fish in a barrel."

In the world of urban planning, however, the pot shot just does not work. The duck will not sit still, the fish will not climb into the barrel. The target, the city, is moving all the time—never the same in two days. So you have a moving target. And your plan must aim to lead it constantly and by an appropriate amount. The philosophers of kinetic planning (which seems to be a good name for it) will disagree about how much of a lead you should give. Perhaps ten years is good, with the auxiliary financial planners programming six years ahead in order to hit the target. Too great a lead—the ancients to the contrary notwithstanding—makes it impossible to develop a program that will ever reach the target.

The problem with quail shooting is that the bird is accelerating all the time. The speed is not uniform and this makes aiming difficult. To a great extent, this corresponds to the expansion of many communities since World War II. No matter how fast you thought it was growing, the statistics a year later would show that you had underestimated the growth. This made the sitting duck technique, the fixed target, even sillier.

Nevertheless, in spite of the puzzlements and problems, a number of cities are producing planning that is practical. Many are keeping on target. Many city governments can pace planning operations to the speed of urban developments, even though that speed may be constantly increasing.

But to pull one final hunting analogy. A game bird even more difficult to bag than the quail is the jacksnipe. A spindle-legged little number with a voice like a rusty hinge, the jacksnipe, according to frustrated hunters, flies like a corkscrew. A duck flies with constant speed. A quail flies with constant acceleration. But a jacksnipe swerves and swoops, dodges and dives, and even completely reverses its direction of flight.

In a few places, just as planners and plan commissions are beginning to get the hang of it, something happens to make the government or the people of the area reverse their direction—at least reverse their philosophy of movement. Instead of an honest effort to understand, to cope with and accommodate to the change around them, they panic, dig in their heels, and refuse to believe.

This makes the most difficult environment of all in which to try to plan, to foresee and forestall the problems of the future. Because the future in these circumstances is not what will be tomorrow, but what has been yesterday. And if you refuse to believe that there will be any change, that there can be any change, that you will permit any change—you have no reason to plan for it. You might as well put your gun back up in the rack.

Replication: or Double the Trouble

Condensed from the ASPO Newsletter
editorial, February 1966.

Science, the Journal of the American Association for the Advancement of Science, published an article describing an experiment in extrasensory perception. Identical twins were used in the experiment on
the chance that their transmitting and receiving apparatus might be
more likely tuned to an identical extrasensory frequency. One twin sat
in one room and was signaled to blink his eyes. In another room, an
observer watched the second twin, and timed *his* eye-blinks to see if
they were made at the same time as those of his brother. Experimenters also recorded alpha waves in the brains of the twins.

The experimenters thought that they may have found some evidence of extrasensory perception. The eye-blinks and alpha waves
corresponded closely enough, after much mathematical examination
of the results, to be beyond what might be expected by pure chance, or
so the experimenters thought.

As soon as the article describing the experiment reached the members of the AAAS, letters started pouring in to the editor. The majority of scientists are highly skeptical of everything in parapsychology
(the scientific version of the old psychic research) so this reaction
could have been expected. The tenor of the letters was similar. The
conditions of experiment were not described accurately enough, not
enough variables were considered, there were no control subjects, *the
experiment could not be replicated.*

"Replication" is an ugly word, but dear to the hearts of scientists.
Most of us would use the word "duplicate," but there may be a subtle
difference.

Anyway, the rules of the science game call for replication. If you
carry out an experiment and you think you have discovered something new or interesting, you must provide *all* the necessary information on what you did: "I did a, b, c, . . . n; I got result R," so that any
other scientist can go through exactly the same steps a, b, c, . . . n. If
he also comes up with result R, you are partially vindicated. If you
found something particularly unusual or offbeat, it may be that your
experiment will have to be replicated over and over. But unless you

can be, and until you have been, replicated, your discovery cannot be accepted.

The occasion for this excursion into the methods of science is a letter I received. The writer spoke of a study which investigated a certain standard that is widely used by planners. The report stated that the investigation had found the commonly used standard was too high and suggested a new one as being more appropriate. Our correspondent wrote: "I am not convinced that the study was accurate." If he had been a scientist, he might have said, "I'll believe it when I see it replicated."

There could have been no reason to question the credentials of the person making the study nor to doubt the integrity of the person who commissioned it. And the planner's standard that had been investigated was one of those intuitive, rule-of-thumb figures that abound in the planning mythology. But planning is trying to take on the trappings of science, and if it is to succeed, it must follow the rules of the game, one of which is replication.

If planning is to become more nearly a science, or partially a science, it will be an ambiguous situation. Because planning deals with physical things such as automobiles and land and air and water, it seems to be properly treated as a physical science. Even in its dealing with people, it is often primarily concerned with numbers and with the natural processes of birth and death, which is the field of biometry.

Yet because planning aims to understand and to cater to the needs of people, it must also hope to be accepted as a social science. Replication in social science is notoriously difficult, and because replication is less often possible than in physical or natural science, the reliability of a pronouncement in social science is more often questionable. Some will be based on "the considered judgment of reasonable men with experience in the field." Others will be based on studies, investigations, perhaps even experiments. We cannot avoid using the considered judgment of experienced men—this is necessarily the only way we can carry on most of the business of government. But any figures which claim scientific validity must be able to be tested for scientific probity. We must describe how we arrive at them so that they may be replicated.

Planning has a long road ahead before it can become eligible to play a game that calls for replication. Which means that we should have plenty of grains of salt handy with which to take some of the stuff that we will be seeing in the future.

The Workable Program Game

Condensed from "Planning for a Workable Program for Community Development," an address to the New Jersey League of Municipalities, Atlantic City, November 21, 1957.

I started my adult life right at the beginning of the Great Depression. As youth and man I have seen the beginning and the increase of federal aid programs in many parts of my life. I have observed these as a state bureaucrat, as a federal bureaucrat, as the mayor of a small community, and most recently as a private observer not directly involved in programs at any point. Over the past 25 years I have learned to see a few things—through a glass dimly, to be sure—which seem to characterize many of these programs and the actions and attitudes of both recipients and administrators of federal aid.

To be quite blunt about it, I think we must all be alert to the possibility that federal aid programs can do harm as well as good— can, in fact, accomplish just the opposite of what they are intended to do. This is not the fault of the original conception of the program, nor is it the fault necessarily of the beneficiaries of the program. It is, in fact, just a sort of law of political nature that gets in the way of doing the things that we want to do.

One of the dangers of any federal aid program is that it quickly takes on the characteristics of a game. Not a game in the sense of two opponents fighting to put a ball on the other side of a goal line—more a guessing game. It goes this way:

As a prospective recipient of federal funds, the first step is to get a Workable Program certified by the Administrator. A Workable Program has seven points—we must get credit for all of those seven points.

I am sure that I am being grossly unfair to a great number of people and to a great number of cities. But the more I see of urban renewal operations around the country and the more I read about urban renewal programs in the cities, the more I feel that urban renewers are acting according to that old school aphorism: "It isn't whether you win or lose that counts, the important thing is how you play the game!" It isn't important whether anything ever gets renewed, redeveloped, rehabilitated, or conserved—it is how clever and adroit you are in playing the game and getting things through to that nirvana of all nirvanas—"the loan and grant stage." I fear very much that most of the urban renewal schemes are based upon the hope that the powers-that-be will rule the documents and assurances submitted acceptable—rather than upon any real serious desire to have urban renewal as a part of the community total planning scheme.

An overwhelming yearning for "free" federal money plays an important part in federal aid programs. This is matched by an equally overwhelming desire on the part of federal bureaucrats to push the money out for fear some might be left over at the end of the fiscal year, which would militate against getting additional and equal or larger appropriations in subsequent years.

It is quite difficult to avoid playing a game, to avoid matching local wits against federal wits. It is difficult for the local agency to avoid the necessity of having to try to guess what will be acceptable in Washington; or for Washington to avoid having to try to guess whether the local agency is accurate, or is sincere but overly optimistic, or is just plain hypocritical in its claims.

It is also difficult to avoid game playing in view of the lushness of the prize that is offered. But those responsible for the administration of local affairs will find themselves caught in something about as productive as a bingo game unless and until they decide the principle objective is to get on with a job: the job of cleaning up old blight and putting a stop to future blight. Blight is definitely not something a municipal official can be neutral about. He either gets to work positively to do something about it, or he aids and abets the spread of blight by doing nothing, by being apathetic. One of the first things to do is to strike out the capitalization of those two words, "Workable Program." Make it small w and a small p.

What are the distinguishing features of a small w workable, small p program to eliminate and arrest blight? Is it determined by the seven lovely virtues that the federal government has so conveniently listed in the little yellow booklet: sound local housing and health codes, general master plan, neighborhood analysis, administrative organization, financial capacity, relocation housing, citizen participation? No, the workable program, without benefit of capital letters, is simply what the words mean: a program that works, a program that gets about the job of eliminating blight, a program that prevents blight in the future. The program may have one or none of the stigmata listed or it may have all of them and a dozen others they never mentioned.

I know one small city which has no blight at present, but is headed for it as sure as the Lord made green apples. All this city needs to prevent blight—all it needs for a program that will work—is for the city fathers to have guts enough to fire a superannuated city attorney who keeps them from adopting the kind of subdivision regulations the city needs and is empowered to enact under the state statute. I know another city where the most important single act needed to prepare a workable program against blight would be to clean house in the police force. They have approval on a "Workable Program" which does not mention this item. I know another group of cities—all of the cities in one state—where the most important single step in eliminating blight would be to get the state constitution altered so that they could have municipal home rule.

If you want to see the most catastrophic producer of urban blight that you can imagine, go to a small city that lost the one big factory, or a medium-size city that depended upon an industry which became obsolescent. The resuscitation of the economic base of such a city is the overwhelmingly important part of any program to fight blight. Or take a clearly demonstrated example: the most important weapon in the program to eliminate blight in Pittsburgh undoubtedly has been the air pollution control ordinance and its enforcement.

A related problem arises in the use of minimum standards in governmental regulations. It is almost certain that any standard which is set up in a law or in an administrative rule as a minimum acceptable condition almost immediately becomes, instead, the maximum that people will undertake. There is great danger that the standards for the "Workable Program" will be taken as the maximum necessary to produce a "workable program."

In the game of "Workable Program," played according to the seven rules of the road, somebody has to win the prizes and it might as well be you. At the same time, I hope you will make it your business to produce a program that works, regardless of whether or not it is granted the imprimatur of the Administrator.

ADP and the Planning Agency

An ASPO Newsletter editorial, October 1965: Excerpts from the luncheon address at the Third Annual Conference on Urban Planning Information Systems and Programs, Northwestern University, Evanston, Illinois, September 16, 1965.

An early experience of mine was with a primitive type of computer. I refer to the WPA, Works Progress Administration—a sort of War on Poverty, 1935 version—and one bit of work it performed. If one current model electronic computer adds one and one at the rate of one operation per microsecond, the result at the end of one second will be exactly the same as you would get by having one million 1935 model WPA project workers performing the same operation at the rate of one addition per second for one second. A million is a million is a million.

I did not have a million WPA workers—only 30 to 50, depending on the budget, the weather, the length of the bread line, the incidence of influenza and a few other factors. However, I did have a machine that could turn out an enormous amount of work if the individual operations were kept simple enough and the whole contraption were programmed properly. My primitive WPA-type computer was employed in planning research (that's what we called it then) for state planning. My function was to program the machine on instruction from above, keep it oiled, replace defective units, and check the print-out.

My machine and I turned out hundreds—perhaps thousands—of "interesting" charts and maps. We charted and mapped school children, brick plants, births, deaths, railroad mileage, interurban trains, crime, incidence of malaria, building permits, streets—name it, we made a picture or a graph or a table of it. I would show my boss our latest bar chart and he would say: "Hm-m, that's an interesting bar chart." We also produced interesting pie charts and interesting scatter diagrams and interesting S-curves and interesting matrices.

We did not produce any plans, interesting or otherwise. So far as I have since been able to determine, we had no effect whatsoever on the development of the state, other than to feed and clothe and keep alive my boss, me, and the individual components of our WPA-type computer. The moral of my story is that although there have been some remarkable advances in hardware since 1935, I have a sneaking hunch the printout has not changed all that much. I do not claim to be completely *au courant* with what is being turned out by data processing-oriented planning staffs, but I have flipped through a number of reports and I get a feeling that great effort and much machine time is being devoted to turning out interesting—and sometimes not-so-interesting—information.

I see this as one of the great dangers of this data processing age: the proliferation of research for research's sake. In research for planning conducted by planning agencies, I am an irreconcilable pragmatist. I want to know exactly how that research will be used to guide and improve the development of the community which the planning agency serves. I am not so complete a Philistine that I advocate starting from a preconceived result and then gathering statistics to prove my point. I do, nevertheless, advocate that you set forth, before you ask the machine to add the first one to the second one, the possible range of results; and that you make an honest effort to determine what effect any of the possible answers will have on the business of plan preparation or plan administration.

Nor am I against "basic" research, which is often better described as "far out," rather than basic. I just happen to believe this sort of stuff is not a proper function of the local planning agency. Perhaps I might feel different if I believed that any local planning agency had really exhausted the possibilities of the traditional tools and methods and was forced to seek exotic new *modi operandi*. I have yet to see that agency. A related danger for planning agencies experimenting with data processing is empire building, or letting the data processing operation begin to dominate the other operations.

I also detect a great danger of working to a spurious accuracy with a computer. A fundamental tenet of research is that the results you get can be no more accurate than the data you work from. Yet I see data on dilapidated houses and tourist expenditures and unemployed middle-aged people calculated out to two decimal places. Even if it is possible to achieve accuracy to one or two or ten places, how will you use the results? Do you really need to know that land zoned for single-family housing is 27.34 percent of all the land in the city? Or will your knowledge be precise enough if you use 27.3 percent? Or 27 percent? Or merely that single-family residence is about one fourth of all the land?

The almost infinite capacity of a computer to ingest, digest, and deliver data makes it awfully tempting to feed it and milk it beyond all reason. It seems to me that the greatest weakness in the planners' use of data processing is that they do not plan for it. They dream about the use they can make of data processing, and all its potential, both known and unknown. This is a type of planning, but at the same time I think planners forget one of their basic principles. A plan to be effective must be comprehensive—which means it must cover everything within the realm of authority of the government for which the plan is made.

The planner sees data processing in terms of what it can do for him. This is wrong. He should look at this miraculous new gadget as a tool that can work for every department, every agency in his government. The use of it in planning should be secondary—almost a fringe benefit. There are several quite logical reasons for this, reasons which are well known to planners. A computer installation is a capital expenditure, whether it is purchased or leased. As such, it should be subjected to cost and benefit analysis. The planner should consider the relative place of planning in the total governmental scheme. One way of approximating this relative place is to compare his budget with the total municipal budget. This does not mean that the planning application of data processing should be considered as trivial, but it does mean that in the comprehensive plan for data processing, 99 or 99.9 percent of the city operations should be primary and determinant.

I believe that the planning agency should be involved in making the plans for the total municipal use of data processing. I know that some planners will not agree because they see this as a function of management planning, and they believe management planning is outside their field. It is my observation that the most successful planning agencies are those deeply involved in management planning—and, in my opinion, properly so.

A third reason for total planning of data processing might be classed as enlightened self-interest on the part of planners. The effective use of data processing in planning calls for up-to-date and accurate information—perhaps most of which must come from other agencies and other city departments. Unless those other agencies and departments are convinced that the computer can return very useful information to them, the data they furnish will be neither accurate nor current. Also, the printout must be immediately useful to their ongoing operation.

Data processing has a fine future as a planning tool. There should be further study and experiment to advance its use in planning in line with its potential, provided that study and experiment does not preempt time and energies and funds that should be devoted to the regular business of planning.

We must not forget that we know more about cities now than we have been able to use effectively. No mathematical model that I have heard of has been able to account for all of those things that make urban planning so difficult, factors such as ward politics, birth control, Viet Nam, the personal idiosyncrasies of councilmen, and the condition of the weather on the day a crucial vote is taken.

Data processing is on the wave of the future, but let's be sure we know how to swim when we dive in.

Begin at the Beginning

Condensed from the ASPO Newsletter
editorial, November 1965.

The Occasion: A subregional public hearing on alternative metropolitan land-use plans.

The Actors: Staff members of the metropolitan planning agency, mayors, councilmen, plan commissioners from communities in the subregion, and a chubby woman in a flowered dress who saw Communism lurking in every comma (and who will not be mentioned again).

The Props: A slide strip showing the need for metropolitan planning, three diagrammatic maps of three alternative land-use plans for the metropolitan area, and three large-scale, broad-brush sketches of the particular subregion and how it would look developed under the three alternative plans.

The First Incident: After the presentation by the metropolitan planning staff, there was a brief intermission. The mayor of East Westville (pop. 5,263) walked up to one of the sketches of the region.

"Where is East Westville on this map? It sort of looks like it should be here, in the middle of the purple patch. What does purple mean?"

"Purple is industry."

"You mean you are going to develop all of East Westville and put it into factories?"

"Oh, no! In the first place, the only way this or any metropolitan land-use plan can come about is through what you do in your own city, through what you do with your own land-use plan and your own zoning ordinance. In the second place, this is only diagrammatic. Under this particular alternative, there would be just a general concentration of industry in your area."

"I don't understand. We've got lots of nice homes, and a brand-new shopping center, and good schools, and . . ."

The Second Incident: Following the intermission, the audience got a chance to ask questions and comment. A man rose.

"I am the chairman of the Pugsburgh Planning Commission. You said that in order to carry out metropolitan planning you are going to change the tax system so that towns that can't raise enough taxes to take care of themselves will get money from other towns that are paying their own way. Well let me tell you, we are not about to pay for schools and streets and sewers in other towns. We've got a good plan and we are going to follow it and we are going to pay for it and we couldn't care less about what happens in other towns. Let them make their own plans and let them tax themselves to pay for it, just like we have done."

*   *   *

If your village has just been wiped out by the planner's prismacolor pencil, you are not apt to take kindly to his metropolitan plan. If you have been persuaded by one planner to buy planning for your own community, only to find that another planner has a superscheme that

ignores what you have done, your support for the metropolitan plan
will be less than enthusiastic.

What is the answer?

First, it would seem reasonable to recognize that metropolitan
problems are being solved only (a) in those very few places with
metropolitan governments; (b) in regions where a single-purpose
authority is created to attack its assigned problem; (c) for
highways, where the state moves ahead because it alone has the
(federal) money to carry out a metropolitan highway plan; and
(d) in those areas in which there is a regional quasi-government
through a voluntary governmental council. But even in those
areas where there is one or the other kind of regional action
agency, there is a notable absence of any grand rearrangement of
the land-use pattern.

Second, with our display of total comprehensive metropolitan
patterns we are contradicting one of our most sacred cliches—
that plans to be effective must come from the people, must be
built from the bottom up, not from the top down. We do not
remedy the defect by discussing alternatives with the people,
after the fact, if those alternatives were not devised by the people.

Third, the problems most amenable to regional treatment are
those that are kinetic rather than static; they embody movement
to, from, and through a community and are therefore more
demonstrably joint problems of neighboring independent governments. Movement is a prime characteristic of air and water
pollution, floods, water supply, traffic, and transit. Movement
is not a characteristic of land as a resource, and this is what the
local community sees.

Fourth, if a metropolitan plan is to succeed, it must contain a
strong dose of immediate usefulness to the individual community. This is why regional highway plans will be carried out. In
spite of frequent bickering on alignment, local governments can
endorse the objective of a highway plan because it clearly
benefits the hometown. Other successful metropolitan accomplishments such as flood protection and waste disposal similarly
produce immediate local effects.

The present land-use pattern in metropolitan regions is largely
accidental. The land-use pattern of the future is being deter-

mined by the transportation authorities which, despite some lip service to producing a more rational development, are working almost entirely with conditions as they are, not as the metropolitan planners would like to see them.

We are not going to start over and do a total reconstruction job. It is time that we stopped asking for total repeal of local plans. It is time that we also pay attention to what exists, and to work with it and to work to improve it by helping local governments, by trying to help with the dirty *little* problems in which we can prove that a joint approach can produce immediate beneficial results. Boundary-line zoning conflicts, annexation and incorporation disputes, joint utility undertakings—micro as well as macro land-use planning—these are some of the realities of life.

When will we learn that we must begin at the beginning and not at the end? Or do we believe that if we make our plans big and broad and diffuse enough, we will avoid ever being asked to carry them out?

Plans and Anti-plans

**An ASPO Newsletter editorial,
December 1965.**

Since I wrote of the problems of exhibiting a metropolitan land-use plan, the unfortunate impressions that local public officials get from such a plan, and the questionable usefulness of a metropolitan scheme that had little chance of being carried out, I have learned of other situations that make me believe there is a problem even more serious than I had thought, the buildup of a dilemma that may soon bring planning to an impasse. To review some of the evidence:

The General Neighborhood Renewal Plan (GNRP) was promoted by the Housing and Home Finance Agency as a device to give a broader and more balanced method of handling urban redevelopment projects. The relation of a redevelopment area (or several redevelopment areas) to a larger area was studied, and plans for rehabilitation and conservation in the entire neighborhood were tied in with redevelopment. However, in many instances, when the GNRP was published—and even before it was published—the residents of the neighborhood claimed that the plan itself was blighting the area. They not only claimed it, but they proved it. Real estate transactions came to a complete halt, except for distress sales. In many cities the GNRP was therefore outlawed by the council.

Recently the planning staff in a large city presented a plan for a new parkway. The parkway had been proposed publicly several years earlier. This new plan finally showed the location with some precision, but still without a definite schedule for construction. At a public hearing, property owners from one end of the route to the other screamed "blight" and "confiscation of private property." The screams were heard in the council chamber, heard and heeded. The plan was withdrawn.

In another large city, the preliminary hearings on a comprehensive plan are under way. The city ordinance requires that the plan be adopted by the council. It is clear from the preliminary hearings that there will be substantial and potent pressure to get the council to turn it down. Again, the indication of new expressways and the broad-brush, no-detail, designation of future land use are cited as blighting and confiscatory. Assurances by the staff that everything is "diagrammatic only" do nothing to calm the opposition.

Then there is the San Diego experience. After two years of careful, conscientious public hearings and work with the citizens, a comprehensive plan was presented to the council. It was adopted by a unanimous vote, backed by practically every organization and civic group in the city. Within two weeks of adoption of the plan, a petition for a referendum was circulated, and the plan adoption was placed on the ballot of the next election for decision by the citizens. In the face of strong support *for* the plan from a number of important organizations, the vote was nearly two-to-one *against* it in the election and the plan was thrown out. The opposition to the plan used lies and the typical dirty tactics of the Radical Right. Supporters of the plan used truth and sweet reason. But the opposition prevailed and San Diego had no official plan.

It should be pointed out that planning is not a Johnny-come-lately in any of these three cities, nor in many of the cities repudiating the GNRP device. Planning is respectable with a history of acceptance of its past works by the people.

It is a truism in American planning theory that the people must participate in planning if it is to be effective. There is considerable experience to show that a plan sprung on the people as a *fait accompli* is in for a rough time. This fits with the strong prejudice in American democracy against secrecy in governmental affairs. While plans are customarily first devised in the sanctuary of the planning department drafting room, their "advisory" status is always stressed and they are, by one method or another, subjected to public review. Still the current humor of the public indicates that if a plan is likely to be effective, or the public thinks it is, the plan is also likely to be vetoed by the public.

Another dilemma arises from the question of procedure. The early planning theorists held that a comprehensive plan was merely a guide. Because of this, it was better that it were not adopted by the legislative body—this would make it too rigid and give it a false air of accuracy. But later theorists have pointed out that because it did not give the plan official recognition by adoption, the council usually ignored the plan completely. Adoption was, therefore, necessary.

The subtlety of this distinction is lost on the public. The public knows that if the legislature adopts a no-parking ordinance for a particular street, this is not a guide, it is quite something else—park on that street and you get a ticket. At the same time there is endless documentation for the view that a not-adopted plan is also a not-followed plan. So why bother to plan at all?

Probably the most important factor changing the public attitude on plans is the increasing likelihood that a certain plan *will* be carried out—regardless of whether or not all of the formalities of legislative adoption are observed. This is the result of the massive federal intervention. Years ago a planner might come out as strongly as he wished with a plan to tear down an area he called blighted and rebuild it with modern structures. No one took him seriously because no one could possibly see where the money was coming from. Nowadays, all a planner needs to do is walk through the neighborhood with a piece of paper on a clipboard and the residents hear the crash of the wrecking ball against their walls.

For the same reasons, those who ignored the fine, inner-loop, outer-loop, spiderweb thoroughfare plans of the '30s are now painfully conscious of any map showing expressway routes, no matter how strong the claim that it is only "diagrammatic." When the $50 billion Interstate Highway System is completed, who doubts that another $50 billion will be forthcoming?

So there we are with a hatfull of contradictions. We state that authoritarian plans are both improper and unworkable, but even when we use citizen participation, we do not thereby also get citizen support. We hesitate after we have prepared our plans so that citizens may comment, and by our hesitation aggravate the problems we are trying to solve. We decry plans that are not effective, that are not carried out, yet our strongest opposition to plans is because the public believes they *will* be carried out. We say that urban development without plan brings chaos, and the public immediately votes for chaos.

Four or five swallows may not make a summer, but they are harbingers. There are several hundred cities in which the dilemma has not showed up because the citizens have not reacted in violent opposition—yet. But there are also a number of cities that the purist may classify as antiplanning, because no plans have been presented. In these cities no plans will be presented because the political leaders have anticipated the public reaction. If you are a gambling man and you gamble with your head rather than your heart, you might do well to place your bet on antiplans to pull ahead of plans.

The resolution of the dilemma is not apparent. What is apparent is that we are not going to get out of this by reworking the old planning axioms and remouthing the old planning cliches.

A Broad Brush with a Sharp Edge

**Extracted from the ASPO Newsletter
editorial, June 1967.**

A favorite indoor sport of metropolitan planning staffs is the preparation of comprehensive regional planning alternatives. Which means constructing from three to a dozen maps on which are shown ingenious—or ingenuous—arrangements of residential, commercial, and industrial land patterns, parks, greenbelts, new towns, urban corridors, nuclei, all laced together by hypothetical rapid transit lines that will probably never be built, and expressways that, unfortunately, probably will be built. The alternatives are tested by picking great quantities of numbers off the maps and pushing them through a mysterious formula in a computer, and then further testing by exposing the maps to public scrutiny.

Except for the one alternative which shows the planner's estimate of how the area will look in the future, if it continues to sprawl just as it has in the past (the one alternative that regional planning is supposed to prevent), the public is assured that the alternative regional land-use plans are merely broad-brush representations of the general character of the proposed land uses and the details will have to be worked out locally, by the local governments. Of course, if one of the prettier patterns is ever to come about, there will have to be some, a great many, changes made.

Our real choices, then, are two, the public says. One, to submit to a great number of violent disruptions of our present community if we choose one of the fancy plans. Or two, to leave things as they are. So long as you, the planners, cannot identify and specifically describe the changes, it makes more sense to choose the known rather than the unknown. And if this is the obvious choice, what point was there in drawing up all of these alternatives, what point in regional planning at all?

You must be persuaded, the planners answer, by our logic. Scheme A shortens the average journey to work by 0.31 miles—multiply that by x thousands of trips per day and look at the gasoline you save! Scheme B makes mass transit economical! Scheme C makes the extension of sewerage and water supply cost less! Scheme D puts a cultural center within 10 miles of every home! Of course, the public must realize that it will take some time to achieve these benefits. But with Scheme X your choice, you just go on living as you are now, only more so! Is that what you want?

So long as planning for urban regions continues as it is now practiced, this fatuous exercise in public participation will continue. In the first place, general promises of economy and spiritual uplift are not persuasive. If the planners could say, "You choose Scheme Y and we will guarantee to reduce your property tax by 10 percent in 10 years," the public would view the alternatives differently.

In the second place, so long as the planner works without a clear idea of how his plan will be carried out, so long as he is divorced from any responsibility for the consequences of his recommendations, so long will his plans be only pretty pictures. The effect of responsibility, or accountability, can be seen in the work of the city planner who knows his plans will be translated into sewer lines and urban renewal projects and zoning amendments.

And in the third place, the further the plan is removed from the details of the immediate environment of the individual human beings, the less valid is citizen participation, decision by popular vote. When someone is ill, the doctor does not call in the family to vote on whether the treatment should be penicillin or Aureomycin or sulfanil-amide.

Nevertheless, the broad-brush technique is appropriate in regional land-use planning, for the decision can only be competently made by a few well-informed persons who have the time and the resources to weigh alternatives. Their attention must not be distracted by wrangling over neighborhood details. But the broad brush must be used with a sharp edge and the color must be indelible. We must be able to say that this plan will be carried out because it is both necessary and sufficient.

Sufficient, because within the broad-brush land-use categories, the public will have as much freedom to shape their own communities as they now have and still will be able to conform to the plan.

Necessary, because planning on this scale is no longer merely for convenience and economy and social welfare, but is a matter of life and death. We cannot continue to exploit and abuse the land, water, and air resources in our metropolitan regions and hope to maintain human life. The deterioration can be slowed and the date of complete exhaustion postponed by technological tricks, but with our present wishy-washy approach to resource conservation, it can only be a postponement.

We have got to stop playing childish games and get to doing man's work.

The Baby and the Bath Water

**Extracted from the ASPO Newsletter
editorial, October 1959.**

A certain suburban newspaper is regularly running editorials critical
of a proposed county zoning ordinance for the environs. The principal
criticism is directed toward industrial performance standards. The
editor doesn't understand these standards, nor does the group of industrialists whose whines he echoes. (Or perhaps the industrialists *do*
understand. Some of their present plants, even though untouched by
the proposal, could not now comply with the proposed or any other
decent standards of public behavior.) But take the editor at his word:
regulations to govern industry will discourage industry! We don't
want to scare them away! We need factories, we need more tax base!

His argument is one heard from 10,000 cities. The unexpressed
alternative is that if the industry is frightened away because City A
establishes minimum standards, the industry will choose to locate in
City B where it will be welcomed with open arms and no questions
asked. City B will then be free to live high off the hog because of the
generous flow of income from property tax.

The simple question—what are we going to do about taxes?—remains unanswered. To avoid wrestling with inequitable tax assessment and distribution we are willing to go to extremes. The fault lies
not with the industrialists or the suburban newspaper editors, nor
with the citizens, nor planners, nor most governmental officials. The
fault lies with an antiquated, creaking tax system and those who have
vested rights in keeping it intact. The solution is clear: public revenue
collection and distribution not on the basis of artificial political boundaries, but on the obvious basis of areawide needs.

Until we get courage enough to adopt the remedy, whatever it may
be, we shall continue to toss out babies with the bath water.

The Plan's the Thing

**An ASPO Newsletter editorial,
August 1967.**

Gatekeeper: And on earth you were . . . ?

New Arrival: I was a planner.

G.K.: You were a planner. What did you plan?

N.A.: Cities, I planned cities. And regions. I planned regions, sometimes. But mostly cities.

G.K.: I see. That city over there . . . not that one . . . the one under the pinkish yellowish grayish cloud . . . that's where you came from, isn't it?

N.A.: Yes, that's it, good old . . . .

G.K.: Did you plan *that?*

N.A.: That's where I came from, all right. I was the head planner there, but no, I didn't exactly plan it.

G.K.: I don't understand. You planned cities . . . .

N.A.: And regions. . . .

G.K.: And regions. . . . You were the head planner. But you didn't plan the city?

N.A.: Well, no. You see, a planner doesn't exactly *plan* cities. He makes plans *for* cities.

G.K.: Maybe I'm a little rusty . . . all these languages, you just wouldn't believe it, six hundred from Africa alone. Anyway, I thought a plan meant you say this is how we are going to do it. Then you go ahead and do it. They say the Other Fellow has a grand plan for sparrows and the like.

N.A.: Well, yes and no to your definition. A plan is like saying, "This is how we are going to do it," all right. Only we don't do it.

G.K.: I'm afraid I don't . . . .

N.A.: You see it's this way. Planning is a process, it's continuing, it's ongoing. You have to keep updating the comprehensive plan. . . .

G.K.: Comprehensive plan?

N.A.: Maybe you heard it called the master plan.

G.K.: Master plan?

N.A.: Well yes, the general plan. Once you've made it, you've got to revise it, because things change. You can't beat change, can you? You've got to accommodate to change.

G.K.: So you make a master plan, or a comprehensive plan, or a general plan. Then you fix it up a little, erase a line here, add a line there . . . .

N.A.: It's not quite that simple. First you make a plan in, say, 1950. You start it in 1950, that is, and you finish it in 1955. But by 1955 it is out of date, things have changed, your data are obsolete. That's why the data bank.

G.K.: Then you erase a line . . . .

N.A.: No, it's very technical. In 1955, you start to prepare another plan. You have to more or less start from scratch . . . .

G.K.: From whom?

N.A.: Not *Old* Scratch. That's just an expression. Means you start over.

G.K.: Then nothing is worth saving?

N.A.: If you had a good base map, you don't have to do that all over. Don't stint on the base map, I always say, do it carefully the first time and you can use it for a lot of plans. Except consultants, of course, consultants always have to make a new base map.

G.K.: So you start a plan in 1950, then another one in 1955, and a completely new one in 1960. . . .

N.A.: Except for the base map. . . .

G.K.: . . . except for the base map. Then still another one in 1965, and then . . . .

N.A.: We were really just getting going on the next one when I had to leave. I expected to have it ready for public hearing in 1968 or early 1969—data bank and simulation models and all those new techniques speed things up. I wouldn't be surprised if someday we got things so we could turn out a new comprehensive plan annually.

G.K.: A new one every year?

N.A.: PPBS too.

G.K.: I beg your pardon?

N.A.: PPBS. You've got to have it if you want any federal money.

G.K.: I see. Let's get back to that city of yours. From here it looks pretty messy—when the smog clears enough for me to see it. Now it looks that way because it got rebuilt according to a new plan every five years, is that right?

N.A.: Oh no, you don't seem to understand. You see, a plan is an *ideal.* You never expect the city to look like the plan. You aren't *supposed* to achieve it, as the saying goes, just use it as a guide to what the city would look like if you implemented the plan, which you don't. At the same time, the plan must be realistic, it must be based on what exists at the time you are making it. In five years there will be a lot of changes made. So you've got to start over.

G.K.: From scratch?

N.A.: From scratch.

G.K.: Except for the base map?

N.A.: Except for the base map.

G.K.: Well, I think I begin to see how you came here. You meant well, didn't you? Even though your plans weren't implemented, as the saying goes?

N.A.: Oh yes, all my intentions were good.

G.K.: You did a first-rate paving job.

N.A.: Paving . . . ?

G.K.: The road to hell . . . .

N.A.: . . . is paved with good intentions! So that's where I am, I thought . . . .

CURTAIN

3
Laws and Prophecies

Editor's Commentary

With his fresh method of looking at things, such a predominant and constant DOH characteristic, it was inevitable that he would use his knowledge and interest in the laws and principles of biology and the physical sciences to illuminate human activities and urban systems. This characteristic led also to an especially famous illumination—what 100 families mean to a community in terms of the public services needed and the costs—a "crib . . . from the boys who whoop it up for new industry," using calculations in a way that could be easily pictured by those "who don't know and don't care about things like age-sex pyramids." (This 1955 ASPO Newsletter editorial, "One Hundred Families," became the most cribbed of all his writings. Reprints appeared on the editorial pages of metropolitan dailies; in periodicals such as *Changing Times* and *U.S. Municipal News;* in planning agency publications; and in pamphlet form for distribution by the New England School Development Council. Reprints from reprints, often with figures altered for a specific city and sometimes with the original source omitted, were spotted and sent by ASPO members for years after the editorial originally appeared.)

With DOH his observations, theories, and predictions were often—as he would say—"intertwingled." Those combined in this chapter include a selection of editorials, extracts from speeches, and a sprinkling of quotes. Numerous other "laws" and "prophecies" have not been extracted from papers on specific subjects treated in other chapters for the sake of a more complete grouping here. They will be discovered and enjoyed in their rightful place in their original context—for example, in "What Price Half-Life" (see Chapter 7) in which he used the half-life concept for measuring the rate of decay of radioactivity as a measurement of the continued usefulness of printed and spoken words. Another example is in his warning against using traditional methods: his solutions for New York City's traffic problems were based on the need to discard the Euclidean axiom and use Rieman geometry (see Chapter 6).

The prophecies made in the last paper express his deep concern about the discrepancies between the have and the have-not nations—a concern heightened by his increasing involvement with professionals and public officials around the world as a member of the Bureau and then vice president and president of the International Federation for Housing and Planning.

One Hundred Families

An ASPO Newsletter editorial, April 1955.

Planners worry about population. They worry about people also—people as human beings. But their working material is people as statistics—population. Planners spend days and weeks extending curves, extrapolating figures, calculating fertility rates, and building age-sex pyramids. Then in the end they come up with just those things: curves, figures, rates, and a queer drawing that looks like a stylized Christmas tree.

Valuable as these population statistics must be (or planners wouldn't spend all that time on them), they don't make for lively reading. They are particularly dull when you try to work them into a speech. So I suggest we crib an idea from the boys who whoop it up for new industry. I suggest we adapt one of their reports in which they have tried to figure out "What 100 New Factory Employees Meant to Their Community." Only we talk about families.

What do 100 new families mean to the community? What do we have to do to supply all the public services that urban residents need and demand? How much will some of those things cost? It seems to me that these figures would come in handy many times. It seems to me, too, that they would be quite easily pictured by those who don't know and don't care about things like age-sex pyramids.

Here's how they will look:

One hundred new families mean about 450 new people. One hundred new families will put about 100 new children in our schools. About 67 will be in grammar school and 33 in high school. If you operate on the 6-3-3 system, it will be 50 in grammar school, 25 in junior high, and 25 in senior high school.

To follow this school business, which is mighty important, a little further: You will need 2.2 new grade school rooms and 1.65 new high school rooms, which will cost about $120,000. *[Note 1955 cost figures.]* You will need four new school teachers and they are hard to find. The 100 families will add about $30,000 a year to the school operating budget. The city will have to buy about four acres of land: one acre for grammar school, one acre for high school, one acre for parks, and one acre for playgrounds and playfields.

Besides school teachers, the 100 new families will require you to hire other municipal employees. The city will need 0.84 new employees in the police department and two thirds of a new fireman. The police budget will have to be boosted $4,510 each year and the fire department budget increased $2,820.

You will need all sorts of additional jobs done like cleaning streets and cleaning more windows on the city hall, like collecting garbage and collecting taxes, like looking after the city parks and the city health. You will probably need four new persons on the municipal payroll besides the policemen, firemen, and school teachers, at $12,000 to $15,000 added to the annual payroll.

The water department will have to figure on pumping about 10,000 additional gallons of water each day. The 100 families will own 140 automobiles and trucks that will be added to your present traffic. The way it looks now, however, you can't count on the 100 families increasing the number of public transit riders in your city at all.

There are all sorts of odds and ends of things the 100 new families require. Like a new hospital bed (price $10,000); 500 new volumes in the library (add $675 to the library's annual budget); a fraction of a visiting nurse; and a fraction of a cell in the jail.

Before anyone starts questioning these figures too closely, I will say they are based on a sort of composite of the family that lives in the modern merchant-builder, mass-produced suburb, and the operating figures are for the three best administered medium large cities (I will plead the Fifth Amendment to anyone who asks me to name the cities) plus miscellaneous unidentifiable sources too numerous and obscure to mention.

Oh yes, the 100 new families will increase the planning budget $98.83 and will have to be provided with 0.02017925 persons added to the planning staff. But even that little of a planner is scarce these days.

From Biology and Physics—On Urban Systems

"Homeostasis," an ASPO Newsletter editorial, July 1954.

Homeostasis is a biological term; it is that tendency of a living organism to maintain, within itself, relatively stable conditions. It is the ability of the organism to adapt itself to variations in conditions and still survive.

When a human being eats sugar in any form, the proportion of sugar in the blood rises. When the concentration goes above 0.18 percent, the pancreas secretes insulin and the blood-glucose drops down to normal. If the blood-glucose concentration goes below 0.07 percent, adrenalin is secreted. Adrenalin stimulates the liver to transform its glycogen into glucose, brining the blood-glucose *up* to normal.

While homeostasis was first used to describe this adaptive character of living organisms, it applies equally well to systems of any kind, including nonliving. A simple illustration is the action of Watt's governor on steam engines. The steam engine is designed with the governor adjusted to a normal speed. When the speed gets above normal, the spheres on the governor fly out because of centrifugal force. In so doing they close a valve, reducing the steam entering the cylinders, and the speed drops. When the speed goes below normal, the spheres drop, the valve opens wider, more steam enters the cylinders, and the speed of the engine picks up.

Homeostasis is a characteristic of any self-adjusting system. The processes of urbanization have systems showing homeostasis. As an area builds up in new homes, the school load increases, school rooms become overcrowded. New schools are built to bring pupils per room down to an optimum. When the families become older, the children pass on beyond the local school system, schools have too few pupils per room. The school board abandons or consolidates schools. Pupils per room increase back to the point that the board feels is efficient.

There are two vital requirements of a homeostatic system. The first of these is *feedback*.

A system has feedback when the parts affect each other. Blood-glucose stimulates the production of insulin; insulin changes the quantity of blood-glucose. Steam engine speed controls the governor; in turn, the governor controls the speed of the engines.

The second requirement of homeostasis is that the processes controlled must be *essential* to existence; not trivial. Coma and death, for example, will result from prolonged excess or deficiency of blood-glucose. Prolongation of overcrowded schools means the degeneration of the educational system, while uneconomically small classes will lead to bankruptcy of the school district.

What happens when homeostasis fails and the system no longer adapts to changes? Because in homeostasis the matters are essential to the continued function of the system, failure to adapt must always mean eventual collapse of the system. One common process of failure in a homeostatic system is called *runaway*.

A runaway system is one that behaves as the name implies. If, for example, the linkage on a Watt's governor were reversed, as the engine gathered speed and the spheres flew outward, the steam valve would open wider instead of closing, more steam would enter the cylinders, the engine would operate still faster, the spheres would fly out still wider—it would be difficult to find a more descriptive term for this than *runaway*.

Some sytems in the urban organism get into a runaway state. Variance and spot amendment in zoning is a runaway state in many cities. As a consequence, the zoning and land use system has collapsed completely. It is impossible to revise or revive. All that can be done is to start over.

It is possible that we may not always recognize a runaway system. Many urban processes are slow, and we cannot be sure at just what stage they are in. There are a few things, however, which show some symptoms of runaway—or in which, at least, it is difficult to find any governing feedback.

The most optimistic estimates on new housing production show that we face a mounting deficit every year. The economic system of the housing market does not show signs of adjusting to this need. Motor vehicle registrations and mileage increase about two or three times as fast as population. At one time we spoke about leveling off of this increase. No one mentions this now—there is no slackening in sight. Traffic congestion could be expected to act as feedback, but we exert great efforts to short-circuit this—to keep the automobile complex in a runaway state.

Applying the idea of homeostasis, and its related ideas, to urbanization may offer a fresh method of looking at some of our problems.

"Faster, Faster," extracted from the ASPO Newsletter editorial, January 1963.

Each year goes faster than the year before. This is a characteristic of biologic time, and each human being becomes sensitive to it sooner or later. Frequently, he realizes it suddenly and with a shock. Even though we might like to think otherwise, biologic time is just as real as solar time or sidereal time, or whatever it is we measure with clocks and calendars. But biologic time is not always understood, especially is it not understood as it applies to nonbiologic institutions as well as to those things, such as human life, which are clearly biological.

To explain biologic time briefly: Between his first and second birthdays, a child doubles his age. This is a very long time and the child makes remarkable progress. But between his second and third birthdays, he increases his age only 50 percent. The time is much shorter, his progress toward maturity is great, but relative to his entire lifetime up to that point, the progress is much less than the year before.

This ever-decreasing increment also operates in the institution of urban society, including the environment which surrounds urban society—the city. In short, each year becomes a smaller proportion of the total life of the city; each year we have a greater problem to solve, a greater amount of inertia to overcome, than we had the year before.

One way to show this is to imagine what might have been the effect in an earlier year if we had exerted the same amount of effort on a particular problem that we did in a later year. Imagine how much more $50 million for open space purchase could have accomplished if it had been authorized when we had only about half the number of people living in cities, when much more open land was available, and when prices were only a fraction of what they are now.

You cannot beat biologic time. The best you can hope for is to find some way of speeding up your reactions to keep pace with it. To do this in urban affairs takes some effort to speed up, or make more efficient, the things that you are trying to do now. In 1916, zoning was just such a breakthrough—a new way of handling the public interest in land-use problems—more efficient than had been the previous nuisance abatement-private convenant-public censure methods.

Perhaps urban renewal has been such a breakthrough, although it is not yet clear that this is true of it in its present form. If the public transit aid program is successful, it could very well be a device that would help us catch up. The federal interstate highway program, however, may have as many negative effects as it has positive.

All in all, last year probably was a reasonably successful year. But if we are to have any hope of keeping up with urbanization, we have to do a lot better in the future. There are some things that we haven't dared to dream of, Horatio, that we had better get incorporated in our philosophy.

The Angle of Repose, extracted from an untitled paper given at the Third Annual Conference of the Southern Association of State Planning and Development Agencies, Louisville, November 29, 1949.

Scientists have the uncanny knack of taking what would seem to us to be a most insignificant fact or phenomenon and studying it and examining it and measuring it and in the end coming forth with something of amazingly practical value. For instance, many years ago, some fellow got himself some sand and a bucket and a smooth floor. He then proceeded to pour the sand out of the bucket onto the floor. He found that the more sand he poured on the pile the higher the pile grew, but also, the wider the sand spread over the floor. Anyone who ever poured sand out of a bucket knows that! But the scientist saw that sometimes, when he poured the sand out of his bucket very carefully, the pile for a few seconds would increase in height more rapidly than it increased in width. However, sooner or later, no matter how carefully he poured, the heap of sand went squash! and slipped down the sides of the pile and spread out at the base.

This scientist measured the angle that the side of his pile made with the floor. He made this measurement hundreds of times with hundreds of piles of sand. He found that if the angle were steeper than the average of his trials, eventually the pile would slump and the top would slide down the sides. He called his angle the *angle of repose.*

After he had measured and determined the angle of repose on sand, he tried it on other materials—on sugar, on wheat, on clay, on gravel, on loam. He discovered that certain materials could be piled higher before they slumped, others that were quite fluid could be piled not so high. There was a different, but a definite, angle of repose for each material.

The most obvious practical use of this very simple business of piling sand on a smooth floor is its engineering application to the construction of fills and embankments. If you pile your earthfill so that the slope of sides is sharper than the angle of repose for the material, sooner or later, your earthfill will go squash and all of your work will be undone.

I will lift the idea of an angle of repose completely out of its context and apply it to the principles of human and economic activities. I am not using it entirely as a figure of speech, for I believe that if we were smart enough to understand all of the factors which influence human activities, we could measure the angle of repose for those human activities with as much accuracy as the engineer does his piles of sand or gravel or loam.

The clearest illustration of this slithering effect in human affairs can be shown in the spread of large cities. In our metropolitan areas, as you pile up people you get the same cone shape that you do in a pile of sand. The population is more dense in the central city and it tapers out to the suburbs, then to the subsistence farms, and it finally disappears in the agricultural sections. The more people you put in the metropolitan area, the wider becomes the geographical base.

For a time, under unusual circumstances such as the housing shortage we have had since World War II, you increase the pile of people in the central city to a dangerous height; but eventually, the slumping effect takes place and the people move away from the excessively dense concentration in the central city.

The angle of repose in any material depends principally upon the fluidity of the material. Thus dense, nonflowing stuff like wet concrete can be heaped up with fairly steep sides. A quite fluid material like molasses can be piled hardly at all. The fluidity of our population is, of course, directly related to its method of transportation and has increased with modern mass transit, automobiles, and airplanes.

Another aspect of human affairs which is obeying my newly invented law of an angle of repose is industrial activity. Industrial activity that for several decades had been piling higher and higher in the Northeast quadrant of the United States exceeded the angle of repose and started to slide out into the rest of the United States. Because of this, industrial development is taking place throughout the entire nation.

My angle of repose law doesn't tell anything about the conditions in the center of the pile or underneath the pile. All it says is that if you pile things high enough, sooner or later, they're going to slide down and spread out.

A bunch of new piles has started. Some of them are mighty big already and are beginning to slide out into the surrounding area. We should observe well what has happened to cities, to people, and do what we can to avoid some of the effects of being at the center of the pile.

**The Threshold of Obnoxiousness, quoted
from the ASPO Newsletter editorial "Observations on Air Polluting," January 1959.**

Among the interesting twists to the problem of urban development is
one you might call "threshold of obnoxiousness" or "the straw that
breaks the camel's back."

The horrible dust storms of the '30s, when the airborne dust particles crossed everyone's threshold of tolerance, were greatly influential in producing our federal soil conservation programs. If it had not
been for the junk that motor vehicles poured into the Los Angeles air,
it is possible that the Herculean efforts Angelinos are making to clean
up would not yet be started, because the threshold of obnoxiousness
would not yet be crossed.

This "threshold of obnoxiousness" applies to a lot of things in urban
development—to stream pollution, to traffic, to uncontrolled development, to inefficient public administration, even to lax enforcement
of school fire-safety rules. Something drastic has to happen to bring
the malaise across the threshold of obnoxiousness so that the public no
longer stands still and takes it. The trouble is, of course, you can't stop
in your correction of the problem with merely pushing it back just
beneath the threshold of obnoxiousness. You have to clean it all
up—which costs a lot more than if you never let it get beyond the
threshold in the first place.

On Solving Problems

**The Balloon in the Shoe Box, quoted from
"Overall Planning," a speech to the
Municipal Association of South Carolina,
Greenville, February 16, 1953.**

Frequently I get the feeling that running a city is about like trying to
put a partly inflated and slightly too large balloon in a shoe box. You

get it shoved down in one corner, only to have it push up in another corner. You never seem to get it all stuffed away so you can clamp on the lid.

In a city, just about the time you think you've got one problem licked—or at least under control—another one pops up. And, quite probably, like the balloon in the shoe box, the cause of the second problem can be traced to your solution of the first problem.

A Prophecy Made with Certainty, quoted from "Every Man His Own Prophet," a guest editorial written for *Better Roads* magazine, December 1954.

What service to human beings has the most ready sale? If I were asked this question, my answer would be "prophecy." It would be hard to prove, but I am sure that the business of predicting the future would be high up on any list of human demands.

One prophecy we can make with absolute certainty: If we wait until tomorrow to solve tomorrow's problem, that problem is bound to be there waiting for us. If we cannot solve tomorrow's problem completely now, at least we can make the solution of today's problem a first step toward the solution of tomorrow's problem.

There Is Some Sort of Law, quoted from "Are Fringe Areas 'Free Riders'?" a speech at the Annual Meeting of the Municipal Finance Association, Washington, D.C., June 5, 1956.

I am sure that there is some sort of law of political science which says that if you neglect an obvious need long enough, sooner or later the next higher government will step in and take the whole thing away from you.

**Discussion Belongs in the Public Domain,
quoted from "Pattern and Progress of
Development in the Nation and in the Mid-
Continent Area," from a speech to the Mid-
Continent Council of Development
Agencies, Denver, 1949.**

I do not believe that decisions are any better for having been arrived at in secrecy. In fact, I am of the opinion that they are not nearly so good as if the whole discussion had been brought out in the open.

Important problems should be in the public domain. They should be the common property of and the subject of discussion by the people. The solutions to the problem should not be something arrived at in a back room and then justified before the citizenry by an adroit public relations expert.

**A Prediction, quoted from "Special Districts
and Authorities," a speech at the American
Public Works Association Annual Congress,
Fort Worth, September 26, 1956.**

The problems resulting from urban growth in the next 40 years will be magnified in direct ratio to the number of independent single-function districts and authorities trying to solve them.

**"Progress Is People," quoted from the
ASPO Newsletter editorial, May 1964.**

In this world, advances, innovations, are almost entirely the result of the ideas produced by individuals, by single human beings. We all know the old jokes about committees, how they design camels and things—and we know that there is usually more truth than humor in the jokes.

It is the work and the ideas of individuals and not of committees that have shaped the world—Buddha, Christ, Mohammed, Newton, Pasteur, Einstein. In some cases, the work and ideas of individuals have shaken the world—Napoleon, Lenin, Hitler.

These are the big names in history. Everyone knows about them.

But the contribution to progress by individuals goes on all the time. The contributions come from persons with all sorts of backgrounds, producing ideas having all possible degrees of import to civilization.

No "Best" Way, quoted from "Fighting the 'Urban Problem'," a guest editorial written for *Public Management*, May 1967.

"The urban problem" is how to produce a city in which everyone is reasonably well housed, reasonably well educated, reasonably fully employed, and reasonably happy. It is how to rid the city of pockets of slums, ignorance, disease, unemployed, crime, and misery. It has taken us about a generation to recognize that we have to do something about education and jobs and health as well as fix up the buildings in which the poor live.

There is no "best" way to solve "the urban problem." The object must be to unify the forces that work on the problem.

Urbanization in Developing Countries, quoted from the introduction to a symposium on "Urbanization in Developing Nations," on April 5, 1967, at the ASPO National Planning Conference, Houston.

There is reason to believe that urbanization in the new countries poses a potential problem for the developed nations which, in the long run, will equal or be greater than the urban problems the developed nations have within their own boundaries.

The Problems of Unrest, quoted from "Some Thoughts on Evolution," a speech presented at the formal dedication of the new headquarters building of the International Federation for Housing and Planning, The Hague, Netherlands, December 13, 1965.

The most powerful institutions for dealing with problems of human unrest are the political institutions. The world has made substantial

progress here. Most significant has been our creation of the United
Nations. There are other cooperative ventures: the Common Market,
the Organization of American States, the Pan-Arab or Pan-Moslem
movement. But established governments are notoriously difficult to
change. Surrounding every nation there is an invisible, but impenetra-
ble, political wall that prevents a truly free flow of ideas and
assistance. You may call it nationalism or self-interest or self-
protection, or what you will. The wall exists, and evolution in the
direction of removal goes ever so slowly.

But there is a way to pass through political walls, and there is a way
in which men of goodwill can work together to help others who need
their help. This is through their association, free of political pressure,
in such organizations as the International Federation for Housing and
Planning. IFHP and the many other organizations—in health, in public administration, in education, in science—are each punching their
own little hole through the political walls.

The Middle Future

Extracted from the ASPO Newsletter
editorial, February 1954.

I am concerned about a period that I call the Middle Future. I believe
that planners are neglecting this Middle Future, and that we cannot afford to neglect it.

Beginning with tomorrow, I would divide the future into three
parts: Near, Middle, and Distant. The Near Future begins tomorrow
and ends 15, 20, 25 years from now. It begins with the first new day of
overcrowded schools and ends, perhaps, when the babies born today
have finished college. The Near Future begins with the step we take
tomorrow, or fail to take, to lick today's traffic problem, and it ends
with the completion of the last traffic project in that catchall group at
the end of the public works program, called "for future construction."

Descriptions of the Distant Future can be found in an assortment of
publications, some quite respectable, others not quite so respectable.

The description lies buried in ponderous articles in the scientific journals, or pictured in comic strip colors in a science fiction magazine. It will be found in mathematical equations, in philosophical works, in poetry, in religion.

The Distant Future is risky to describe, but it certainly includes voyages into space. It includes a diet of algae. It includes the actual creation of "life" from inert materials. It probably includes unthought of political readjustments. It includes the conquering of all or nearly all of today's diseases—and the evolution of new ones. It includes a myriad of events beyond anyone's dreams today. All in all, the Distant Future will be a strange and wonderful era, judged by today's standards—and perhaps a disturbing era. But there is no exact description of it. It is all too hazy to worry about now.

This brings us back to the Middle Future. The best way to describe this middle period is to say that it is a waypoint, in some cases a terminal point, for certain inevitable processes. Population growth is an inevitable process. In the Middle Future, we shall need to supply urban facilities for twice as many people as we now have. Each year there are more motor vehicles than the year before. Each year we add hundreds of miles of highways, thousands of parking spaces. We reshape our lives around drive-in theatres, drive-in restaurants, super drive-in shopping centers. What proportion of our national economy are we devoting to the care and feeding of the motor vehicle? How does this compare with the portion of our national efforts spent on education or on health? The answers to these questions are not easily available. But we can be sure that one day, in the Middle Future, we must face up to this situation. In this case we have a terminal situation—the absolute upper limit of our substance that we can afford to give to the automobile.

A third example is that for some years now, the proportion of workers employed in industry have been decreasing. This has come from the improvement of manufacturing efficiency and from the substitution of machines for men. To offset the decrease in proportion of industrial workers, we have had an increase in the proportion employed in services. Thus far, the change has been relatively slow. But now we are in for a speed-up. There is no end to the changes that may accompany automation. We can feel reasonably certain that in the long run the old bogey "technological unemployment" will not bother us. Nevertheless, we shall have a shorter work week, maybe even 20 hours. We shall have more leisure and shall need to confront the problem of catering to that leisure: outdoor recreation, adult education, more auto travel and the facilities therefor, earlier retirement for workers, increased migration to the better climates, etc.—all in an amount far beyond anything we are thinking about today.

It is my feeling that we in planning are spending so much of our time on problems of the Near Future that we have no time left for this inevitable Middle Future. Granted, there are powerful reasons for trying to fix up tomorrow so that we shall be rid of the problems of today. But the problems of day after tomorrow will be on us before we are ready for them.

The problems of today and of the Near Future are being worked out by a host of technicians and specialists—traffic experts, civil engineers, housing technicians, architects, redevelopers, social and political scientists of all sizes and shapes. But the Middle Future is neglected by the specialists. The person who must start thinking about it is the generalist, who is the planner. No single person is going to tell us what we should expect and how we should prepare for this Middle Future. It has to be a cooperative and cumulative effort. Probably no city can now do a great deal to be ready for that day after tomorrow. So many of the descriptive measurements of that era are statistical. But the events are no less probable for being statistical. If planners do not help to prepare for this Middle Future, we shall have failed.

The Shape of World War III

Extracted from the ASPO Newsletter editorial, September 1965.

During the 1950s there was speculation as to when the cold war would change to a hot one. The pessimists believed the next war would be a hydrogen bomb affair. The optimists could do little more than hope that the pessimists were wrong. Even the most optimistic felt that the world was only being given a breathing spell, an interval to allow for tooling up for World War, Mark III.

The mistake that both pessimists and optimists make is to assume that World War III has not yet commenced. On the contrary, if we look objectively at the situation, we are well launched into a world war. There are the obvious international trouble spots: any of these could explode into total war, but probably will not. There are the shooting-type uprisings: since the end of World War II, there has been a constant succession of bloody revolutions. There are the complete splits in some nations, and the tense international situations in many nations.

This is the shape of World War III, and we are well into it. Trouble, resentment, conflict in a hundred different forms and a thousand different places. Unrest in not only nations, but in entire continents. We must expect the war to increase in intensity until we are willing to admit that we are truly in World War III and that we must fight in it with the same dedication and singleness of purpose that we used in World War II.

In oversimplified terms, war is a struggle between the haves and the have-nots; although sometimes what the have-nots have not, is power over their fellow man and over lands they covet but do not need. The only way any war can conclude successfully is for the have-nots to win so that they, too, become haves. If the have-nots are defeated, they sink back, lick their wounds, and prepare for another assault when they have regained strength and their enemy has become weaker. The only possible way for World War III to be ended is for the have-nots to become haves. But this need not—must not—be through killing of the haves. This would indeed be a Pyrrhic victory.

The United States and her prosperous friends are plainly the haves. It is safe to predict that the Soviet Union will sooner or later join the ranks of the haves and change her anti-Western tune. The nations of the rest of the world are the have-nots. The haves must fight World War III by seeing to it that the have-nots gain their objective. The haves must bring this about not by shooting and being shot, but by *helping* the less fortunate, with as much energy and thought and money as they put into *fighting* during World War II—or even more.

No nation can hope to fight a successful war if it has major internal problems. No man's posture of uprightness is convincing if he spends money at the race track while his children go hungry. World War III must be fought on many fronts, including the home front of the affluent nations, and especially the home front of the United States.

The President and Congress have declared war on poverty. This is a positive step in one World War III battle. As in every new massive program, there will be many false starts, much inefficiency and waste of money. Inefficiency and waste are among the loudest cries against our foreign aid program. But are these programs any more inefficient and wasteful than a shooting war? Not by half.

Perhaps our greatest handicap in solving our internal problems is our real ignorance of how to do it. If, to learn how to help people live, we had spent one tiny fraction of what we spend on learning how to kill people, our World War III prospects would be much better. We must realize that "business as usual" is just as impossible in fighting World War III as it was in previous World Wars. For the new weapons of education and health and welfare and economic development and urban reclamation, both on foreign and domestic fronts, we must spend funds of the same order of magnitude as we would to fight a shooting war.

Until we do that, we shall be losing World War III.

4

What This Country
Needs . . .

Editor's Commentary

A principal Dennis O'Harrow concern was *land pollution* and what he called
our "namby-pamby attitude" toward land-use policies. His forceful statement
on the need for a national policy for land, at a 1967 conference sponsored by
HUD and the Department of Agriculture, reached the White House: Leonard
Garment, special consultant to the president, quoted it at the 1971 ASPO Conference and reported that the need had been recognized by the administration
and given priority in legislative proposals. Among necessary policies and actions to achieve this goal, DOH stressed that we must convince the people of
the need for measures that are "currently just not a part of the American tradition." This he strove to do in a variety of ways.

In his strong focus and strong arguments on the urgency of conserving
natural resources and controlling pollution, he was also very much aware of
the conflicting claims of economic growth and a pollution-free environment.
"Smoke means work," as he put it in a 1961 editorial which commented on a
situation still being debated both nationally and internationally.

In the '50s, he wrote frequently on the effects of air pollution, noise, traffic
congestion, and the nationwide grabbing of open space park land. In 1954, he
warned "if you think the problems we have now are tough, just wait about 20
years! If there is any one key symptom that points to whether or not the
modern city is livable, it is the migration to the suburbs." (As early as 1949, he
had pointed out that "cities are bankrupt—or on the edge of it. They are losing
their tax base, losing their industries, losing their leaders.")

Better quality in government was an underlying need stressed throughout
his admonitions and recommendations. He also defended public servants. In a
widely acclaimed editorial, he said that the public official had to fight extremism in order to truly represent the great majority of the citizens, and that
when the hate-mongers showed up, it was "no time for softness."

The speeches, reports and editorials in this chapter deal with these matters;
with the growth and change and problems that began in the post World War II
years, with the observations of "Mr. Planning" on what this country needs.

We Need a National Land Policy

Land Pollution, extracted from the President's Address to the International Federation for Housing and Planning, 28th World Congress, Tokyo, May 14, 1966.

It is only within our own lifetime that we have recognized that there is a limit to the amount of water we have to use for drinking, for irrigating our crops, for transferring into steam, for using to dispose of our wastes. Even more recently have we come to see that there is also a limit to the air that is available for us to breathe. We recognize water pollution, we recognize air pollution, but we do not often recognize—or think of—*land* pollution. We pollute the land with slums, we pollute the land with speculative development, we despoil the land with hectares and square kilometers of highways and parking lots, we waste the good crop land with urban development, we litter the land with paper and trash and beer cans and billboards and ugliness of a thousand different kinds.

Two peculiarities with land make it difficult to solve the problems. First, land does not move, as water and air move. Because land does not move, it is not easy to show that what one man does with or to his land will injure his neighbor. When a man throws sewage waste into a river, he can see it flow past his neighbor and make his neighbor's drinking water unfit to drink. It is also easy to appreciate that the air he poisons will kill people downwind. But it is not so easy to convince a developer that by despoiling the land he injures the entire community.

The second great problem with land pollution is the psychological one related to landownership. The Englishman has said that his home is his castle. Which is to say that each landowner becomes an absolute monarch of the fraction of a hectare that he owns, and no one may direct him, force him, or even suggest to him how he shall use that land. Which has made it extremely difficult to make progress through government action in our efforts to eliminate land pollution.

We must eliminate pollution in all three natural resources, because for none of them is there unlimited quantity. We now know how to conserve all these resources, we have both technical ability and sufficient money, at least in the industrial nations, to produce the kind of world we should live in—that is the hopeful aspect. The discouraging aspect is that although we are able to produce the better world, we have not yet produced the philosophy of government, the administrative procedures, the understanding by our people—that is also necessary to bring about the better world. This is the point at which the technical planner must turn to the leaders of our communities and of our nation and say, "We are prepared technically. Are you prepared, also to ask for and support the necessary government action?"

Regulation of Land Use for Urban Growth, condensed from a paper presented at a University of Chicago seminar, March 21, 1967.

I propose a reason for land-use regulation that differs from the reasons usually given. Planners say that our goal in planning and land-use regulation is the optimum human environment: to create an urban pattern that gives human beings the opportunity to realize their full potentiality, that makes possible a full range of choice, that eliminates as much as possible the undeserved penalty of being born of parents of the wrong color, or of being born into the wrong economic groups. The goal I propose to substitute is stated, in shorthand terms, as the conservation of land. In slightly extended terms, the goal is to adjust man's use of land to produce and maintain a balanced ecological system on the earth. The goal is neither more nor less than the survival of the human race. I recognize that human survival requires much more than the conservation of land, but land conservation is necessary.

In the Netherlands, the most densely populated nation in the world, slightly more than 12 million persons are living on slightly less than 13,000 square miles of land—an average density of about 945 persons per square mile. To the Dutch, land is probably the most precious of all natural resources. They not only conserve it and preserve it, they also create land out of whole cloth—or rather—out of the submerged ocean bottom. The Polders, the Zuyder Zee reclamation, rank among the greatest engineering feats of all time. In spite of the very great density of population, the Netherlands is not a crowded nation. There are great stretches of pastures and meadows, fields of wheat and flax, even forests and national parks. You never have a sense of being overwhelmed by urbanization, by man and his artifacts and urban excrement.

If you took the outline map of the Netherlands and plopped it down over the American eastern seaboard area, with a slight judicious warping of the boundary line, you would have enclosed the Greater New York-Northern New Jersey-Philadelphia area, all of the states of Connecticut and Rhode Island, the Boston area, and about half of the state of Massachusetts—the same amount of land as in the Netherlands, slightly less than 13,000 square miles. But you would have enclosed slightly more than twice as many human beings, 25 million instead of 12.2 million. The average density of this Netherlands-in-the-United States would be 1,900 per square mile instead of 945. Another difference is that among the enclosed population you would find little or no appreciation of the value of land as a natural resource.

If this were only an aesthetic failing, it could be shoved aside. But the situation is much more serious than aesthetic myopia. The problem arises from an indifference that in turn comes from a lack of understanding, a misconception of the amount of land we have available, and an ignorance of what we are doing with our land. The degree of our present interest in conservation of the three basic natural resources may be just the inverse of the long run need.

At present, our greatest conservation efforts are directed toward water. With prods, and enticements, from the federal government, we are mounting a massive attack on water pollution, and we are beginning to push for water management: flood water retention, recharging of ground water acquifers, greater reuse of water. We already are moving water enormous distances to bring it to where it is needed. We are spending millions of dollars in research on desalinization of sea water. In conservation we have thought of water as the scarcest of the three natural resources, yet the outlook for the future is not at all discouraging.

The attack on air pollution—which is better stated in the positive, the program to conserve air—is underway. One of the determining factors was the invention, or discovery, of the "airshed." An airshed is analogous to a watershed; air available for use at any one place (for example, the air for any particular city or metropolitan area) can flow from only a limited region—the airshed, a region that is difficult to define precisely, but is determined by the topography, land and water conditions, and prevailing meteorological patterns. If the development on the land covered by the airshed is all of the kind to pollute the air above it, the city served by the airshed will always have polluted air, the citizens will always be breathing poisons.

The metropolitan region of Chicago, northeastern Illinois, and northwestern Indiana measures 960 square miles. The air that it uses comes from an airshed about twice that size—some 2,000 square miles. And the water, including the source waters of Lake Michigan and of underground acquifers, is the drainage product of at least 10,000 square miles. The region has a smaller resource reservoir of land than of either water or air. The 1960 population of this 960 square miles was about 6 million, about 6,209 persons per square mile—six times as great as in the Netherlands, three times as great as my eastern seaboard example.

There is reason to believe (although I cannot yet document this) that in our great urban concentrations we have already passed the capacity of the regional natural resources to continue to sustain life in these areas for another 100 years.

Water, air, and land resources are interrelated in such a manner that you cannot carry out a complete conservation program for one unless at the same time you have a conservation program for the others. Thus water conservation requires measures to slow runoff, which means less impervious surfaces, less highways, roofs, and driveways, less urban development, less intensive land use. Similarly, air conservation also requires decreasing industrial, domestic, and transportation waste—all products of urban development.

Moreover, during the rest of the 20th century we shall add about 100 million to the present population. There is at present no indication that there will be any substantial increase in population in central cities. Instead, we shall build new urban facilities in the periphery of central cities—in an amount equal to such facilities now existing in all cities of 25,000 population or more. In this process we will consume 18 million acres of land, of which some 5 or 6 million acres alone will be devoted to the automobile. This new urban development would be about twice the size of the Netherlands, with a density about three and one half times as great. And I speak only about the *next* 100 million population. After that comes the second 100 million and the third 100 million—each falling faster and faster on the heels of the previous one. Assuming in all this, as we must, that there is no nuclear war.

The scale on which conservation is needed to let urban man live at peace with nature, even just to continue to live in a balanced ecological relation with his environment, cannot possibly be satisfied with only the land we can afford economically to set aside for recreation and nature preservation. We need open space on a scale far greater than anything we have yet contemplated—open space interspersed throughout the areas that we urbanize.

We must stop concentrating our urban growth as we are now doing, we must thin out and scatter urban development in the future. I do not know that anyone has made any quantitative determination of this scatteration; my guess is at least one acre of open space for, and closely associated with, each acre of developed land—the ratio might eventually become as much as four or five open acres for each developed acre. There are several methods by which we can achieve this thinning-out:

1. We must use the full potentiality of zoning.

2. We must encourage and perfect the use of the nouveau-zoning devices such as planned unit development, holding zones, land-use intensity ratings, density zoning, performance standards, and so on. Here we need further experiment and ingenuity in perfecting methods and probably a frontal attack on the courts to prove that the devices are constitutional.

3. We must get rid of the idea that the administration of land controls can be carried out by amateurs. The British Land Commission Act, for example, is generally regarded as about the most complex law ever adopted by Parliament. Our laws, and the technical background necessary for sane administration, can be expected to be every bit as difficult. This statement carries with it the implication of a greatly stepped-up training and research program in land-use administration.

4. We must recognize and cash in on the socially created development value of land. This is a very iffy type of control, and I would not presume to say just how it could be used. Fortunately, the British are doing our experimenting for us. Their first experiment failed. We shall watch the second experiment with interest.

5. We must overcome the idea that it is evil for society to try to control its own destiny by owning the land on which it builds its habitations. To return to the very useful example of the Netherlands: all of the land on which cities have expanded in the Netherlands during the past 60 or so years has been owned by the government. The Dutch people have no problem in accepting this policy, and I defy you to find a more fiercely democratic, independent people than the Dutch. Governmental

ownership of land for urban development is common in Europe and is a major feature of the British Land Commission Act.

6. We must embark on a program of real new towns, or new cities. I do not mean more Restons, which are really a prettier, better-designed type of metropolitan sprawl. I mean completely independent, self-sufficient cities of 100,000 and upwards, far removed from any existing metropolitan areas. I see new cities as primarily a responsibility of the federal government and not something that can be undertaken by private enterprise.

7. We must design and create governmental units with power to carry out the land conservation program. I am not suggesting metropolitan government in the usual sense. We should set up regional resources authorities—to use a term that I am not ready to define, but which I might model to some extent on the Tennessee Valley Authority. In general, the regional resources authority will have responsibility for conserving and allocating the three basic resources—water, air, and land. And because of the overwhelming influence of transportation on resource use and conservation, I think we must also give the regional authority veto power, if not full control, over transportation.

8. And last—or perhaps it should be first—we must convince the people of the need for these measures. The suggestions I have made are currently just not a part of the American tradition. The American people must be convinced.

We still have today in the United States a wide range of options for the human beings who live here. However, unless we start putting some curbs on our obsession that we who are now alive have an inalienable right to do as we please with our land—and our air and our water—we shall steadily and surely decrease the options available to our descendents, including, to put it bluntly, the option to live.

I have always thought the philosophy expressed by a Nigerian chief is one that we, who consider ourselves more sophisticated, could do well to adopt. When asked by a visiting anthropologist about his conception of property rights, the chief said: "I conceive that land belongs to a vast family, of which many are dead, few are living, and countless numbers are still unborn."

Using Every Governmental Power in the
Federal Arsenal, extracted from a discussion
paper of panel presentations at the Conference on Soils, Water, and Suburbia,
sponsored by HUD and the Department of
Agriculture, Washington, D.C.,
June 15-16, 1967.

The most neglected (and I think most serious) resource problem we
have is the conservation of land. There is a sort of inverted reason
why most metropolitan-regional agencies are not really thinking
about land conservation. They are not being paid to think about it. I
do not make a moral judgment, but it is a fact that most regional agencies draw their principal financial support from the federal government, and the work that they do depends very largely on what sort of
project, what sort of study, what sort of planning the federal government will pay for. (Fred Bair, one of the most cynical members of the
planning profession, has defined planning as anything for which you
can get a federal grant. And the federal government has not yet really
taken a wholehearted interest in land conservation.)

This conference reveals a stirring of interest. The Department of
Agriculture, through the Soil Conservation Service, has recognized
that it has skills and knowledge that are vitally important to the solution of urban development problems. I do not criticize the Department
for the delay in this recognition. I am a farm boy myself and I have a
vivid recollection of the psychological gap—truly a canyon—between
farm folk and city folk. That difference was bound to cause some difficult engineering problems when the gap needed to be bridged. But I
suggest that bridging this particular chasm, important though it be, is
only one step on a long journey—I might even say a desperate
journey.

So long as the land-use plan is advisory, so long will its chance of
realization be illusory. Even more important, however, is the magnitude of land conservation yet proposed anywhere. So long as we continue to think of land conservation as merely setting aside areas for
recreation—and this is practically universal among public officials
and planning agencies—we shall never get to the real job. The Southeast Wisconsin study does go well beyond the stereotype of parks and
playgrounds to include "wetlands, woodlands, wild life, scenic, scientific, and historic sites," but it is still all linked to recreation. The

Wisconsin environmental corridor concept is far in advance of most of the nation, and if it can be carried out is a real step forward. But still, it is not enough.

Everything that I have heard thus far in this conference takes for granted that concentration of human beings and urban devastation will continue forever. The suggestions have all been addressed to how to make it safer, prettier, more efficient. No one has suggested that we are probably already overdeveloped beyond the capacity of the land in these great, sprawling, urban regions.

In my opinion we are, in our metropolitan regions, pushing the environment beyond the point of no return. We are altering the ecology of these areas to such an extent that they will become completely uninhabitable. How long it will take to reach a state of uncorrectable toxicity of air, water, and land, I do not know—perhaps 200 years, perhaps only 100 years. If you think that the odds are now against my being correct, I can answer that each year we continue in our ruthless program of despoilation of land resources in urban areas, the better are the odds in favor of my pessimistic view.

I see a great national program mounted against water pollution. I hear a hue and cry against air pollution, which presages another outpouring of federal funds. But I see no comparable concern over our pollution of the land—which is really the scarcest of the three basic resources of human life.

The solution is simply stated, but not easily carried out. We need a national land policy, a policy for all land, urban and nonurban, a policy with teeth in it, a policy laid down by Congress and administered by the White House, using all the tools and every governmental power in the federal arsenal. Similarly, state and local governments will need to use all their powers—the police power, the power of eminent domain, the taxing power. In my opinion, the time for half measures is past.

We Need Action on Environmental Pollution

The Tea Party Shift, extracted from "City Planning and Air Pollution," a speech to the Midwestern Air Pollution Prevention Association, Gary, Indiana, October 16, 1953.

At the mad tea party in *Alice in Wonderland*, there was a large table, with many places set, but there were only three persons occupying it—the Mad Hatter, the March Hare, and the Dormouse. When Alice approached the party, the Mad Hatter insisted there was no room for her. Alice protested, because she saw so many vacant chairs. The Hatter's explanation was simple—when the dishes got too dirty and the tablecloth too messy, everyone got up and moved to a clean place at the table and started all over.

This tea party shift is exactly the same technique being used in developing our cities. When a portion of a city gets too dirty with smoke and dust and grime, and gets too messy with traffic and overcrowded land and insufficient utilities, the property owners pull up stakes and move to another and, temporarily, cleaner and less cluttered section. They hate to wash the dishes. It's easier and cheaper to throw everything away and start out fresh. That which is left behind, we call "slums" and "blighted areas."

Besides the people who are moving on to a new place because the dishes are all dirty, there are new people who refuse to sit at our table because they see all the dirty dishes.

I was once a member of a team of city planners making a comprehensive plan for a medium-large industrial city. In our analysis we found that the economic base of the city was deteriorating rapidly. The first step we recommended—the step without which there was no chance of stabilizing and diversifying their industrial base—was cleaning up the smoke and dirt nuisance in the city. While the abatement of the air pollution is not the only step that will be necessary in that city if they are to regain their economic health, it is quite obviously the key step, without which all other activities will be futile.

It was in this city also that I gained a greater respect for the science of semantics and its theory that people confuse words with the things that they stand for: if someone says that a book is red, you have to question him to find out whether he is referring to the color of the binding or the political views of the author. In this town, 95 percent of the people believed that *smoke* and *work* were exactly the same thing. The choking blanket of smoke that lay across the industrial valley most of the time was a symbol of work in the factories. But they mistook the symbol for the thing symbolized. And they automatically fought air pollution abatement because they felt it was getting rid of the work to get rid of the smoke.

In the introduction to the model smoke abatement law of the American Society of Mechanical Engineers, there is the following statement:

> All differences of opinion and all controversy relative to a smoke ordinance are basically economic. . . . It can be assumed that no one desires unclean air: the question is how clean an air can the community afford? Engineering can provide it. [Many schemes] are not ordinarily considered because of the cost. What is considered is some economic compromise.

Air pollution problems always get mixed up with economics. But what kind of economics? For what period of time are you making your economic comparison? Air pollution is bad enough in itself. Its effect, and potential effect, on public health is well documented. From an aesthetic viewpoint it is obviously bad. The effort that goes into dusting and cleaning and sweeping and laundering, all because of excessive air pollution and dust fall, is economic waste. And there are not only the primary effects of air pollution but the secondary effects—its part in the creation of blighted areas. The tea party shift— the getting up and moving to a newer and cleaner spot when the old becomes so bad that we can't stand it—is an economic luxury that we cannot afford.

"Smoke Means Work," extracted from the ASPO Newsletter editorial, March 1961.

City governments—which is a shorthand way of saying all the people that live in the city—find themselves with Gordian knot problems. The classical solution, to wack through the knot with a sword, is not very attractive. *The Wall Street Journal* of December 8, 1960 carried the story of one of those knots, most inextricably entangled. Under the headline "Sheet & Tube Bids Youngstown Choose a Smokier City or Less Work at Plant," it read in part:

> Youngstown, Ohio—More smoke or fewer jobs?
>
> That, in effect, is the choice Youngstown Sheet & Tube Co. is offering this industrial city.
>
> The company, seventh biggest American steel producer, wants to install oxygen roof lances . . . to speed up production and make the plant "more competitive." The roof lances would cut in half the time needed to melt a batch of steel, but also would pour more smoke into the air than Youngstown's smoke control ordinance permits.
>
> Youngstown's Mayor has proposed a compromise under which the city would relax its smoke control regulations for three years while Sheet & Tube installed the roof lances and attempted to work out a method for controlling the resulting smoke. But Sheet & Tube's president turned down the proposal with a warning that the Youngstown area faces a loss of jobs if the company is not allowed to go ahead with the roof lances. "We could not proceed with the oxygen method under a time limit so short. I believe the choice is a simple one. Does the city want the new and more competitive oxygen process to be adopted here or would it rather take its chances on the area falling farther behind in jobs and prosperity? It is for the city to decide whether we are to proceed."

It is about as Gordian as a knot can be.

At first there seems to be a clear conflict between the public and private interest, as when a property owner asks for zoning changes so that he can make money. But this is not truly the case. The conflict is between two mutually exclusive courses, both of which can be shown to be in the public interest, and both can be shown to be against the public interest.

Steel production is the dominant industry of Youngstown, even more important than it is to Pittsburgh. Steel management means what it says. Unless the plants can be modernized, it will become more and more necessary to cut back, perhaps eventually to abandon them. This would be fatal to the economy of the city of Youngstown.

Yet if you slice the Gordian knot in the other direction—by enforcing a good smoke abatement ordinance—you have a better than even chance of hastening the complete abandonment of all steel plants.

The nub of this problem is perhaps that it deals with one of the great natural resources of the nation, the atmosphere. Is local government able to handle this problem?

The Right Hand and the Left Hand, extracted from the ASPO Newsletter editorial "The Lord Gave and the Lord Hath Taken Away," November 1966.

In a certain city there are two large redevelopment projects, both completed and operating successfully. Both projects are built on sites that were formerly badly blighted, mixed-use areas. Both projects are now apartment complexes, 100 percent residential except for very minor service uses. Both projects represent great improvement over their predecessor slums—except that in one project the air pollution from the heating plant is about half what the site produced as a slum; the air pollution from the second project is about 50 percent greater than the area produced when it was a slum.

While the Congress has worked itself into a lather about air pollution and is financing studies and giving money to clean up the foul atmosphere, it is also handing out funds to encourage building that produces even greater pollution.

This inconsistency applies not only to urban renewal grants. In every city, institutions and public buildings—hospitals, schools, universities—can always be counted on to be among the worst offenders in dirtying the air. And the federal government is more and more paying the bills for constructing these public and quasi-public structures.

The tax-relief program to encourage industrial construction, now temporarily halted, puts the government and all of the citizens heavily into the financing of new factories. Fortunately, relatively few industrial plants are air polluters. But there are a few; and some of the few, such as steel mills, are awfully large and can be awfully dirty.

The solution to this problem is quite simple: *No federal assistance unless the completed project meets strict standards on the emission of air pollutants; no tax relief unless the new plant is clean.*

Perhaps we are not politically ready to require a good local air pollution abatement program before federal largesse of any kind is bestowed on the community, but this should come eventually. Haven't we required a local housing code as a prerequisite to urban renewal assistance?

We cannot promise that the planners will be completely satisfied. After all, a planner is never satisfied with things as they are. But it would be a great help if we did not have to watch Washington giving us clean air with the right hand and taking it away from us with the left.

Noise Pollution, extracted from "City Planning for Reduced Noise," a paper given at the Fourth Annual Noise Abatement Symposium, Armour Research Foundation, Chicago, October 23, 1953.

Every profession must have its own squad of apocalyptical horsemen. In city planning they are war, greed, population increase, and technological progress. The four of them manage very handily to keep city planners on their toes and out of breath, if not actually trampled underfoot. We are a little better equipped to fight the fourth of these—technological progress—than we are any of the others. At least, we can be a little more objective about this struggle.

We have been planning cities for reduced noise for the past half century or so, without knowing it. We have used the simplest (and probably the most expensive) sound insulation material available—space.

By putting enough space between you and any noise yet created, you are bound to eliminate its effects on the auditory nerves. So we pushed the noisy factory over to one side of the town, and put the residential district as far away on the other side of the town as possible. Based on the single factor of noise nuisance, the value of the property was in direct ratio to its distance from the noise producer.

In setting up requirements within residential areas, planners specified side yards, which, among other things, kept the noise of your neighbor's children and his quarrels with his wife out of your house—and vice versa. Yards in front and between the houses and the streets deadened the clop-clop of horses' hooves on the cobblestone pavement.

The city planner's use of space is not caused solely by his desire to provide noise insulation. We make a multiple use of the instrument. We use space to isolate sources of air contamination, to give the sun a chance to reach the ground, to separate people from eyesores and psychologically unpleasant operations, to give them a chance to see and use the earth in an unwrapped, unconcreted condition. We have specified buffer strips between railroads and the adjacent residential property. We are designing buffer strips along either side of high-speed, high capacity expressways, and specifying them for the borders of off-street parking lots. We are also beginning to call for landscaped buffer strips between industrial districts and adjacent residential districts. .

Performance standards are, without doubt, the most scientific approach to city planning for reduced noise. City planners are badly in need of help from the acoustical engineers. We need general agreement on tolerable limits of noise generation. We also need simple instruments and simplified procedures for measuring noise, a sort of Ringelman chart. I realize there isn't much hope of simplifying the measurement of noise to this point, but I am confident that it can be made a lot simpler than it now is. It must be simple enough for the relatively untrained type of person in our municipal building departments.

We must also have, in addition to standards and measuring devices, some method of prejudging noise generation. Physicists and acoustical engineers must be able to tell us, merely by looking at a set of blueprints and specifications, whether a factory, after it is built, will meet the noise standards we have established for the area in which it is to be located. I haven't the slightest idea how this can be done. Nevertheless, it must be done; we cannot afford to wait until after a factory is built to find out whether or not it complies with our regulations. It would be not only unfair but politically impossible to tear down a plant after it was once built, just because it was 10 or 15 decibels noisier than we thought it was going to be.

Disturbing noise is one of the unpleasant concomitants of urbanization. We have been planning cities to reduce noise for many years, perhaps mostly in an unconscious manner. We now hope that we are moving into such planning in a more conscious manner, taking advantage of the more accurate techniques now developing. However, if we are to avoid slipping further and further behind, we must have, on the part of scientists and technologists, an awakening to social responsibilities for the ideas they loose on the world.

"Cities Don't Need to Be Ugly," quoted
from the guest editorial written for *Kiwanis
Magazine*, June 1958.

Cities build and rebuild continuously and their form follows from the decisions of millions of different human beings. We have created ugliness not beauty. Civic beauty comes only with conscious effort that includes beauty as an objective. With the same effort and the same money that now goes into the production of urban ugliness, we could—if we would—produce urban beauty.

In spite of the enlightenment of some manufacturers, businessmen, and developers, it takes no trained aesthete to know that development since World War II has produced square mile after square mile of ugliness, desecrated land, and despoiled landscape. This is not democracy; this is anarchy!

Unless we stop this spawning of horrific countryside, we shall produce a sickness in our land, in our cities, and eventually in our people—a sickness that may be impossible to cure. We are only beginning to understand the psychological effects of urban congestion, blight, and ugliness. What we do understand makes it urgent to correct our development policies before it is too late—if, indeed, it may not already be too late in many cities.

"Clearings in Prefab Jungles," extracted from the ASPO Newsletter editorial, September 1956.

On my desk there is an envelope stuffed with newspaper clippings. It is marked "Parking versus Parks" and is filled with stories of the erosion of open space by expressways, Nike installations, civic centers, armories, schools, housing projects. Some of the articles have happy endings: "Near East Siders Win Battle to Save Highland Park" (Indianapolis). Some are grim: "How the Hopkins Park Playground Will Look When It Has Lost Half Its Present Land to Louisquisset Pike" (Providence). The raiding goes on in all cities. In this batch of clippings there are reports from Milwaukee, San Francisco, Louisville, Washington, Los Angeles, Baltimore, Boston, Philadelphia, and Portland. The theft is not confined to city and county parks; it threatens even our national parks and monuments.

Surrounding every major city and most smaller cities are carefully engineered housing developments, monotonous reaches of cubicles flowing irresistibly over every acre in sight, flooding farm lands, flattening trees. This, I believe, is even more disheartening than the loss of established public open spaces. I feel much as though I were sitting at

the bedside of someone I love, watching the progress of some in-
curable disease, helpless to do more than watch.

Why do we have this annihilation of openness? Certainly, if we do
not have open spaces, we breed generations who know nothing of
their beauty and necessity, and who may be even more callous than
we.

I have often thought of the peculiar religion we all seem to have, our
national belief that glorifies the remains of the dead above the happi-
ness of the living. A cemetery is sacred above all things, holiest of
holies. A park is a reservation of land until the time we need it for a
cloverleaf expressway intersection. I do not suggest that we release
our cemeteries for the benefit of automobiles, because that seems to be
the one open land use we can hang on to. I just ask why we can't make
parks as sacred as graveyards, why the quick are not just as good as
the dead?

The newspaper stories do not give the impression that planners or
planning boards are at fault in this raiding of our open space. Some
may be too apathetic, but in many cases it is the planning agency that
is fighting the last ditch battle. No, the forces seem to be economic—a
handy term for activities that you can't quite pin down. If they are
economic, if they are the results of prosperity and population pressure, then we should be warned. These forces are now puny compared
with what they will be.

We need a policy to give us clearings in the prefab jungles we are
planting. What shall it be?

"Expressways and Parks: A Suggestion," extracted from the ASPO Newsletter editorial,
January 1966.

The reasons why highway builders prefer park land for right-of-way
are simple. Parks offer long, uninterrupted runs to meet the supreme
highway economic principle: A straight line is the best route between
two points. Park land is cheap because the city already owns it and,
therefore, it is free. And nobody lives in parks so you do not have the
problem of relocating irate householders. The problem can be expected to increase as the federal highway program continues into the
distant future.

Some years ago, the Regional Plan Association of New York suggested a clear statement on the use of park land for highway (or any other nonpark) construction. Briefly, the RPA recommended that cities adopt a two-point policy: (1) avoid using park land for highway purposes wherever possible; and (2) where it is absolutely necessary to use park land, replace the land taken by establishing a new park, as nearly as possible equal in size and equally well located to serve the same neighborhood.

There is no way of knowing how many communities do subscribe to the RPA policy either by overt statement or in practice. But it is clear that a number of communities do *not* subscribe to it (Chicago officials, for example, ignored the policy until they were forced to change).

There are two factors today in the problem that were apparent 10 or 15 years ago, and which suggest a new approach to the solution. The first of these is that a public policy, or a plan, is a sometime thing. This needs no elaboration, since planners have preached on this subject many times: plans-gathering-dust-on-the-shelves, a council cannot bind the action of later councils, political expediency, and all that. That is to say, adopting a policy is not the same as carrying it out.

The second factor is federal aid and the role of the United States government. In urban renewal the story is clear. Without federal insistence on an effective relocation program, the entire urban renewal program would long ago have stopped. Relocation is just as much a part of urban renewal—just as important—as code enforcement, clearance, rebuilding, rehabilitation, or conservation.

Unless the federal government extends the same insistence (and probably the same financial aid) to the relocation of parks massacred by highways, we can expect that the high-handed expropriation of park land will continue. I therefore suggest the following amended policy:

1. Any construction not for park purposes that uses any federal financing, should, if possible, avoid the use of any park land.
2. Where for such projects, if it is found necessary to use park land, *the land so used must be replaced, at the same time and as a part of the same project,* by an equal amount of land suitably located to serve the same purposes as the original park.

If such a policy becomes an integral part of the law of federal largesse, the highway economists will wake up to the fact that Chicago's lakefront parks, and Central Park, and Balboa Park, and a thousand other parks can no longer be considered as unlimited reservoirs of free land.

We may like to think that the increasing weight the United States government has been giving to relocation in urban renewal is a sign of our increasing humanitarianism. If we are cynics, we will point out that the government learned that persons displaced by slum clearance projects were also voters. It is now being discovered that although trees and green lawns in parks do not yet have the vote, people who sit on these lawns under those trees are full-fledged and highly articulate voters.

Of course, getting such a policy adopted by the United States government will not be easy. We can expect torpedo attacks by the same group of highway lobbyists that emasculated the highway beautification bill. Except one: we might get support from the outdoor advertising industry because the operators know that they cannot put billboards alongside expressways that run through the parks, so that if they force the expressways to go outside parks, there will be more mileage open to billboards.

Strange bedfellows!

Meeting the Irresistible Force, extracted from "A Place for Everything," a speech given at a symposium on "The Maine Coast: Prospects and Perspectives," Bowdoin College, New Brunswick, Maine, October 20, 1966.

When an irresistible force meets an immovable object, will the force prove to be not irresistible? Will the object turn out to be not immovable? When the encounter takes place, one gives way; either the force is stopped or the object moves. But until the two meet, you don't know which.

The citizens of Maine are now facing this very same situation—the irresistible force and the immovable object. The irresistible force is the automobile, fueled by ever-increasing affluence and leisure time and manned by an ever-growing urban population. The immovable object is the land of Maine, blessed by unsurpassed beauty and anchored by a New England tradition and way of life that does not accommodate easily to change. The invasion by the irresistible force—the force has many aspects of attack and conquest—has already overrun much of the land, destroyed too much of its beauty. It is a sort of scorched earth policy: as the invaders spoil one section of the seacoast, they move on to take over and spoil the next section, leaving behind a desecration that even they cannot stomach.

The state of Maine is a suburb of the largest urban agglomeration in the world: the 20 million people in a great sprawling city that extends from Boston to Norfolk—20 million today, 40 million before the end of the century. Maine will be a principal recreational area for megalopolis.

You cannot count on having the remaining years of the 20th century to meet the doubled invasion force. The boat and auto population is growing much more rapidly than the human population. This is because of increased wealth and increased leisure time and because of finer highways and improved navigational facilities. I give you ten years, at the outside, before the irresistible force will be doubled—doubling the tourists and the ruthless exploiters of Maine's land and seacoast.

The state legislature will have to pass some new laws. It will have to appropriate money for buying back the birthright of its citizens. Zoning is a good tool, but it cannot be relied on to avoid continuation of the unpleasant pattern that is developing. Nor will "planning" solve the problems.

The enabling statutes for local land-use regulation should be modernized. This is one action. A second piece of legislation is a law to establish some form of state review of local zoning and land-use regulation. State review does not in any way interfere with local autonomy, local government competently administered, but it does put a damper on local government selfishly administered, or maladministered.

But state review of zoning is not enough. The state itself must take over land-use regulation in a number of areas. In those areas in which local government is not able or does not wish to regulate development, the state must step in. The state must regulate the use of land in other areas where there is clearly a statewide interest that overrides local interest. This could include the area around intersections on expressways, it could even include the entire shoreline.

You must have legislation enabling both the local community and the state to assume a degree of control of development that is not possible under conventional zoning and subdivision regulation. To preserve open space and views and areas of great natural beauty under the police power—the legal basis for zoning—would be a violation of due process. Therefore, you must have legislation that permits partial compensation, permits the purchase of scenic easements and development rights in land, leaving the fee title to the land itself with the original owner. You also need the power of partial compensation to begin to get rid of the most offensive nonconforming uses and to correct some of the worst mistakes in earlier zoning.

These measures are primarily directed toward the preservation of natural resources and the prevention of abuse. Essentially they are negative—prohibiting, in one way or another, inappropriate development. They are necessary, but not sufficient to accommodate to the inevitability of the irresistible force. They are also quite vulnerable to attack for economic as well as legal reasons, unless they are at the same time accompanied by a much bolder program to provide accommodations for the temporary refugees from megalopolis.

I therefore propose that the people, working through the state government, go into the business of recreational development. I do not mean a token operation which provides picnic tables on roadside turn-offs, a few cabins in state parks, or an occasional public pier. I do mean cottage developments, motels, restaurants, ski runs and ski lodges, full-scale marinas and harbors with all shore facilities, camping and trailer parks, and all of the facilities that the tourist needs and wants. I mean that the state should go into the recreation facility development business with the object of preempting an ever-increasing proportion of all such development for the entire state.

There are terrific problems that such a program would face: financial problems, management problems, political problems. But these problems can be solved if the people wish to solve them. I firmly believe that if the people abdicate the responsibility for development of their state and turn it over to national motel chains, national oil companies, and the busy, busy hoard of fast-buck developers, they will lose their state.

**Planning, Zoning and Aesthetic Control,
condensed from a speech at an American
Bar Association seminar, Chicago,
June 3, 1967.**

Over the years I have observed that lawyers, along with priests and
doctors, are a triumvirate of the most realistic of professionals,
realistic in their recognition of the foibles and weaknesses of human
beings. Yet like doctors when they speak of a health regimen, and
priests when they exhort the saintly life, lawyers are inclined to get
idealistic when they speak of laws and the rule of law. It is not that
lawyers believe the passage of a law automatically puts an end to
whatever particular sin that law forbids. Rather, lawyers seem too
often to pass over lightly the intermediate state between the law and
the sinners, a process involving standards, permits, review, records,
inspection, investigation, and prosecution—details of which cannot
be spelled out in the statute. Most important, administration is a process that must be carried out by human beings.

I think we can stipulate—to use the lawyers' term—that our objective is to make our nation and its cities beautiful. I hope we can also
stipulate that the majority of the people are in favor of beauty and
that it is not unconstitutional to try to give them their druthers. There
are three types of action we can use to achieve our objective. We can
eliminate, we can preserve, we can create. I refer to the administrative
process by which we accomplish our ends, and I use the pronoun *we*
to mean "we, the citizens, acting together through our government."

1.   **We can eliminate ugliness.** As a temporary expedient, assume
that part of beauty is the absence of ugliness. We do not need to say
that we are producing beauty by getting rid of ugliness, only that we
cannot have a beautiful environment so long as part of that environment is ugly. We have the problem of defining ugliness; nevertheless,
there are some things on which we can agree as objects of undoubted
ugliness—slums, for example. The effect of the underlying aesthetic
objections to slum property should not be underestimated as a major
factor in the original motivation for clearing slums, and slum clearance does eliminate ugliness. There is also a fairly large consensus on
the inherent ugliness of billboards, where the remedial action can only
be, of course, elimination.

2.   **We can preserve existing beauty.** Again we have the problem of
defining beauty, of deciding what to preserve. Perhaps it would some-

times stretch the idea of beauty to include historic districts and structures, but it is not stretching the idea of aesthetics. We have made headway in historic preservation in many cities. We also have a history of preserving natural beauty in national, state, and local parks— and man-made beauty—by erecting a legal fence around the objects and saying, "Keep out! This will remain as is—forever and ever."

3. We can create beauty. We can create beauty by designing and building beautiful public structures, beautiful monuments, beautiful parkways and highways. We can even create natural beauty by landscaping, improving our parks, our seashore, our riverbanks. We must also include in our creative activities any efforts (and sanctions) to encourage and guide private development to be beautiful.

Eliminate the ugliness of the past that is still with us, preserve and hold safe the beauty that we now have, create in and for the future a still more beautiful environment: a simple prescription, but extremely difficult to administer.

The first problem is the one of standards. How do you define what is aesthetically pleasing, what is aesthetically displeasing? Thus far our most successful efforts in aesthetic control have been those in which we did not attempt to define the abstraction, "beauty," but by using concrete terms describing secondary characteristics, have implied that anything having these characteristics was beautiful. This has been the operation of historic preservation. We have said, "You may not demolish any building constructed before 1850," for example, implying that all buildings constructed before 1850 are *ipso facto* works of art. Or we have said that all buildings within a certain section of the city, which we describe accurately by naming the boundary streets, shall remain as is or be replaced only by buildings of a certain architectural style, as we have done in the Vieux Carre in New Orleans. We can describe that style in fairly unequivocal language, and we imply that that style is beautiful.

We have also been successful in defining standards when we set about to eliminate ugliness, although we do not come right out and say, "This is ugly, therefore, you must get rid of it." We merely say, "All junk yards must be moved away from residential and commercial districts and must be screened from public view wherever they are located." The successful campaign to rid Hawaii of billboards used the very simple and unambiguous principle, "Billboards must go!" The implied definition of beauty is a landscape without billboards, but it is not necessary to spell it out.

When you come to the third administrative process, the creation of beauty—or the prevention of ugliness—in the future, you run into trouble. You are no longer dealing with something of beauty or ugliness that already exists. You must try to put into words some limits to the truly infinite variety of man's creativity.

One generally accepted mark of aesthetic fitness is compatibility. This is the justification for demanding the Old Pueblo architecture in Santa Fe. A Cape Cod saltbox would be a jarring note, incompatible with its adobe neighbors. There is an equally valid mark of aesthetic unsuitability: monotony, too much sameness. This is a universal complaint against the mass production houses that characterize suburban sprawl. You have two exactly opposite aesthetic objectives: houses must look alike for compatibility; they must look different to avoid monotony.

From these contradictory ideas we have had a number of architectural control ordinances. One type holds that you must prevent monotony by changing the window pattern, the roof design, the construction material, the exterior dimensions. Houses that duplicate each other in two or more of these characteristics must be separated by a prescribed number of intervening houses of dissimilar characteristics. The other type of ordinances holds that the sin is creating incompatibility by plopping down a bunch of houses that are too different from those already built. Therefore, if you want to build in that community you must follow the prevailing architectural style—in material, roof line, number of stories, fenestration, and so on.

From the viewpoint of administration of aesthetic controls: if we can agree on what now existing is beautiful, it is not too difficult to describe and preserve those things; if we can agree on what we now have that is ugly, we can describe that, too, and eliminate it. (I refer only to the administration of such laws, not to their legality or constitutionality.) But when we come to some statutory device to assure that the future works of man shall be beautiful, we must inevitably stray from the rule of law and get into rule by men. And, of course, here we run into trouble.

Aesthetic control is land-use control, and land-use control ordinances have, from their beginning, been recognized as laws that can be unnecessarily harsh on individuals. While relief from any law is available through the courts, the fathers of modern land-use regulation—zoning—felt that it should have a simpler, more rapid, less costly method to get substantial justice for the injured property owner.

So zoning ordinances always include a device to permit deviation from the letter of the law—the variance. Zoning also provides for a comparatively fast amendment procedure that in effect authorizes a private bill for the relief of an individual property owner. While zoning gives the appearance of a law that rules, it has become largely an enabling statute, authorizing administrators to receive petitions and to use their discretion to grant or to refuse.

I favor land-use regulation by administrative agency. But the basic requirement for successful and fair rule by an administrative agency is that the agency be manned by experts, and this has not been true of land-use control administration. Boards of zoning appeals are made up by citizens whose only claim to expertise in land-use regulation is that they have all their life lived in houses or apartments built on land. The record of zoning appeal boards has been spotty, with the spots being the good boards and most of the record being bad. The expertise of the city councils who are called upon to amend zoning ordinances is not better than that of the zoning appeal boards.

In my opinion, adding aesthetic controls to a land-use regulatory system that is already archaic is only compounding the problem. In fact, the difficulty of judging aesthetic values will be even greater than the difficulty of passing on our present, more prosaic land-use questions. If there is one thing we can be sure about, it is the absurdity of trying to make aesthetic judgments by popular vote.

Yet, with all my dissatisfaction with the administration of land-use regulations, I am as certain as I can be that we shall have fewer hard-and-fast standards in the future and more discretion lodged in the persons administering the regulations. And whether we call them aesthetic controls or not, our land-use regulations will have a large measure of aesthetic implications.

Long before we faced the problem of beautifying suburbia, and long before we publicly admitted that beauty might be an appropriate public concern, we had written into our zoning codes several provisions that could only be honestly interpreted as aesthetic standards. Chief among these were the standards for required yards: front, back, and side. We justified yard standards on the basis of light, air, and the provision of a free passageway for fire engines to go between buildings. We talked about public health and safety, but what we really meant was that we thought it was prettier to have yards surrounding single-family houses.

The second half of the 20th century brought the urban explosion and along with it a lot of architects and urban designers with fresh ideas which could not be fitted into the numerical straightjacket of conventional land-use control. The designers invented the regional shopping center, the industrial park, the cluster subdivision, the high-rise apartment, the townhouse, the atrium house, and the ziggurat. We had to face the difficult fact that true aesthetic creativity nearly always starts off by kicking over the traces, by violating rules and ignoring standards.

Another problem in the administration of land-use regulations must be recognized if we are to be realistic. This is the widespread lack of enforcement and reluctance to prosecute. The problem is most noticeable on violations that are considered minor, and sadly for the aesthete, violations of such aesthetic controls as we now have are considered minor.

The administration of land-use controls is generally unsatisfactory, even where standards are not ambiguous. It is messy because of the confusion between administrative, legislative, and judicial acts. It is amateurish because it is being carried on by amateurs. It is also inefficient because the present laws are inadequate for regulation and development as it is now being done. Until there is general modernization of land-use control laws and their administration, we cannot be sanguine about either the effectiveness or the equity of aesthetic controls written in a similar manner and administered by the same machinery.

Thus far I have assumed that we were using the police power as the basis for aesthetic controls. The courts now say it is proper to include aesthetics among the factors that you consider in planning a city and controlling development—a change from early decisions that arbitrarily threw out aesthetics. When the appearance of an area, its architectural style, its beauty, can be shown to have economic effects related to the means of livelihood of the citizens, the relation to the general welfare is obvious. But I see no likelihood of aesthetics being added in full status to the quartet of public health, safety, morals, and general welfare. We will need to continue to find primary justification in the original four, and let aesthetics tag along. I do not find this unreasonable.

I also believe that we must use other governmental powers more than we have done to achieve, among other objectives, aesthetic goals. For example, I suggest that we step up sharply the use of the taxing power to control billboards. The power to tax is the power to destroy, and while it is not considered nice to use taxation to this extreme, it would not be difficult to justify stringent regulation of this form of ugliness by levying greatly increased taxes in return for the offense to the public eye.

Then there is the very difficult question raised in the case of the Seagram building in New York City, where the owners claimed that they were penalized because they had made their building beautiful. It would be worthwhile to consider the opposite—a temporary tax bonus for excellence of design—if you could ever get any agreement on what constituted excellence in design!

I believe we must also increase the use of public purchase, backed up, of course, by the power of eminent domain. Public purchase is certainly the indicated treatment in many situations involving historical buildings and districts. It is also indicated in certain areas of natural beauty. Parenthetically, I do *not* recommend purchase or compensation for controlling billboards.

To some it may seem radical, but I believe that we shall only achieve effective aesthetic control of our exploding suburban areas when we realize that we must have public ownership of all outlying land having urban development potential. In other words, when government is the landowner, government has the indisputable right to say what is built on that land. Aesthetics is not the only justification—in fact, there are other and more persuasive reasons for advocating such a policy. Extensive purchase of land to be used for private construction could not be supported if control of aesthetics were the sole objective. Also, from the aesthetic viewpoint, you might question whether government administrators were any better to judge beauty than would be a miscellany of private contractors and lending institutions. I happen to believe that a properly organized and staffed governmental agency will do a better job—it certainly would be hard put to do a worse job.

For natural areas, the assumption is that nature undisturbed, or relatively undisturbed, by the works of man is beautiful. I agree with this assumption. The preservation of natural beauty is the objective of most land conservation efforts today. Another reason for conservation that carries more weight, but that takes less land out of the private market, is the need to provide recreation areas, principally for overcrowded cities. In my opinion, preservation of natural beauty is not a sufficiently compelling motive, nor can we justify preservation of open space in the amount required and in the locations necessary, if we rely only on the needs for recreation and the preservation of natural beauty.

Continuation of the present pattern of urban proliferation actually threatens the survival of the human race, by disturbing the balance between air, water, and land resources—the ecology of our urbanized regions—beyond the point of no return. I am not alone in my fear that while the catastrophic climax may be 100 years ahead, the point of no return may be less than a generation away. If we can document this statement—and I am confident we shall be able to do so—we certainly have full justification to use the police power to take whatever steps are necessary. As a side benefit, we shall preserve and promote beauty—more natural beauty, and more beautiful people.

We Need Better Quality in Government

The Fight Never Ends, extracted from the ASPO Newsletter editorial "Virtue Begets Its Own Punishment: or The Bigger They Are, the Harder They Fall," December 1959.

People have a quirk that makes them root for the underdog. It may be because of their sympathy for the little guy struggling against great odds—most of us are also little guys and are also struggling. But a lot of it is that we dislike the big fellow, we despise his high and mighty airs (whether or not he has them), and we always see him as fair game. Of course, we all don't feel like this all of the time, but a lot of us do act this way a lot of the time. Some of this attitude transfers to our attitude toward government.

For example, there are a number of awards and citations for good city government. They are almost always given for spectacular achievement, some overcoming of great odds. The rewards are particularly likely to be given for spectacular political reform, where righteous citizens revolt against corrupt political machines and throw the rascals out. The amateur political David is particularly beloved if he can lay the professional Goliath in the dust. Or the small town rounds up all citizens to put in a park and start a recreation program, and gets a pat on the back for doing something it should have done 20 years earlier.

When solid Cincinnati rebelled in 1924 and threw the gang out, it was magnificent. The city deserved some sort of prize, of course. But doesn't it also deserve recognition for having maintained good government in the decades since?

Nowadays, the city that has for years avoided slums and blight, using and enforcing good codes and ordinances, will not be given urban renewal grants, whereas into the city that has let things go to pot for the last 50 years shall be poured all sorts of money from above.

It is not easy to sort out from our actions those that stem from our irrational dislike for the successful and the efficient and those that come from the truly charitable wish to help the weak and faltering, to give a hand to the lowly.

When you have a successful reform movement and want to throw the rascals out and set up good government, the greatest threat to continuing such government is voter apathy. It is difficult to rid yourself completely of the old city hall gang, since we frown on capital punishment for political shenanigans. They always lie there under the rocks waiting for signs of a slackening of interest on the part of the reformers, then out they creep.

It is generally held that good government lulls people into a trance. It is said that this is because good government is usually so inconspicuous and efficient that the voters forget the old days. They forget that the fight to maintain good government never ends, just as the fight to maintain freedom never ends.

"No Time for Softness," condensed from the ASPO Newsletter editorial, January 1965.

Almost everyone who tries to be decent, considerate and tolerant, sooner or later reaches a point where he says, "How much more of this do I have to take?" There comes a time when brotherly love and self-preservation are at odds. Freedom of speech does not mean, either legally or morally, license to lie.

The members of the Radical Right start operating at the first mention of anything that smacks of an effort to improve health, government, or urban life. They lead the fight against flouridation of water, against improvement of mental health. They are the violent antivivi-sectionists that threaten to upset medical research and retard the fight against cancer. Those in the Radical Right are anti-Negro, anti-Catholic, anti-semitic, and anti-foreign. In spite of their habitual use of the national flag they are also violently anti-federal government.

Harry and Bonaro Overstreet in their book about these groups, *The Strange Tactics of Extremism,* say that the philosophy of the Radical Right can be summed up in three axioms: (1) Those who are on top in government, education, church councils, etc., must be pulled down; (2) Those who are on the outside of the citadels of advantage and ex-clusiveness—the Negroes and other minority groups—must be kept outside; and (3) All alliances, treaties and agreements with other na-tions—the Organization of American States, NATO, United Na-tions—must be disavowed and broken.

The same names keep showing up among the national extremist or-ganizations. Nevertheless, there is as yet no single, identifiable na-tional organization which houses them all or acts as a front. The *American Mercury* at one time seemed to serve as a rallying point, but even there, the most vicious and prolific of the professionals seldom appeared, except as they were quoted by lesser hacks.

One touchstone on the national scene seems to be money. Can the propaganda be produced and distributed widely, so that its author makes money? One of the pros, Gerald L. K. Smith, does quite well. Herman Pope [then president of Public Administration Service] wrote in *New Peas in an Old Shell Game,* that "reporting under the Federal Corrupt Practices Act reveals that Smith, through his Christian-Nationalist Crusade, has grossed as high as $202,359.71 and never less than $155,135.82 in each of the seven years ending with 1958, demon-strating that hate-mongering is, in more ways than one, definitely not a labor of love." Later reports on Smith's activities indicate even larger takes.

On the local scene also, the faces are hardy perennials. In *Nation's Cities* [November 1964], Arthur Prager of the New York-New Jersey-Connecticut Metropolitan Council describes the behavior of the hate-mongers in their public appearances and gives some suggestions for public officials [reproduced at the end of this editorial]. Prager calls them "Klansmen without nightshirts," and in at least one instance the lack of a nightshirt at the public meeting was only temporary—at other times the man appeared in the nightshirt as a leader of the Klan.

Members of the Radical Right are great writers of letters to the *vox pop* of the local newspaper, particularly the suburban locals. Most editors spot them quickly and refuse to print the stuff after the first letter. If the local paper continues to print the letters, this can mean that the newspaper too has joined the Radical Right.

The standard claim of the Radical Right to respectability is that they are fighting "Communists." However, in their vocabulary "communist" has included every president in the United States since Hoover. In fact, if you as an individual are ever singled out for their venom, you will find yourself in the company of some of the most distinguished and honorable men and women that the United States has produced in the last century.

It is surprising that anyone can take most of the hate literature seriously. It is so obviously phony. Much of it seems to have been written by illiterates. However, we must admit that it has been quite effective in disrupting and disorganizing the efforts of intelligent and honest civic action.

There are three late additions to the ranks of the Radical Right that make the situation more dangerous than heretofore. First is the group of men of very great wealth that support the extremists. Great wealth, coupled with unscrupulous writers and communications experts, is dangerous.

Second, respected professors from at least three major schools appear to have thrown in with the Radical Right. The writing skill of these persons is greater and more effective than that of the long-time professional hate-mongers. Until recently the falsity of the extremist writing was easily spotted by an educated person. However, the publications by the professors are not nearly so crude nor so easily identified as spurious. The literature now takes on an air of scholastic respectability.

The third, and perhaps potentially the most dangerous of all, are the professional organizers who have joined the ranks of the Radical Right. Perhaps the word should be professional "disorganizers," because their technique is to move into an area where there is tension and effectively disrupt local government action to alleviate the conditions causing the tension. Their technique, inadvertently revealed by one of their dupes, is to "rub salt in open wounds."

Certainly not everyone who joins one of the Radical Right organizations is inherently vicious from the beginning. Why, then, do they get taken in? Except for those leaders who are clearly in it for money or power, the motivation seems to be fear—fear of change. This is the emotion that the propagandists work on. Even the status quo is too progressive, the Radical Right would go even further back, returning to a historical past that never did exist.

Because fear of change is the dominant emotion of these people, it is easy to see why municipal government in these days is particularly susceptible to attack. The total effect of urbanization is change— change from farm boy to city boy, from farm land to urban land, from scattered small stores to great stores in shopping centers. The tools and ideas that we have developed to accommodate to change: planning, zoning, urban renewal, new towns, expressways, slum clearance, public housing—these terrify the little members of the Radical Right, so they attack us. It cannot be emphasized too much that the leaders of the Radical Right and their followers are implacable enemies of all public officials and the friends of none. Our sympathies for those poor, terror-stricken souls who have fallen for the propaganda must not interfere with our better judgment. The Radical Right is extremely dangerous and is quite effective, as anyone who has tangled with it, and lost, will testify. The Radical Right may hate communists; but to gain its own ends, it has adopted all the communist tactics of subversion, infiltration, and exacerbation.

It is the duty of the public official to listen to the citizens, especially to those who honestly differ from him. The Radical Right does *not* honestly differ. It *dishonestly* seeks to overthrow him and everything he stands for. It is therefore also the duty of the public official to fight extremism whenever and wherever it shows up. Only in this way can he truly represent the great majority of the citizens. He can also expect this same great majority to back him up. Most Americans still will have no truck with the hate-mongers.

The public official must also realize that he can expect no quarter from the Radical Right. He must be fair, but he, too, must give no quarter. If he tries in any way to mollify these enemies, he is certain to lose. No one can afford to be tolerant of intolerance.

The following material is reprinted from "Here Come the Hate Groups" by
Arthur Prager in the November 1964 issue of *Nation's Cities*.

What to Look for

Organized Disruption. Begins with audible signs of approval or
disapproval of whatever is said. May be sharp intakes of breath,
gasps, *sotto voce* groans, sighs, shuffling feet, or muttered phrases.
Usually starts at prearranged signal by group leader.

Monopolization of the Press. One or more will suddenly rise and
bellow an eccentric slogan calculated to galvanize reporters. They
know that little space is allotted in large newspapers for local issues
and less than a minute prime time on big TV channels. Extemists' objective: Grab the lion's share of the limited coverage. During breaks in
hearings, they try to buttonhole press so no one else can be inter-
viewed.

Circuit Rider Technique. No matter where a meeting is held, the
same faces always show up. In different areas, they assume different
quasi-political or patriotic organizational names, associated in some
way with issues to be discussed.

Professional Antagonism. They never appear except to oppose.
Target for the day may be a piece of legislation, election of a school
board member, establishment of some administrative innovation, or
efforts at regional cooperation. Among their dislikes: National Municipal League, League of Women Voters, International City Managers' Association.

Anonymity. Except for a few leaders, rank and file are reluctant to
identify themselves. Membership lists are secret; financing is not ex-
plained. Attempts to find out are rebuffed in short order.

Misuse of Patriotic Symbols. U.S. flags much in evidence. Letter-
heads, pamphlets, and releases bear representations of the American
eagle, escutcheons, Great Seal, and other symbols. Implies their principles and issues can't be opposed by other than un-Americans.

Blind Accusations. Charges without evidence are invariable, at
meetings and in literature. Proposals may be termed "a trick to raise
your taxes." When proven otherwise, tactic is to call it "the thin end of
the wedge," implying that it may lead to other dangerous proposals.

Invisible Experts and Documents.   Famous but nameless people are always cited as support ("A group of well-known engineers says . . ."). These folks are never present, of course. Documents are vaguely identified, but never distributed and no one may see them.

How to Maintain Order

First. Expect them.

Second. Know them and keep your information about them up-to-date and timely.

Third. Explain simply and politely the rules and procedures which govern your meeting, and warn them that those rules will be strictly adhered to.

Fourth. If they have the right to participate under the rules set down, insist that they adhere to the point, that they offer factual information, and that their evidence be real and acceptable.

Fifth. Take steps to see that they do not monopolize the press coverage of the meeting by unfair tactics.

Sixth. Be firm. Do not waver and do not compromise with them. Take rapid action on any infraction of rules. And don't worry about losing their votes. They won't vote for you anyway, even if you give in and let them run riot over your meeting. On the other hand, a firm and unyielding policy with these people will gain you the respect of the citizens of your locality. For every voter or customer lost, a dozen new partisans will appear. Don't be worried about the "or else" clause in their threats. They can't enforce it.

"A New Contest," extracted from the ASPO Newsletter editorial, August 1962.

Awards and citations tend to be for positive accomplishments or characteristics: Oscars for the *best* movie actress; Emmies for the *best* TV program; Nobels for the *finest* accomplishments in medicine, physics, peace, and so on. As well as for human beings, we also have awards for cities, again slanted toward the positive side. Which city has made the *most improvement,* what city has *overcome the greatest handicap.* It is time for rebellion. Let us give awards for the worst, the least, the poorest.

It would be difficult to name the worst cities without some objective method of scoring.

Schools being so much in the mind of citizens these days, let us start there. We will give several points for the school system that is dominated by athletics, where the high school gym is big enough to hold the entire city and then some. Also, a big batch of negative points to the city that has a crusading citizens' committee for censoring textbooks, a committee that sees a communist hiding behind every arithmetic problem.

Recreation areas: If you take ten acres per thousand population as proper, you could run a reverse scale like five acres per thousand rates 50 down-points, 2.5 acres per thousand rates 75 down-points, etc. Special bonus points would go against the city that had parks but refused to spend any money for recreation supervision. We would also give a bonus to the city in which the school and park boards continued on their own separate courses and refused to pool facilities.

The police department: Where a good police scandal has come to light, we should take this into consideration in downgrading a city. On the other hand, more demerits should be awarded to the city that has burglar-police cooperation, but does not bring it into the light of day.

In lining up the ten worst cities, we would not overlook the water and waste situation. Chronic water shortage in the summer is a good sign of bad operation. Even more important is the waste disposal. On our reversed scorecard, points are to be inversely correlated with the effectiveness of sewage treatment—complete treatment, no points; raw sewage in the river, 100 points. Open dump disposal of solid wastes also rates a healthy number of points.

Scoring on traffic congestion will be difficult. Practically every city rates a lot of down-points here. You would probably give a bonus related to the public transit situation: no public transit, lots of points. You can also do a lot of demeriting on the traffic control system—flashing neon signs on corner filling stations, no timing on traffic lights, speed traps, council-businessman conspiracy to prohibit one-way streets. In the larger cities, of course, you can get any number of down-points on an expressway system, how effectively it disrupts neighborhoods and bisects school districts, how completely unrelated it is to the local street system, how it dumps its load on the unprepared central business districts.

Of course, when it comes to planning, zoning, and urban renewal:

no planning, no zoning, no urban renewal—that city would be just about a perfect candidate for the nadir. Another good sign of a bad city is one in which zoning variances and amendments can be purchased, although this city would be only slightly lower than the one in which everything that anyone wants to do to circumvent zoning is freely given to them by the board of appeals or city council. There are many technicalities in these fields that an expert can use to downgrade a city: no capital improvement program, chicken-hearted off-street parking provisions, beauty shops as home occupations, low planning budgets, property manipulation by planning board members, planning technicians working both sides of the street, and so on and on.

This is a complex problem and I have touched on only a few of the points that must be studied. I have said nothing about low public salaries, or even about the *form* of the city government—both very important factors. How much weight would you give to closed council meetings or closed meetings of other commissions and boards? What about the newspaper situation in a one-newspaper town, either the newspaper that sees all government as a invention of the devil, or one that because of certain personal connections, can never see anything wrong with the local politicos? Bad hospitals should be rated, as should bad libraries, and bad smelling city halls. How completely has the local waterfront been fouled up? What is the attitude of the local business group toward new industry? Keep it out because it might raise wages? What is the local attitude on minority problems?

This is no little undertaking I propose. To be chosen for one of the ten worst is a dishonor not easily arrived at nor one to be taken lightly by a winner.

So with these few notes we leave the proposition up to our readers. If we ever get this contest rolling, we know just exactly the kind of vessel that would be a suitable trophy to present to each of the ten worst cities.

**"What This Country Needs Is a
Good . . .," extracted from the ASPO
Newsletter editorial, September 1966.**

Why don't we have some standard of rating city government?

The American Council of Education issued a ranking of graduate schools and universities. The ranking in each field of study was based on the combined opinion of scholars in that field—where they would like to work, which schools they would choose if they were young men starting out graduate training at this time. The ACE rating generated anguished wails and loud denunciations. But the ratings will stick.

Back in 1938, Edward L. Thorndike published a rating of 295 American cities on the "goodness of life" that they offered. Thorndike's ratings were based on objective measurements such as average family income, population growth, illiteracy, and so on. He even included the going price of cabbage and permanent waves. While the figures he used were objective, the weight Thorndike assigned to various factors was his own idea. The rank of the city went up, for example, as the infant mortality rate went down. Thorndike's study is now hopelessly out of date—he based most of his index on 1930 figures—and besides, he had no real factor for local government, no figures on quality of government that he could throw into the formula.

There are special ratings at present for cities, however, that are widely used and are influential, and which are partial measurements of the quality of government. One of these is the National Board of Fire Underwriters' fire insurance classification. Cities are assessed deficiency points when conditions fall below standards prescribed by the Underwriters. They are then given a classification—Class 1, best, to Class 10, poorest—and the cost of fire insurance in a city is based on the classification.

The other important city ratings are the financial ratings made by Standard & Poor and by Moody's Investors Service. These ratings are consulted by banks and other investors before they bid on local government bond offerings. The lower the Moody or Standard & Poor rating of the city, the higher the interest rate. Financial ratings are based on a number of factors, including some that Thorndike used, such as diversity of employment, so they cannot be considered strictly as indicators of the quality of fiscal administration in the community.

You have some tough problems if you try to rate governmental functions objectively. Crime statistics, for example, are so notoriously unreliable as to be useless in comparing police administration in different communities. Hospital beds per thousand population can be accurately determined, but the need for public hospital beds—if you are judging quality of public health administration—is dependent on the supply of private hospital beds, and the need for local public hospitals is tempered by the proximity and availability of regional and state public hospital facilities.

Nevertheless, I believe that it is possible to judge and compare the quality of local government. Some combination of the ACE rating of graduate schools (a census of the informed judgment of experts on separate governmental functions) and the Thorndike use of pertinent objective measurements, should be possible. Then the rated departments should be classified in groups, A, B, C, as the financial raters do, or 1, 2, 3, as the Underwriters do. I don't believe you can give a numerical rank to individual cities like the U.S. Lawn Tennis Association does with tennis players—1, 2, 3, and on down the line: no hand-to-hand combat between cities on which to base your judgment.

I believe that the citizens would take an interest. I can hear them asking, "What's wrong? Why do we spend all this money on planning and get only a C rating, while over in such-and-such, they spend less and yet the planning department is rated A. How come?" I think that sort of public inquiry would be helpful.

5

New Goals,
New Techniques,
for Urban Problems

Editor's Commentary

We need new attitudes, new techniques, Dennis O'Harrow kept warning. And he spelled out his observations and advice on some issues and problems that the country is still trying to resolve.

The massive federal financing of urban development required, in his view, new federal, state and local roles. The population increase—the need to build additional cities and urban facilities—called for new governmental, and planning, goals and techniques. The expanding social and economic implications of planning called for new knowledge and new relationships.

"You cannot be sure what form the creature will take," he said, "that is the way with evolution." But he pointed out and analyzed significant mutations.

When he "looked at planning with a cold and fishy eye," he said in 1963, "there are four areas in which weaknesses show up. There are four horsemen that the early scribes failed to mention in the planning apocalypse." He labeled them "in academic fashion":

1. Planning administration, quality of
2. Government, integrity of
3. Taxation, equity of
4. Citizen faith, amount of

Administration of planning had been revealed as the greatest single weakness of agency operations and the planning process during the many detailed studies the ASPO staff had been requested to make in various cities. No wonder! Added to the new social and political demands and the new technology, there were also the burdens of growth and sprawl, of federal programs, of fractionalized, autonomous, and uncoordinated governments—*and* the critical shortage of professional planners.

"The truth is," DOH said in a 1958 paper given to the annual meeting of the National Health Council, "we know a great deal more about the technical solutions to urban problems than we have ever been able to put to use."

DOH made specific suggestions on the problems, and on the emerging issues for federal financing, for state responsibilities, for metropolitan areas and central cities, for new towns and renewal programs, for planning in relation to public and private institutions. He sought to bring more understanding; he urged experimentation; he pressed for quality and cooperation. And he stated emphatically in a 1963 lecture to college students: "The 'minority problem,' to use a nice euphemism, is probably the most important unsolved problem in America today. If we are to save our cities, if we are to save our nation, we had better get about solving the minority problem."

Federal Tunes

Extracted from the ASPO Newsletter
editorial "A New Tune for the Piper,"
March 1966.

A paradox of the federal grant program during the Great Depression was that the greatest rewards went for municipal mismanagement. The rules were such that the federal government stepped in and gave money for public works only if you were in hock up to your ears and over your bond limitation and preferably when you already welched on debt-service payments. If your government had spent carefully, programmed wisely, budgeted its expenditures according to its income and had been conscientious about meeting its obligations, your hope for federal help was slim. Help was only for those who were both poor in pocket and poor in management intelligence.

The Great Depression was a catastrophe situation, so the federal government had to act fast and to give priority to those most threatened by disaster. There could be no stopping to inquire whether the victims had been baptized in the waters of good government. Although they were paying the piper, the feds were very permissive about the tune they played. But times change, and the irreversible process of evolution takes over. He who pays begins to get sticky about the tunes he likes to hear. In some cases it is Congress that calls the tunes; in most cases the agency that hands out the money also hands out the music. The rules by which you get federal aid evolve and get more definite. And also, as time goes on, enforcement of the rules becomes more strict.

When the "workable program" was introduced into the Housing Act of 1954, you got it accepted merely by professing good intentions, not by doing anything. But as time went on, the paving bricks of good intentions were recognized for where they led. A dozen years later, you had to deliver on your promises, or the purse out of which urban renewal grants are paid was closed to you. The 1966 "comprehensive city demonstration program" act eventually will go beyond demonstration to continuing practice. And the name of the operation will later change, perhaps to "comprehensive city program"—or more likely to "Comprehensive Metropolitan Program," with the dignity of initial capitals, and finally to "CMP." Ground rules for taking advantage of CMP aid will be set up: proof of financial ability, proper administrative organization, nondiscrimination in housing, modern building code—these will be some of the prerequisites.

We can guess the course of evolution, although progress will be traumatic. Someday a federal coordinator will be able to say: "You get no money for urban renewal until you clear up the pollution in your river, until you stop pouring guck into the air, until you set up a decent education system, until you build adequate medical facilities."

Perhaps someday, too, the rules will include a requirement that you rationalize your own local tax structure or you get no federal money to supplement it.

State Responsibilities

**Extracted from "Land Use Planning—The
Role of State Government," a paper
presented at the Annual Southern
Governor's Conference, White Sulphur
Springs, West Virginia, August 19, 1963.**

There are three areas or aspects of land-use planning in which state government, and only state government, can function.

The first is the review of local actions in land-use planning and regulation. I do not favor overcentralization of power in federal government vis-a-vis the states. I strongly advocate that as much as possible, local planning be done by local citizens and local governments. Many local governments are doing outstanding jobs in planning. Nevertheless, many communities, for one reason or another, are not doing an adequate job in land-use regulation—especially, the local administration of zoning and subdivision ordinances. To the case for a state-level review commission on the basis of the present chaos in the administration of land-use regulations, and the obvious inequities for property owners, developers, and even the municipalities themselves, I would add that such a state body is needed from the viewpoint of the state government itself, in its job of getting along with preparation to meet the future. In addition to being unfair, the current situation is grossly inefficient. It will definitely interefere with the optimum development of the state, both socially and economically.

The second area in which state government must function is in metropolitan regions. Since the problem is essentially one of a lack of coordination, even downright conflict, among the multiplicity of local governments, it is capable of solution only by a senior government—in this case the state. There is no single infallible, universally desirable, method of attacking the metropolitan problem. In a few areas a form of metropolitan government may be possible, but I would rank this as the least likely solution, and not necessarily the best. Instead of metropolitan government, the problem must be approached through metropolitan planning, through the establishment and encouragement of voluntary regional councils of local governments, through study and reform of taxation and governmental financing for the region, through modernization of laws on annexation, through reexamination and tightening of laws on municipal incorporation and special districts, and through legislation permitting joint action by two or more communities in any number of fields of governmental activity.

The states must adopt a positive role in this situation. Governors and legislatures must assume the leadership in attacking the problem. The very fractionalization of government in metropolitan areas prevents local officials from seeing the area as a whole. It is a perfect illustration of not being able to see the forest for the trees.

The third function for state governments is statewide land-use planning as a part of general state planning. Although we have had what we called state planning in a few states off and on, relatively little has been accomplished. We have little precedent for specific recommendations on procedure in state land-use planning. Looking to the future, however, there can be no doubt that we must get into it. Statewide problems are becoming so complex and so costly that we must face up to the situation if we are to assure economic survival. Some of the major objectives of a state land-use planning program are protection of watersheds for public water supply; lessening the costs and danger of flood; preserving recreation areas to meet the enormously increased demands of the future; preserving prime agricultural land; protecting the natural resources and raw materials vital to industrial development; coordinating development in subregions that are not heavily urbanized; and deriving a rational urban development pattern.

The most disheartening aspect of the future urban expansion is that at this moment, we can see no end to urban sprawl. The arch-example of sprawl that we point to is Los Angeles. The truth is that we have a hundred other areas that are headed down the same primrose path of thousands of miles of superhighways, bordered by endless acres of tract housing, bound for the same Hell of monotonous formlessness. We have not yet faced up to this future of endless sprawl. The open space program sponsored by the federal government is a gesture toward stemming the flood of mass-produced housing, or at least building green islands in the midst of the flood. But it is not enough, nor can it ever be. Furthermore, I do not believe the federal government is the proper agency to solve the problem of controlling urban sprawl. I believe a solution to this problem is the responsibility and duty of state government. One of these days a state governor and a state legislature will begin to change this pattern of sprawl to something that makes more sense. When this happens, we shall mark another stage in our national development, a coming of age.

States cannot do a proper job of land planning unless at the same time they are coordinating and planning for water and air and utilities and transportation and recreation and education and finances and the host of other functions that are the responsibility of government. The state is already contributing to and guiding the development of land through state programs for highways, parks, forests, and conservation, through state aid for education, health and welfare, through industrial development programs, and so on. State government must become aware of the implications of current programs on the urban land pattern of the future, and that much can be accomplished merely by coordinating at the state level—by tearing down the walls that seal off the several state departments and bringing them out of their splendid and often self-centered isolation, by pushing them to work together.

Metropolitan Questions and Answers

**"Are Fringe Areas 'Free Riders'?" extracted
from a paper presented at the Annual Conference of the Municipal Finance Officers
Association, Washington, D.C.,
June 5, 1956.**

The simplest definition of the fringe area is that it is what is immediately on the other side of the imaginary fence—the political boundary—from where you live. This is a double-edged definition, of
course. It not only puts Evanston in a fringe area for Chicago, it also
puts Chicago in Evanston's fringe area, Washington in Arlington
County's fringe, Los Angeles in Pasadena's fringe, and so on. The
definition leads me to ask, quite seriously, who is riding free on
whom?

We usually hear this problem stated primarily from the point of
view of the central city squawking about the suburbs riding free, the
spillover into unincorporated territory with those spilled over demanding services but refusing to pay for them.

Central cities do have problems caused by fringe development. The
great American bogeyman, traffic congestion, is largely a creation of
the morning invasion and the evening retreat of surburbanites. The
vital leadership of many central cities has washed its hands of civic
responsibility for the central city and has moved its families beyond
the city limits. The fringes scream for water and sewage disposal, but
seem not inclined to pay. They expect emergency fire protection, but
don't put cash on the barrelhead to pay for the long hours of standby
time that is the essence of an emergency readiness.

However, there is another side, reasons why I believe there *is* a
question as to which is the free rider.

In briefest form, municipal finance consists in finding enough
money to pay for all the services people demand. In a typical city, the
largest single source of revenue is the property tax, although its proportion of total revenue is declining. A man pays property taxes in
three distinct ways.

1. He pays directly to the tax collector, taxes on the house he owns
   (or through his landlord, taxes on the house he rents).
2. By his labor in a factory, he adds a value to raw materials, part

of which value his employer pays to the tax collector (or in business, he creates a gross profit for his employer, which also includes a portion for property taxes).

3. When he purchases goods from a merchant, he pays an over-charge which the merchant collects to pass on to the property tax collector.

When a man's home is in the same city as his employment and his purchasing, he gets back a share of the property taxes that he has paid through his employer and his merchant. When he works and buys in the city, but lives beyond the city limits, then the taxes collected by virtue of his labor or his shopping are not returned to help him pay for an adequate standard of services.

There are two general theories of taxation—two general approaches to the problem of financing a governmental undertaking. One is the benefit theory: taxes should be paid in accordance with the benefits received. The second theory is based on ability to pay: taxes should be paid in accordance with the taxpayer's ability, whether or not the taxes are greater than the benefits received from the governmental services.

In the United States, we operate under both of these theories, but in general, we are inclined to prefer to base tax bills on the ability to pay. In some cases, this is absolutely necessary for the preservation of the nation. For example, it would be impossible to finance education on the benefit theory. Large families with low income would find it impossible to educate their children and we would rapidly build up illiteracy in the nation to the danger point.

I believe that we must push this ability-to-pay concept beyond its application to individual taxpayers. We must extend it to what we now think of as individual political units—individual taxing bodies. Until we do so, our fringe area problem will be with us, and probably in ever increasing virulence.

Countywide school financing is one method. Grants-in-aid of all kinds are another method. State grants for education, state and federal assistance on streets, bridges, redevelopment, public housing are efforts to distribute tax receipts more equitably. But too much increase in free funds from Washington, or the state capital, weakens some of the local independence that I believe is much of the strength of the nation.

From a theoretical viewpoint, annexation by the central city would be a simple way of solving the problem. But that is politically impossible; what would happen if Philadelphia started extending its city limits up the Main Line, like a devouring amoeba, to gobble up one suburb after another? And regardless of whether it is politically feasible, I believe that it will not produce the best government.

I am completely convinced that there is no one way which will solve our "fringe area" problem, because there is no one single cause—except the fundamental one of rapid population growth and urbanization of the nation. But I am equally firmly convinced that we have to rid ourselves of the notion that we can solve the problem by looking at it as a search for some trick to catch the "free riders." The problem is mutual and must be solved cooperatively.

Metropolitan Planning, extracted from the ASPO Newsletter editorial "Metropolitan Planning—Now and Later," February-March 1967.

The emphasis the federal government is putting on metropolitan planning makes it appropriate to take a look at the state of the art. The feds are pushing to make metropolitan planning a prerequisite for a long list of federal aid programs. Metropolitan planning is asked to coordinate the federal grant programs so that the grants will be used to complement and supplement each other, and not to conflict and contradict.

We are tempted to say, *physician, heal thyself,* because the federal government has proved to be hopelessly inept in coordinating its own actions, and we see in the push for metropolitan planning a passing of the buck: "You straighten out this mess for us, we cannot do it here in Washington." But if we assume that there is a real need for rationality in metropolitan development, it is probably all for the best that the coordinating be done close to the spending.

We shall be charitable and say that metropolitan planning is still evolving—not that it is pretty sad. And we should be charitable because when we look at city planning, which has had more time to evolve in this country, we see in too many cities an undertaking just as feeble as the present planning for the larger metropolitan regions.

Metropolitan planning is now primarily an exercise in futility. Some technically excellent analyses and proposals have been made for regional resources, other than land. The acceptance of the proposals has not matched their technical excellence. Metropolitan highway plans have been made and are being carried out because of the power of the almighty grant-in-aid, but the quality of the plans, and especially their relation to the proper development of the region, is questionable. As for metropolitan land-use plans, they seem to be the ultimate in futility.

If evolution is to proceed to any good end, we need more mutations, several rearrangements of the genes.

Leaving aside the question of how to tie metropolitan planning to a government that can and will carry out plans, another common weakness in organization for metropolitan planning is the voluntary status of affiliation in most metropolitan planning agencies. The local community can join in the metropolitan agency or not, just as it pleases. This particular characteristic is vestigial, a carry-over from the "purely advisory" niche assigned to the protean city planning board. Closely allied to voluntary affiliation is the financing of metropolitan planning by voluntary contribution. In some areas the local governments must contribute according to a formula, if they desire to cooperate at all with the metropolitan agency, but in others it is the rankest kind of tin cup charity—give only what you want to give and threaten to withhold all money if you don't like what the metropolitan agency does.

If the need for metropolitan planning is as great as we say it is, then all local governments should be required to participate and there should be no question about money, no hint of begging. If we are not sure enough about metropolitan planning to pull all governments into participation or to give the agency an assured income, perhaps we should forget it.

What is the definition of *all* when we say "all governments"? *All* seems to mean only the city and county governments in the area. School districts, drainage districts, and a host of other special governments and independent taxing units are conspicuous by their absence from involvement in metropolitan planning, and equally conspicuous in the presence of their influence in shaping metropolitan growth.

To say nothing of the state. The state is the one government pervasive throughout the whole of each metropolitan area. Through state programs, especialy state highway construction, the state undoubtedly has more influence in metropolitan area development than any other single government.

Then we have the voluntary councils of governments (that word *voluntary* again!) This device is being touted as the way to get from plans to accomplishment. Thus far, the relation between the voluntary councils and the metropolitan planning is at least ambiguous. Thus far, the governments represented on voluntary councils are, with very few exceptions, the same 25 percent in metropolitan planning: cities and counties. And thus far, the councils seem to be plagued by political Golden Rulism: *I'll vote for whatever you want in your county because I expect you to vote for whatever I want in my county.*

You cannot be sure what form the creature will finally take. But this is the way with evolution. Some mutations in an evolving species prove to be lethal. *Voluntary* affiliation, *voluntary* financing, absence of special district participation—these all seem destined to be fatal to the individual.

Federal grant review requirements; some feeble, still polite, but mandatory review of local zoning by metropolitan or state agencies; elected officials involved in the planning; some rumblings for metropolitan control of truly metropolitan functions (especially for air pollution)—these mutations point to the shape of metropolitan planning in the future. There's life in the old girl yet.

City Planning Experimentation and Coordination

"Strength Through Diversity," quoted from the ASPO Newsletter editorial, May 1955.

European planners visiting the United States for the first time are nearly always amazed—even shocked—at our lack of standardization and our lack of hierarchy of control. There are no central planning agencies in state governments to say yea or nay to local activities and schemes. Nor is there a national planning agency to say yea or nay to either state or local plans. Each municipality, from the smallest village to the largest megalopolis, is free to make its own plans, its own mistakes.

This attitude exists because of the basic feeling in this country that there is greater strength in diversity than there is in uniformity.

This is not to say that there is absolutely no review of planning proposals. There are two reviews: one by the courts and one by the citizens. The court's attitude toward planning matters must be confined to those subjects that are appealed to it—not all planning activities, by any means. And the courts are learning about planning. The final review of planning, however, is made by the citizens. They review planning schemes in several ways. They vote for or against bond issues. They vote for or against mayors and councils, frequently because of the plans the candidates propose or the plans they fail to propose. The citizens review the actions of appellate courts by amending constitutions or by insisting on something so frequently and so vehemently that the courts finally understand.

We will do it one way in one city and another way in another city. We will be experimenting in half a dozen or half a hundred places. We will make many mistakes and we will be slapped down frequently. But in the end we will learn how to do what the people want us to do.

Planning for Messopolis: A Neglected Problem, condensed from the executive director's annual report at the ASPO National Planning Conference, Philadelphia, April 18, 1966.

There is a new unit of urbanization, which is sort of the "forgotten man" among urban forms. To impress on the public mind a special and particular kind of urban form, we look for some descriptive prefix to attach to the Greek root, *polis*. We have *metropolis* and *megalopolis, necropolis,* and *parasitopolis*. Recently we have been given *dynamopolis* and *ecumenopolis*. I searched through the colorful changes that have been rung on this idea and could not find one that fitted my needs. So I invented and now give to the world another variation: *messopolis*. I have added to the Greek suffix, *polis*, which means "city," the American root word, *mess*, which means "mess." I believe the use of the American root is appropriate because we in the United States invented this particular urban form.

A messopolis is a city, a single urban entity with clearly defined boundaries, to which we have given an unambiguous name like the city of Philadelphia, the city of Chicago, the city of Phoenix, the city of North Ipswich; which has a city hall, a mayor, councilmen, perhaps a city manager, a city planning department; but which harbors within the clearly defined city boundaries anywhere from 2 to 25 separate, uncoordinated, often antagonistic, independent governments. The final criterion for identifying a messopolis is that the citizens, to a great extent, and the outside critics to a man, see the messopolis as a monolithic structure, all of whose problems can be blamed on city hall, the mayor, the councilmen, the city manager, and—especially—on the planning department.

The most ubiquitous of the independent governments is the school board, usually with the largest budget and the largest bite out of the property tax dollar. But there are many others: park boards, sanitary districts, water utilities, hospital commissions, urban renewal agencies, housing authorities. In many communities, even the board of zoning appeals has begun to act like a separate government, making its own rules, owing no allegiance whatsoever to the city government that created it.

The extra intramural "governments," as I have termed them, may even be nominally a part of the city government and be partially supported by the general city tax levy, but they still act independently and live a smug and cozy life of their own.

It is my opinion that messopolis is the most neglected area in our present-day planning, that we in planning are getting a bad name because of this neglect, and finally, that unless we direct our attention to them, messopolitan problems are going to get worse instead of better.

One reason for our neglect of the *messopolis* is our obsession with the *metropolis*. Metropolitan planning agencies have proliferated like guinea pigs. We recognized metropolitan problems by creating in the new Department of Housing and Urban Development the post of an assistant secretary for metropolitan development. But take a look at the figures. There are about 240 metropolitan areas in the United States. How many messopolitan cities are there? I do not know of any demographers who have tried to count them, but I would guess that there are between five and ten thousand.

Even in metropolitan areas there is tunnel vision in an analogous situation. In Chicago, for example, we view with alarm (and maybe just a little pride) the fact that we have more than 1,000 separate taxing units in the metropolitan region. But when we think seriously about the metropolitan problems of the region, we are really working with only 230 or so incorporated communities and 6 counties. We expect to achieve coordination and togetherness by working with less than one-fourth of the public bodies involved.

How did we get our cities in this peculiar, inefficient form? Why did we create messopolises? There are several reasons. We invented the separate school board because we wanted to keep schools out of the dirty business of city politics. We used the independent agency as a method of trying out a new public service that we were not quite sure of, like running public parks. And, of course, we legislated ourselves into an impossible tax muddle and then invented a hundred different forms of special districts to help us squirm out of the muddle. Sometimes we have established a new intramural government, then after a shakedown period during which it proved itself, annexed it to the regular city government. This is what we did to city planning itself. But too often something happens, the umbilical cord is severed, and we have another independent government in messopolis. However, in perpetuating messopolis the most important single factor is money— independent money. If you look at the city department that is a law unto itself, you will find earmarked funds or a so-called proprietary function that pretends to operate on a profit-and-loss basis. The position of the truly independent government with its own taxing authority is stronger yet.

From our perhaps selfish viewpoint, the sad part of the messopolitan scene is that planners, which means the city planning agency, are being blamed for everything that any government in a messopolis does. Planners are responsible for school ills, although most school boards could not care less about how they fit into a comprehensive planning operation. Planners catch it for all of the mistakes, both real and concocted, that the urban renewal agency makes. The sorry plight of public housing is the fault of the planner—although I cannot think of any unit of messopolitan government that has been less influenced by community planning than has the average public housing authority.

If we could be sure that nothing would be added to messopolis to make it messier than it now is, we could say: "Give us time, and we will work it out." But there is good reason to believe just the opposite, that we are entering an era in which there will not only be more independent governments in each city, but the independent units will be stronger.

I think it is time to get moving toward the introduction of rationality and some sort of order in all government operations within the city limits.

We can make progress with messopolitan problems. We have tried, and we have had some success—my remarks to the contrary notwithstanding—urban renewal agencies, with park districts, and even with school boards. We must do more. We must try harder. Because if we do not, I think we are moving straight toward the next urban form, which I have tentatively christened, "Godawfulmessopolis."

"The Planning Commission," extracted from the ASPO Newsletter editorial, July 1961.

The planning department is an administrative device that has particularly recommended itself to the newer types of municipal organization, the strong mayor and the manager-council forms of government. It has had appeal because it integrated planning with the executive function. The independent commission and staff had been apart and aloof from city government and, except for certain statutory review powers, had not been too effective.

The planning department is proving successful. All questions on organization, however, have not been answered. The first question is what do you do with the old lay planning commission? Has it completely outlived its usefulness? Is there any advantage in having a group of lay persons mixed up in planning? If you keep the lay commission, what status do you give it?

A common answer to the question of status has been the creation of a "planning advisory commission" or board. The commission is relieved of any appointing and supervisory authority over the staff. It is retained as a committee to counsel and advise the staff or the city fathers. Actually, planning commissions in the United States have always been primarily advisory groups. At the same time, their advice has been something more than "we think you should do it this way." They have been given the legal responsibility to pass on zoning amendments and subdivision plats and to adopt the master plan or the capital improvement program. In all cases, the municipal legislative body has been able—properly—to overrule the planning commission, but not to ignore it. If the new look in planning organization is only a setup to get seven or nine very nice men and women to come in and make complimentary remarks about staff planning work, it probably should be forgotten. A big fat citizens' advisory committee would be easier and less hypocritical. A planning commission must be given some authority and responsibility if it is to be worth having.

But why have a lay planning commission at all? If for no other reason, because it can serve as an objective body to coordinate the actions of overlapping governments. It has often been suggested that the planning commission is a useless appendage to city government, that municipal planning can be done by the city council, that, in fact, it is the council's *duty.* Only the politically naive could imagine that the city council could get very far planning for the school board and other independent governments. But a planning commission, even though it is a creature of the city, can and does do a lot of planning for other units, and the planning is accepted.

Why plans by a planning commission are accepted by independent governments leads to perhaps the most important reason for retaining the commission. In spite of our real progress in municipal government since the days of Lincoln Steffens, we are still not sure of the incorruptibility of municipal government, or the ability of the mayor and council to view problems in an unbiased manner. So the original reason for making plan commissions independent, outside of politics, still exists. There is still need for a commission, that will attract the services of leaders who are unable or unwilling to get into active politics, but who are interested in serving their city. There is still need for an official agency that any and all governments can approach with some assurance of an unbiased hearing.

I grant that some of the early experiences with planning commissions were exercises in futility. I am fully convinced that the integrated planning department is superior to the aloof commission and staff. I am equally certain that the strong lay planning commission will continue to be necessary for planning to be accepted and used as it should be.

"A Department of Urban Development,"quoted from the ASPO Newsletter editorial, February 1961.

We have approached urban development from two directions. In planning, we started with the dream of the City Beautiful and became more practical until we were preparing capital budgets. From the other direction, we started with the demolition of our worst slums (a close connection with the City Beautiful) and have progressed to the preparation of a community renewal plan. The two movements meet in urban development, which is merely the sum of all public and all private activities which make up the growth and changes of the city as it adjusts itself to the passage of time.

In some cities the two lines of evolution have already met: renewal activities are in the hands of the planning agency, or the only true planning is being done by the renewal agency. Division of the urban development function of the city must be eliminated. Planning, without the use of the powers of taxation, bonding, eminent domain, and the police power to see that plans are carried out, is purely an intellectual pastime. Urban renewal, which also requires all these governmental powers, is just speeding up chaos unless it is based on sound economic, social, and physical background knowledge, comprehensiveness, understanding of the problems of interrelations, and clear goals—the contribution of true planning.

We have learned that planning without implementation is futile. We know too well that implementation without planning is chaos. I do not believe that it is out of line even to divide all municipal functions into two categories—operation and development. It has already proved a useful division of the municipal budget.

Inevitably, we must come to a department of urban development. There is a lot in a name if it will help us to unite activities that should no longer be divided.

Rejecting Projectitis, extracted from "The Challenges and Achievements in Planning and Development Administration," a speech at the opening session of the ASPO National Planning Conference, Atlantic City, N.J., April 30, 1962.

Projectitis is defined as the construction of an individual public project as though it were the only thing in the city, as though it were related to nothing else and nothing else were related to it. The principal carping about projectitis is directed toward urban renewal and urban redevelopment projects. Planners were quite influential in bringing urban redevelopment into the world. It has been advocated in the proceedings of planning conferences for the past two generations. But once the baby got born, its planning parents were so frightened they disowned it. Urban renewal is not *planning.* It is *operating*—a nasty word!

Urban renewal is also *action* not conversation. Federal grants are hanging on whether the city can make up its mind to do something. Federal grants pay for action and they get it. But the planning process, in its standard basic research and master plan aspect, has just not been up to moving fast enough. So the master plan, if any, gets passed over and projects get built in spite of the planning process, not because of it. The beginning of projectitis, then, is the need for action in the face of ineffectiveness of the planning process to give guidance to the action.

I firmly believe there has to be more acceptance of new administrative forms. There is no question that change to departmental status for planning is the most rapidly spreading reform in the United States. The department-commission scheme has improved the quality of planning by making it a great deal more realistic. The department is also bringing mutual respect between planners and the other government administrators. Other department heads now appreciate the planning approach to problems, while the planners begin to understand the practical problems the others face.

But making a department out of the planning staff does not solve all problems. There is still the missing master plan. There is still projectitis.

While projectitis can infect any part of government, it became most noticable in redevelopment. A policy of easiest-sold, first-cleared resulted in the pillar-to-post relocation technique—relocate them out of one project into the site of a second project, then relocate the same families out of the second project into the site of the third project, and so on ad infinitum. Such treatment, in addition to being inhumane, will stir up a big political ruckus. There were other errors in redevelopment: misplaced projects, wasted public works. Or if mistakes were not yet made, it was easy to see that conflicts were inevitable unless some orderly planning was done for the entire city.

The spectacular effects of urban redevelopment, the great cost of the projects, the intense emotional conflict involved, the gravity of the social problems sought to be corrected and the special problems inadvertently created—all of these may cause some of us in the large cities to lose perspective on total urban development.

As of this moment, I would not care to describe an ideal organization for planning. The political situation—the balance of power—in a particular community at the moment of reorganization will influence the form of the organization. I am not willing to say that a planner, as we know him now, should necessarily be the chief professional employee. It will be many years before we get an ideal organization for planning fixed. A lot of professions, a lot of different backgrounds, must be called in to help solve the terrific urban development problem that lies ahead of us.

After all, what we really want to do is to produce the best possible urban environment for the hundreds of millions of people who will live in this country in the future. We cannot afford to cling to pet ideas and outdated forms that do not further that purpose. Nor can we afford to have jurisdictional disputes.

"The Future of the Central Business District," condensed from a speech at the Annual Convention of the National Retail Merchants Association, New York City, January 8, 1964.

The central business district is the lineal descendent of the old market place, the Greek agora, the Roman forum, the New England town square—the rallying point for the entire urban agglomeration, for urban life, yea, even the focal point of civilization. As modern cities grew and distances from its outlying parts lengthened, we developed mass transit. Creating the need for—and created by—mass transit, the central business district reached the pinnacle of dominance as the site of business, professional and financial service, entertainment, culture, and government.

Then came the automobile. For a while the situation in the central business district improved. The automobile made it easier to get downtown so more people could come oftener and stay longer. However, it was like a box of candy. One piece is good, the second piece is also good. But if you eat the whole pound at one sitting, you get a belly-ache. The central business district started to get belly-ache symptoms. The streets became strangulated with traffic. More and more automobiles, fewer and fewer places for them to park.

We were quick to accommodate to the new order. We developed

the outlying shopping center, designing it with one thing in mind—to give tender and loving care to the automobile. Soon the downtown stores were losing ground, not only relatively, but absolutely. We sought ways to reverse this direction. We built parking garages above ground and below ground, so that more automobiles could be stored—like in the suburban shopping centers. We built expressways at fantastic costs in order to make it easier for people to get into the downtown section. We experimented with malls. With our private means, we built new office buildings. And with both our private and public means, we did redevelopment: Charles Center in Baltimore, Penn Center in Philadelphia, Mile High Center in Denver, the Golden Triangle in Pittsburgh. To bring the population back closer to the central business district, we started building downtown high-rise apartment buildings.

Have our efforts thus far been successful? Not particularly so. What are the prospects for a renaissance of mass transit? With the possibility of a few exceptions, they are not very good. What about the increase in office space downtown to bring more daytime population to the city? The new office buildings are in large part creating vacancies in the older buildings. What about urban redevelopment? Many of the projects give every evidence of being successful—in themselves, at least—and this may be enough to justify them. But what are they doing to the rest of the central business district? Downtown high-rise apartments? What profiteth it a city to bring in 10,000 middle- and upper-income persons, if at the same time 100,000 in the same income group move further out in the suburbs? Expressways and garages? How do these jibe with mass transit subsidies? More important yet, what good is it to make it easier for persons to drive downtown when there is less and less, and still less reason for their coming downtown at all?

It is no longer necessary to go downtown for medical services, or for financial services (except for very large corporate deals) or for entertainment.

The location of governmental activities in the central business district has been one of the strongest supports and drawing cards that downtown had. But Los Angeles has branch city halls scattered throughout the city; New York City has a mobile mayor's office which travels around the city and stops in neighborhood business centers; Chicago courts, instead of being concentrated, are now scattered throughout the county.

As for employment, a great deal still remains in the central business district and may even be expanding a little, but the real expansion is in the outlying areas—the expansion in all of the businesses and services that have migrated or grown up out there. Even more important, it is the expansion in industrial employment. Industries, too, seek areas in which they can provide parking for employees. Industries have also gone horizontal; they can no longer operate in lofts, or in five-and-ten story factory buildings, they must spread out. And there is also the decentralization of office employment.

It seems to me that central business districts must undergo a metamorphosis. If we work with nature, we can expect to see a beautiful butterfly emerge from the chrysalis. But we cannot expect to see an eagle come out. Our whole urban pattern is undergoing a violent change and there is nothing much of the old pattern that is sacred—least of all the central business district. To survive, the central business district must accommodate itself to its new position on the urban scene.

Each city is unique. There is no single formula that can be applied to central business districts to bring about their adjustment to the new urban pattern, although the citizens of any community can learn a great deal by seeing what the citizens in other communities have done—the unsuccessful as well as the successful things they have done.

In a few cities, a half-dozen or so "world cities," we can expect the dominance of the central business district to continue. These cities have many problems, but the overall future is reasonably well assured. There is another group, cities with a population of up to 50,000, perhaps up to 100,000, where the general outline of a program for adjusting the central business district to the realities of the times seems reasonably clear: conversion of the central business district, at least the core of it, to a shopping center, with all that term implies, with both private and public expenditures.

Between these two groups are cities which do not, and will not, fit into either category—either the world city or the shopping center conversion. Probably this middle group contains about half the urban population in the United States. In these cities, we must concentrate on developing those functions and services in which the central business district of a medium or large city does have some advantages—activities that are most appropriately located in the center of the local transportation network and that require a large population for support.

There is another, more crucial problem. The primary market area of central business districts in medium and large cities is getting to be more and more an area for housing the disadvantageed of our population. Until this trend is stopped and reversed, the prognosis for a healthy downtown area is not good. Businessmen will not accomplish anything by laissez faire or just plain singing the blues. They can do some good through urban renewal in its three manifestations: conservation, rehabilitation, redevelopment. In particular, they must move toward open occupancy, *not only in the central city, but also in the suburbs.*

They must also throw their weight behind some social and economic betterment programs. They must support education, retraining, everything that will lead to an increase in the job opportunities and the ability of more persons to take advantage of those opportunities. They must make the central city a desirable place to live in. They must work to make it possible for all persons to have a freedom of choice where they live. They must work to make certain that everyone—man, woman, and child—will have an opportunity to develop to the limit of their capabilities.

The central business district problem is only one part of the larger urban physical, social, and economic problem that we face. There is a limit to what can be accomplished through rejuvenation of the physical plant. The social and the economic plant also need rejuvenation. It is a whale of a big job.

**Schools and Community Responsibility,
quoted from "The Community and the
Family," a speech to the Annual Convention
of the National Congress of Parents and
Teachers, Cincinnati, May 20, 1957.**

There have been countless discussions of the share of the child's education that is the responsibility of the school and the share that is the responsibility of the family. But have there been parallel discussions on the responsibility of the community for the education of the child?

By "community" I mean the physical urban environment, the streets, the stores, the parks, the houses, the factories. I mean the slums and the mansions. I mean the dirt in the streets and the litter on the lawns, as well as the clean garbage trucks and the efficient fire apparatus. I also mean the mores and the values we have in public affairs as we express them—through honest, efficient government and dedicated public servants; and also as we express them through corrupt and bungling administration, or through inadequate pay scales that label public servants as second-class citizens.

It is particularly difficult for any of us to see the effects, because we, too, have been shaped and molded by the self-same community until we fail to recognize what it has done to us and is doing to our children.

New Towns or New Sprawl?

**Extracted from the ASPO Newsletter
editorial, October 1964.**

The logistics of providing housing and urban facilities for our future population, coupled with the gross diseconomics of our present system of housing by sprawl, will inevitably force us into construction of large-scale communities. The question is: Is this wave of the future going to produce communities of permanent value? Or is it to be sprawl on a grander scale than ever before?

Large-scale developments are inevitable. It behooves us to make them decent. They will not be decent if they are just cases of sprawl jumping over an intervening area in order to avoid speculative land prices. If they are not to be sprawl, they must be reasonably self-sufficient and self-contained—"new towns" in the English sense. In order to be self-sufficient they must be large enough to contain and support:

1. A commercial center;
2. A reasonable range of cultural activities (short of grand opera and such);
3. A reasonable range of recreational facilities;
4. Sufficient medical and health facilities to include a general hospital and a psychiatric clinic-hospital;
5. All necessary public facilities, such as schools, water, *complete* sewage treatment, etc.;

6. A range of residential facilities to accommodate all economic classes;
7. A range of residential types, from the free-standing house to the apartment building (but not necessarily five-acre lots, nor high-rise flats); and
8. Employment opportunities for at least 90 percent of the labor force.

There are two other requirements for a new town in the United States:

1. There must be absolutely no discrimination because of race, religion, or national origin.
2. There must be, eventually, true self-government by the citizens of the new town.

The need for nondiscrimination is obvious. The need for self-government, however, may not be so obvious, particularly to some of the developers playing around with new towns. It is only through self-government that any sense of community can really be imparted to an urban development. Without this sense of community, the development will be a failure. Homeowners associations are successful on a small scale, but in order to be self-sufficient, the new town will necessarily be housing a population of at least 50,000. Governing this is beyond the capability of any citizen's organization without true governmental powers.

There is still another essential of a proper new town. This is that *from its very beginning* the new town must have a clearly stated maximum size and some assurance that the maximum will be respected. To be sure of limiting the eventual size of a new town, it would seem that the most logical method is by means of a permanent green belt.

How are we to get new towns, to assure ourselves that they are going to be properly done? Who must be ultimately responsible for producing them?

The current wave of interest in new towns is 100 percent private. Certainly, we want to encourage private initiative in this field. But except in very rare instances, the new town as I have described it cannot be accomplished privately. Many of the essentials are possible only through government. Only through the cooperative aspects of governmental action will we be able to:

1. Initiate the new towns in optimum locations;
2. Assemble (through expropriation if necessary) the land needed;
3. Marshal sufficient capital for all public and private facilities; and

4.   Establish and maintain necessary controls.

There needs to be a lot more discussion (and there will be) before we in this country are really producing the kind of new towns we want and in the quantity that we need. At best, we will make a great many mistakes. But in the long run, we will be better off if we recognize that government and only government is the proper agency to assume the initiative and responsibility for producing our future urban nation.

New Tools and Techniques

"Flexibility in Planning—The Present Problem," condensed from a speech at the Annual Meeting of the International City Managers Association, St. Louis, October 28, 1959.

In Arizona there is a plant that is the pride of the state. It is the saguaro cactus, a tall, slender, regal plant that grows in the desert and on the mountainsides. The saguaro cactus is a slow grower—almost unbelievably slow. It takes about 15 years to get six inches high, 100 years to grow as high as your head, 200 or more years to get its full growth, which is 15 to 20 feet high.

In the Middle West, there is another plant that contrasts sharply with the saguaro. This is the common cultivated morning glory, usually called Heavenly Blue. It is truly a Jack's beanstalk breed of vegetable. When you plant them, you almost need to drop the seed and dodge to avoid being overwhelmed and strangled. With only desultory care, you can expect the main stalk to grow 50 feet in one season, with 50 to 100 branches 5 to 25 feet long.

You don't need to be an expert gardener to know that in your backyard gardening you would have two different problems in using saguaros and Heavenly Blues. With the morning glory, you have to beware that it doesn't engulf the house and black out the windows. With a saguaro, the only danger is that the house will rot away and fall in before the cactus comes to full growth.

Urban growth has reached the morning glory speed, while our planning ideas and techniques are too frequently predicated on the saguaro growth.

The most difficult problem in guiding urbanization is caused by the speed of urbanization, the speed and unpredictability of technological and population changes. It is the question of how to maintain the proper balance between flexibility and rigidity of control methods so that we have security, protection, stability and, at the same time, do not stifle growth nor impede progress by freezing the city in a rigid and inefficient pattern. The trends and developments in planning today can be almost universally analyzed as experiments—not always successful—in solving this problem: rigidity, but not too rigid; flexibility, but not too flexible.

Take the major document of planning, the master plan. When it burst on the scene in this country, it was an extremely complete scheme, even to minor details. The famous 1909 Burnham plan for Chicago included a great number of beautiful renderings, complete down to the architectural details of the buildings proposed and to the location and variety of the trees in the parkway. The Burnham plan set a master pattern for master plans that lasted for nearly half a century. Happily, that era is now drawing to a close.

The workable master plan of today—we even steer away from the word "master" and call it a general plan or a comprehensive plan— consists of (1) a set of goals and policies; (2) charts or maps *illustrating* the hypothetical working out of those goals and policies; and (3) a set of first steps, first projects consistent with those goals and policies, that can be and are scheduled within the financial capacity of the city to carry them out. The most important part of this new general plan, the set of goals and policies to guide the recommendations of the planning staff and the decisions of the legislative bodies when specific projects and questions arise, are as definite as we can make them, and at the same time, they allow us latitude to meet changing conditions, to roll with the punch.

The new tempo of urban growth caught us in a most embarrassing inflexible position with our two most powerful planning tools: the zoning ordinance and the subdivision control regulations. For all the years since we invented these tools, we had based them upon the construction of buildings by individuals, building a single structure at a time—a single residence, a single store, a single factory. Then along came the production-line builder. Our inflexible land-use controls just were not designed to handle this type of operation. We have worked this particular problem out pretty well by introducing provisions that are analogous to the goals and policy provisions of the master plans. As the policy, they set the maximum density that will assure the public official of a limit on the utilities and services necessary for the area. At the same time, they give the developer and the architect freedom to experiment with new visual forms and with efficient construction methods.

It has been necessary to set limits on some individual rights through governmental action and the police power of the zoning ordinance. We must come to a similar policy for our municipal rights. Securing proper flexibility by improving the adaptability of local plans to metropolitan goals is more complex than obtaining flexibility in zoning. The form of organization, the method of financing, the authority given to metropolitan planning agencies will be nearly as varied as the areas for which they hope to plan. Some agencies will be namby-pamby, others will be strong, well backed, well financed. Some will do nothing, some will do a little, some will do much. Some will be liked, some will be hated. I will not try to predict what these agencies will do, or in general how effective they will be, but I will predict that they will increase in number every year until every metropolitan area or quasi-metropolitan area has a metropolitan planning agency.

Another phenomenon that has brought up the problem of rigidity and flexibility is urban renewal. It is an outstanding example of the speeded-up processes of urbanization. Normal urban processes of decay, demolition, and rebuilding that used to take 25 to 100 years now take place in 2 to 5 years. This has introduced a new set of problems, not only in functions customarily related to planning, but also in nearly all areas and functions of municipal government. Our techniques are still far from being perfected in urban renewal.

The moral of this sermon is that municipal executives should take a searching look at planning in their city. In particular, they should examine the tools and techniques.

Long-Term Operational Budgeting, extracted from the ASPO Newletter "The Next Step," October 1958.

In the '30s the National Resources Planning Board, after some trial runs, sent technicians about the country to carry the torch for public works programming and capital improvement budgeting. Capital budgeting—laying out a long-time plan for public works and how you will pay for them—was not an invention of NRPB. But the federal agency deserves a lot of credit for getting it accepted as a normal way to carry on municipal affairs.

Capital budgeting is not accepted by nearly all cities. Yet it is generally accepted by planners as a tool for carrying out development according to plans. Now we should take the next step. Call in the next planning tool: long-term operational budgeting.

One compelling reason that the National Resources Planning Board had for promoting capital budgeting was to avoid adding to the roster of white elephants created by emergency public works programs: the auditoriums that were too expensive to heat for winter use, the sewage treatment plants that stood in isolated grandeur not connected to the sewer systems, the incinerator with no public funds available for lighting the first fire. If a city is to work out a plan for financing its public works over a long period, this can only be done effectively if there is also a long-term analysis of the costs of operating and maintaining the new facilities. And the city must be able to pay for this operation and maintenance at the same time it operates all of the older facilities and carries on all of the activities of the regular departments—police, fire, health, welfare, and what have you.

This simply means that a city has to have a long-term operating budget as well as a long-term capital budget if it wants to avoid embarrassing situations. There is no question that embarrassing situations will come. The pressure of population and rapid development has pushed a number of cities a long way out on a limb. They have been forced to build capital improvements to the point that there is doubt that the improvements can be maintained.

It is time for the planner to start working for long-term operational budgeting, to throw in with his municipal finance officer, who is also conscious of the need. This means that we must get out of the installment buying mood, which has led us (personally) into buying houses and appliances and autos that make us scratch to keep up and that has led us (politically) to the erection of lush structures of glass, stainless steel, and writhing concrete, which also make us scratch to get tax money to keep up.

Our object is to build cities that are viable and that serve the economic and social purposes of urban machines—not monuments for the glorification of political machines or even for the glorification of planning machines. The logical next step is the long-term operating program as an integral part of public administration.

"Tools for Planning," an ASPO Newsletter editorial, November 1961.

Fortune (October 1961) had an interesting article on the outlook for advances in the design of computers. The search is for a method to make the electronic behemoths behave more like human brains which, although slow, are still infinitely more brilliant than the largest Gimmiac yet built. The article, "Problems, Too, Have Problems," opened with two provocative paragraphs:

> Ever since man started making tools to tinker with nature one to two million years ago, he has been getting into—and, so far, out of— more and more elaborate kinds of trouble. Many of the problems he is now trying to solve and now creating overtax even his prodigious capacities for coping with complexity. There are more products, more people, more laws and loopholes, more nations, higher risks of head-on conflicts. Furthermore, events unfold so swiftly that decisions had better be right the first time; you may never have a chance to check the answer.
>
> We are transforming a world and shall soon be transforming a solar system, and there is only one possible way to deal with the rising flood of problems of our own making. To avoid painting ourselves into a corner, we need, of course, more education, but we also need more thinking aids.

The relevance of these words for the job of guiding our cities and regions into the complex future is painfully obvious. I cannot believe that there exists a planner or planning commissioner who does not at times—often—groan and wish he were seven people with the wisdom of seven Solomons. The technical problems are complicated by, even dominated by, the never-diminishing problems of relations with human beings. There are the mayor and council, the department heads, the county, state, and federal governments, the civic organizations, and the special interest groups.

As the *Fortune* article points out, we need more education, but education is not enough. We also need more and better tools, for the tool is the extension of the hand that has made civilization possible to build and maintain. We need more and better tools for our urban and regional planning, if we are to keep up with the times or have the breath of a chance to get slightly ahead.

The new and glamorous tools of today are the computers. Planners have started to use them for transportation, land use, economic and population studies. They are proving their value and they will surely prove more valuable in the future and for other studies. We should prosecute with all diligence our research in how to use them.

But there is another group of planning tools, less glamorous than the Univac, Eniac, and their cousins. They are less glamorous but more effective because they are the products of the more powerful machine—the human brain. I refer to standards, model regulations and checklists.

There are great philosophic objections to the use of model regulations and to standards, not so much to checklists. It is argued that no two situations, no two cities are the same, therefore standards or model ordinances are dangerous, should not be used. It is true that no two situations are the same. In fact, no two physical objects greater than a molecule are identical, and there may be some question about the identity of two molecules. But this argument can quickly be reduced to absurdity. Followed to the end, for example it would call for individual treatment of each wheat grain when we milled the flour. In government it would be the abolition of laws because each instance of criminality was different from every other instance of criminality, and therefore, you could make no general rules.

Actually, much of the superiority of the human brain lies in its ability to classify events and objects on the basis of broad, significant criteria and not to be confused by having to give heed to insignificant details. Grains of wheat, burglaries, flood hazards, billboards, and filling stations are more importantly alike than they are different.

Then there is the very practical question: Why repeat all the work that has gone into producing a model ordinance or some other standard? There is another practical consideration. Whether the purists like it or not, standards are going to be used. Regulations in one city will be picked up and used by another city. Where such borrowing is done without thought, considerable damage may result. But if the provision is intelligently *adapted* instead of blindly *adopted*, the borrower is wisely using a valuable tool.

Standards and models are useful and will be used. They are tools that permit the planner and his commission to multiply their own effectiveness. The tools deserve improvement, however, and extension into fields for which they are not now available. Perhaps most important of all, standards need constant rechecking for validity, because they can become dangerously harmful if they are not observed in practice so that errors may be corrected.

But under any circumstances, we need a larger arsenal of these planning tools if we are to have any hope of meeting the future.

"New Techniques for Shaping Urban Expansion," condensed from a paper prepared for the Housing and Home Finance Agency Conference on "The Problems and Needs of Urban Expansion" June 7-9, 1962. (Subsequently adapted, with the permission of HHFA, for ASPO Planning Advisory Service Report No. 160.)

New techniques for controlling and guiding urban expansion have been initiated recently, and still other new techniques have been proposed. The very fact that innovations are being tried or suggested indicates that all is not well with present techniques. We are not satisfied with the operation of conventional planning and development controls now. But the impact of urban expansion in the near future makes the situation even more dismaying. A population increase of millions within the next few decades, all to be housed, employed, entertained in urban areas; urban renewal needs in the magnitude of a trillion dollars. It is little wonder that the adequacy of our techniques for shaping urban environment are being examined with a jaundiced eye.

This paper attempts to assume an objective, if negative, viewpoint on the "ideal" pattern for urban development. Many forms of urban development will be tried out. Some will be successful while others will not. But it is doubtful that success or failure is inherent in any particular form.

The mix of housing between private single-family dwellings and multifamily structures is assumed to remain about the same as during the past few years, and both types to be significant. The relative importance of either type may make some difference in the weight assigned to one or another technique of government control, but it will not alter the need for a variety pack of controls. Multifamily structures will be mainly in-town, calling for redevelopment devices; single-family houses will be suburban and require related techniques.

A basic weakness of present land-use control techniques is an inadequacy to handle development on the modern scale. Zoning and subdivision ordinances are out of scale, their administration is out of scale, even picayunish, to cope with today's mass buildings and construction methods. Present-day subdivision regulations have tended in practice to fix maxima where it was intended to fix minima. The regulations are not rigid, nevertheless, they have tended to stereotype development, producing whole developments of identical lots—all of the minimum size.

Land-use controls have been ineffective as techniques to preserve those assets we wish to keep, or to carry out a predetermined pattern of land use. After more than a half-century of experience, the conventional master plan is accepted by a legislature so rarely that it becomes top news in planning when one is followed. Faced with the forces of the market, zoning districts and regulations have given way, have been unable to withstand onslaughts by the land speculator and the merchant builder.

The present techniques have been particularly ineffective in securing metropolitan coordination, in getting local government bodies to give any heed to regional repercussions of their acts.

A grave weakness in present techniques is a lack of method to maintain continued concern and responsibility for urban developments. The merchant builder will build an isolated, unbalanced residential project that is unable to support itself. Then he runs out, leaving the individual buyers to hold the bag, to try desperately to make a viable community when the makings are not there. This is in contrast to the shopping center promoter or the industrial park promoter who, because of his unliquidated financial investment, continues to maintain standards and to police covenant restrictions. There is also a continuity-of-interest problem in urban renewal. In the redevelopment process, it occurs in the complete letdown of interest in the project once the contract has been signed. It also comes in the difficulty of assuring, on the part of the city, continuity of outlook and maintenance of zoning standards in rehabilitation areas.

Another problem is the difficulty of maintaining an overview by all government agencies of the entire urban situation, so that all programs are coordinated, so that the benefits of one action are not negated by another action.

The difference between a new technique and an improvement in an old technique is difficult to define, however, new techniques have inevitably been foreshadowed by existing techniques in the field. There are a number of ways that techniques can be changed:

Federal—Local Agency.   Present urban-shaping techniques are in the hands of several governments. The controls can be shifted up or down the line. We can have more or less federal intervention, more or less state intervention, more or less metropolitan or regional intervention, more or less local intervention. Zoning, for example, is completely in the hands of local communities. It could be shifted to a metropolitan agency or to a state board. Local planning assistance projects are financed by a mixture of federal, state, and local funds. These arrangements can be changed, the division of costs shifted.

Incentive—Prohibition.   There is a continuum in the method of guiding development that runs from incentives offered to a private developer to encourage him to follow a chosen course, to laws prohibiting the developer from doing something considered undesirable. The range of incentives and regulations is wide. In some instances, one or the other seems to be the only possible method. In other instances, it is a matter of judgment whether incentive or regulation will be most effective.

Regulation—Acquisition.   Those who would shape urban growth must decide between guiding development by using regulation (under the police power), and guiding it by the more positive and certain acquisition of the fee or some lesser interest in property (eminent domain). This decision must necessarily be influenced by considerations of feasibility (Is it possible to get the necessary control through police power?); questions of finance (Is the government able to afford the purchase of land?); and questions of politics (Will the temper of the electorate permit condemnation and government ownership?).

Control—Free Market.   The whole gamut of urban development control techniques is a collection of methods of government intervention in the free market of real estate. How far this manipulation of the market should go is a question that will probably be answered in political terms. There is no chance of the one extreme: complete abandonment of market intervention by the government. This would certainly lead to anarchy and chaos in the urban scene. It is more likely that we will move steadily the other way, toward increased control and manipulation of the market through many governmental techniques and devices. Such manipulation may be *direct* (housing code enforcement) or it may be *indirect* (tax penalties on slums).

This paper divides the possible new techniques—or the improved version of older techniques—into seven categories. Admittedly, the differentiation between types is not always clear and any one technique may fall into two or more categories, however, the division aids in canvassing the field. The degree of detail of the discussion is variable. In several instances, it was necessary to invent terminology.

1. *Plans and Programs.*   It is generally believed that if we are to attempt to shape urban growth intelligently we need a clear picture of the ultimate shape we wish to achieve. Traditionally this picture has been the master plan.

Prodded by federal local planning assistance programs, we increased our stock of master plans enormously.

It is doubtful that there is much correlation between the production of number of master plans and their actual use. For most large cities they do not exist, for most small cities they are not used.

The most hopeful outlook for a usable master plan, or master plan substitute, is the document which consists of policy statements, which has little or no specificity, no maps. This has been called a *community development policy.* An important feature is that it will be formally adopted by the local legislative body, giving it the status of a law, in contrast to the traditional procedure in which the master plan is rarely adopted by the local legislature. The traditional master plan, because of its specificity, has proved a nuisance and a handicap in those few places in which it has been formally adopted. Strong caveats against adoption abound in planning literature. Formal legislative adoption of the community development policy version of the master plan will be a sharp break with tradition.

The *community renewal program* falls somewhere between an existing technique and a new technique. Completed programs are too rare and too new to give us information as to their effectiveness. There is evidence that the planners will for some time be experimenting with several approaches. However, if we assume the objective of the community renewal program is valid—i.e, a technique to fill the interstices in the master plan, tied in with a program including method of financing—then we should consider a further step. On the basis of area covered and persons cared for, the greater part of future urban expansion will take place in the fringe areas of cities. It might be well to consider extending the CRP concept into the undeveloped areas of metropolitan regions, it might be called a *community* or *metropolitan development program.*

The fields of environmental engineering and environmental health may bring emphasis on *community facility capacity.* This is the concept that in any area there is an absolute limit to the capacity of certain community facilities to serve urban development, and that this capacity limit can be accurately measured.

The critical facilities will certainly be, at first, water supply and sanitary waste disposal. The capacity of any facility could change. For example, there would be one development limit so long as an area could be served only with septic tanks, but this limit would be greatly increased with the installation of sanitary sewers. Air supply is one important community resource for which definite capacity limits will eventually be established. The research in Los Angeles on the capacity of the atmosphere for disposal of airborn wastes clearly points toward this type of control. The concept of capacity limits may be someday extended to such community facilities as schools, hospitals, or streets.

The idea of community facility capacity has been implicit in most reputable master plans. The difference suggested here is that with the birth of environmental engineering, the idea is now in the bailiwick of engineers, who are accustomed to working with enough precision so that they feel quite sure of themselves, and of health service technicians, who are accustomed to establishing and administering the very strong control measures permissible under the powers given to health agencies. As the environmental engineering or environmental health concept gains strength and funds, there could be a dramatic shift in the agencies and personnel administering development controls.

2. Regulatory Measures. Most of the techniques discussed in this paper are regulatory measures in some degree, however, this classification is used to discuss only zoning limitations.

Zoning, with its precise measurements and standards, is a tool designed for the individual lot. It is most effective, for example, in guiding "in-filling," as the British term it—construction on and use of the vacant lot that lies in the middle of an already developed area. Zoning can be particularly useful to maintain the amenity of an historical preservation area. However, zoning has not been effective as a means to preserve the integrity of the land-use plan for an undeveloped area. Nor has it been effective to control and yet to allow reasonable freedom to the builders of shopping centers, industrial parks, large residential projects, or balanced community developments.

Whether done formally or not, the trend is toward the limitation of zoning to developed areas and small parcels. Instead of designating undeveloped fringe land as "agriculture," or limiting it with extra large "estate" zoning, we can expect the use of an "uncommitted" zone designation. The legislative body would say: "We have not determined the proper use of this land. You may continue to use it as you now use it, but when you want to change the use, you must come to us with your proposal for a permanent zone designation. At that time we will hear you and grant or refuse your request." Hopefully, the legislative decision would be guided by a rational land-use policy and plan.

Once the classification is fixed and development has taken place, then conventional zoning would take over maintenance of control of land uses.

3. Licensing Measures. The increase of licensing is a fact. It is bewailed regularly and at great length by the pioneers of zoning, but their objections seem to have no effect in slowing the trend. In addition to licensing through special exceptions and floating zones, the modern zoning ordinance and the modern subdivision regulation will both contain provisions for large-scale or planned developments that need not necessarily adhere to standard provisions for lot size, yards and setbacks, use segregation, building type, etc. The one control customarily maintained is that of overall density of development. If the scheme as presented meets with the approval of the reviewing body (which may be the board of zoning appeals, the plan commission, or the legislative body), the developer is given permission, is "licensed" to go ahead with construction.

Another type of licensing, which also is offensive to the purists in zoning, is the free-and-easy rezoning by the local legislative body. In fact, in many areas where the local legislature has been inclined to be reluctant to change zoning classifications too easily, the courts have taken over and ordered reclassification.

In the days before large-scale construction, there was a clear distinction between the functions of the zoning ordinance and the subdivision regulation. With the rise of the merchant builder who controls the development operation all the way from buying the raw land to selling the finished house, the distinction is lost. This melding together of zoning and subdivision control is particularly apparent in the floating zone and the large-scale development provisions of the two types of ordinances. We can be sure that the distinction between zoning and subdivision regulation, at least as far as new development is concerned, will be lost and there will be a widespread use of the *development ordinance*. It is probable that the ordinance will go beyond a combination of zoning and subdivision control in fringe areas to embrace the full zoning ordinance for developed areas. Eventually, there may be a possibility that the development ordinance will also include the community building code and housing code.

4. *Land Acquisition.* The acquisition of land for public purposes, in advance of need, has from the beginning been a desired end-product of planning. The object is to get properly located parcels of land at a time when the cost will be lower than if purchase were delayed until the land is actually needed. For example, in 1959 the city of Cincinnati reported that as a result of a 1948 master plan, land for parks had been purchased well in advance of need; the city had saved approximately $2 million by virtue of advance acquisition.

In general, communities have the legal authority they need for the advance purchase of land, although they are frequently short of the necessary funds to make such purchases. There is also reluctance on the part of the city officials to commit the city irrevocably to a scheme far in advance of the time the scheme can be carried out. In part this is due to the lack of a long-range plan of development or to the lack of understanding of the need to follow such a plan, if one exists. It is also due to an understandable lack of faith in the ability of any public official, including—perhaps, especially—planners, to foresee the future with any reasonable degree of certainty.

A technique that, like the community renewal program, falls somewhere between old and new is the purchase of interests in land less than the fee simple title for open space purposes. These interests are known variously as development rights, scenic easements, and conservation easements.

The object of the purchase of *development rights* is to give the local community the unquestioned right to prohibit intensive development of open areas. Supposedly, it can be done at a lower cost than if the community were to purchase the land outright. Also, the prohibition against the development will be done in a manner more palatable and more fair to the landowner than if the right to develop had been taken by zoning or some other ordinance under the police power. Enabling statutes to permit the purchase of development rights are still too new to make possible a fair judgment of their effectiveness.

(An interesting variation on development rights purchase is discussed later in this paper, under "Metropolitan Development Commission.")

The development rights program can be used to assure permanent open space in expanding urban areas, which would be considered a public purpose (morally, if not legally); or it can be used for development timing, for restraining development of an area until the community is in a position to furnish the necessary municipal services. If the purpose is development timing, then the land is slated for eventual private use rather than for public use. Until recently, such an idea would have been politically unacceptable and impossible to carry out legally. Because of the pressure of expanding population, particularly on schools, there has been a shift in the political and juridical philosophy to a more liberal viewpoint. There has also been definite legislative action, plus a reasonable assurance that courts would look favorably on government purchase of land eventually to be resold for private development. It is no longer treasonable to comment favorably on the Scandinavian practice by which cities own not only the developing fringe lands, but also large areas within the built-up city. The universally cited example in the United States of a similar situation is Mountain Lakes Borough in New Jersey: the borough itself owns 35 percent of its entire area, and sells it for private development only as rapidly as the borough officials feel their government is able to finance the public costs of private expansion.

A suggested instrument for handling property to assure properly timed development is the *land bank*. Land is purchased by the community and held in the land bank until such time as it is ready for development—when the community is ready and able to accept the responsibility and cost of serving the property after it is developed. Or, what may be more important in some cases, the land is held in the land bank until the market is ready to absorb it for the purpose which the community has determined it should be used. This latter situation is particularly important for the preservation of outlying industrial land. A master plan may determine that a particular outlying parcel is both suitable and needed for industrial growth. However, at the time the plan is made there is no market for the parcel as industrial property. Under existing laws and court decisions, it will be almost impossible to freeze the parcel for exclusive industrial development, so long as it remains in private ownership. The owner will claim violation of due process. The courts will almost certainly support him if regulations freezing his land for industrial development prevent him from selling it for any other purpose.

The land bank can also be used to hold areas cleared through redevelopment. A substantial and growing proportion of redevelopment clearance areas (whether or not the clearance has actually taken place) are proving to be unsalable at present. Naturally, the areas most attractive for private rebuilding will be cleared first because they can be resold easily. Areas for which no developer can be found will remain uncleared or, if cleared, will remain unused. The land bank can be a useful device for handling this problem.

5. *Recapture of Betterment.* The value of land in the environs of a city is enhanced by public acts. A new expressway, a new school, the extension of water and sewer facilities—all of these will increase the value of land in the vicinity. However, none of the increase in value will be returned directly to the local community which paid for the improvements that caused the increase. The only way in which part of "betterment" value is recaptured for the public is through the federal capital gains tax—if the property is sold. And this tax goes to the federal government rather than to the local government.

The British government has tried by the use of development charges to collect some of the socially created increment. This has not proved particularly successful. The land bank mentioned earlier could be used to recapture betterment. To do this, the community would simply buy property at one price and sell it later at a higher price, with the government taking the profit. An extension of this idea would be for the government itself to redevelop clearance sites, the profits from which would eventually reduce the costs of clearance. As well as being a method to recapture betterment, this redevelopment by government agency may be the only way that certain submarginal sites can ever be redeveloped.

An older technique for the recapture of betterment is *excess condemnation.* There has been no widespread use of excess condemnation, partly because it has not fared well in many state courts, and partly because the name has a bad ring—it is a politically dangerous tool. The idea, nevertheless, has particular merit as a means to protect expressway interchanges. The public investment in an interchange structure can be seriously depreciated unless there is positive control of land use and access to the interchange for some distance in all directions. Such control is most positively assured if the government actually purchases the adjacent land. Protection does not mean complete absence of any use. Certain selected and carefully controlled operations can be placed in an interchange area, preferably on the basis of ground lease. The enhancement in value of land because of the intersection would in this way accrue to the public. It is questionable whether zoning alone could ever assure the degree of protection at a highway interchange that is desirable or that could be gained through protective purchase.

6. *Financial Incentives.* Perhaps more important in the shaping of urban areas than any programs, ordinance, or control that has been discussed thus far are financial incentives. The federal government is, by all odds, the most important purveyor of financial incentives. It operates through FHA and VA mortgage insurance, FNMA mortgage purchase, the depressed areas program, urban renewal grants, community facility loans, public housing grants, open space grants, public transit aid, and—although completely beyond the scope of this paper—the national fiscal policy.

It is also beyond the scope of this paper to discuss the subtleties of this financial incentive program. A few points might be made, however. In private residential development, the most important financial factor is the FHA mortgage insurance program. It is suggested that FHA might well examine its policy on approving developments that have sandbagged zoning changes, that are contrary to local land-use plans, that have leapfrogged existing development too far, or that will clearly make an excessive drain on the community's ability to provide urban services. The reverse of this situation also might merit favorable treatment from FHA (and from VA)—a situation in which the development was clearly lining up with a community development program or master plan.

A few students of urban renewal advocate the abolition of noncash contributions as a credit from the local public agency. It is stated that the whole situation would be better, even if the federal writedown were increased to 80 or 90 percent, with the local contribution of 10 to 20 percent being demanded in cash. It is difficult to calculate the pros and cons of this proposal, but it seems worth investigating.

The Pittsburgh ACTION-Housing program for the East Hills project is based on financing development from a revolving fund, plus direction of the operation by a quasi-public corporation dedicated to the public interest. This is a model that should be studied closely. It seems to offer a possible method to assure continuity of interest in a private residential development. It may be an effective way to fight the hit-and-run developer, who caters to the same lower middle-income group that the East Hills project will serve.

In the general field of land-use planning and control (other than construction and development) the federal government embarked on a program of aiding local communities to purchase open space, or to purchase development rights to maintain open space. This technique was first authorized in the 1961 version of the Federal Housing Act. If the open space program is taken up with any enthusiasm, it can play an important part in shaping future urban developments. The open space program is necessarily a metropolitan program. Because of this, a major obstacle to its complete success is the scarcity of metropolitan planning of value or effectiveness. Experience with the open space program should be reexamined. It may be found that, even with the federal subsidy, local governments will not to any great extent be financially able to take advantage of the program.

7. *Tax Assessment Policy.* Property tax policy is important in shaping urban growth. The tax payment as it relates to the true value of land is important in determining whether the land can be held for a speculative rise. An important factor is the policy of the assessor on weighting the zoning classification of property. Shall he assess at the value for the use permitted by the zoning classification, perhaps agriculture; or shall he assess at the value for urban development, for development into tract housing? The general practice of assessors has been to ignore the zoning classification, except where mandated differentially by state statute. They have adopted a realistic, if blase, attitude that zoning ordinances were only temporary deterrents.

The most important current proposal in property taxation is the use of the *land tax* or *site value tax.* Under the land tax, only the land is assessed—never the improvements on it. However, the land is assessed at its highest use value. The tax rate for the taxing jurisdiction is adjusted so that the total property tax income will be the same as under the customary land-and-improvements tax scheme. This is actually Henry George's single tax, although the present-day advocates seem to want to soft-pedal this origin.

Under any circumstances, a rational assessement policy would be helpful in guiding a rational urban development policy. In cities where the assessed value of property is extremely low, perhaps as low as 5 percent of the true value, the city is badly handicapped because of a lack of bonding power. The full effectiveness of any federal programs for shaping urban development will certainly be lost in such low assessment areas.

A major problem in fringe area development has been the financing of schools and parks for new suburban development. A number of local communities have attempted to meet the problem by requiring that the developer dedicate land for school and park purposes, or by charging him a fee in lieu of dedication. In New York and California, the state legislature has authorized such practices. However, courts in the majority of the states where the question has arisen have declared park and school site dedication requirements or payments-in-lieu to be illegal.

A suggested solution for this problem is the use of a school or park *benefit district*. This would operate under the customary laws governing other benefit districts which are financed on the basis of special assessment against property owners in the district. Streets, sewers and drainage improvements are quite generally financed in this way.

The operation of a hypothetical school benefit district would be: The community delineates the service area of a proposed school. The plan states that a school will eventually be built somewhere near the center of this area, a school to serve 500 families. The cost of the land and the building is being set at $100,000. A benefit district is formed. Each dwelling unit to be built in the district will carry a special assessment of $200, perhaps payable over a period as long as ten years. The period of the assessment starts running when property is subdivided into lots or when house construction is started. Construction on the school will start when the school authorities consider development has gone far enough to warrant building. If the cost of the school is more than was raised by the benefit district charges, the community undertakes to make up the difference. If more than 500 dwelling units are built in the district, each would still pay the $200 special assessment on the theory that more than 500 families will require a school larger than was originally planned.

Administration of Land Development Techniques.   Thus far there has been little discussion of the problems of administering the land development techniques listed. New, or improved, administrative techniques and agencies are important in themselves, whether or not there are substantive changes in the actual development incentives and controls.

1. Department of Urban Development.   There has been more than a little criticism of urban redevelopment because of the craze to get something torn down and something new to replace it regardless of whether the project fitted into a rational development plan, and because it has caused double and triple relocation of families. The cause of "projectitis" can be localized in the gap between the philosophy of urban renewal, an action program, and a philosophy of planning which avoids any contact with action. The cure has been to amalgamate the two into a single *department of urban development*. As an organization form, it is getting more popular. It augurs well as a means to get a more rational renewal program and a more realistic community plan.

2. *Development Control Agency*. In spite of the fears of excessive discretionary powers, there can be little doubt that we shall have an ever-increasing use of the licensing philosophy in the administration of land development controls. A most promising suggestion for handling this problem is the *development control agency*. (A better name might have been selected, but an attempt was made to differentiate clearly between this proposal and the Krasnowiecki-Paul "Metropolitan Development Commission," discussed later.) The agency would be analogous to the federal regulatory commissions: Interstate Commerce Commission, Federal Communications Commission, Federal Aviation Agency, etc. It would be under the direction of perhaps three full-time commissioners, persons with expertise in planning, law, real estate, public administration, construction, or similar fields, who would administer a development ordinance—a combination of zoning, subdivision control, and large-scale development control ordinances. The agency would be guided by a community development policy, rather than a conventional master plan, although the commissioners would also be guided by a detailed program, such as a community facility plan.

The agency would (a) replace the board of zoning appeals and the zoning administrator; (b) take over the plan commission functions relating to zoning and subdivision regulations; (c) replace any architectural review board; and (d) have delegated to it legislative authority to establish zoning regulations and delineate use districts, under the guidance of general policy laid down by the legislative body.

An important aspect of local regulation of urban expansion is that local government is regulating an industry, the home building industry, in addition to regulating land use in the public interest. An attitude that balances concern with the public interest and understanding of the industry problems is more likely to be found in a full-time regulatory commission such as the development control agency than it is in the congeries of lay boards and commissions that now administer a mishmash of ordinances, plans, programs, and personal prejudices.

Also, the development control agency can be most effective if it has metropolitan or submetropolitan jurisdiction.

3. *Superior Review Boards.*   Metropolitan or state boards are being proposed for review of local decisions on land-use regulations. The proposals call for review, either automatically or upon appeal, of local board of adjustment rulings on variances and special exceptions and planning commission decisions on subdivision control. Some proposals even call for automatic review of local legislative action on zoning amendments or on original zoning and subdivision control ordinances.

The chances are good that superior review boards will be established in some states. The pressure for such boards will be coming principally from the real estate and home-building industries, whose operators are alarmed by behavior they consider irresponsible and discriminatory, and by policies clearly inconsistent with related policies in adjacent communities. The home builders get some support from planners and expert zoning lawyers, who are especially alarmed by the chaotic administration of land-use controls in metropolitan areas.

4. *State Planning Agency.*   While state planning can hardly be called a new technique, there is a revival of interest that may make it an important factor in shaping future urban growth.

State planning had been dead since the abolition of the National Resources Planning Board. In fact, there are legitimate doubts that state planning ever amounted to anything even under the NRPB aegis. However, there is definitely a return of interest, triggered by the state plan of Hawaii (probably the first true state plan ever to be completed), and by the top priority to state planning given by Governor Nelson of Wisconsin in his whole administrative program.

As a result of this interest, a special report on state planning was prepared by the American Society of Planning Officials for the Council of State Governments, and the 1962 Governors Conference endorsed its recommendations. The principal thesis was that urban and metropolitan growth (and decay) will be the number one state problem in the coming years. It urged that state governments take positive steps toward meeting this problem by using state planning and by taking definite action to ease the metropolitan situation. It seems reasonable to expect that in some of the more populous states, state government will move into the urban situation strongly, although it is not possible to predict what form state intervention will take. The state zoning in Hawaii indicates that some extremely powerful steps can be taken: for example, the limits of urbanization are definitely controlled; the state-controlled land-use pattern has resemblance to the British greenbelt and "white area" scheme.

5. *Suburban Development District.* In an article appearing in the *Journal of the American Institute of Planners* (May 1960), Marion Clawson proposed a new form of organization which he called the "suburban development district." Clawson's proposal was to surround and enclose the city with a series of ad hoc districts, distantly modeled after drainage districts. He would give the districts the power to "perform any function ordinarily performed by local units of the government, including such matters as provision of water supply, sewage disposal, fire-fighting organization, schools, parks, roads and streets, and the like." The major power he denied the district was that of eminent domain. The district limits were to follow natural or artificial boundaries in some sort of logical fashion. A district would contain from one to ten or more square miles, the size varying to some extent directly with the size of the city surrounded.

The basic power of the suburban development district would come from an authorization to acquire all the land within its boundaries, if necessary. Clawson felt that complete purchase would not be necessary, but that most of the land could be controlled by options, voluntarily given. (Where necessary, the state was to condemn property or property rights for the district.)

The major activities of the suburban development district were (1) to plan urban growth of the district, as needed; (2) to acquire control over the land area by purchase or option to the extent necessary; (3) to enter into contracts for actual development of the area, at optimum rate, with private developers; and (4) to undertake, either in its own name or by contract with local government units, to supply necessary local governmental activities. Six interest groups were to be represented on the control board of the suburban development district: counties, special local governmental districts, neighboring city or cities, private real estate developers and builders, present landowners in the district, and leading citizens of the general area. These various interest groups were to be "permitted to subscribe from 10 to 25 shares of 'stock' each." How this "stock sale" was to be arranged was not clear.

There have been some sharp criticisms of Clawson's proposal. One of the most serious would be that the additional governmental units only increase the balkanization of metropolitan areas. While it is not likely that the suburban development district exactly as Clawson proposes it will be adopted, the proposal does have some pertinent suggestions to offer as a method of administering a land-acquisition program.

6. Metropolitan Development Commission. In the December 1961 issue of the *University of Pennsylvania Law Review* (Vol. 110, p. 179), there appeared an article by Jan Z. Krasnowiecki and James C. N. Paul entitled "The Preservation of Open Space in Metropolitan Areas." In this article, the authors propose the establishment of "metropolitan development commissions," and they offer a tentative draft of an open space act to use this device. The proposal attracted a great deal of attention. The device is too complicated to discuss in detail in this report. However, it is generally an adaptation, and, according to the authors, an improvement over the British scheme of nationalization of development rights. (This aspect of the British system has not been particularly successful.)

The authors described the system as follows:

1. When the area to be preserved or developed for open space purposes has been chosen, through procedures and within a governmental structure which best assure maximum benefit to the community, the properties in the area are valued.

2. The valuation is based on the same principles and is accomplished under the same procedures as is the valuation of property for purposes of just compensation in condemnation.

3. The values thus established for each property in the area are guaranteed to the owner by the government authority.

4. The aggregate of these guarantees for the whole area is equal to the compensation which would be payable if the whole area were condemned in fee on the date when the open space program goes into effect.

5. The fee, of course, is not condemned.

6. Instead, detailed regulations controlling the uses of the property for open space purposes are imposed against the guarantees.

7. To the extent that such controls depress the value of the land for uses actually being made of it at the time they are being imposed, the owner is permitted to draw on his guarantee for damages.

8. To the extent that such controls depress the value of the property for other than existing uses—depress or eliminate development worth—the owner may draw on his guarantee through an administratively supervised public sale of his property, in an amount by which the guarantee allocable to his interest exceeds the proceeds received by him from the sale.

9. The guarantee established for any property in the area is reduced by each payment of damages or compensation. Thus the damages and compensation payable by the community cannot exceed the guarantee established for each tract. What this means, in effect, is that development values not existing on the date when open space controls are imposed are not compensated.

The proposal is ingenious, particularly in view of the probability that the natural long-term rise in suburban property prices would minimize the need for ever actually paying any money for the development rights. While full criticism of the proposal has not yet been heard, one critic suggests that the danger of the metropolitan development commission scheme is that the principle behind it, once accepted, might be extended to already built-up property, instead of being confined to open space control. Under these circumstances, even if the proposal surmounted constitutional objections, there would be great opportunities for discriminatory treatment of similarly situated landowners.

7. *Metropolitan Government.* A realistic appraisal of the situation in the United States indicates that true metropolitan government has little chance of being widely adopted in the reasonably near future. Metropolitan cooperative agreements may be successful in some areas. Some city-county consolidation may take place, and some county governments may be modernized enough to handle urban problems (several are so equipped now).

As some of the problems, such as water supply or sewage disposal, get critical enough, we can expect additional ad hoc metropolitan authorities to take over these specific functions.

Metropolitan planning is the only administrative device which has fairly wide acceptance. The history of metropolitan planning gives us nothing to be particularly pleased about. The most successful metropolitan planning has been in small metropolitan areas where the urbanized area is enclosed within the boundaries of a single county. In these areas, there are several variations of the city-county joint planning operation which have been reasonably successful. Where the metropolitan area includes several counties or spills over into more than one state, the record is not encouraging, so far.

This is essentially a negative report on metropolitan government and metropolitan administration, but it is a situation that should be reckoned with when considering the problems of shaping the future urban expansion. The awakening of state interest in metropolitan problems (mentioned in connection with state planning) offers some encouragement. Other techniques discussed in this report are also essentially directed toward remedying the problems of metropolitanism.

8. *The Federal Role.* The federal government will probably play an increasingly important role in shaping urban expansion. If for no other reason, this can be inferred from the safe prediction that federal grants-in-aid, subsidies, and loans to local agencies involved in urban development will continue to increase.

It can be assumed that a number of federal programs, quite important in shaping the urban future, will be administered by agencies other than the federal department most directly involved, which will require coordination of all programs affecting urban development. The cooperation between FHA and the Federal Aviation Agency on the policy for mortgage insurance on property in the vicinity of airports is an illustration of the coordinated approach. Federal aid for school construction would be an extremely important factor in shaping urban growth; unthinking disbursement of school construction aid fund could undo a great deal of the work of both federal and local agencies.

In addition to the direct influence of federal financial incentives on urban development, the federal agencies are influential in the rules and standards set to qualify local agencies for federal assistance. It is always difficult to decide how far the federal government should go with its rules and regulations, since this strongly smacks of intervention in local affairs. There must be a compromise between the need to protect the federal funds and the need to preserve local autonomy.

The seven-point "workable program" is an illustration of the type of federal requirement that can strongly influence local policy. The workable program did much to improve local operations in the field of urban renewal and planning. At the same time, there was relatively little review of the quality of the various elements involved. There is need for expanding the concept to include a judgment of the quality, balance, and completeness of the arsenal of local development control techniques.

In fact, the good work of one control device, such as zoning, can be completely offset by the harm done by another device, for example, the assessment policy. It is suggested that there should be a method of making an objective survey to analyze and evaluate all aspects of city ordinances or city policy that have an effect on urban development. If such an analysis could be presented impartially, it would aid local government to inaugurate an integrated program to improve its tools for shaping urban development.

A Development Guidance System, extracted from "The Future of Planning in Puerto Rico," a speech presented at the 25th Anniversary Conference of the Puerto Rico Planning Board, San Juan, August 10, 1967.

The standard talk on planning reveals the secret that solves all problems, makes all troubles vanish, lets everyone live happily ever afterwards. All you need is a master plan which is based on a careful analysis of economic, social, and physical data, designed to make the optimum use of resources in the light of well-defined goals for the future. The master plan nowadays comes in several different flavors: multitowns, radial corridor, satelite cities, etc. The standard procedure is to hand the citizens all of the alternatives, the entire menu, from which they will make a choice by democratic vote.

The tricky thing about the master plan is that when you hear about it, it makes sense, it is logical. The problem comes when you start preparing it. It never seems to be finished, there is never enough staff to do the job, never quite enough data. You need improvements in the simulation model. You still have to test it against this road network and that sewerage system; against low, medium, and high population projections; low, medium, and high economic conditions; low, medium, and high residential density; and low, medium, and high nearly everything else.

Upon occasion—usually the occasion is some rough talk by political critics—preliminary versions of the alternatives are released, but they need refinement. When refinement starts, you learn that the information is inadequate and out-of-date and must be gathered fresh. In the meantime, while the master plan is gestating, life goes on, new factories are brought in, hotels go up, highways are built, utilities are extended, rural folk flock to the city, residential projects are erected, schools get overcrowded, health needs mount, land is used, water is used, air is used. We can lump this all together under the heading of development.

I fear that development never waits for master plans.

The pattern of development in any one area is determined by countless hundreds, and even thousands, of decisions, some governmental, most of them private decisions. Development takes place because of the working of a system—a sort of great institutional machine that is guided by the collection of decisions—seemingly random decisions; but decisions which actually add up to a totality that makes the system operate.

The system works, but the system also wastes. In my opinion, it can be fatally wasteful if it is not guided for the benefit of all the citizens. This—the guidance of development for the greatest benefit to *all* the citizens—is the basic reason for planning. By determining the public purposes and adopting policies consistent with those purposes, you are in a position to identify and to make those decisions that will be the key to influencing a whole chain of subsequent decisions—decisions that will shape development in the form it should be.

This, a sort of system-within-a-system, is a "development guidance system." That is, development takes place by virtue of actions: house construction, road paving, factory building. The action system is guided by a decision system, and here is where government intervention takes place.

When you look at it this way, the conventional master plan begins to assume its proper role. It is not the supreme guide to development that it was once thought to be. It is only an expression of the physical pattern that is determined by the development guidance decisions made to achieve public purposes.

While public objectives are customarily rather general, policies can be, and must be, more specific. Thus, if the goal is the conservation of land in the island of Puerto Rico, one policy would be to limit the wasteful consumption of land through urban sprawl by prohibiting development in certain areas. For example, you might draw one line around the present urban limits of Ponce, and a second line five miles out from the first and say: "Within this five-mile belt, no more than 10 percent of the land may be used for urban purposes—90 percent must remain open in agriculture or a regional park." At this point the master planning technique comes in, to arrange the development pattern in the belt area and to uncover the remaining decisions that must be made regarding highways, public transit, residential density, schools, water supply, sewerage, and so on, in order to carry out the pattern. But always observing that strict 10 percent limitation. The important decision has been made within the development guidance system, not on the drafting board in the planning office.

6

A New Approach to Moving Goods and People

Editor's Commentary

Dennis O'Harrow made some strong and memorable statements about the need for a new approach to moving goods and people.

He kept warning that we are obsessed by and engulfed with the problems of moving private vehicles, that we are spending money and trying to solve problems using methods that are self-defeating.

He pointed out that one of the rarely recognized costs of the increase in auto population is land consumption: "The land we consume per auto is greater than the land we use per human being." A policy to control this land consumption, he said, means a policy of "birth control for rubber tires . . . compensated for by a positive program of adequate public transportation."

He recommended that we reexamine our assumptions on public transportation. We would solve the problem, he said, only when we approached it "as a public utility, a municipal service, that must be provided no matter what it costs—because no matter what it costs, it is going to cost less than trying to move people in and around and through our cities entirely by automobile."

One of the papers in this chapters on moving goods and people contains his demonstration of the inadequacies of Euclidean geometry, and his proposals on solving New York City's traffic congestion which, the *New York Herald Tribune* said, "punctured virtually all the conventional approaches."

Another new approach, a proposed new institution at the state level for settling highway disputes, is outlined in a paper prepared for a meeting of the Highway Research Board.

DOH warned but, as always, he also recommended.

Mass Transportation—The Forgotten Stepchild

Quoted from "The Place of Mass Transpor-
tation in the City," a speech to the Citizens
Public Utility Committee for the
Metropolitan Area of Chicago, 1952

The central business district is the focal point of traffic problems: too many automobiles for the streets and no place to put them except on the streets. One way we have attacked the problem is to devise a method for getting automobiles out of the business district as rapidly and efficiently as possible. We have invented the limited-access expressway. The expressway not only empties the central business district rapidly, it also fills it up just as rapidly—which has led to our desperate search for methods of increasing the downtown parking areas. It is a self-defeating process. Good roads and ample parking space generate more driving and more parkers.

For the most part, our thinking about today's municipal problems almost completely ignores mass transportation. If there ever was a forgotten stepchild in American municipal government, it is public transportation. We are so obsessed by and engulfed with the problems of moving private motor vehicles that we completely overlook some of the obvious facts. Our principal interest should be in the movement of people, not of vehicles.

Yet where are we spending our money? We are trying to solve problems of traffic and parking, using methods that are not going to solve anything. We could do the job much more cheaply and much more efficiently if we were to divert a greater share of money to the improvement of public transportation, and a greater share of our energies and talents and thoughts to getting it accepted as an economical and sensible means of traveling.

"Desire" Lines for Transit Passengers

Quoted from "Town Planning and Public
Transit," a paper given at the Canadian
Transit Association Annual Meeting,
St. Andrews, New Brunswick, Canada,
June 15, 1954.

All the evidence indicates that every year we learn to get along on less
and less public transit. Down underneath I have a feeling that it's like
the farmer who started mixing sawdust with the oats that he fed his
horse. He kept decreasing the amount of oats and increasing the sawdust in the mixture each day until he finally achieved success. He got
rid of the oats altogether, feeding the horse 100 percent sawdust.
However, the day that he achieved success was also the day that the
horse died!

Trying to educate the public as to the value of public transit is in
competition with what must be the most stupendous "educational"
campaign the world will ever see—that being conducted by General
Motors and Ford and Chrysler and the oil companies and the rubber
companies, on the urgent need we have for a private automobile,
preferably a new one each year.

Until we approach the business of providing public transit from the
viewpoint of providing what the public needs and *wants*, we will continue to let our public transit get in worse shape. Our approach must
be one of service first and finances second.

In origin and destination surveys for limited-access highways and
expressways in a city, we map "desire" lines, we plot and design and
construct our facilities for private motor vehicles on the basis of the
"desires" of the passengers. That is the primary consideration. There
are many things wrong with origin and destination surveys and traffic
studies as we now make them. We don't know nearly as much about
the situation as we think we do. Nevertheless, there is not much
wrong with our method of "educating the public" as to the need for expressways. We don't really educate, of course; we find out what the
public desires and we provide it.

Only as we find out what the public wants from its transportation,
and how we can supply that want with public transit, will we ever

start public transit back on the way up and halt its wild toboggan ride toward oblivion.

Public Transportation Axioms

Extracted from the ASPO Newsletter editorial, April 1954.

There are many transit operations—too many—that lie mortally ill. If we make our prognosis on the basis of the headlines appearing from coast to coast, we must inevitably conclude that public transit is headed straight for extinction, like the dodo. This is not a quiet passing from the scene. There is great hullabuloo and outcry. There are accusations and counteraccusations. There are proposals and counterproposals. There are schemes and more schemes. There are studies and super-studies. But the patient loses ground every day.

There are many suggestions concerning what we should do about mass transportation. These cover routes, headway, equipment, fares, finances, and a host of countervailing measures directed toward lessening competition from private vehicles. Because therein lies the heart of the matter—the competition between private and public transportation.

We don't know whether some of the proposals will work or not, because we have never given them a full trial. Nevertheless, it seems to me that no scheme will succeed until we back it up and take another look at some of the *a priori* assumptions on which we base our attack on the ailment. And these assumptions are economic.

The first assumption we should examine is our method of figuring the cost of what we call the "journey to work." We have shown quite accurately in several studies the cost of driving an automobile to our employment. We show that it is expensive, much more expensive than fares by public transportation. Then we bewail the fact that economic man is behaving in an uneconomic fashion, because he continues to drive to work, and in greater numbers every day.

What does this mean? It means that if we have any thought of reviving our ailing transit systems on the basis of immediate cost to the consumer, we're going to have to get back to nickel and dime fares. We're going to have to adopt the token payment in more than one meaning of the word.

The second *a priori* assumption is also in accounting and economics. This is the axiom which holds that public transportation is essentially a self-contained activity, and that we can do our accounting on a closed system. We point to certain cities where the operation is still in the black. We point to other cities where, if we were to remove the tax burden, we could show self-supporting operation. In other cities we are able to meet the costs of operation, but need somebody to carry depreciation and replacement of equipment.

But I refer back to the dozens of articles each month on the sad state of affairs. And I refer to the ever-swelling flow of chromium-striped models coming out of Detroit. And last, but not least, I refer to the mounting urban highway and expressway construction program.

As the planner knows, the problem is one that he has aptly named "circulation"—the moving and shuttling of people and goods into, within, and out from, a city. If we are going to treat the entire problem of circulation as a unit, then our economics must be based on the entire problem. Our accounting system must be set up for the entire problem. We are being completely illogical if we try to strike a balance in any way on public transportation alone. In fact, we must make a stab at an economic and an accounting system that will go beyond circulation and include all of the other facets of urbanism: housing, industry, trade, recreation, etc.—in one grand bookkeeping operation.

The third and last assumption I would question is partly a matter of economics and partly a matter of semantics. This is the suggestion that pops up in more and more places, i.e., that we should grant to public transportation a "subsidy." To me, a subsidy is a payment of money that we make in order to keep an uneconomic, but necessary, operation going. If we think we can solve the mass transportation problem with the type of reasoning that I believe lies behind the idea of *subsidy*, we are going to continue to be in hot water for a long time—for as long as we use that philosophy.

We will never solve the circulation puzzle in our cities until we start all over again and approach public transportation in the same manner in which we approach most of our other municipal services. We are going to have to look at it just about the same way we look at fire protection. We never consider that we are "subsidizing" the fire departments, we don't ask them to come out in the black each year. Perhaps most significant of all, we don't ask the property owner to put a nickel or a ten dollar bill in a coin box before he calls out the fire department to save his house. The public transportation problem must be approached first as a necessary municipal service, before we inject any accounting into it. This is almost saying that we should even consider free public transportation as the starting point. There are operational drawbacks to such an offer, but I have a feeling that an honest appraisal will not disclose an economic disadvantage.

Traditional Methods and Conventional Thinking Won't Solve the Problems

Condensed from "Physical Aspects of the Traffic Problem: What Can Be Done in New York City?" a speech to a conference of traffic experts in New York City, January 19, 1956.

I will start my observations by stirring around in some principles of modern day physical science. In high school you studied Euclidean geometry. It was logical, clear, and it made good sense. The problems worked out neatly and if you had reason to use it, the geometry fitted the world outside. You could measure the height of a chimney by the length of its shadow. You could measure the area of a room merely by measuring the length of two adjacent sides. You probably remember that there were some axioms or basic assumptions that you didn't have to prove. As we used to say, "They just stood to reason." One of these axioms related to the number of lines you could draw through a point that were parallel to another line outside the point. Euclid said you could draw only one such line.

It seems, however, that a couple of mathematicians named Lobachevski and Riemann disputed this assumption. Lobachevski said that you could draw an infinite number of parallel lines through the point. Riemann said that you couldn't draw any parallel lines at all. So each man used his own assumption regarding parallel lines, worked back through all of Euclid's propositions, and proved each and every one of them.

These trick geometries just don't "stand to reason." Nevertheless, Einstein picked one of them up to use in his theory of relativity, and it was found that only by using Riemann's geometry were you able to explain the operations of the universe; the kind of geometry that was adequate for all our operations on earth just couldn't be extended to include the entire universe.

The moral of this story is this: ideas, tools, methods that are generally appropriate for operations on one scale break down completely when you try to apply them to something on a much greater scale. The application of this moral is that you are not going to solve the urban problems of New York by traditional methods and conventional thinking. You must look for the Riemann geometry that fits.

During a five-minute traffic stoppage in the garment district, one vehicle space in the street—200 square feet—handles one vehicle and is used at 100 percent capacity. There is no way to increase the number of cars occupying that space for that five-minute period. If we put that 200 square-foot space on an expressway, we use it to only 15 percent of occupancy capacity and yet put 100 vehicles on it. Cars traveling at 30 miles an hour and passing three seconds apart occupy the space for less than one-half second each.

An analysis such as this has shown us that streets can be used to 100 percent occupancy capacity only to store stationary vehicles, not as channels to move people and goods. It has also shown us that when we reach 100 percent capacity, we shall have a complete breakdown of street transportation.

Then this has led us to say that the solution to the problem is to divide the handling of motor vehicles into two parts—movement and stationary storage. Move the cars into the city by efficient expressways, one-way streets and tubes, double-deck bridges; store them off the street in lots and garages. In a ten-story parking garage, for example, you can put ten cars on 200 square feet of land, stacking them ten feet high.

Thus far, this is pretty much conventional thinking—the Euclidean stage. Let us follow this analysis further, using these same figures, which are conservative.

Instead of using the 200 square feet on the expressway as the base, we now use one in-bound expressway lane. As we approach maximum use of this one lane for moving vehicles, we also approach a need for vehicle storage space in the order of 5 million square feet. To provide off-street parking space, at $20 per square foot, each in-bound lane would require a $100 million investment in storage facilities.

Traffic engineers will say that we are far from using our expressways to the maximum, since this requires a steady flow of vehicles 24 hours a day. Yet all of the steps we propose lead to the same end—that of increasing the vehicular traffic poured into the central city.

We propose that trucks limit deliveries to the hours from midnight to dawn. This moves us closer to maximum 24-hour use of the streets. We propose that working hours be staggered, again to spread the input and output hours. We use our greatest ingenuity in traffic flow design: one-way streets, turn restrictions, traffic lights—all to move more vehicles. We plod steadily on, increasing our off-street storage space so that we can use our streets for moving vehicles instead of storing them. Finally, when we see that in spite of our best efforts we still have peak overloads and on-the-street storage because of traffic jams, we add more expressway lanes, more tubes under the Hudson, another deck on the George Washington Bridge.

In short, our Euclidean axiom is that the greater the number of motor vehicles we can jam into Manhattan, the better off we are.

The axiom does work out in certain instances. It works out on the scale of the regional shopping center: the greater the number of vehicles you can get to the center and provide stationary storage for, the more sales you will make within the limits of your staff and sales area to handle the trade. It even may hold good for small- and medium-size cities. But when you come to an operation on the scale of New York, the Euclidean axiom is no longer valid.

I suggest a Riemannian substitute, which is antithetical to our current axiom: the fewer motor vehicles there are in Manhattan, the more efficient and successful will be its functioning.

Until you get rid of the idea that you can solve the traffic problem by providing for more traffic, by increasing thoroughfare capacity, providing more passages across the river, and more auto storages in the business district—until you have discarded that axiom—you cannot hope to have any success in easing New York traffic congestion.

The things we do now *generate additional traffic*. It is crucial that a substitute policy rest firmly on consideration of and control of traffic generation. You don't have traffic unless you use your land in a manner to generate it. And until you control the traffic generation potential of your land, you will never make one inch of permanent headway against traffic congestion.

Since the end of World War II, New York has already *built* as much *new* office space as there is in the entire city of Chicago. This same action has generated additional traffic in an amount equal to that generated by all of the offices in the city of Chicago. It is certainly a thrilling exhibition of initiative and faith in the city of New York. But did the city, at the same time, think to add transportation facilities equal to those of the city of Chicago (chaotic and inadequate as those particular facilities may be)?

The potential traffic that can be generated by another activity is probably even greater. Nothing attracts new manufacturing enterprises like a large market and other manufacturing. In both of these, New York is in a class by itself. So there seems to be no limit to the potential for industrial growth. While I have no idea what part of the commercial area is already devoted to manufacturing, I feel sure that it could be doubled with little effort. I also feel sure that this potential traffic will make that added by new office buildings look puny.

The great advantage over all other cities that New York offers is the astounding range of activities and contacts. The city must provide for the easy and efficient circulation of goods and people between and around and among all parts of the city. We have been so accustomed to equating motor vehicles with this movement of freight and human beings that we cannot separate the two in our thinking. But New York has two of the most effective and efficient means of transportation that have ever been invented. One is the transport of people by underground railway. It would be impossible to operate the city without the subways and the commuter trains coming in below the surface. The other effective vehicle is the little pushcart that carries women's dresses about the streets. Can you imagine the expense and the impossible delays in trying to ship one of those loads of dresses by trucks?

To me these two forms of New York transportation symbolize the basis on which the city must build its future plans: off-surface public transportation for bringing people and freight into the city; and the design of an integrated, intra-central area circulation system on the surface that gives all priorities to pedestrian-type movements.

In my youth there was an acrid political campaign in which one party claimed that if the other got in office there would be grass growing on Broadway and Fifth Avenue. Someone had a good idea there and did not realize it. I am not ready to commit myself on Broadway, but I believe that if the pavement on Fifth Avenue, say from Washington Square to Central Park, had been replaced by grass and trees with moving sidewalks in both directions, we would have made real progress.

Projects to "relieve the traffic congestion" will be proposed and built and will temporarily bring minor relief—but not with minor expenditures. Nothing that has yet been carried out has permanently relieved the Manhattan traffic mess. I feel certain that such will be the future experience until we back up and start off in another direction.

While New York is the highest flowering of modern civilization, it is also a pioneer city. By the end of this century there will be a dozen or more cities in the world as large as New York is today, two or three of them in the United States. But New York will have gone on to even greater superlatives. New York is pushing into the frontier area of the super-giant city of the future. You can't be stymied by small ideas or by conventionalism.

The Pedestrian

Quoted from the ASPO Newsletter editorial "On Walking," August 1957.

"Pedestrian" is a term of opprobrium we apply to any person who is at the moment forced to transport himself without benefit of rubber-tired wheels. He is a molecule of resistance to the smooth flow of auto traffic. It is a misdemeanor to hit him and can be quite expensive.

Traffic engineers have studied the fallen pedestrian quite statistically. From 50 to 70 percent of the time he is permanently still, and this is what makes it so expensive to hit pedestrians. About 85 percent of the cases where a pedestrian interferes with the forward progress of a motor vehicle, the pedestrian seems to have been perfectly normal. He had no handicaps, he was not ill, he had not been drinking. His only sin was that he was walking.

What to do about the pedestrian is a puzzle. Drastic jaywalking laws have not worked very well. The present recommended treatment is one of moderation. The emphasis is on education. Pedestrianism is really a reversion to more primitive times, an anachronism, a manifestation of infantilism. Anyone who is unfortunate enough to have to walk must be given instructions on the dangers of such activity, a course on how to survive in cities.

Humpty-Dumpty said of words that they should serve man, not that man should serve words. He said that the question was simply who was to be master—man or the things that he created. This is an attitude that needs digging out and polishing. Are we to be masters of the things we build, our gadgets, our machines, our cities? Or are they to be our masters?

The right to walk naturally without fear and without disgust is as good a place as any to start being master. But we will have to do some revolutionary thinking. We must think of human beings as creatures whose natural method of locomotion is walking. Rubber tires must be secondary to human feet.

The Planner's Approach to the Urban Highway System

Condensed from "The Roles of Engineering and Urban Planning in the Urban Highway System," a paper given at the Ninth Pan American Highway Congress, Washington, D.C., May 6-18, 1963.

Urban highways rank high among urban needs, high both in importance and cost. They are important not only for the new urban areas that must be created, but also for the modernization of existing urban areas. The planner's approach to the urban highway system is to see it as part of a complex of many types of projects, of private as well as public activities, as a part of an economic and social environment as well as a physical environment, and as an undertaking that can raise thorny legal questions that threaten basic constitutional rights.

The motor vehicle and the highway system on which it moves are only one part of an urban transportation system that includes railroads, aircraft, ships, bicycles, elevators, and—quite importantly—people themselves when they are pedestrians.

By far the most serious conflict between parts of the system is that between urban highways and the special form of railroad known as public transit: rapid transit, subways, elevated lines, commuter railroads, and perhaps, someday, monorail. The trend in the United States is clearly to subordinate public transit to private automobile and truck transportation, in spite of some obvious inconsistencies. It has been demonstrated that public rail transit on separated right-of-way is more economical and more efficient than private motor transportation; the physical limits of private motor transportation are considerably below that of public transit, and the capacity limits for handling private vehicles are being reached in many cities at a point well below the eventual needs for the movement of people and goods.

Still another and relatively new aspect of motor vehicle transportation that is disturbing planners and public administrators is the limit to the capacity of the air above cities to handle the noxious fumes exhausted from gasoline motors. This limit has already been exceeded in at least one great American city.

The question that the planner asks is: Should the urban *highway* system be seen as ever-expanding, or should the available funds be used to improve the urban *transportation* system? Which means that for the best results in the future, when cities are two or three or more times as large as they now are, improved pedestrian facilities and public transit must be studied as alternate and perhaps better investments of public funds. Extremely important decisions on a proper balance of the entire urban transportation system should be made prior to any decision to proceed on the urban highway system.

The motor vehicular transportation system includes collector and service streets, a street system too often neglected. The glamour of the expressway and the easy availability of nonlocal funds for building it have too often blinded local and public officials. They have constructed a monster that has made the overall situation worse, that has induced more persons to speed the course of a modern expressway—at the end to transfer to a local street system that is even more congested, unsafe, and ill-maintained than before the expressway was built.

Just as important as the collector street system for moving vehicles is the storage system for stationary vehicles. To concentrate on the high-speed highway, while ignoring the parking capacity at both ends of the highway, is to build an unbalanced, and therefore inefficient and costly, motor vehicle transportation system. The planner again raises the question of priority: Should not the available funds be distributed among the several parts of the system so that the collector streets and the parking facilities are carried along in a balanced development?

The motor vehicular system is not only part of a whole urban transportation system, but a part of an even larger public facilities system that includes parks and recreation areas, schools, public buildings, sewers, water supply, refuse disposal facilities, hospitals, low-cost housing—in short, every building, structure, and facility within the urban area that is constructed and operated with public funds.

It is extremely difficult to weigh the relative merits of a hospital against the merits of a highway, the need for a sewer against the need for a school. The device used by planners and administrators to solve such dilemmas, the capital improvement program, gives city officials a single picture of the complete needs of the city, it sets up a program that the city is able to pay for, and it avoids costly conflicts between projects and improvements proposed by different departments or agencies.

(In the United States, however, certain revenues are earmarked for specific types of expenditures and may not be used for any other purpose. Almost universally, special funds are reserved for highway purposes, the expenditure on urban highways has been dictated by the laws. There are inequities in this financial arrangement.)

It is the intensity and type of urban land use that creates the need for urban highways. It is also the configuration of this land use, the urban pattern, that determines the general route of urban highways. But part of an urban highway system, if it is properly designed, will serve areas that are not now developed. By bringing access to new areas, it also creates the future land-use pattern. It is in this area of future urban development that the urban planner is likely to find himself at odds with the highway planner. The highway planner too often sees the undeveloped periphery of the city merely as an undifferentiated area in which to end the urban highway. Or, he sees it as an area in which he can place the circumferential expressway, because the right-of-way is relatively cheap. But once an urban highway moves into an undeveloped area, it opens up the area for development. In fact, this potential development is taken into consideration in making a cost-benefit analysis and is reflected in the highway design. The estimate of new traffic generated by future development must enter into the calculations.

The planner asks which should be determinant, the land-use plan or the urban highway system? Which is better for the city, that its future form be planned and the urban highway system fitted into the plan; or that the location of the urban highway system, not based on a future land-use plan, arbitrarily determines the future form of the city?

After World War II there was a rush to buy and build on land bordering on highways, particularly on the bypass and circumferential routes. Filling stations, drive-in restaurants, outdoor cinemas, furniture stores, souvenir stands, golf driving ranges, motels, trailer camps, used auto sales lots, billboards—an endless string—lined the new highways, destroying the usefulness and efficiency of mile after mile. The remedy for this wasteful destruction of highways was to limit access, to permit ingress and egress only at widely spaced interchanges. For further efficiency and safety, the interchanges were designed to do away with all cross traffic. The modern urban highway has eliminated roadside clutter (with the exception of billboards) and the danger of rapid deterioration.

There remains, however, a vulnerable point—the off-highway portion of the interchanges. On the approach routes for a half mile or so before the actual turnouts that connect with the urban highway, there are border areas that have not been controlled by limiting access. These are attractive to the developers of roadside junk. Traffic bottlenecks and hazardous off-and-on movement near interchanges greatly impair the efficiency of the new thoroughfares. While the usefulness of today's urban highway will not be as completely destroyed as it was on the earlier highways, the financial loss may be even greater because of much greater investment in the modern highway. Those bottleneck conditions are not necessary. Modern planning and land-use control techniques—zoning, subdivision regulation, development rights acquisition—can prevent roadside litter. But the pressure to build urban highways has been enormous, and these planning techniques have not been fully, nor properly, used.

The planner asks: Should we continue to ignore the lessons of the past? Should we even start to build an urban expressway until we have assured ourselves that the tremendous public investment is protected as fully as we can possibly protect it? (Part of the problem here

comes from divided governmental jurisdiction. The design and construction of the highway is the responsibility of the state and federal
governments; land-use controls are the responsibility of local government.)

One of the most serious criticisms of urban highway location is that
the designers have ignored urban communities and the importance of
preserving a community wherever possible. The danger of the straight
line principle of design for urban highways through developed areas is
that urban communities can be destroyed. Churches can be amputated
from their parishes. Community shopping districts can be cut off from
their market areas. Urban highway designers are getting a reputation
for being ruthless. The social costs of many highways have been ignored. At times there have been indirect public costs that also were
ignored, such as the cost of making a school building obsolete by
dividing its district. The planner knows that any structure on the scale
of a modern urban highway cannot always avoid injuring and disrupting urban communities, parishes, and school districts, but he asks a
softening of the straight line principle of location to preserve some of
the irreplaceable values of urban communities and to avoid unnecessary bisections of other areas.

Closely related is the problem of the highway and the individual
property owner. With right-of-way widths up to a thousand or more
feet, with interchanges requiring hundreds of acres of land, the size of
the urban highway is such that hundreds and thousands of people
must be dispossessed.

So-called slum areas have special attraction for urban highway
locations: first, because slums are generally found ringing the central
business district, the chief traffic generator in a city; and second,
because there is a feeling, in large part justified, that in the destruction
of slum dwellings, the highway destroys the least valuable buildings in
the city. We have learned through bitter experience that relocating the
persons whose homes and stores are demolished in a clearance operation is so difficult, and so politically explosive, that because of it the
whole urban renewal program has been killed in many cities and has
been slowed down in nearly all others. The magnitude of the urban
highway program is such that the number of persons who must be relocated may eventually exceed the number relocated through the urban renewal program, if indeed, it has not already done so.

The social—and the political—implications of relocation are much
greater than highway planners had generally realized. The planner

asks: Should not the relocation plan be worked out as carefully and as completely as the design of the interchanges? Should not the same attention be given to equitable compensation for the appropriation of social values and human rights as is given for the appropriation of property values?

There is probably no highway department in the nation that commits all the sins I have catalogued. The purpose of this paper has been to isolate and give emphasis to the general planning factors, to serve as a checklist of the many nonengineering considerations that should enter into guiding urban development. Many of the questions raised call for decisions that are not in the province of the engineer or the highway department—they are decisions that can only be made by a legislative body. This may be the city council, but it also may be the state assembly, or the Congress of the United States.

Improved motor vehicular transportation is indispensable in the life of the city and of the nation. The motor vehicle has completely reshaped our cities, and the future of our cities will be determined by it. The magnitude of the motor vehicle as an economic force makes it particularly important that we take special precautions to avoid needless injury to cities, our institutions, and our people.

A State-Level Board for Highway Disputes

Condensed from "Organization of Intergovernmental Relations," a paper given at the 43rd Annual Meeting of the Highway Research Board, Washington, D.C., January 16, 1964. (Prepared with the assistance of Jack Noble, editor, ASPO *Zoning Digest*.)

A particularly familiar and important type of intergovernmental problem is the potential (and too often realized) conflict between a state highway department—the action agency in most highway programs—and a community affected by a highway department proposal: the disagreements over route location, over whether a freeway should be depressed or elevated, or just where an interchange is needed.

How should our institutions seek to resolve these conflicts? The primary objective, of course, should be cooperation among the affected governments. There has been general recognition and widespread discussion of the need for all units of government to cooperate in meeting urban transportation needs, and we have made some progress. By formal devices such as public hearings and informal ones such as continuing staff contacts and very early consultations on project proposals, many differences between state and local viewpoints have been compromised before conflict ever came to a head. Perhaps more important in the long run, a great deal of education has taken place, with the result that planners and engineers are now doing at least a slightly better job of understanding each others' viewpoints. We seem to be on the right road; all we must do is move along it faster.

A significant push in the right direction was provided by the 1962 Federal-Aid Highway Act, the section requiring federally aided highway projects initiated in urban areas after July 1, 1965 to be "based on a continuing comprehensive transportation planning process carried on cooperatively by States and local communities." There is some question as to how effectively the act can *force* cooperation or truly adequate planning. The workable program requirement of the urban renewal legislation was not a notable success in those communities whose only interest was to meet minimum federal requirements. Too often the form of planning is present but the substance is missing. The highway act provision should nevertheless be of great benefit, if only because it calls attention to the need for cooperative planning and causes states and local governments to set up additional channels within which cooperation can take place.

What happens though, if state and local officials do not reach agreement? At present, if we look only at the state statutes, it appears that the state highway department will prevail in one group of states, the local government in others. Statutes in a number of states give state highway departments authority to build certain types of highways within cities despite objections or disagreement by city authorities. The statutes may require various types of cooperation with city officials—perhaps notice or various kinds of hearings—but the final decision is left to the highway department.

Other statutes go to the opposite extreme. They require municipal approval of state highway projects within cities. A substantive municipal veto power may result even in the absence of such a statute if certain local action—such as the vacation of a local street—is required before the new highway may be built, and the locality has complete discretion to take or refuse the needed action.

In practice, of course, the statutes do not tell the whole story. The highway department facing a local veto may exert pressure by threatening to abandon the project or to place it low on the priority list. On the other hand, the objecting local officials may invoke political pressure by running to legislators or congressmen. The important point, though, is that there is no formal mechanism available to resolve these disputes, nobody to act as judge or arbitrator. There should be.

In the first place, any given stretch of major highway in an urban area is likely to be an integral part of an overall statewide or regional transportation net and also part of the transportation net within the urban area. Under these circumstances—and the division of metropolitan areas into many small localities intensifies the problem—it seems an oversimplification to let either the state or local view prevail automatically in the event of disagreement. It seems equally unsatisfactory to permit the decisions to be made through shadowy, informal or political channels. In the second place, there is more at stake in these disagreements than state and local transportation plans. Many of the disputes resemble the most common kind of land-use disputes. That is, they represent a conflict between the need for a particular facility and the objections to that facility because of its effects on the adjacent community.

There are, of course, elaborate legal procedures to deal with an impasse in land-use dispute. A regional shopping center, for example, a project that has the same enormous impact on its surroundings that a freeway has, will be subject to local zoning. In practice, some form of legislative zoning decision by the local government—an amendment of the ordinance, a review and acceptance of the design—will ordinarily be needed before the center can be built. This will subject the proprietor to an "ordeal by public hearing," during which his views, those of his neighbors, and those of local officials will all be aired. Thereafter, the local governing body will make its decision. Although serious doubts have been expressed about the adequacy and fairness of zoning procedures, and numerous suggestions have been made to improve them, the existence of the process is worthy of note. As is the fact that the decision is subject to judicial review—a very searching judicial review in some states.

There is a difference between public and private projects, but it is easy to exaggerate the difference. Controls of private development are justified on the theory that private developers are usually selfish and without concern for the community at large. But public projects, this argument would run, are designed to benefit the public and are proposed by boards or individuals ultimately subject to the electorate. This approach must be rejected. We had better recognize the fact that a public agency responsible for a particular project can generally be expected to weight the importance of building it more heavily than the detrimental effects that its construction may have on the surrounding area. Local governments have been known to build garages for their garbage trucks in the midst of their own best residential areas just because the site was convenient and the land was cheap. And when a government agency, such as a road building agency, spends most of its time on a particular type of public facility, it is understandable that the agency develops a certain momentum—or bias—that is extremely difficult to overcome.

Some state road-building agencies have done a creditable job of integrating planners into their organizations—a better job, probably, than many local planning agencies have done in using engineering in the preparation of their local traffic plans. Hopefully, the addition of planners has increased the concern of highway agencies for community effects of proposed facilities. The fact remains, though, that the primary responsibility of highway departments (and this includes the planners as well as the engineers) is to build highways. And it is not clear that the decision between getting the most road for the public dollar, and considering the welfare of the adjacent community, is always best reached by an interested highway department official. The problem is made no easier when it is realized that money for highway building normally comes from earmarked funds, which results in a definite reduction in the legislative control compared with that which exists in some other areas of governmental activity.

I do not argue that state highway programs should be subject to local land-use controls. Anyone who has dealt with many local officials will recognize that they (and sometimes their planner employees) too often fail to see the big picture—too often want to protect the status quo even it means excluding a vitally needed public project. As the interests of individual suburban communities increasingly diverge from those of metropolitan areas as a whole, this problem becomes increasingly serious. In fact, in such areas we must recognize three parties of interest in a state highway program: the metropolitan community as well as the state and the particular city.

The impracticality of complete local control has been recognized by the one group of statutes that has established machinery designed to reconcile the need for particular public facilities with the adverse effects of those facilities. These statutes, based on the Standard City Planning Enabling Act issued by the Department of Commerce in 1928, require that plans for any type of public facility—often including state highways—be submitted for approval by the plan commission of each affected locality. If the plan commission disapproves, however, the proposed facility may nevertheless be built if two-thirds of the membership of the governmental body proposing the facility votes to overrule the commission. Thus, it appears that the drafter of the standard act recognized, quite properly, that a local veto is not practical.

These considerations, then, lead me to conclude that neither the action agency nor the objecting municipality should be given the power of final decision in those cases reaching a true impasse.

What is needed is a new institution not specifically identified with either contending agency; one with a breadth of view enabling it to see all sides of the picture. This new institution should be a board at the state level, modeled on federal regulatory commissions such as the Interstate Commerce Commission or the Federal Power Commission. Like these agencies, the board's power should be subject only to broad policy standards established by the legislature. The board would be required to consider presentations by the action agency, municipal objectors, and others. The board would then have power to make a final and binding decision.

Although I know of no exact precedent for such a board, there are some useful analogies. In some states, although public utilities are subject to local zoning regulations, state public utility commissions are authorized by statute to grant exemptions from local regulations. In New Jersey, for example, such an exemption may be granted if the board of public utility commissioners finds that "the present or proposed situation of the building or structure in question is reasonably necessary for the service, convenience or welfare of the public." And New Jersey court decisions have spelled out fairly precisely the nature of the matters that the board must consider in applying this standard.

We can infer that the legislators wanted neither the utility nor the locality to make the final decisions. Statutes such as this are particularly interesting for our purpose because of the great similarity of the land-use questions presented by, say, an electric power transmission line and a highway.

The Ontario [Canada] Municipal Board offers another analogy worth studying. That board considers a variety of municipal questions—annexation, assessments, bond authorization, various planning decisions, and zoning. The procedure is simple enough. Certain municipal decisions must by law be submitted to the Municipal Board for approval. The board gives notice to all concerned, hears evidence and arguments, and hands down its decision. There is no doubt that the Municipal Board and its work are highly regarded. It is usually possible to obtain a hearing before the board within a month or two. In minor cases, board decisions are frequently handed down right at the hearing. And in important cases, decisions are usually forthcoming within a few weeks.

Still another analogy may be the boards established in a few states to pass on annexation questions. These boards, like the Ontario Municipal Board, are primarily concerned with review of actions contemplated or taken by a single municipality, although intermunicipal conflict is often involved.

An institution of the type proposed, if established to deal with highway disputes, would rapidly come to be used for a number of other state-local and intermunicipal disputes as well. At present, although there is an increasing realization among planners of the need for some land-use control authority other than local governments—particularly in metropolitan areas—no agency is now available to perform the needed review functions. For the resolution of controversy, the courts are the only recourse, and their experience in intergovernmental disputes is not extensive nor particularly sophisticated. In addition to land-use control questions, annexation matters could also very easily be assigned to such a board.

A board of this type will not be an unmixed blessing. There will be a danger of the board being biased (as regulatory commissions are often accused of being) or of abusing its broad powers. The method of appointment of board members can become a seriously debated point, although this problem has been faced—and apparently resolved—in the case of the federal and state regulatory agencies. As the boards become more experienced, it would presumably become possible for state legislatures to lay down more detailed policy standards to guide board decisions.

There would also be—and this could easily be the most serious problem of all—a problem of delay. Existing procedures sometimes delay private developments for years, and such delays of vital links in urban highway networks would not be acceptable. The magnitude of administrative delays would have to be continually examined as the boards operated. Certainly, highway disputes should be assigned higher priority than most of the other types of disputes that these boards might be assigned. And an adequate staff to handle the disputes would have to be provided by state legislatures. However, in view of the vast amounts of money being spent on urban highways, and in view of the incalculable effects these highways can have on our cities for decades or even centuries to come, there is a strong argument for instituting such a formal process even if *some* delays do result. With expeditious handling, the delays should not be so long that the processing would do more harm than good.

To be realistic about public planning, inadequacies exist—inadequacies in staff, in preparation, in real knowledge of the variables. There is often a complete lack of local consensus on a particular problem and its solution. The intuition of local politicians is no match for the precision of an engineering presentation. Yet this should not discourage us. The doctrine of "put up or shut up" will be invoked. Planners as well as highway engineers will be forced into a deeper and more accurate understanding of the urban development process.

The hope is that, in conjunction with the state-local cooperation now developing in the highway field, it may be possible to devise a new institution to settle disputes when cooperation fails. Once established, this same institution could also turn part of its attention to the increasingly serious intermunicipal disputes which there is now no machinery to resolve. We have long had tribunals to regulate conflicts among private interests and conflict between private interests and public ones. We should at least try a similar approach in reconciling disputes between public agencies that have differing views of the public interest.

The Automobile

Quoted from "The Future of Planning in
Puerto Rico," a speech to the Puerto Rico
Planning Board, August 10, 1967.

The most insatiable appetite for land is that of the automobile. It takes
only about five lineal miles of expressway to consume—literally eat
up—one square mile of land. The land we consume per auto is greater
than the land we use per human being.

Auto population has skyrocketed. It will continue to increase as the
economy continues to improve, demanding more highways, more
streets, more parking lots and garages. And more highways and more
parking lots breed more cars which in turn demand still more streets
and parking lots. It is a vicious circle, one that is especially fright-
ening.

The automobile not only uses excessive quantities of land itself, but
the auto is also responsible for making sprawl possible, for making it
attractive. So the land consumption effects of a runaway increase in
motor vehicles are multiplied. It is a clear example of a factor that affects development, that extends throughout the economy, and that
has terrific social overtones.

An obvious policy is to keep down auto ownership: birth control
for rubber tires. The decision to carry out this policy could be to keep
the auto population under control by taxation—auto license fees,
gasoline tax. Of course, a limitation on private auto transport must be
compensated for by a positive program of adequate public transportation.

7

Communicating: What We Need and What We Don't

Editor's Commentary

Dennis O'Harrow as communicator was continually acclaimed by hundreds of congratulatory letters, by frequent press coverage, by extensive reprinting and distribution of his speeches and articles. As commenter on communicating, he had specific prescriptions—and prejudices.

The planner as educator is a recurring prescription. These selections deal with how, as well as why, the planner must attend to this high priority.

On poor writing and jargon, his plain talk is almost merciless. DOH was a determined foe of planners' gobbledygook, of such tortured phrases as "empirically verifiable relationships in the goal-program-consequence triad." When a Vocabulary Drill was established in the 1967 ASPO *Newsletter* as a follow-up to his "Notes for Webster," he was an ardent contributor to the list, discovering new favorites such as *tutee* (which he suggested should be defined as "the person who is tuted—or tutated—by a tutor"); *prioritize the work* (which "then would lead to a system of prioritization"); and *underincomed, statisticized* and *committeeized* (his comments on which are unprintable).

On the avalanche of words he was prejudiced, but he also prescribed. His "What Price Half-Life" turned out to be one of those instances when a concept of his coined a phrase: "What's its half-life?" is still being asked when a new book or report appears.

As for humor, he thought it particularly essential for planners, who "are always exposed to the danger of taking themselves too seriously—the problems they try to solve are serious and progress slow." His own sense of it, and the response to his use of it, are a persuasive demonstration that we need it.

For some specific other needs, DOH was able to go beyond commenting and act through innovative ASPO programs. For example:

To encourage more effective newspaper reporting of planning and thereby improve understanding and support, ASPO established an annual award "for public service rendered in the advancement of city and regional planning through outstanding journalism."

To increase communication of U.S. planning knowledge to planning students in developing countries, the ASPO Conference Book Exhibits of some 200 titles were donated to a planning school.

To assist communication between planning students and pros, the annual conferences featured sessions including students as speakers.

Two other actions on communicating should be noted—programs and policies instituted by ASPO's first executive director, Walter Blucher, and continued with high priority by DOH: use of plain talk in ASPO's own publications, readiness to travel, to prepare speeches, and to serve as educator and communicator over and over again.

The Planner as Educator

**Explaining Planning, extracted from
"Simplicity in Planning" a speech at the
annual meeting of the Stark County
Regional Planning Commission,
Canton, Ohio, January 14, 1959.**

I am sometimes sheepish about the behavior of my fellow planners. I find many of them less than clear in their writing and speaking.

The overwhelming majority of practitioners in the planning profession are intellectually honest and are not deliberately trying to confuse the citizens. What we often do, however, is to get so involved in trying to solve the problems that are handed to us that when we speak about them, write about them, or seek public action on them, we forget that our audience has not been steeped in our problem in all of its ramifications for 24 hours a day, 7 days a week, 52 weeks a year, as we have been.

If a planner spends one month making surveys and digging up statistics to get background data on a particular problem, then presents the information to a plan commission for their advice and decision on a course of action, he had better not present it in such a manner that it would also take his commissioners one solid month to understand and digest his researches before they make their decisions. They don't have that kind of time. Nor can the planning commission or planner give a problem to a group of citizens and expect them to get a background in planning before they give their advice. In all of the contacts between planners and plan commissioners and zoning board members and citizens, planners must be sure that the conversations are in the same language, that when people are asked for opinions, they are asked in areas in which they have competence and background to *have* opinions.

What this adds up to is that a most important aspect of a planning operation is education. I do not believe in the idea of "selling" planning. I do believe in *explaining* planning proposals as clearly as possible. And by "planning proposals" I mean those rational government action proposals that seem to be the best solution to public problems, either today's or tomorrow's. This is one type of education: the people who must make governmental decisions have learned—have been given the best possible background education on which to base their decision.

There is a second phase to education in planning, however, that I think is neglected. While the basic ideas in planning are always simple, the methodology, the techniques, the legal tools of planning, are most complex. If you want these tools used wisely and efficiently, in the best interests of the city, the county or the region, then you had better train those citizens and board members directly involved in using these tools.

You can get a lot of good help on community problems from citizens, particularly from citizen members of advisory committees and zoning and planning boards. You can improve the quality and increase the quantity of this help by stating your problems and possible solutions clearly so that people can understand them. You can get even better help by making a conscious effort to train interested citizens in the techniques of planning and zoning.

"Information Theory," an ASPO Newsletter editorial, October 1961.

A recent mathematical tool that is being used to rescue us from some of our excesses is *information theory*. One application of this theory is in the storage of written material. For example, it is now theoretically possible, because we understand something about units of information, to store all the words in all the books in the Library of Congress in the space of one cubic yard—about the storage room in five four-drawer files.

There is little prospect that the Library of Congress will be condensed to sardine status. Nevertheless, scientific knowledge in the more active fields is doubling each five years. The problem of storing and making accessible this quantity of material is one of the most difficult we have. But information theory can give us some insights into other problems of communication besides storage.

Information theory starts off simply, but quite rapidly gets involved in mathematics of a high order of difficulty. The use of the ideas has gone far beyond fields we customarily associate with the word *information*. In biology, of all places, the theory promises to aid scientists immeasurably with their most difficult problems in understanding disease.

There are three ideas of information theory that are reasonably easy to explain, without the benefit of mathematics, and which seem useful in many ways.

The first idea is simply that a communication requires both a *transmitter* and a *receiver*, and that you cannot have any measure of the effectiveness of a communication unless you consider both ends of the operation.

For example, take the following message:

FNAR EEEA MMHP IDTR TOOI EOTE HGEH TLMT SLOF IACO WROX OODY NTIT

The transmitter is perfect, the message has been sent without error. But the receiver (which is you, the reader) has been unable to translate it. It is a simple cipher and can be broken pretty quickly by anyone with a rudimentary knowledge of cryptography. But certainly there has been no communication to begin with.

If we look at the following message, however, we decipher it almost immediately.

NXW IS THX XXMX FOR AXX GXXD MEX TO COXX TO THX AIX XX THEXX PAXXY.

Here 20 of the 51 letters are incorrect, yet the message comes through without difficulty. Why? Because you, the receiver, were able to supply from your own knowledge the information needed to complete the message, whereas in the first message, the receiver is not immediately able to rearrange the letters into recognizable English. (Incidentally, the facts intended to be transmitted are the same in both examples.)

A second basic idea in the information theory is that of *noise*. Noise is extraneous, irrelevant matter that gets mixed up with the transmission of all information. Noise is confusing and distracting, and when it gets bad enough, we are unable to receive and interpret the message.

In our second example, there was noise (the letter *X*) but it was a monotone (always the same thing) and did not confuse us too much—

NXW IS THX XXMX . . .

If instead of a monotone, the noise had been varied, with random signals in the place of the silent spaces between words—

NKWRISETHMTEOML . . .

we would have had something completely unintelligible and unrecognizable.

In the first of these two phrases, we had a *signal-to-noise* ratio of 2 to 1—10 intelligible characters (including silent spaces) to 5 unintelligible characters. In the second, the signal-to-noise ratio is 7 to 8, noise outweighs the valid characters.

The third simple idea is that *redundancy* can be an aid to the transmission of information. If you say the same thing two or three different ways, you have two or three chances to get the information across and to counteract the effect of noise that might mask out part of your message. This is an old idea that is pushed to the ultimate by one of the formulas recommended for composing speeches: "First, tell 'em what you are going to tell 'em, then tell 'em, and finally, tell 'em what you told 'em." The value of redundancy is also the excuse for the slavish devotion of hucksters to the repetition of advertising slogans.

There is more, a lot more, to information theory than these three ideas. But these three can be useful in preparing and transmitting information—information on planning, for example.

First, there is the transmission and reception problem. The planning commission, its directors, a consultant—these are the transmitters. The citizens, the mayor and council, at times the planning commission itself—these are the receivers. The message that goes forth from the transmitter must be one that the receiver is capable of accepting and understanding.

You cannot send a message in a strange code and expect it to deliver information to anyone not equipped to translate that code readily. In short, the message must rid itself of planning jargon which is not intelligible to anyone but another planner—and frequently not even to him. Also, information must be in language as specific and concrete as it is possible to make it. Sweeping generality is one of the great weaknesses of planning talk. Sweeping generalities induce sleep, not understanding.

Then there is the problem of noise which obscures the meaning of the message. The signal-to-noise ratio must be as large as we can make it. Some noise is generated by the transmitter. This is the planning report that is fat and full of tables, most of which are sound and fury, signifying nothing other than that the planner spent hours in front of a calculator. This also will jam the transmission so that the receiver finds it difficult to sort out the bits of information that are important.

Another source of noise, however, comes from outside. This is the noise created by those who do not understand or do not wish to understand, the irrelevancies of the special interest groups, the wails of the myopic. This noise is not easy to avoid, often it is impossible to avoid. The ideal solution is to prevent the noisy ones from broadcasting. But usually this cannot be done, so that the best hope is to present the planning message as clearly as possible—and to repeat it.

Repetition of the same message can become boring and actually produce the opposite of its intended effect, Madison Avenue to the contrary notwithstanding. Continuous verbatim repetition is not the type of redundancy that necessarily follows from information theory. Instead, the effective method is to say the same thing in several different ways.

Your plan calls for a new park sometime in the future. It is first shown as a part of the total recreational plan. Then it shows up in the appropriate neighborhood plan. Again, the park appears as a future project of the capital improvement program. It appears in published reports and in the speeches of the planner and his commissioners. It may be combined with the plan for a new school, it affects the thoroughfare plan. It is brought up in relation to zoning amendments and new subdivisions. It can even enter into political campaigns. This is redundancy, but not hypnotic repetition.

The effective transmission of information requires conscious effort. It does not take place automatically as a by-product of human effort. Transmission and reception are separate and apart from the content of the message. They cannot be left to chance. A little thought given to the problems and techniques can pay dividends in increased understanding.

"Sharon Biedelmaier's Grandmother," extracted from the ASPO Newsletter editorial, April 1963.

A basic responsibility of a newspaper editor is to select news stories that will interest and that will seem important to his readers. Take these headlines from a suburban weekly:

Junior High Will Present Mikado

Church Women Plan Dinner for Husbands

Pi Omicron Pi Alumnae Hold Annual Meeting

Biggs Road Residents Question Sewer Costs

Sharon Biedelmaier Plights Troth

High School Board Ok's Purchase of 30 Tables

and, of course,

Trojans Face Vikings in Crucial Match.

Nary a word about Cuba, the Common Market, agricultural sur-
pluses, or the population explosion.

These news items seem pitifully insignificant. Who cares what the
POP girls do, except another POP girl? Who takes seriously the purchase of 30 tables for the high school except the salesman who got the
order, and the other salesmen who did not get the order?

A lot of people. If they are not POP girls or table salesmen, they are
the proud parents of the quavery soprano who will sing the part of
Cho-Cho-San, or the irate residents of Biggs Road, or Sharon Biedelmaier's grandmother. A small-town editor who overlooks this will not
keep his job very long.

In the metropolitan newspaper there will be stories on the Common
Market and the corn surplus. But there will also be the little stories.
The Trojans and Vikings will still face a crucial match. Sharon Biedelmaier will still plight her troth, and although Sharon may have had a
$50,000 coming-out party instead of getting married the day after high
school graduation, Sharon Biedelmaier's grandmother is still as important to the metropolitan editor as she is to the small-town editor.

Bad editing or, more accurately, insensitive editing is a weakness
that planning agencies must beware of. Burnham to the contrary notwithstanding, the hearts of most men are stirred less by the plan for a
multimillion dollar sewage treatment plant than by the $20,000 sewer
improvement that will run by their own front doors. The blobby "gen-
eralized land-use plan" is much less interesting than the proposed service station in the next block. In even the largest cities, the planning
agency (if it is not too independent nor too extramural) is going to
hear from its constituents. The city council will take a personal interest in any proposal that involves spending city funds, and in any proposal that will affect the voting pattern. The neighbors will want all

the little details about any monkey business with zoning in their neighborhood.

When the editor forgets Sharon Biedelmaier's grandmother too often, his publisher gets a new editor—the mayor replaces his planning director. In the world of newspapers, excuses are not acceptable, nor will they continue to be acceptable (if they even now are) in the world of planning. A city plan must eventually be related to the individual lot, the individual taxpayer, the individual voter. A metropolitan plan must be tied into each city and village in the metropolitan area.

If we want planning to succeed, not to be a fascinating intellecutal exercise, we must make it interesting and meaningful to people whom we expect to live by, and to carry out, our plans.

We must not forget Sharon Biedelmaier's grandmother.

"Newcomers to Planning," extracted from the ASPO Newsletter editorial, January 1962.

What we are likely to forget about persons discovering planning, or coming into a planning agency, is that they are newcomers. Those who have been longer in the business must teach, must consciously help the newcomer to understand. But planning is a peculiar activity and there can be a great deal more to this than just instruction for the newcomer.

In planning there are few, if any, absolutes. And the questions of the young planner, or the new commissioner, can serve another purpose besides the enlightenment of the questioner. All of us who have been a long time in planning should be put through a catechism by our juniors with some regularity. Otherwise, we get to mouthing the same old platitudes without using a single gray cell to think about what we are saying. We who preach that only by planning can we keep up with the change of the world are apt to be outstanding examples of the *status quo* in our own ideas.

So welcome the newcomer and talk to him. Tell him what he wants to know. Maybe in the telling you will learn a few things yourself.

The Planner as Communicator

**Ideas and Honesty, quoted from "Plan Talk
and Plain Talk" a speech at the Southern
California Planning Congress, Pasadena,
January 7, 1958.**

A city plan is a collection of ideas, and these ideas are presented symbolically in words, charts, maps. These ideas—when they are worth anything—are the results of investigations and calculations, of tight logical thinking and inspired dreaming. First and most important, there must be ideas—honest ideas, honestly arrived at. When you put them into the symbols of language and pictures, present them honestly. Don't try hocus-pocus, don't pretend that you have something that you don't have, don't try to impress people.

**Notes for Webster 4, extracted from the
ASPO Newsletter editorial "From the Backs
of Old Envelopes," December 1966.**

Dialogue. Originally *dialogue* meant a conversation between two persons. Plato reported the dialogues between Socrates and his pupils, one at a time. There were many teams that specialized in dialogue: Potash and Perlmutter, Weber and Fields, Burns and Allen, Mutt and Jeff. The meaning of the word was warped later to include all the conversation in a drama, or in a novel or a short story, where it was good or bad according to whether you were entertained by it, realistic or unrealistic according to whether you thought people really talked that way.

Now *dialogue* has been taken up as the name you give to yak-yak by any number of persons on any subject that is vague enough to make sure that nothing of value can come out of the yakking. *Dialogue* sounds better than the more descriptive, but less elegant barnyard term. Dialogues are usually conducted on a high level, which is further assurance of vacuity.

The cause for the change in meaning of this word is not clear, but it may have come from the famous Abbott and Costello dialogue (origi-

nal meaning) about "Who's on first," or from an older exchange between two persons that went like this:

"What've you got on under there?"

"Under where?"

"Under there."

"Underwear."

"Under there!"

"Underwear!"

"Under there!!!"

And so on.

Concept. The word *concept* is used as a substitute for "thought" or
"idea," and is highly favored in planning jargon. It is a word remarkable for its propensity to expand by accretion. *Concept* has already
passed up the classic *comment—commentator—commentating* and
should set a record that will stand for a long time.

From *concept* we went to *conceptual*, which apparently means
something that really does not exist except in someone's mind. Next,
we had *conceptualize*, which probably means to think about things
that really do not exist except in your mind as you think about them.
From this we naturally got *conceptualization*, which could mean the
act (mental) of thinking about things that do not really exist except in
the act of thinking about these things. It becomes more and more difficult to understand the meaning of the word as it adds more and more
suffixes, but we should try to distinguish *conceptualization* from the
actual things that do not exist except as we think about them, which
are *concepts*—an important distinction if you can make it.

The next step, of course, is to form the verb *conceptualizate* from
the noun *conceptualization*. From this it is only a short step to the *conceptualizator*, one who *conceptualizates*.

Some may say that if the *concept* means "thought" or "idea," then a
conceptualizator is a person who has thoughts and brings forth ideas,
and you might even call him a *thinker*. However, it should be
recognized that what issues from a *conceptualizator* are *concepts* and
the production of concepts has little resemblance to thinking. Therefore, it appears that the term will and should survive.

Other planning words that appear ready for expansion are *imple-
ment—implementator*, *viable—viabalate*, and *thrust—thrustization*.

The Sign Is on the Land, quoted from the ASPO Newsletter editorial "Publish or Perish," February 1963.

One of these days, we shall have urban research funds measured in the millions of dollars, perhaps tens of millions. Who knows, perhaps hundreds of millions of dollars. Out of this fertile compost heap we shall grow a group of urban scientists. They will have all the characteristics of the physical and biological and space scientists. They, too, will obey the immutable law of researchers everywhere: publish or perish. They, too, will publish, publish, publish. They, too will belabor the obvious.

The jargon journals will proliferate, the mail bags will sag lower with printed reports. The output of drivel will mount and mount. The sign is already on the land.

Dear Author, quotes from some manuscript reviews.

If it can be revised, cut to half or less its present length, shorn of technical terms, repetition, and lengthy excursions into the theory of administration and government, it can be a useful and salable book.

*   *   *

As I think back over my reading of the manuscript, I believe that I was unconsciously trying to edit out an enormous amount of irrelevancy, searching for the ostensible subject of the book. This was hard to find through the jargon, nevertheless I kept hoping it was there.

*   *   *

Is there a shortage of periods—or is it that there are just too many words?

*   *   *

While I do not believe it needs to be written in a popular vein, I do suggest that if possible you lighten the prose up. It is pretty heavy going, especially after a hard day at the office.

**At the Top of the List, quoted from the
speech "What Kind of Training Do Public
Agencies Require of the Planners They
Hire?" given at a conference on planning
education at Wayne State University,
Detroit, Michigan, October 15, 1953.**

I believe that the success, or lack of it, that a planning director has will
have less relation to his technical training than to certain other abilities which are rarely mentioned when a city seeks to employ planners.
At the top of this list I would put, approximately equal in importance,
the ability to write and the ability to speak in public.

Public agencies hire planners as persons who devise, propose, and
accomplish improvements in city operation and development. The
first step, devising the scheme, calls for technical city planning training and experience. But presentation and the accomplishment of the
scheme calls for abilities in communication and persuasion which are
not customarily listed as requirements for a planning job.

You don't have to write like John Steinbeck or Red Smith, and you
don't have to be able to speak as well as Adlai Stevenson II. But unless
you can do a better than passable job in both of these, you aren't going to function very well as a planner. And I will say unequivocally
that the graduates of city planning schools that I have seen recently
have had this part of their training shamefully neglected.

The Avalanche . . . and Ways to
Avoid Engulfment

**"Form and Content: or You Don't Have to
Eat the Whole Egg," quoted from the
editorial in the Association of State Planning
and Development Agencies Newsletter,
November 1949.**

Over my desk there passes each year an avalanche of words. During
the course of a decade, the amount of printed material received would

literally bury this office building, if it were not for frequent and strong-minded disposal. I must select. And that means I must have standards by which to choose to read some publications, scan others, and put the rest in the circular file under the desk.

The form influences me. The first purpose of any published material is to get itself read. The publication must, by its form and appearance, make me want to read it.

But form includes more than physical appearance; it includes also the organization of the work and the style and level of writing. I may be drawn into the examination of a booklet by its layout only to bog down for lack of a table of contents or readable English.

Ideas that are not clearly communicated are not worth the psycho-electric energy that generated them.

"What Price Half-Life?," an ASPO Newsletter editorial, March 1965.

In 1898 the Curies discovered the first new radioactive element, which they named *polonium*. They then found that within six months *polonium* had lost half its radioactivity. At the end of the second six months, the radioactivity was halved again, down to one-fourth of the original potency.

When you measure the loss of radioactivity this way—half lost after a certain period of time, then half of what is left lost in the next similar period, then half again in the same time—you never actually come to an end. But eventually you come to a stage where the radioactivity is so minute that you can no longer measure it.

The Curies' second element, *radium*, proved to have a much slower rate of decay. They calculated it would take about 1,600 years for radium to lose half of its radioactivity.

The concept of a geometrical rate of decay has been given the short-hand term of "half-life." In the 70 or so years of investigation of radio-active phenomena, the half-life concept has proved its usefulness over a remarkable range—from *Uranium I*, with a half-life of 450 million years, to the *theta meson*, with a half-life of one ten-billionth of a second.

Measurement in terms of half-life is a concept applicable to things that are not actually consumed by being used, but which do lose their usefulness with the passage of time. Thus you would not need the half-life concept for bananas, because a banana is gone when it is eaten. But half-life is the only proper way to measure the continued usefulness of a book—or rather, of the ideas contained in a book. The ideas are not consumed the first time someone reads the book, they can be transmitted again and again from the same book.

The medium used to transmit an idea gives an easy first approximation of the value of an idea. Thus the half-life of a newspaper is quite short, perhaps no more than four hours. (Use of one-star, two-star, late-market, late-race results, and other editions seems to cut this half-life even more.)

The half-life of speeches has a wide range. The Independence Day oration that The Hon. Philemon T. Bugsby gave at Tompkins Grove in 1911 probably had a half-life considerably shorter than the time it took The Hon. Philemon to declaim it—especially if the speech was followed by fireworks.

But take the speech given by Patrick Henry in Richmond on March 23, 1775: "As for me, give me liberty or give me death." Who knows what the half-life of this would be—500 years? 1,000 years?

In any measurement of the usefulness of ideas we must also recognize that the timing is quite important. Certainly the beginning of the last quarter of the 18th century was a remarkably appropriate time to talk about liberty. For ideas on a less-exalted plane: 1916 proved to be an apt time to introduce comprehensive zoning, 1933 was appropriate to get cracking on slum clearance.

It often seems impossible to escape the flood of printed and spoken words that pours out of the presses and over radio and television and at endless meetings and congresses and seminars. The only way to avoid engulfment is to recognize the fact of geometrical rate of decay, that the average half-life of the ideas in this flood is quite short, that any worthwhile idea will come to the top, and that in the long run you are not likely to miss anything important.

In the documentation of material—in the classifying, indexing, and storage of printed matter—the concept of half-life is quite important, but not often adequately appreciated. Documentation tends to embalm and preserve great quantities of stuff that were better left to disappear through the natural processes of decay. There is much to be said for book-burning.

As a finale, we indicate how this editorial would fare when we measure it by using its half-life.

First, the single idea that this article intends to set forth: The ideas contained in books, speeches, articles, reports in planning (or any other field) are forgotten and tend to become useless very rapidly; they lose their value at a geometrical rate, best expressed through a measurement of their "half-life."

We now assume that this article will be read by 4,000 persons, half the circulation of the *ASPO Newsletter*. We also assume that it has a half-life of one month. By the end of April, only 2,000 persons will remember any part of the idea; by the end of May only 1,000 persons—in 12 months only one person will recall the idea.

The magnitude of the half-life of an idea is more important to its continued existence than the number of persons exposed to it. Thus, if we doubled the number of readers to 8,000, it would take only 13, instead of 12, months to get to that last person; but if we doubled the half-life to two months, we would have 62 persons recalling the idea of the editorial at the end of the year, instead of only one.

While this idea may be a little depressing to someone who hopes to write deathless prose for the edification of posterity, on the whole, the idea should be encouraging to most people. What it implies is that it really is not all that serious if you *never* get around to ploughing through every deadly dull article in every deadly dull publication that shows up on your desk. The trick is not to judge a book by its cover, but by its probable half-life.

What We All Need: Humor

From a review of *And on the Eighth Day . .* **by Richard Hedman and Fred Bair, Jr., 1961.**

No man who can, and does, laugh at himself occasionally can ever become a tyrant. And it follows, therefore, that if a profession finds time to poke fun at itself, it also cannot become tyrannical. Of course, a "profession" is an abstract concept and the humor must come from certain individuals. Planners are always exposed to the danger of taking themselves too seriously—the problems they try to solve are serious and progress slow. But planners are fortunate in having Bair and Hedman to keep them from going off the deep end. *And on the Eighth Day* is in the noble tradition of planning humor, a logical successor to *Mr. Arbuthnot, The Pharoah and His Planning Board,* and that masterpiece, *The Planners Cul-de-sac.* It is a hilarious (sometimes ghastly) satire, based on the truth, as good satire must be. It should help us, but I am sure that a few planners are going to be shocked into crying "blasphemy!" Nevertheless, we all need it and it should help most of us.

8

Zoning: Why Are We Going Where?

Editor's Commentary

Dennis O'Harrow reported, and was widely publicized for reporting, the flaws of zoning—the theories and techniques he believed basically wrong and the evidence of zoning for sale. But the core of his writing on land-use controls deals with zoning as a creative process; with the need to reject standard answers and "think these things out, painful as it may be"; with ideas on new forms of land-use regulation; with the thesis of the 1961 paper on "Why Are We Going Where" that "tradition must be violated radically if we are to meet the future successfully . . . we may need to violate certain principles of land-use regulation, even of legal philosophy, that we have hitherto held to be sacred."

Another thesis pertinent to current land policy issues is a 1957 comment on the diffidence of government as a competitor for land: government—the people acting through their government—"has permitted itself to be crowded out . . . there must inevitably be a change."

The people, their public officials, and a widening assortment of professions are now coming around to views such as these, and some action is being taken.

A popular current tool, *community impact measurement*, was second nature to DOH—used tellingly, for example, in his 1954 editorial on 100 families (see Chapter 3); in the demonstration of the effects of alternative zoning classifications on a quarter section of land (in this chapter's extracts from the 1955 paper on "Steps to Secure Sound Zoning"), which also includes an early reference to nongrowth policies; and in his 1951 paper on performance standards.

Dennis O'Harrow profoundly changed zoning in 1951 when he formulated a new concept and method—the classification of industries in accordance with their environmental impact. Neither the scientific measurements and specific standards for environmental effects that he proposed, nor application of the theory to commercial and residential uses, have reached their potential, but the principle of performance standards has become an integral concept and component of zoning.

The 1951 seminal paper, and its 1955 follow up analyzing progress and incorporating several caveats on the practical problems of administration, have been only slightly condensed. (The complete texts, plus extracts from zoning ordinances and charts and tables in the 1955 report, are available as ASPO Planning Advisory Service Reports.)

A 1962 paper on the relation of land-use regulation and comprehensive planning pointed to three basic problems: an ever-increasing volume of work due to the change in land-use control administration from a *policing* operation to a sort of *licensing* operation; the division of responsibility among many agencies, not just those directly involved but also the agencies involved in highway construction, school location, water and sewerage, public transit, airports—including those in adjacent jurisdictions; the lack of communication and the lack of understanding of the other fellow's problems and his viewpoint. His proposal (certainly one of the earliest) was "organization of a new planning body, a planning council." He specified a representative body that met regularly to discuss mutual problems, to question and criticize the plans and policies presented by each organization or agency, and stated: "I am completely convinced that more effective comprehensive planning will take place through the means of face-to-face contact and mutual understanding on the part of all persons involved in making decisions that affect land use."

Through his writings on zoning, DOH was an educational force—inventive and with a clarity that extended his reach well beyond the professional planner. Much of this material has been widely quoted or reprinted by newspapers and by magazines in nonplanning fields.

Writing was only one aspect. His educational reach (and his back-up experience) included extensive and direct work on land-use regulation: as a member of numerous committees in government and industry—especially the National Industrial Zoning Committee, and the American Law Institute Planning Law Project to reevaluate public control of land use and draft model legislation; as the author of zoning and subdivision ordinances; as a consultant-critic, expert witness, planning commissioner, and member of a zoning board of appeals; and as a "clearinghouse" for the zoning experiences of individuals and agencies.

For several years, DOH had planned to write a book on zoning, but he found time only for some chapter outlines and a few pages of notes. Thus his contribution to this field remains fragmented, and only glimpses of his book can be seen in the following pages.

Some Principles and Trends

"Principles of Zoning," extracted from the
address to the Women's City Club of New
York series on **"Zoning for a Better City,"**
January 15, 1958.

We know that we live in a world of change, a world ruled also by
Einstein's theory of relativity and Heisenberg's principle of uncertainty. Yet as human beings we cannot be satisfied with change or
with relativity and uncertainty. We demand somewhere some absolutes, something unchanging, something we can depend on for that
feeling of security which our human nature requires. We do not all of
us need, or even believe in, the same absolutes, but nevertheless, we
all select changeless values from among a few categories. We find our
absolute values in God and religion, the family, in learning and
wisdom, in our nation, and—to a greater extent than we realize—in
land. There is reason to believe that as science and civilization have
eroded other absolute value systems, more people have looked to land
as a replacement for those values that have been irretrievably lost.

This attitude toward land as one of the absolutes has given it a
sacred character that makes land-use regulation difficult—always a
touchy subject. As wise judges have learned, there is really no sharp
dividing line between *human* rights and *property* rights. Zoning, the
name we give to a system of regulating the use of land, can be described as a system of governmental interference with property rights.

Zoning is a government regulation imposed on private landowners,
but an even more basic statement of the principle is the conscious control and differentiation of land use, which we find evidence of in even
the most ancient of cities. The idea of segregation was basic to the
whole early theory of zoning. Zoning ordinances that established
zones to segregate and confine the dwellings of minority groups have
been regularly struck down when challenged in court, but the principle of segregating and confining certain kinds of land use to certain
zones is still a dominant principle in all zoning. We do not believe—or
we are learning not to believe—that it is wrong for the laborer or the
man with a different skin color or the man who speaks Spanish to live
next door to the patrician. However, we do have good reason for
believing that businesses and residences, factories and residences, do

not always mix well, and that segregation is indicated. And we have progressed in our land-use controls from complete reliance on the principle of segregation to the idea of *compatibility:* whether two uses are compatible or incompatible determines whether they both should be allowed in the same zoning district.

Segregation, compatibility, what goes in a district and what doesn't go, the rights that a property owner surrenders to (and gains from) the government through zoning—this is the most obvious part of zoning, the effect that the property owner sees and approves of, or objects to. But this is not all that zoning is or does or tries to do.

The zoning ordinances based on a *land-use plan* becomes a legal tool for carrying out the plan—which is actually a general design for the city as we *expect* it or *want* it to develop in the future. While the plan for land use purports to cover only such things as location of residential, business, industrial and recreational areas of the future city, it must be based on and actually recommend a general plan for other urban functions. A sensible recommendation for the location of residential, business and industrial areas must have considered how the residents were going to get from their homes to the factories to work; from their homes to business districts to shop; from their homes to schools and to parks and amusement areas to play. Factories without proper sewer, water, gas and electric services aren't going to function—aren't even going to be built.

This studied, careful approach to future urban development is the prerequisite for good zoning, but there is a growing mass of evidence that we do not have much good zoning in the United States. With the exception of a few and relatively small cities, we have only begun to realize the potential of land-use planning and zoning. This is not something for which we try to find a culprit. The problems of urban expansion have come so fast and are so severe, and our knowledge of how to deal with them has come so slowly and painfully, that it is remarkable we have handled the problems and built our cities as well as we have.

The zoning ordinance applies to the *controllable* future, which is often quite short. The land-use plan applies to the *foreseeable* future, which should be as long a period as we can make it. Some zoning ordinances include provisions that the ordinance be completely reexamined and revised once every five years. I believe that reexamination and revision should be a constant process, started the day after the ordinance is adopted. A new zoning resolution is like a big housecleaning and tidying-up. You get the closets straightened up and the rugs cleaned. You throw away a lot of junk that you thought might come in handy someday. But no matter how clean the house is today, tomorrow there will be a film of dust on the tabletops. The work is never done.

"Steps to Secure Sound Zoning," extracted from a paper given to the Great Lakes States Industrial Development Council, Notre Dame University, South Bend, Indiana, January 7, 1955.

What zoning means can be illustrated by applying zoning to a specific tract of land. Visualize, for example, a quarter section, 160 acres, lying in the direction in which the town seems to be growing. The tract is alongside a principal highway. The topography is reasonably flat, so there are no particular construction problems involved. It is a little beyond the present built-up or building-up section, so there is no obvious pressure on the land at the moment for classification in any certain type of zone. But, it is land that will be developed within the next few years.

If the tract is zoned for single-family residence, at the current popular density of residential development, this 160 acres will eventually house 750 families—slightly less than 5 families per gross acre. In 750 families, there will be 2,500 to 3,000 persons. What does this mean?

For one thing, it means about 750 school children. To meet reasonable standards of education will require 16 to 17 new primary school rooms, 10 to 12 new high school rooms, and about 15 to 20 acres of school land. To serve this residential area, the city will need to supply an additional one-third million gallons of water per day, and it should provide about 15 acres of additional parks and playground just for these 750 families.

(If the 160 acre tract is zoned for apartments, say up to a density of 20 families per acre, you would multiply all these figures by four.)

What is the impact if this quarter section is classified as commercial zoning, and the 160 acres used as a regional shopping center? If you provide the proper amount of off-street parking on the tract, you would be able to get only about 35 to 40 acres of retail sales space, approximately 1.5 million square feet. For such a center to be successful, it would need to be the primary shopping center for a population of approximately 200,000 people living not more than 30 minutes driving distance, and not separated from any of its potential customers by a major natural boundary such as a river. Nor should there be any serious competition for shopping goods within that distance. There would be 5,000 to 6,000 automobiles driving into and out of the parking lot each day, and the roads to the center must be able to handle that kind of traffic.

When we try a third alternative on the quarter section, zoning for industry, it isn't possible to generalize about what will take place, or what is required, as it is with residential or commercial development. Industrial types are much too diverse. Nevertheless, there are some ranges. With modern practices in factory design and location, the quarter section of land would end up with somewhere between 0.5 and 3 million square feet of factory floor space. The number of employees would range somewhere from 2,000 to 25,000.

The facilities needed to supply an industrial development will vary widely. The development may need only enough water for domestic use of the employees while they are on the site, which would run 20 to 40 gallons per day per employee, plus enough reserve water for fire protection. Or it might be a heavy water-using industry requiring a supply on the order of 50 million gallons per day. (The tract is too small for an integrated steel plant, otherwise the range would be 750 to 1,000 million gallons per day.) The problem of industrial waste disposal might be nothing more than minor sanitary waste, or something requiring a phenomenal engineering structure. No matter what industries go in, there must be rail and truck facilities to handle raw materials in and finished products out. Assuming there would be 5,000 employees on the site, the U.S. Chamber of Commerce says this would mean 15,000 more people, 5,600 households, and 5,035 new automobile registrations. The 5,600 new households are about eight times as many as would be on this quarter section of land if it were zoned for residential use. That means two square miles of new residential land, 5,000 more school children, 175 more school rooms, and so on and so on.

You can see from these figures why certain New England towns are desperately seeking for some legal method (they don't even care too much whether it's legal) to halt development of all kinds completely. I wouldn't blame a city for deciding that the highest and best use of this particular quarter section of land is its present use as sheep pasture.

But if the land is in the logical path of development, that 160-acre tract of land will be developed, the city is going to have these problems.

Zoning in a city partially developed takes on exactly the same type of interrelationships, although perhaps on a lesser scale. Rezoning a fully developed area brings up some other problems which are even more difficult to solve. Zoning is not and cannot be an isolated operation.

A weakness in newer zoning regulations—a weakness that has been introduced into the ordinances by planners and zoning experts themselves—is the attempt to include, in one legal document, controls and standards in fields that are not properly within the sphere of zoning and land-use regulation. Most of the time, this is an inadequate job of regulation, these subjects should not be forced into a zoning ordinance. For example, off-street parking requirements should not be in a zoning ordinance, but should be in a traffic control ordinance.

Planners have gone far out on the limb in loading a zoning ordinance with extraneous material because necessary regulations are not being handled in other municipal ordinances. In some cases, the planner may have been able to slip into the zoning ordinance a regulation which would not be accepted as a separate ordinance; in many cases, the planner has not even tried to discover whether a separate control ordinance would be accepted. Thus in many zoning ordinances there are elaborate regulations and controls for air pollution, noise abatement, housing, trailer camps, tourist camps, drive-in theaters, and drive-in restaurants, filling stations, and a host of other matters. The planner has pioneered establishing standards for new and different uses, nevertheless, when these ideas are beyond the experimental stage and well established, they should be the subject of separate ordinances. A requirement for sound zoning is that a zoning ordinance should properly embrace only zoning, and should leave smoke control to an air pollution ordinance, sirens to a noise abatement ordinance, and trailers to a trailer ordinance.

The Nonconforming Use, extracted from the ASPO Newsletter editorial "The Dilemma of the Nonconforming Use," January 1956.

Everyone involved in planning and zoning knows what a nonconforming use is and that all such things should be eliminated. Or do they, and should they? Know, and be eliminated, that is?

First, what is a nonconforming use—or what is it defined to be? The standard definition states that a nonconforming use is a use of land that exists in a district at the time the zoning ordinance is adopted, but that could not be put in as a new use because of the zoning rules. It is something that happened in the past but that the author of the zoning ordinance has resolved shall not happen again. Why do we not like it? Because it is contrary to our instinct for orderliness and segregation and "runs down" the neighborhood? Or because it violates the rules we have established?

When we define a term in an ordinance, that is what it shall be; for in this our power is absolute. At the same time, our legalized definition does not necessarily describe the meaning that we intend to give. Because a use is "nonconforming," it does not follow that it will run down the neighborhood. For that matter, neither does the violation of the principle of segregation—like things together—mean that an area will deteriorate. A better word to express our idea—but a tough one to define for an ordinance—is "incompatibility." Will this use fit in with the neighborhood? If so, it is a compatible use; if not, it is incompatible.

There are many compatible nonconforming uses (and many incompatible ones, too). One of the compatible uses is the little corner grocery store, which keeps odd hours and has saved the lives, socially speaking, of millions of desperate housewives. To the chain operators, these are known as "mama and papa" stores and are responsible for clipping chain profits in the fourth place behind the decimal point.

If we could reliably distinguish between the compatible and incompatible, we could have a better index as to whether we should eliminate the use. We have sometimes based elimination on the absence of substantial investment. This reasoning would seem to be like saying euthanasia is permissible if the person's income is less than $2,000 a year.

There has been an increase in planners' courage to require elimination of nonconforming uses. But nonconforming use elimination has brought a peculiar problem. The entire districting plan will be based on the strength of the elimination provision. To illustrate: if we were to include a provision that all nonconforming uses were to be removed within 30 days, then we would gerrymander district boundaries at every point to eliminate the need for eliminating the nonconforming uses. Even with a mild nonconforming provision, there is a record of a mayor telling his zoning commission, "I want those boundaries drawn so there isn't a single nonconforming use in this city." *a* We don't want them but *b* we don't want to face the political heat that will come when we try to eliminate them.

When the provision is mild to the other extreme—no elimination of nonconforming use—then we should be able to set zoning district boundaries freely and follow the land-use plan without inhibition. But if we don't rid ourselves of the incompatible uses, our zoning will fall short of our good intentions. If the use is incompatible and does run down the neighborhood, why should we want to continue it?

We must not forget that a nonconforming use is *a* vulnerable spot. We usually prohibit expansion, but at the same time *b* we have granted the operator a neighborhood monopoly. There is every chance that his favorable environment will increase his business until he seeks (and too frequently gets) a variance that gives him a chance to make himself even more incompatible with his neighbors. It reminds you of the bootlegger who fought to maintain prohibition.

If there are solutions to these problems, they are not obvious. But the time is here when we should no longer be content with standard answers. Painful as it may be, we are going to have to think these things out.

The Buffer Idea, extracted from the ASPO Newsletter editorial "Buffer Zones," July 1959.

The idea of a bumper, a fender, a buffer appears in endless places. There are the chrome-plated bars of steel at either end of an automobile, the ingeniously knotted hunks of rope between the ship and the wharf, the no-man's land between World War I trenches, the neutral zones that sometimes appear athwart Latin American national boundaries. The idea may even be used as an advertising gimmick that claims to protect a person's stomach from the ill effects of aspirin.

In the popular mind as well as in the definition, the buffer functions to protect something that lies on one side of itself from something that lies on the other side. Frequently it protects both sides, each from the other. This is the situation when two belligerent states snarl at each other across their mutual border. The protection afforded by a buffer is not always *a* physical. It may also be *b* psychological. The proposal that a band of trees be interposed between residences and an expressway was done so in the hope that it would furnish a buffer to protect the residences from traffic noise. The decrease in noise proved to be insignificant; nevertheless, the band of trees furnished a visual and psychological barrier.

The idea of a buffer in zoning also aims to protect. But protection has gotten itself mixed up with another—and pernicious—idea in zoning. It has gotten mixed up with the idea of higher and lower land uses, the idea that the noblest use of land is for single-family houses and the most ignoble is for industry, and that there is a clearly ordered progression down the scale from good to bad.

Under the hybridized theory of these two ideas, an intermediate use protects a high use from a low use, a two-family district protects a single-family district from an apartment district or anything lower. A commercial district prevents the evils of industry from impinging on the senses of apartment dwellers. At least this is the implication.

There is also another aspect of the hybridized theory. It is implied that buffers are only for the protection of the higher use, the good guys. Of course, there would be no reason to protect the lower use, the bad guys, from the good guys. Mutual protection is not reasonable under the circumstances.

Although the zoning buffer idea, in the eyes of its advocates, is valid for the entire high-low range of land uses, it appears most frequently as the apartment zone used to protect single-family houses from industry. We might ask some questions about this.

If we are trying to protect a single-family district, isn't it conceivable that the traffic generated by a multidwelling area may be more destructive than that from a designed and controlled industrial district? As for air pollution, wouldn't people prefer the modern, cleaned-up factory to the modern, not-so-cleaned-up apartment incinerator?

If there is really something about industry that makes it an undesirable neighbor, which is better: to have it as a neighbor to 4 families on a residential acre, single-family district; or as a neighbor to 40 families on a residential acre, apartment district? Or is it true that apartment dwellers are really second-class citizens not worthy of protection?

If you believe there is value to industry in a community and that it deserves promotion, then again: would the industry be better off sharing a street with the traffic coming from 4-families-per-acre dwellings or from 40-families-per-acre dwellings?

The "Highest and Best" Use, condensed from "Things to Come in Land-Use Control," a speech at the Annual Convention of the Society of Industrial Realtors, Miami Beach, Florida, November 14, 1961.

The famous bit of real estate jargon, "the highest and best use," has been pretty much of a red flag to a number of planners. It seemed most exasperating when it was invoked, as it invariably was, by some high priest of real estate expertise as he tried to get a corner lot in a residential district rezoned for a filling station. And, of course, we are familiar with that piece of property which Expert *A* testifies will achieve its highest and best use when it is converted to industrial use; Expert *B* swears it can reach its highest and best use only if it is zoned for commercial purposes; while Expert *C* is certain that residential is the highest and best of all possible uses.

In checking on what real estate theorists have said was meant by "highest and best use," I found, somewhat to my surprise, a rather clear definition of the expression. First, the description that appears in Preston Martin's text, *Real Estate Principles and Practice:*

> The fundamental principle of land use is that all sites in the long run (over many years) tend toward their highest and best uses. The highest and best use for a given parcel of land is that one which produces the highest future net income. . . . Economic forces of the community will provide the answer to the question: What use shall the land have?

Professor Arthur Weimer puts it quite directly:

> The term *highest and best use* has been defined in terms of *greatest net income, highest land value,* and *largest return in money or amenities over a period of time.*

I have no quarrel with this definition, since "highest and best use" is a real estate term and real estate experts are entitled to define it in a certain way. When a phrase becomes fixed in technical jargon, then for the purposes of technologists, the individual words no longer may be interpreted in their literal sense, but must be interpreted in their new sense. So highest and best use to the real estate man means the use which begets the highest price, the use which results in the greatest total income.

But it appears that there may not be one single highest and best use, in spite of the definition which says it is *the* use which results in *the* highest total future income. Or at least if there is one *the* highest and best use, experts can disagree honestly as to what it is. And experts also are willing to modify the definition, as when they plead for a zoning change on the residential corner lot because a filling station, if not the highest and best, is at least a higher and better use, since it will make the value of the lot greater than it would otherwise be.

The trouble is that there are some major flaws in the philosophy that insists on always putting land to its highest and best use, in this technical, economic sense.

EX

CENTRAL PARK

There is a very famous parcel of land in New York bounded by 59th Street on the south, 110th Street on the north, 5th Avenue on the east, and 8th Avenue on the west. New York has named it Central Park. This parcel is not put to its highest and best use, and the Lord willing, never will be. Remember, "highest and best use" means that use which will create the greatest net income, the highest value for the tract of land. Central Park brings in no return. It costs money to maintain and to police. It takes 840 acres of the most valuable land in the world off the tax duplicate.

But no one really doubts the value of Central Park as a park. It is much more valuable, much more important, as a park than it can possibly be as a site for high rise apartments, hotels, and office buildings. This is true in spite of the capitalized value of the income it would produce if built in apartments, or the price it would sell for. But this true value can only be expressed as community value, a community asset. The total value of the community would be decreased if there were no Central Park. Perhaps this could be put into dollars:

New York, as is—X billion dollars.

New York, with Central Park built to apartments and offices—Y billion dollars.

The value of Central Park to the community—$(X - Y)$ billion dollars.

Who could possibly calculate this? No one! But the citizens of New York feel sure the X billions (New York with Central Park) is much greater than Y billions (New York without Central Park). This very obvious example clearly illustrates that something is lacking when you insist on pushing real estate towards it highest and best use.

EX

In the example of the tract of land about which the experts disagreed, Expert A said industry would be the highest and best use.

He based this judgment on the physical characteristics of the site, on its location, and strangely enough, the contribution it might make to the economy of the community. He could capitalize the future earned income of the property itself to set a price, but he could not capitalize on that boost to the community economy. Expert *B* fancied the tract as a shopping center. The income he foresaw for this use could be capitalized for more than *A*'s future income from industrial development, and *B* did not have to monkey with any theoretical boost for the community. His figures were clear and easily demonstrable: the value for a shopping center was greater than the value for an industrial park. So *B* got the land because he could prove, with money, that his was the highest and best use.

Let us say that in this case, industry was the *proper* use of the tract—"proper use" meaning that use which will be of greatest value to the community as a whole. If *A* were to prevail, he needed more than the capitalized value of the future income on the land to get it set aside for its proper use; he also needed a good strong assist from the community and its land-use controls. Real estate operations under a pure highest and best use concept are inadequate for determining *proper* land use.

After the real estate doldrums of the '30s, we passed through the construction moratorium of the war and emerged into the '50s with an enormous shortage of urban facilities and an enormous appetite for converting nonurban land into urban uses. The creators of urban facilities quickly adopted new techniques and new forms of urban development, the production-line suburb, the shopping center, the industrial park. But communities were not equipped to handle these new forms of development, not equipped to add intelligently the ingredient of community interest that was necessary if tracts of new land were to be put to *proper* use. We were working with stodgy out-of-date plans and zoning controls. As a consequence, the community in many cases had to abdicate its responsibility. Much of the postwar development has been for the "highest and best use" in the worse sense of that phrase—the fast buck.

There have now been numerous attempts to update community land-use controls and to inject the community interest into the land-use pattern that is developing—devices such as provisions for planned unit developments calling for review of development plans, and regulations that pass on to the new development a larger share of the cost of community services or prevent land from being developed until the community is ready and financially able to furnish the facilities that are needed. There is also a hidden type of land-use control: the control or limitation of competition. (For example: a plan commission has before it three separate requests to rezone property for a regional shopping center; all three parcels are within a half-mile radius; there is not—neither now nor in the future—a market large enough to support more than one center and if the commission permits all three, at least two of them will flop and probably all three; if the commission decides the community is better off with one flourishing shopping center than with three droopy ones, and selects only one—this is the control and limitation of business competition.)

The final control is the community plan. The new concept—a statement of goals and objectives and the policies necessary to achieve those goals and objectives—is a flexible instrument, not precise. Because a developer does not *know* whether or not his proposal is in agreement with the plan, he will have to ask the planning administrative agency to rule on his case.

Review under planned unit development provisions, and for development timing, is a foretaste of the type of administrative review to come. As for limitation of competition: in many areas, economic justification reports are required when there is an application for shopping center rezoning; this is administrative review, even now. Metropolitan or statewide land development commissions are other possibilities to come in the future. My prediction is for an increase in administration, more governmental supervision, and the tendency for land to be put to its highest and best use *in the community interest.*

**"Why Are We Going Where?" extracted
from a paper given at the Second Annual
Institute of Planning and Zoning, Southwestern Legal Foundation, Dallas,
October 26, 1961.**

One fact that is basic to the problem of the future is that we face a population explosion: between 1960 and 1990 we shall add a population equal to that of every city in the United States whose population is now 2,500 or more. The logistics involved in caring for such a population increase are unbelievably complex, the quantities involved are stupendous. Of particular interest, however, is the quantity of land needed for *lebensraum.*

We will be converting to urban use an area approximately the size of all New England. Land available for conversion to urban use is not plentiful. The reasons are complex but the fundamental reason is that land, to be usable for urban development, must be so located that it already has a number of urban facilities or has reasonable access to them. Because of this requirement we can expect that almost all development of living facilities in the future will take place in and around our present cities and metropolitan areas. These are the areas to which the basic civilization needs are now accessible, where the lands that now have potential for urban development lie.

We have been using traditional methods to regulate the flow of land resources into urban uses, trying to adapt these methods to an accelerating change in civilization, but tradition must be violated radically, if we are to meet the future successfully. In the course of alteration we may need to violate certain principles of land regulations, even of legal philosophy, that we have hitherto held to be sacred.

I will use a series of statements to outline the form I believe land development regulation must take, if it is to meet the needs of the next 100 million urban dwellers. These propositions apply most cogently to large cities, to metropolitan areas, and to counties; they presuppose a level of administrative sophistication and of organization size that will not ordinarily be possible in the small city or village. Each statement is properly subject to modification, but by looking at some of these ideas realistically, I think we can begin to work ourselves out of our present position regarding land development controls—a position I believe to be untenable:

(1) For built-up, generally stable areas we shall continue to use the traditional zoning ordinance, but we shall change the administration and appeal procedure.

(2) For small subdivisions and resubdivisions, we may need to continue the traditional subdivision control procedure but, again, with altered administration.

(3) For the majority of future urban development, which will take place through merchant-builder developments, shopping center and industrial park construction and urban redevelopment, we should prepare a new control device. I will call this "a development ordinance."

④ The development ordinance will include some standards, perhaps similar to the intent statements that we now use in zoning ordinances. The development ordinance will also be refinement and consolidation of the floating zone and planned large-scale development provisions we now use in zoning and subdivision controls.

⑤ We shall create an appointive zoning and development commission to act as an industry regulatory commisson, a board of development appeals, a board of zoning appeals, and a zoning legislative body. In large jurisdictions, I see this as a three-man commission, probably full-time and paid. In smaller jurisdictions, I see it as a five-man commission, part-time and, perhaps, paid.

⑥ As a general guide for large-area action, we shall continue to use the comprehensive plan prepared by the planning agency. The principal guide will be the land-use plan, and not so much the map that illustrates it but the policy statements on which the land-use plan is based. Guided by the plan and policy statements, the zoning and development commission will establish the detailed regulations, including the boundaries of zoning districts.

⑦ We shall use the office of zoning administrator in all except the smallest jurisdictions, and perhaps should call him "development control administrator," since he will review applications under the development ordinance as well as under the zoning ordinance.

⑧ The development control administrator will be the principal staff technician for the zoning and development commission. In some cases he may act as a hearing officer and he may be given authority to rule on certain matters, such as variances, special uses for which fairly definite standards can be set up, and minor zoning map changes.

⑨ One of the most difficult problems in administering a development ordinance will be to get an intelligent review of plans submitted by the developer, because standards can be established only in the most general terms. For this reason it is important that the development and zoning commission and the administrator be highly competent, preferably because of training and experience.

(10) The development and zoning commission will review and pass on all applications under the development ordinance, on major large area special exceptions such as airports, and on all zoning amendments.

(11) Appeal of decisions by the development and zoning commission may be taken by the legislative body at that body's option, or appeal may be confined only to court review.

(12) The development and zoning commission may, also, be the planning commission. Under any circumstances the recommendation of the planning agency must be taken into consideration in every decision made by the development and zoning commission.

The People Through Their Government, extracted from "Zoning for Industry," a speech to the American Railway Development Association, Milwaukee, May 15, 1957.

In spite of what we planners might wish to do, there will still be much zoning done by the free market. Land development today is in the hands of big developers using large hunks of land, big home builders, big department stores and retailing promoters, big industries—all with plenty of capital and big ideas. They are all competing for suitable land, and frequently the one that gets there first with the most is the one that gets the land—and calls the shot on the zoning. Occasionally, there is a fourth type of big developer competing. That is government itself.

If we were able to do a perfect job of allocating land to the various uses, it would be most regrettable to see our perfect planning subjected to these forces. But we readily admit that we cannot make a perfect distribution, nor accurately foresee all the changes in urban development that call for changes in the land-use pattern. We are forced, therefore, to recognize that the free market must determine the development pattern to some extent, and the zoning to some extent.

While I believe that in many instances, land use can be determined by the free market, I also believe that in many other instances this has produced conditions that are most unhappy, errors that will take a long time to correct—if we can ever really correct them. For the ambi-

tious farmer is not the only one to succumb to the blandishments of
high pressure development. I do not believe that any corporation or
private individual, no matter how high-minded it or he might be, has
the right to dictate the development pattern of a city. That right must
remain with the city.

The forces that make the free market, and that shape our sprawling
cities, are filling every crack and cranny, every nook and crevice, with
one kind or the other of their developments. There is no space for
relief, no place to breathe. The diffident fourth party in the free
market—the people acting through their government—has been
crowded out or has permitted itself to be crowded out.

This state of affairs is not good, and there must inevitably be a
change. As a sort of forecast, I believe that over the years we shall
have an increase in the strength of land-use controls. I believe that
cities are going to be reaching out farther and farther to control
undeveloped areas and that they will be buying a great deal more land
to retain in public open spaces. As the years go on, I believe that there
will be increasing difficulties in changing the land-use plan, once it has
been established.

Assorted Sin . . . and Salvation

**A Trend Can Be Down, quoted from "Trends
in Planning," a speech at the 41st Annual Conference of the International City Managers
Association, Bretton Woods, 1955.**

A trend can be down as well as up.

You cannot watch zoning activities in the cities around this country
for long without concluding that zoning changes are now done by
pressure. The use that is made of a piece of land does not follow any
preconceived plan; the decision is made according to which side can
exert the most pressure. A developer sees a spot that he likes for a filling station. If it is zoned for filling stations, he offers $20,000. If a fill-

ing station is not permitted, he offers $15,000, figuring it will cost $5,000 in attorney's fees—and perhaps certain subventions—to get the zoning changed.

All over the country, in city after city, this is repeated. Filling stations, high-rise apartments, excessive land coverage, inadequate parking, shopping centers—all where they are not wanted. You can get any zoning change you want if you just bring enough pressure. The easiest place to get the change through is the board of zoning appeals. If the board stands pat, force the council. If the council is stubborn, the courts will help to slap it down.

I know very few planners who countenance pressure zoning. But in most cases the planner is low man on the totem pole, even though zoning is supposedly his specialty.

This is a trend in planning—and not a good one.

"Zoning for Sale," extracted from the ASPO Newsletter editorial, June 1957.

The literal sale of zoning favors is not important. In the first place, it is so infrequent among all zoning administration that it is insignificant. In the second place, it will occur only in those cities already so sick that zoning bribery is only part of a morbid administration that includes police-payoff, street paving kickbacks, watered garbage contracts, and a dozen other forms of boodle. The people of these cities have a lot of other messes besides zoning to clean up. Much more important are the zoning sales that are made everyday by upright men for honorable reasons. Sometimes the principals are embarrassingly frank.

For example, in one small community, the school board is negotiating for a junior high school site. The present owner of the site is asking EX $81,000—if! The if: the municipal legislative body must rezone the adjacent remainder of his property to permit its use for a wholesale distribution center by a large national chain. If the rezoning fails, then the price is $150,000. Incidentally, the price of $81,000 is supported by professional appraisal.

The attorney for the community has urged the school board to go on record supporting the rezoning, and the indications are that the board will do so. The attorney points out that if they are forced into condemnation there is no telling what the property might cost.

Besides, the distribution center will make a fat contribution to tax revenues, to the support of the school after it is built.

Who is in the wrong? The property owner, because he wants to make up for the profit he will fail to get if the combination deal is turned down?

The attorney, because he wants to save money for the municipality (which must purchase the land) and take a certain and equitable price rather than risk eminent domain proceedings?

The municipal legislators, because they want to build up the tax base and make it easier for the residential taxpayers?

The school board, because they want to cooperate with the municipality?

The national chain, because they have found a good site for their distribution center, presumably after careful economic analysis, and would like to build on it?

Or are planners wrong because they say "zoning is not for sale," and (from the facts we have in this case) are not able to offer a better reason?

Industry pleads with a voice that is difficult to resist when it asks for a zoning change to build a multimillion dollar plant. We can hardly label public servants as venal if they fail to resist something that is obviously so beneficial to the citizens they serve.

But the most effective weapon of the opposition is the threat of the loss of tax revenue. In metropolitan areas planners can counter this through metropolitan financing and metropolitan planning. In other areas—well, it's a formidable weapon.

1 Our courts have stated clearly that we shall not trade our legislative authority for money. We shall not sell zoning amendments. Yet we 2 would be less than realistic if we pretended it was not happening. If the *quid pro quo* is not always as immediate as in the example, it nevertheless can be discovered with little difficulty.

We will have to reckon with pressure zoning changes for a long time. We should immediately be suspicious of any suggestion that involves bribery (no matter how legal the bribery might be); that involves threats, such as a threat "to take our plant to another city"; or which involves the use of legal technicalities to circumvent the ordinance. These are *prima facie* signals of danger to the public interest. A legitimate need for change can be demonstrated without recourse to such tactics.

We who work for the rational development of our cities must also strengthen our own hand. We must have a clear plan for land use, rather than a vague feeling that we "don't like this proposal." Land-use plans allow for changes, but the changes must be consistent with the interests of the whole area.

"The First Rotten Apple," extracted from the ASPO Newsletter editorial, February 1960.

I reaffirm my belief that the preponderant majority of lay planners are strictly honest, that lay planners have no more problems of ethics and conflict of interest than do professional planners (if as many), and that the ethical level of public administration shows no discernible difference from the ethical level of private business. But after this disclaimer, I must admit that either (a) there has been a marked increase in ethical problems in planning or (b) we are just waking up. I lean toward the first explanation.

It takes only one rotten apple to spoil a barrel, and it is better to throw it out at the first sign of a brown spot. A friend sent this editorial from a California newspaper:

> A reader of this newspaper has asked an interesting hypothetical question which concerns our planning commission. There is a surplus of apartment dwellings in this city at this time, the reader contends. Numerous vacant apartments are available for prospective tenants. The city planning commission is the body which recommends whether or not property should be zoned for apartment construction. Several members of the city planning commission happen to be owners of apartment units.
>
> "Suppose I wanted a piece of property zoned so that I could build a new apartment on it," asks the reader. "Could I get a fair hearing under the circumstances? Or would the fact that some members of the planning commission own apartments that might contain vacant units make them feel unconsciously that the city had all the apartments it needed?"

Another friend from the other side of the country writes:

> Our chief trouble is that the planning commission is very largely composed of, and certainly dominated by, realtors, developers, and large property owners. To them, land is a commodity, the owner of which is entitled to squeeze out the last possible dollar. They hardly realize that land is a national resource, and that every parcel is vested with a public interest.

These are borderline cases—at least there seems to be nothing *illegal*. Nevertheless, decay spreads rapidly.

It is said (and demonstrated) that in one section of the country there is an unwritten rule: all vacant or potentially developable land is to be zoned at least one degree more restricted than its appropriate develop-ment. Thus, a good apartment site is restricted to single-family houses, a good commercial site is zoned for apartments. By this device, an owner is forced to come in for a change of zone if he wishes to develop his land appropriately. The grant of that change becomes the grant of a political favor, to be repaid by the owner in some manner.

The use of planning and zoning to enhance political prestige has taken other forms. One plan commission chairman demanded that the staff make a scrupulous examination of subdivision plats, spotting the most minute variations from the rules on grades, degrees of curvature, irregular-shaped lots, and so on. The order seemed not amiss, until the planning director awoke to the use being made of the reports. Variances for flyspeck changes would be granted as political favors in some cases, while in other cases the letter of the law was invoked against politically unacceptable developers.

Political favors or pecuniary favors—it is only a difference in the coin used. In one city where zoning variances are granted by the city council, you may have to hire a relative of your ward councilman to expedite consideration of your variance. Otherwise it never appears on the docket.

There is definitely an increase of this sort of thing. The cause is not hard to identify. It is the profit to be made in urban land. The supply is short, but the demand created by prosperity, technology, mobility, and fertility is long.

During the last major land boom, in the 1920s, land-use controls were ineffective and comparatively rare, so that there was little opportunity for shenanigans. During the 1930s, the depression pervaded everything, including the real estate market. During the 1940s, wartime building restrictions took away most of the interest in real estate. Only since then has real big money been riding on the vote on a zoning variance or an amendment, on the location of a superhighway, on the number of building lots that can be chopped out of an acre. With big money comes big temptation.

If it were only a matter of stopping illegal actions, there would be no great difficulty. You would keep on decrying it, pushing grand jury investigations and prosecutions. You would hope to succeed, or at least to keep illegal practices to the acceptable minimum. But the truly illegal activities are not nearly so dangerous as are the legal but unethical, unpublic interest activities. What can we do with these? Remove temptation? Remove those persons whose backgrounds make them appear subject to temptation?

Whatever we do, both tempters and tempted should realize that ac-tions against the public interest need not be illegal to invoke retribu-tion. The public has a way suddenly of taking violent notice of attacks against its interests. The remedy is usually stricter, more arbitrary rules and laws—less discretion, less chance to show mercy, left to mere man. Unless we public servants can learn to tell right from wrong, we should expect our master to act positively—no sense letting the whole barrel spoil.

It Is Time We Recognize Publicly, extracted from the annual report of the executive director, April 27, 1965, at the ASPO National Planning Conference, Toronto.

It is time that we recognize publicly that a small—but still much, much too large—group of public officials are engaged in selling zoning favors for a price.

I do not speak of the essentially honest councilman or planning commissioner who votes for a rezoning amendment against his better judgment because he wants to increase the community tax base. This too is a kind of sale, or barter, of zoning, but what this person needs principally is education, not incarceration. I am speaking of the man who takes money for his vote, the corrupt public official who accepts a bribe to pay for his action in the zoning case.

A few weeks ago a planning consultant told me he was convinced that you can buy with money any kind of zoning you want in half the communities in the United States. I disagree with his statistics. I do not know what the correct figure is, but even if it is 1 percent or less—it is still too much.

As in all types of dishonest dealings, the iceberg effect is present in zoning finagling. We see only a small percentage of the cases, because only a small percentage get found out.

For example: a developer plays games with the public officials, but according to different rules than they had planned on. Maybe he con-ceals a tape recorder in his hotel room. Suddenly the councilmen find themselves and their bribes spread all over the front page of the local

EX newspaper. Or a citizen gets his curiosity aroused by the mayor's real estate activities—buying a piece of property just before a rezoning petition is submitted and immediately after the rezoning is adopted, selling it back to the original owner. So a mayor goes to jail; a planning commission chairman gets a suspended sentence because of his age; a councilman resigns; a board of appeals member takes the fifth amendment before the grand jury. Still, most of the dishonesty you never discover because no one squeals, no one investigates.

EX   If you want rezoning in County *A* the word goes out that you must make a contract with a certain well-driller. Maybe you thought you needed only a two-inch well for a single-family house, but he will convince you that you need an eight-inch well. (And don't go checking on the *depth* of the well that he charges you for.) If you want the special permit you need to build a service station in City *B* you must hire a certain lawyer, whose standard fee is $5,000. Do you want a shopping center in Suburb *C*? That takes a planned unit development permit and a review of the engineering and site plan, and *X, Y* and *Z*, local consulting engineers, are the best doggoned engineers and site planners in the area. Quite by coincidence, the firm of *X, Y* and *Z* also acts as city engineer for Suburb *C*.

       It takes no deep analysis to determine *why* zoning has become such a marketable commodity. A single vote on the city council can change the value of an acre of land form $5,000 to $100,000. A million dollars may ride on the outcome of a single public hearing. The stakes are high and if by judiciously handing out $5,000 here and $10,000 there, you can guarantee (no final payment until the goods are delivered) a million bucks profit, why not sell out a little chicken feed for the big bundle?

       Although I am reporting on malingering by public officials, it always takes two to complete a bribe: one to give as well as one to receive. In my opinion, it is not one whit more blessed in these cases to give than it is to receive. I think that no one really knows how extensive is the official corruption in administering land-use controls.

       There are hundreds and thousands of people who spend time, money, and brain power in devising and testing new ideas, or in applying, carefully, old and trusted techniques—all with the objective of bettering their urban environment. Yet all that these people do means nothing unless we route out our handful of Judases. There is no reason to deny that these persons exist. To overcome the handicap they put on us by refusing to admit that there is any dishonesty in zoning administration is like trying to treat cancer by denying the existence of the lesion.

I think that learning how to rid ourselves of the malefactors is every bit as important as most of the esoteric urban research that is going on in the United States today. I therefore propose that we start the job of doing something about this monkey business by going direcctly to the point. I think we need a sort of National Zoning Crime Commission. We need to get the answer to some questions, such as:

- How prevalent is the sale of zoning?
- What are the methods of operation in this field of chicanery?
- How can we bring the bribery that we know is going on out into the open and let people see what is being done to them?
- And more important: how can we prevent this sort of thing, this bribery for zoning favors, in the future?

It is time we pulled our heads out of the clouds or out of the sands—I am not sure which—and took a look around.

Exclusion of the Public Interest, extracted from the ASPO Newsletter editorial "Member of the Wedding," March 1964.

It is not true everywhere, nor is it always true to the same degree—but it is true frequently enough and the consequences are serious enough that it needs pointing out. I refer to ostracism of the public interest at the hearing of zoning disputes, to the cold-shoulder treatment given to consideration of the general municipal good by boards of adjustment and sometimes even by city councils.

Granted that the terms *public interest* and *municipal good* are hazy at best. But nearly everyone has an instinctive feeling that some such thing does exist. "Greatest good for the greatest number" is one way, not very satisfactory, of expressing it.

The existence of a public interest is a basic premise of planning. It is what we are getting at when we say that planning must be *comprehensive,* that we must consider the *whole* city, all of its functions, all of its people, all of its geographical expanse. The idea of zoning, in fact, is that there is a public interest in how land is used that transcends the private right of the individual to have complete freedom to do whatever he wishes with his land.

There are two attitudes exhibited by boards of adjustment as they go about excluding consideration of the public interest. 1 The first is found in the board that leads the attack on the zoning ordinance. Here the board members see themselves as champions of the individual property owner, as the officials whose duty it is to whittle away at the zoning ordinance. Their board is set up to assist the individual in every possible way to avoid complying with the ordinance. The board might better have been termed a "board of erosion." These board members think of the public interest—if they ever do think of the public interest—as having been completely represented, probably overrepresented, when the ordinance was originally adopted. The ordinance at that time was guilty of tyrannical appropriation of private rights, and there is no sense in trying to prove its innocence. It is the bounden duty of the board of adjustment to fight this tyranny, to right the wrong that was done in the first place.

2 The second attitude that ignores the public interest in a zoning case is that held by the board of adjustment that sees itself solely as a judicial body, impartial, aloof; severe, perhaps, but just. It is not always clear whether these boards actually believe they are acting properly or are just playing at being Supreme Court justices. To the members of this board, every zoning petition represents litigation, a conflict between two parties. Usually one party is the petitioner, the property owner, and the other party includes all the neighbors who object to the zoning change that is being sought. The question as the board sees it is not what is the proper use of the parcel of land, but which party will be injured the least if the decision goes against it.

The ultimate manifestation of this attitude is: "We granted his request because no one appeared at the hearing to object to it." It is a plaintiff versus defendant action, and since no one appears as defendant, the board automatically awards judgment to the other party.

When the city through its planning staff does appear before a board afflicted with a super-judicial complex, neither the board nor the petitioner nor the objectors see this as a representation of the public interest. The planner is accused of "siding" with one or the other party, with the petitioner or with his neighbors. When the city planner is the only one questioning a petition, and there are no neighbors objecting, then in the eyes of the board the two parties to the suit are the petitioner and the planner. Although it can be said the planner is representing the public interest in this case, that is not the way the board of adjustment sees it.

These defects in zoning administration are not easily cured. For one thing, there is some justification in both attitudes. The board of adjustment was invented to ease the harsh action of literal enforcement of a zoning ordinance. So it is the board's duty to adjust the ordinance where it creates unnecessary hardship. And there will always be zoning cases in which completely contradictory opinions will be put forth. It does require a calm, an unbiased, yea, a judicial turn of mind to get the straight of the dispute.

Nevertheless, it needs to be recognized that the public interest is *always* entitled to hearing, must always be represented. Perhaps we cannot hope to be sure of this representation until we have recognized that zoning in most areas is getting too complicated for administration by amateurs.

"A Law Can Be No Better Than Its Enforcement," quoted from the ASPO Newsletter editorial, January 1953.

A law can be no better than its enforcement. This is just as true of a zoning ordinance as it ever was of prohibition. When we think of failure to enforce zoning ordinances, we naturally think of the building commissioner, or the board of zoning appeals, or even of the city council itself. It is certainly true that many zoning ordinances have been made worthless by the careless (sometimes illegal) actions of these three.

But there is also a fourth group of public servants who, from time to time, pour their own buckets of sand into the zoning gear box. I speak of corporation counsels—city attorneys. There are many who by their intelligent and sympathetic handling of zoning litigation, strengthen their city's ordinance. The cases they carry through to appellate courts actually contribute measurably to the advance of zoning practice in the United States. However, attorneys with this knowledge of, and interest in, zoning are all too rare. There are altogether too many who neither know nor care.

It is my belief, based on bitter experience, that (a) with very few exceptions, attorneys have not the faintest knowledge of zoning theory; and (b) with the exception of those cities that have had the foresight to assign a special assistant corporation counsel to the planning and zoning department, the chief planner in a city is much more familiar with zoning law than the corporation counsel's office.

So don't let yourselves be pushed around.

Laxities in Litigation, quoted from the ASPO Newsletter editorial "Planners Must Try Their Zoning Cases," March 1954.

I am convinced that planners must take on the additional duty and function of trying zoning cases. This conviction results from the reading of a great many zoning decisions which were decided adversely to the community, simply because an inadequate record had been prepared in the lower courts. In reading the decisions of the state appellate courts and courts of record in the United States, I am literally appalled at the lack of understanding of what is involved in zoning.

Time after time, a particular court will decide against a municipality almost entirely on the ground that the zoning classification creates a loss of value. There is no understanding that if each case is taken individually without relation to its effect on the total neighborhood or total community, it is possible to show in almost every instance that the zoning will cause a loss of value.

How are we going to avoid this? The average city or village attorney has little knowledge of what is involved in zoning. (There are, of course, rare exceptions.) He doesn't realize that in order to win a zoning case the effect on the total community must be shown. He doesn't realize, for instance, that if the court is permitted to shift the boundary line simply because a residential zone abuts a commercial zone, there can be no zoning in the community. The planner has the task of showing the city or village attorney exactly how the case must be built and what the nature of the record must be. He must tell the attorney what kind of testimony must be introduced and what its effect will be. The planner even has to provide the witnesses who will testify and outline the nature of their testimony.

We do an injustice to zoning and planning everywhere when we let a half-baked case go to court.

"The Expert Witness," an ASPO Newsletter editorial, December 1963.

If you have ever watched a good knockdown, drag-out fight in court, either as a participant or as an observer, you must have been confused by the testimony of expert witnesses. It goes like this:

Planner A comes up front, swears to tell the truth, whole and nothing but, and sits in the witness box. Attorney for the plaintiff questions Mr. A to prove that Mr. A is eminently qualified as an experienced authority on zoning. Mr. A has a master's degree in city planning. He has worked as a planner for 20 years. He was city planner for Endsville for five years. He prepared master plans for the cities of Shem, Ham, and Japheth. He has written articles on zoning for the state league of municipalities. He has given speeches at conventions of planners. He belongs to all the right professional clubs.

Then comes the hypothetical question. "Mr. A, assume that in a city with a population of 151,276 there is an intersection of two streets, one carrying an average daily traffic of 8,545 vehicles, and the other carrying an average daily traffic of 325 vehicles. Assume further that at the northeast corner of this intersection there is a vacant lot containing 10,742 square feet . . ." and so on and on for five minutes or more, with the attorney making certain that the hypothetical question is as unhypothetical as it is possible to make it, ending with "Mr. A, assuming the foregoing assumptions, do you have an opinion as to how the lot on the northeast corner should be developed?"

Mr. A: "I do have an opinion."

Atty.: "What is that opinion?"

After invoking all his gods—Accepted Planning Principles, Highest and Best Use, Population Explosion, National Motor Vehicle Registration, Neighborhood Service Needs—it turns out that Mr. A sees the northeast corner lot as an ideal location for a filling station—to no one's surprise.

Following a decent period of heckling by attorney for the defense, Mr. A steps down. Sometime later, when the defendant presents his case, planner B is called to the stand, and the ritual dance takes place again: education, experience, articles, speeches, clubs unhypothetical hypothetical questions.

Mr. B also cites Accepted Planning Principles. But Mr. B prefers to emphasize Gasoline Explosion rather than Population Explosion, and Neighborhood Democracy rather than Neighborhood Service Needs.

Mr. *B* then finds that the northeast corner lot is suitable only for single-family residential use—also to no one's surprise. After receiving his measure of insults from attorney for the plaintiff, Mr. *B* steps down.

If you are not sufficiently confused by this contradictory testimony, then go to the next case. Here you will find the roles reversed—Mr. *B* calling on Mr. *A*'s gods to show the need for a drive-in hamburger joint, Mr. *A* citing Mr. *B*'s authorities to prove that a single-family residence is the highest and best use.

To keep your perspective on expert witnesses, you should try to remember that ⓐ expert testimony is always *opinion,* not fact; ⓑ there is always room for a difference of opinion; ⓒ the facts in two cases are never identical; ⓓ cases at law, especially zoning cases, are almost never black-or-white, yes-or-no.

At the same time, you probably cannot rid yourself entirely of the feeling that an expert's opinion just may be influenced by the wishes of the attorney who first approaches him, the guy who pays his witness fee. "THE BEST THAT MONEY CAN BUY"

The problem is not at all peculiar to planning experts. Land appraisers, engineers, yea, even doctors, are apt to exhibit ambivalence when they appear on the witness stand as experts.

MODEL SCHEME FOR EXPERT WITNESSES & OPINIONS TO APPLY TO ZONING CT. CASES

With physicians, however, the courts are trying out a new scheme. The court itself is selecting an impartial medical expert on personal injury cases in which there will be contradictory medical testimony from physicians hired by the plaintiff and defendant. The fees of the court's expert are paid by the court, or from foundation funds available to the court—not by either party to the suit. Impartial medical experts are selected from a specially screened panel (in Illinois the names on the panel are kept confidential) of physicians of ability who have no affiliation with corporations or employee groups and, especially, physicians who are not notoriously sought after by litigants. The results of the impartial medical witness plan have been excellent. Most of the cases in which it has been used are settled out of court, hopefully with reasonable justice for both parties.

Perhaps such a scheme could be tried in zoning cases. It is difficult to see how it would be less satisfactory than the present situation.

But then it is like belling the cat: who is to select the secret panel of impartial planning experts?

"Divine Rights and Civil Rights," extracted from the ASPO Newsletter editorial, December 1956.

Once upon a time nations were governed by kings because of a monopoly on divinity that the kings carried in their genes. Whatever the kings wanted to do was proper because of this divine gift. At the end of the 18th century there were two bloody revolutions to dispute this idea. The result of the revolutions forced the decision that if there were divinity in the genes, it was shared by king and commoner alike.

The divine right of kings was just another face on the statement that the end justifies the means. Because kings moved under divine guidance, any action they might take, any atrocity they might order, was justified. In short, divine rights supersede civil rights.

I have no notion as to how kings arrived at the idea they were divine and could do no wrong. I am sure, however, that they sincerely believed it. As I try to analyze several recent instances of this same attitude, I believe this is the common thread. The proponents have sincerely ascribed divinity unto themselves. And they are all honorable men.

Take religious organizations. The connection with divinity is obvious. It is not surprising that in a few cases those working for salvation of men's souls slip across the line and believe themselves tinged with divinity. As a result they feel they should not be bound by the rules that govern common, or nondivine, people. They refuse to adhere to such things as off-street parking requirements. They ask a state legislature that churches and all things remotely connected with churches be exempted from zoning controls. This does not happen with all religious organizations nor even with the majority, but it does happen.

Take freedom for education and scientific inquiry. In a large city, the president of the municipal university declared that the plan commission was interfering when it asked to review the university's decision to lease part of the campus to private interests for a parking lot. "A municipal university must control its own destiny," he is quoted as saying. One can almost see the Jovian majesty of the man as he defends the ancient and sacred right of the university.

The relief of human suffering is one of man's noblest occupations. Probably its most effective practitioners are the doctors and dentists. When they extract a hot appendix or an aching tooth, we are grateful.

When they save the life of our child, our gratitude knows no bounds. It is little wonder that the medical profession climbs higher and higher on the pedestal of sanctity. To prevent death is just a negative way of expressing: to give life. To give life—but that is a feature of divinity. So we shall not forbid the doctor's office (plus receptionist, nurse, lab technician) wherever he wishes it. Does not the steady flow of patients who enter suffering and exit cured testify that his is a sacred calling, above other callings?

We thought that when we acted upon our declaration of 1776 we were settling the question of the special divinity of kings. Probably we did settle it for kings of the United States, but in the place of kings we put democratically chosen representatives. We created a federal government that puts post offices and Nike reserves where it pleases. We created state governments that appoint highway and toll road commissions whose word is final. We created local governments that write local laws but are not bound to observe their own laws when they wish to build an incinerator or sewage plant or to open a new dump. Remember, though, that these are representatives of democracy. Democracy is the finest flowering of political justice and equality. It is transcendental; therefore its operators are likewise transcendental.

I think that we shall never have an end to self-bestowed infallibility. It is in the nature of persons dedicated to a cause to identify themselves with the cause until they become one and the same thing. We are able to restrain some excesses. We must always be alert, particularly in times of stress when our efforts may be diverted by other problems—times such as we have now, when the forces of urbanization, of migration, of easy and plentiful money, of frenetic civilization, distract our attention from the appearance of new self-appointed divinities.

Beware of the man who is sure he is right, because that certainty is reserved only for the divine.

"Like Concessions, Man!," extracted from the ASPO Newsletter editorial, August 1960.

One of the oldest dodges of the con man is the false "concession." In bare outline it works this way: the sharpie offers you a gold brick for $1,000. You balk. He likes your looks, likes your family, has to sell in a hurry because he has an appointment on the coast. He makes a concession. He offers to sell you the gold brick for the bargain price of $100.

It was a gilded hunk of lead worth $2 to begin with and it is still the same hunk of lead. He asks you to pay only 50 times its value instead of 500 times its value. (And unless you are a scrap metal dealer or make your own bullets, why do you want a hunk of lead, anyway?) Do you fall for the concession by the con man? If you don't buy, there's always another sucker who will.

The false concession gimmick is not the exclusive property of the professional racketeer. It is now being used with great success to take in plan commissions and city councils. I quote from *Florida Planning and Development* (May 1960):

> A loudly aggrieved applicant appeared again before the planning
> board with a site plan for a shopping center on a large tract. He
> pointed out that he had been in several times with revised plans, each
> of which provided more parking spaces than the one before. The
> board pointed out that the number of parking spaces still did not
> meet the requirements of the zoning ordinance. So the man pointed
> out that he had made repeated concessions to the inordinate demands
> of the board, felt that he was being subjected to unnecessary hard-
> ship, and requested that the planning board recommend to the board
> of adjustment that he be granted a variance to provide less parking
> space than the law required.
>
> In view of the concessions made, the planning board then voted to
> recommend the variance.

EX

Maybe in this case he brought the price of the hunk of lead down to $10, and the planning board couldn't resist the bargain. I still ask why they want the lead in the first place. (It also reminds me of the speeder EX picked up for doing 45 miles per hour in a 25-mile zone. He says you should forgive him because he could have been doing 60 miles per hour.)

It is a crying shame, but it happens every day somewhere in the United States.

Councils and commissions can protect themselves by a simple rule. Any time a developer returns with a second application for the same property that is not completely in compliance with the regulations (or in compliance with *real* concessions that the council or commission granted to him at first hearing)—throw him out!

Don't be a sucker!

Zoning for Industry

Performance Standards in Industrial Zoning, condensed from a paper given at the ASPO National Planning Conference, October 15, 1951, Pittsburgh.

The expression "performance standard" is taken from the building code terminology. Modern building codes are written more and more in terms of what materials and methods of construction will *do*—their performance under stated conditions—rather than in specific descriptions of materials and building methods. This change has been forced on building commissioners because of the great number of new materials and designs.

The situation in zoning is similar. Zoning administrators are asked to rule on new land uses, and on new—and improved—forms of old uses. Factories are making new products, are using new production processes, and are taking on a new appearance. The buildings are kept to one story in height. They are placed well back from the property lines. Factory grounds have neat lawns and beds of flowers. The buildings are windowless and air-conditioned. Many modern industrial plants would be an improvement to the area if they were placed in the center of nearly any of our residential districts. Zoning ordinances need reworking to catch up with our industrial techniques.

Building codes have passed through three stages. In the first, or *primitive*, stage, for example, the code said that a party wall should be made of brick or stone. It was soon found that there are brick walls and brick walls. Some of them withstand burning and some do not. It was necessary to state *how* you wanted the wall constructed and how thick it should be. This was the second stage, the *specification* code. Then along came builders with new materials: monolithic concrete, cinder block, and so on. They were faster and cheaper to build, and the proponents claimed they would furnish the protection we sought.

When we stopped to think, we found that we actually didn't care what the wall is made of—brick, concrete, steel, or tissue paper—so long as it is fireproof. So we established a *performance* code. The party wall must be able to retain its strength and block off a fire produced under laboratory conditions. The fire reaches a temperature of 2000° Fahrenheit in two hours. If the material holds up in this test, it is permissible to use it in building a party wall.

Some parts of our <u>zoning ordinances</u> have reached the *specification* stage—side yards, for example. We don't say "side yards must be furnished," which would be the *primitive* stage. Instead, we say "there will be two side yards, each of which will be not less than five feet in width." This is a *specification* standard, because we have specified a minimum acceptable width. It is not yet a *performance* standard. We haven't said what we want the house to do, which is to assure adequate light and air to its neighbor, nor have we set up an accurate definition of "adequate light and air."

While parts of our zoning ordinance have progressed to specification standards, there are still parts that are back in the primitive stage. Especially is this true of our method of handling <u>industrial zoning</u>. The clause that is best evidence of this primitive stage is probably somewhere in 99 percent of existing zoning ordinances. It goes

> . . . and any other use that is not objectionable because of the emission of dust, odor, noise, excessive vibration or other nuisances.

We have recognized the weaknesses of such clauses and we want to overcome them. Almost universally we have tried to overcome them by setting up groups of uses that we think have about equal powers of nuisance generation. We have outlined districts for "light" and "heavy" industry, but for the life of us, we can't give a clear definition of light and heavy. In some cases, we have limited the horsepower of individual machines—on what justification it has never been clear, except that someone else had done it before. Sometimes we have limited the number of employees, saying that a laundry employing five persons would be permitted in a business district, but that a laundry employing six persons was *de trop.*

In some places we have improved upon our primitive standards by granting conditional use permits. The industry could locate in the district it requested *if* it fulfilled certain conditions regarding the handling of dirty materials, off-street loading, paint spraying, sandblasting, and so on.

Although we can go a long way in writing performance standards into our zoning code, there are several fields in which we will have to continue specification standards for many years to come. Again, this parallels the modern building code, which uses performance as often as possible, but still carries a list of specifications for items on which performance standards are either not available or not practical. However, we can move out of the *primitive* stage at many points in our zoning regulations.

The ideal zoning performance standard will substitute a quantitative measurement of an effect for the qualitative description of that effect that we have used in the past. It will not use the terms "limited," "substantial," "objectionable," "offensive." Instead it will establish definite measurements, taken by standardized methods with standardized instruments, to determine whether the effect of a particular use is within predetermined limits, and therefore is permissible in a particular zone.

There are 11 fields in which we need to look for performance standards for industrial zoning. These are:

① Noise   ⑦ Fire hazards
② Smoke   ⑧ Industrial wastes
③ Odor   ⑨ Transportation and traffic
④ Dust and dirt   ⑩ Aesthetics
⑤ Noxious gases   ⑪ Psychological effects
⑥ Glare and heat

1. Noise. The possibility of setting up performance standards for noise appears both hopeful and difficult. It is hopeful because acoustical research has come up with some new techniques for measuring noise, and with a new unit of noise called the "sone." The older unit, the "decibel," is primarily a measure of the pressure created by sound waves and will not be superseded in the measurement of the strength of individual tones. But the technical difference between "sound" and "noise"—particularly the difference between the decibel measurement of sound and the loudness of noise—is a subject that you want to approach only when you are in the pink of mental condition. Professor G. L. Bonvallet, of Armour Research Foundation, has taken enough measurements of this kind of noise—street and traffic noise, industrial noise, transportation noise—to give limiting spectra for noise.

The control of factory noise through zoning is also hopeful because a most effective means for the muffling of noise is a tool that has been used in zoning for many years—setback. Noise is decreased approximately as the square of the distance. If the noise of a factory is a certain figure at the property line, move the factory twice as far away and it will be down to one-fourth the former intensity. (Don't be too quick to believe that objectionable noise at 10 feet has dropped to a whisper at 20 feet. Common sense tells us that isn't true. Noise measurements are on a logarithmic scale, and they drop slowly in the upper brackets.) But setbacks from property lines give us an extremely useful control for noise. And noise gives us another excellent excuse for setbacks.

The discouraging aspect of performance standards for industrial noise is that factory noise—the noise from industrial processes—is not the objectionable part of industrial noises in 95 percent of our factories. This was first brought out in the famous New York City noise survey of 1930, in which factory noise was considered objectionable in only 1 percent of the cases. This finding has been reaffirmed several times. Objectionable industrial noise is overwhelmingly due to traffic and transportation noises—trucks coming from and going to the plant, steam locomotives puffing and diesel engines thundering, box cars switching and gondolas banging, thousands of self-propelled employees changing shift. The chance of controlling this type of noise through a performance standard on noise generation is not good.

Nevertheless, at least 5 percent of our factories *do* create objectionable noise in addition to the traffic noise they spawn. Any factory noise adds to the overall noise pattern. I believe that we are ready to set up definite standards in this field.

2. Smoke. The second needed performance standard is a limit on smoke emission. We have excellent standards and simple methods of measurement. The simplest and most popular is the Ringelman chart. On this chart are five designs, each representing a degree of smoke density. When you are far enough away from the chart, the designs merge into shades of gray, all except No. 5, which is solid black. The shades are numbered from 1 to 5. Multiply the number by 20 and you get the percentage density of the design. Thus No. 1 is 20 percent, No. 2 is 40 percent, No. 3 is 60 percent. The model smoke control ordinance forbids the emission of dense smoke, and dense smoke is defined as equal to Ringelman No. 2 or darker. A few ordinances set the limit as Ringelman No. 3 or darker. We thus have our performance standard on smoke emission already worked out. All we have to do is to apply it.

There are, of course, some problems in bringing the smoke standards over into the zoning ordinance. For example, if our city smoke control ordinance forbids smoke more dense than Ringelman No. 2, we may want also an area in which we set No. 1 as the limit, or an area in which we specify no smoke whatsoever, requiring gas, oil, or electricity as fuel. However, there is no doubt that we are ready to drop smoke from the ubiquitous list of undefined nuisances and sub-stitute the clear definition that we have available.

3. Odor. Thus far, there have been readily at hand some well-tested standards of measurement. In the field of olfactory offenses, we have to proceed cautiously.

So far as I have been able to determine, smell (and its concomitant, taste) is the most subjective of our sensations. You just can't measure odor. You can't even describe it, except to say that it smells like some other odor, or that it is pleasant, indifferent, or horrible. Odors have been classified in dozens of different ways. Numerous tries have been made to determine odor profiles, but none of them has quite come off. Experiments under way to place odor in the electromagnetic spectrum show promise.

One approach to odors is through measurements of the threshold of smell. These are available for a considerable list of compounds and show the minimum amount needed to give the first sensation of odor. Measurements are made in ounces of the substance per thousand cubic feet of air.

For example: 0.001 ounces of hydrogen sulfide, the old familiar rot-ten egg gas, in a thousand cubic feet of air, is the minimum concentra-tion that can be smelled. Less than this concentration we cannot per-ceive. There is a wide variation in the amount of different substances needed for the threshold of smell. It takes 0.05 ounces of butylene beta, which is the warning odor used in illuminating gas. It takes only 18 *millionths* of an ounce of ethyl seleno mercaptan, which seems to hold some sort of position as the foulest of all smells.

A great many substances have had this odor threshold determined. A list of several hundred, mostly for polysyllabic organic compounds, included, however, only one of the compounds that constitute the peculiar odor that arises from a fish processing plant. At any rate, the list is too long to include, except by reference, in the ordinary zoning ordinance.

If accurate measurement of odor is not now possible, it is only a question of time before it will be. In the meantime, we have some em-pirical methods open to us. There are very few industrial activities in which offensive odor cannot be prevented from escaping. The odor from our old friends the glue factory, the slaughterhouse, and the fish cannery can be completely eliminated—at least as far as escape into the atmosphere is concerned. On the other hand, there seems to be no prospect, present or future, for the elimination of the odor nuisance from a stockyard. In the doubtful list we would also have to put petroleum refining, artificial gas manufacture, and soap manufacture.

Our best approach to the odor problem is to bar no industry by name, because of its odor nuisance. Instead, we would specify that in a certain district, we shall permit no industry to locate that commits an odor nuisance. Then perhaps we should have a checklist of industries that have traditionally smelled bad and specify that these industries must present detailed plans to prove that they are going to eliminate the odor, or we won't let them operate in this district. Of course, we must not forget that if there are some industries not yet able to eliminate odors, they must be located *somewhere*. We must have a district permitting them to be erected in some, if not all, of our cities.

4. Dust and dirt. The fourth in the list of needed standards is one for dust and dirt. The most frequent source of dirt from industrial sections is the smokestack, blowing cinders and fly ash into the air. Here again, we have the work of the smoke-abatement pioneers. They have definitely stated that they would not tolerate fly ash in excess of "0.30 grains per cubic foot of flue gas at a stack temperature of 500° Fahrenheit." This standard would not be difficult to incorporate into our zoning regulations. We may wish to set different limits—such as 0.2 grain or 0.1 grain.

As for other kinds of dust and dirt, there are at present no standards to determine a permissible amount of pollution. I am inclined to the solution suggested for odors. We would not list any industry by name. In those districts that we wish to keep free of dirt, we would require satisfactory proof that an industry will be able to keep all dust and dirt confined within the walls of the building. If there be any industry which cannot keep its dirt to itself, we'll need to find a district for it somewhere—downwind. I have a feeling, however, that there is no industry conducted within a building that nowadays needs to pollute the air with dirt.

5. Noxious gases. By noxious gases, I mean those gases which are relatively odorless, and which can, in sufficient concentration be dangerous to plant and animal life. Hydrogen sulfide, the rotten egg gas mentioned previously, is quite poisonous. But like the rattlesnake, it warns you before it strikes; the unmistakable smell telegraphs its presence in advance of toxic proportions.

When considering our standards for zoning ordinances, we should

not forget that there is another body of law that is always in operation—the law of nuisance. While it is all quite unclear as to what is
nuisance and what is not nuisance, there is no doubt that the discharge
of poisonous gas in toxic quantities is definitely a nuisance. As such it
will be promptly abated. Therefore, I do not believe it is necessary to
concern ourselves with clear nuisances in zoning.

One way of looking at zoning regulation of some of these matters is
that we are trying to regulate processes so that they never become
nuisances. Standards for toxic concentrations of gases are easily available. Carbon monoxide, for example, is dangerous to human life at
about 2,000 parts per million. The maximum safe concentration permissible in plants is set a 100 p.p.m. This is about the concentration
found on a heavy traffic street.

Although we might prefer to forbid the release into the atmosphere
of any noxious gas, it is unlikely that this can be accomplished. We
may have to relegate the poison gas producers to the same district as
the odor producers. We need to examine industries that are noxious
gas producers, to see whether the escape of such gas can be completely
eliminated. If it cannot, then we have at hand definite standards—standards that should be comparatively easy to adapt to zoning regulations.

6. Glare and heat. The steel industry is the most spectacular producer
of glare and heat. To watch a Bessemer converter blow off from some
safe distance does not offend you. On the contrary, it fills you with
awe and respect. Living close to it is not nearly so thrilling. The intensity of the light at night is great enough to make the neighborhood
within several blocks as light as day. But the establishment of new
blast furnaces and Bessemer converters is infrequent enough, and it
presents so many special problems, that the glare and heat nuisance
will never be a crucial consideration.

On the whole, this is a minor problem. It would probably arise
most frequently from welding operations and acetylene torch cutting.
Here I think we can get a performance standard—actually a prohibition. Such operations shall be performed so that they may not be seen
from outside the property. This would mean that they would be inside
a building where they could not be seen from outside. Or if it is
necessary to work outside, as it may be in scrap metal operations, the
work will be behind a tight fence.

7. Fire and safety hazard. Most cities have, in the building code or fire code, a list of "special hazards," operations and processes that are held to be unusually dangerous. These uses are customarily forbidden anywhere within the first "fire zone." If these special hazards were adopted into zoning regulations, there might be some advantage in coordinating fire zones and land-use zones. However, the disadvantages of using the typical "special hazard" list outweigh the advantages. For example, you will probably find "paint spraying" and "fireworks manufacture" on the same list. Although we may wish to prohibit both of these operations in our first fire district, we can't afford to treat them as equal in setting up our industrial zoning regulations.

When we wrote into our zoning ordinance that industries might be objectionable because of fire hazard, it wasn't to protect the hazardous industry from itself, because wherever it locates it will still be hazardous to itself and its own employees. We wished to protect the neighbors, to offer assurance to any present or future manufacturer that he could locate in this area without fear of having a hazardous plant come in next door to him. How can we measure this potential danger?

Fire insurance ratings offer a great body of practical experience to draw on. Fire insurance rates are established by experienced technicians using a schedule that is a kind of score card. There are several in use throughout the country, but the best one is known as the "Analytic" schedule. In this schedule, the cost of insurance starts with a base rate for the individual city, to which are applied several factors in the form of percentages. Some of the factors increase the cost of the insurance and others decrease the cost. The factors fall in four major groups: building construction, occupancy, exposure, and condition. Of these, all but "condition" can be determined before the plant is built.

The effect of type of building construction on the insurance rating is well known. The completely fireproof building carries the lowest rating—costs the least to insure—and frame construction carries the highest rating.

Occupancy factors, which are of particular interest in zoning, depend solely on the use to which the building is put, without regard to the type of building construction, or the exposure of the building because of surrounding hazardous conditions. These factors range from zero—that is, nothing added because of the occupancy—for the ordinary offices, to as much as 245 percent additional for bottling acetylene gas, or even more for other occupancies. Occupancy factors also take into account special features in a plant, such as the use of inflammable gas, enameling operations, and so on.

The third group of factors used to rate the fire hazard of a building covers the exposure of the building to nearby hazards. Since we are interested in setting a standard by which we can predetermine the acceptability of a given use, we are interested in the exposure hazard that is *created* and not the one that the new plant meets. The rating factor applied for "condition" cannot be determined in advance of the construction and use of a building. It is based on housekeeping and general maintenance after the building is actually in use. Although it is important in arriving at the cost of insurance, it is not necessary to establish zoning standards.

In fire insurance rating, we have a method of setting up a definite numerical standard by which we can judge fire hazards. It isn't going to be easy, but it does offer a chance to get away from naming names and still be quite definite as to what we consider appropriate for different industrial zones. We are interested in the hazard to other industries that our permitted uses will create. Therefore, we should recognize that there is no fire hazard we might create that cannot be eliminated by distance. We return to our old zoning tool—setbacks from property lines. Undoubtedly, the required setbacks to eliminate fire hazard caused by certain uses, such as gasoline tank farms, are going to be so great that economic necessity will force these uses to locate in our less valuable districts. This is as it should be, since it tends to direct the more intensive uses to the better locations.

There are some weaknesses in insurance rating schedules, but I believe there is an opportunity to improve our zoning regulations by using them intelligently.

8. Industrial sewage wastes. A municipal sewerage system is, or should be if it isn't, planned for a long time in the future. In some rare instances, it may be possible to expand the system—laterals, mains, interceptors, disposal works—easily in any part of the city. But in the majority of cities, the sewerage system is a miscellany of sections, some of which can handle more sewage than they are taking, others that are up to or over capacity, still other sections that cannot be expanded economically. So it is quite important to plan industrial areas with the present and potential sewerage system in mind.

Industrial sewage is not necessarily a nuisance. Of course, industrial waste discharged raw into a stream can be a nuisance. However, let us assume that state and local health laws are effective in preventing this.

If they are not, the zoning ordinance cannot be a satisfactory substitute. Delineating industrial zones based on the capacity of the sewerage system is primarily a land planning problem. Still, the principal tool for carrying out the land plan is the zoning ordinance. Industrial sewage standards should be in it.

Fortunately, we have excellent methods of measuring industrial wastes and in estimating them before the plant is built. For example: the production unit in a slaughterhouse is one hog. A steer is two and one half hog-units. The amount of industrial waste accompanying the slaughter and preparation of one hog can be converted to a population equivalent. It is equal to the domestic sewage waste of 2.43 persons. A slaughterhouse with a daily capacity of 1,000 hogs, or 400 steers, throws the same load on a sewerage system as would a population of 2,430 persons. The average cheese factory has a population equivalent of 2,000 to 3,000 persons; the average tannery has an equivalent of 18,000 to 20,000 persons; a beet-sugar factory equals 65,000 to 125,000 persons, depending on the process.

We have practically all the basic information that we need for industrial waste standards. In zoning ordinances, they will probably take the form of density regulations. Thus for an area with ample sewerage, we might permit industrial waste up to a population equivalent of 1,000 per acre. In another area we might have to limit waste to a population equivalent of 50 persons per acre.

9. Traffic and transportation. For 95 percent of our factories, the noise from machinery is not objectionable. But for factories that might be objectionable because of the traffic they generate, the figure is close to 100 percent. The possibility of increased traffic bothers the neighbors more than any other aspect of industry in the neighborhood.

Traffic and transport are not objectionable *per se*. It is the effects of traffic that bother us. It is the noise of roaring trucks and banging switch engines. It is the poisonous carbon monoxide pouring from the exhaust of motor vehicles. It is the smoke and cinders belching from steam locomotives. It is the street hazard created by autos of employees streaming to and from work, and the preemption of parking space by those autos. It is the driving hazard caused by improper loading berths. It is the dirt raised, even from concrete streets, by thousands of wheels. In fact, the effects of traffic include most of the annoyances for which we are trying to set up industrial performance standards.

Standards for traffic require some basic thinking. Performance standards, as we have talked about them heretofore, are one step removed from the problem. For example: studies show that doubling the number of motor vehicles will increase the noise level about 3 decibels, which corresponds to about a 40 percent increase measured in sones. If the number of vehicles remains the same, but the percentage of commercial vehicles doubles, we get about the same increase—3 decibels, 40 percent increase in sones. This gives an idea of the overall effect of added traffic and points up the annoyance power of commercial vehicles. It is hardly suitable, however, as a standard to write into a zoning ordinance. For example: standards on smoke production can be applied to railroad locomotives, but the control of locomotive smoke is not properly a responsibility of the industry served by that locomotive (unless it is an industrial locomotive owned by the plant).

It may be that standards on industrial traffic will be called specification rather than performance, but the important point is to get *some* method of describing the limits in traffic generation that we wish to set up for a given district.

The first step is to list the aspects of traffic and transport that we wish to recognize. We have background to set standards for:

- Amount of employee traffic, based on number of employees and number of shifts.
- Amount of truck traffic, based on maximum daily truckloads of raw materials in and finished products out.
- Railroad traffic, based on daily carloads in and out.
- Off-street parking space, based on number of employees, and number of company vehicles.
- Off-street loading docks, based on daily truckloads in and out.

For the last two, off-street parking and off-street loading, modern ordinances now include regulations. These are still rule-of-thumb provisions, but from experience and from the National Industrial Zoning Committee survey, we may be able to improve them.

With the other items in the list, we will have some trouble. In setting limits on number of employees, we run head-on into the weakness present in our attempts to limit industrial activity in commercial districts. It isn't reasonable to say that a plant with 100 employees is all right, but one with 101 employees is objectionable. We may be able to get around this by specifying *density of employment*—number of employees per acre of ground, for example. In this way we would spread out the focus of traffic generation.

A provision in the residence-industry district in Cleveland requires that industries locating in the district must operate only one shift and may not operate on Sundays, normal business holidays, or at night— an excellent method for reducing the objection to integrating industry into residence districts.

Standards for materials and products transportation will be difficult to establish. A provision proposed in New York City states:

> Whatever merchandise is received and shipped has a high value in relation to its size and weight, so that very little trucking traffic will be generated.

This points toward one method of measurement. Here also, a density measurement may be possible—truckloads or carloads per day per acre.

The zoning ordinance is only part of the technique for handling industrial traffic. We must provide the industrial district with thoroughfares, proper truck routes and good mass transportation. The best way to keep a horde of auto-driving industrial employees off neighboring residential streets is to provide them with more attractive methods of getting away from the factory, preferably in public transit, or at least on well-designed major thoroughfares.

10. Aesthetics. It may be questioned why I have included aesthetics as one of the regulations that should be imposed on industrial buildings. Many new factories are handsome, intelligently designed examples of functional architecture. They are set well back from the street in grounds that have been decently landscaped and that are carefully maintained. But not all new plants are built that way. In spite of the obvious advantages in employee satisfaction as well as in company advertising and community relations, we still have industrialists who want to build an architectural monstrosity that covers every square inch of land. And, of course, they can always find an architect to help them.

The truth is that the great majority of our existing factories are eyesores—and unnecessarily so, in most cases. In spite of the fact that aesthetic control is not yet universally accepted, there are a number of legal decisions that recognize the right to control the appearance of buildings. If this were not enough, we need only note the voice of the people as expressed at zoning hearings and in aesthetic control ordinances. Our supreme courts lag behind the wish of the citizens, but they will eventually catch up.

If we are going to rethink industrial zoning, we should recognize aesthetics. This is particularly true if we wish to bring industry up out of the dumps and wastelands and house it among more pleasant surroundings that are now the domain of residences. Like Caesar's wife, industries are going to have to be completely without sin if they hope to live side-by-side with decent folk.

Aesthetic standards are somewhat hazy. For our purpose, they call for simple regulations, specification standards pretty much the same as we now use in residence districts. We should have front yards, side yards, height regulations, and prohibition of monstrous advertising signs. For those combined residence and industrial districts that we shall develop some of these days, we may need review of the plans by a municipal art commission. We should not have much difficulty writing these regulations, nor in getting them accepted. They may be feeble suggestions for aesthetic control. Compared with the complete anarchy that we now permit in industrial zones, they will be a long step forward.

11. Psychological effects. For regulating uses on the basis of psychological effects, I find no method of measurement. Even to illustrate what I am talking about, it is necessary to speak of definite uses.

The clearest cases of land use objectionable because of psychological effects are those connected with the disposal of the dead. Crematoria have never been, and probably never will be, accepted as harmless. People just don't like the idea. They always express fear of odors. Yet for the past 50 years, so far as I have been able to discover, there is not one case of a crematorium having created the faintest suspicion of a nuisance. I feel quite confident in predicting that there will never be such a case in the future.

The same psychological distaste exists for funeral homes and cemeteries, although not to the same degree. There is also strong dislike for mental and contagious disease hospitals, and for prisons of all kinds. The dislike has no connections with any annoyance created by the uses.

These uses are not industries, although some zoning ordinances have tried to relegate crematoria and mental hospitals to industrial districts. However, we will face the same psychological antipathy for certain industries. No matter how sweet and clean we make a slaughterhouse, a lot of people don't want it for a neighbor. There are some other industries that people don't like, including glue factories, breweries, distilleries, and tanneries.

It may seem that these psychological nuisances are principally ones that create odor pollution and haven't shown much interest in cleaning up the smell. They will be permitted only in districts in which we allow a certain amount of odor to escape, and those districts will be as far downwind as we can put them. However, slaughterhouses can be and are being cleaned up. Properly designed, they do not create an odor nuisance. There are very few industries that seem hopeless in their efforts to eliminate odor. Someday only the hopeless ones will be allowed to perfume the air. The uses mentioned are not among the hopeless.

If the zoning ordinance is to function as we should like it to function, industries will be judged only on the effects they produce, and *any* industry will be permitted to go into *any* industrial district—including a combined residence-industry district—if it can comply with our standards. This means that if the slaughterhouse meets the standards, it will be able to move into that combined district. Perhaps we can assume that psychological hazards will be present in only the combined residence-industry district. For that combined district, we may have to prohibit certain industries by name—which is always bad.

In conclusion, the ideal regulation of industry would mention no industry by name. Of course, if I am correct in my analysis of psychological hazard, these will be exceptions. Except for the exceptions then, a zoning ordinance of the future will merely set up the standards for each zone, and any industry that can meet those standards will be permitted to locate in that zone.

"Zoning for Industry," condensed from a paper given at the Annual Meeting of the American Society of Civil Engineers, New York City, October 27, 1955.

The experience in administering performance standard zoning is practically nil so far, so the best one can do is to try to discover, from the texts, how the writers of the zoning ordinance propose to answer certain questions:

1. What are reasonable standards?
2. How can you tell prior to actual construction whether or not the plant, when it is built and operating, will comply with the standards?
3. Can you train the ordinary building inspector to make the necessary and quite complex measurements used?
4. How will you handle future violations by a plant that originally complied with all regulations?
5. How will you handle existing uses which do not comply with the new standards (uses nonconforming as to noise or smoke, etc.)?

My comments on the progress thus far in the use of standards for the control of industrial districts are based on a detailed analysis of 11 zoning ordinances, adopted or proposed, that introduce this concept, the ordinances for Albuquerque, New Mexico; Anne Arundel County, Maryland; Bismarck, North Dakota; Center Line, Michigan; Chicago, Illinois; Clarkstown, New York; Parsippany-Troy Hills Township, New Jersey; Penn Township, Pennsylvania; Rye, New York; Southfield Township, Michigan; and Warren Township, Michigan.

Effects Regulated. In "Performance Standards in Industrial Zoning," 11 effects are discussed and the possibilities of establishing numerical standards for each of them briefly explored. With three exceptions—traffic, aesthetics, and psychological effects—each of these is included in one or more of the performance standard ordinances analyzed in this paper. In addition to those effects listed in the 1951 discussion, three other sources of annoyance—electromagnetic interference, radioactive emissions, and vibration—are listed in some of the ordinances.

Number of Zones. One basic weakness of industrial zoning has been the use of the terms "light" and "heavy" industry. Planners would agree that watch manufacturing was definitely light and blast furnaces definitely heavy, but there was no agreement on the exact point at which light changed to heavy. Besides, industries that might have been considered heavy ten years ago had changed their processes and cleaned up their operations until they were no more obnoxious than industries once classed as light.

In two ordinances, only one industrial district is established. In another, the standards apply to all zones—residential and commercial as well as industrial. This raises a question on a fundamental point in zoning. Is the use of standards in these cases a proper function of a zoning ordinance? Or should this type of regulation be the subject of separate ordinances?

This is more than an academic question. There is evidence that some planners have seized on the idea of performance standards as an opportunity to introduce a type of regulation that has not previously been acceptable to the city council. As an example: a zoning ordinance establishes Ringelman No. 2 as the limit of permissible smoke in its industrial zone. This is a reasonable maximum for smoke for the entire city. But for one reason or another, the city has not been able to adopt a general smoke abatement ordinance, so that in all other districts, residential and commercial, smoke can go to any density to Ringelman No. 5—100 percent opaque—with no legal sanctions forthcoming. There are certainly temptations for the zealous planner to see performance standards as a vehicle by which he can introduce reforms that could not yet stand alone.

On the other hand, the planner may reason that smoke abatement must come someday to every city. It is much less expensive to build smoke control into the plant at the time it is originally constructed than it is to add the necessary equipment later.

The Administration of the Ordinance.   It is believed that in large cities it will be relatively simple to employ inspectors with enough technical training and skill to make the rather complex measurements necessary to determine compliance with performance standards. In Chicago, for example, there is a division of smoke abatement with a trained inspection staff competent to carry out the very complicated measurements of particulate matter proposed in the new zoning ordinance.

But for smaller cities, the Chicago provisions will certainly look forbidding. To forestall anxiety concerning an ordinance he was preparing for Kettering, Ohio (population 28,000), L. Segoe wrote:

> A preliminary investigation made by us indicates that certain of the industrial research organizations in Southern Ohio do consider themselves capable of performing the measurements and evaluations required by the proposed ordinance. Where such services are required, the cost of hiring the research firm is paid by the industry desiring to locate in the city.

The Parsippany-Troy Hills and Penn Township ordinances place on the applicant the burden of proof that he will meet the standards. In these townships, all applications for industrial use occupancy permits are reviewed by the Boards of Adjustment. These ordinances go further on certain industries. They recognize that it is unfair to judge the possible annoyance of a new plant by the annoyance created by the same kind of industry in an old plant operated somewhere else. At the same time, the governing body knows that just because it is possible to minimize noise, odor, smoke, etc., there is no certainty that the proper control devices will be installed. Therefore, the ordinances list groups of uses that have a reputation for unpleasant emissions and require applicants for these uses to submit detailed plans of their proposed control methods. But the ordinances go further and require a *public hearing* on the application, so that the citizens can also be assured of the inoffensive nature of the proposed operation.

While it may be practical to call in outside experts to review original applications, it may not be so convenient to use such consultants for routine inspections after the plant is operating. The Parsippany-Troy Hills ordinance attempts to meet this problem by allowing the Board of Appeals to require automatic recording devices.

Types of Standards Used

Noise. In all of the 11 ordinances analyzed, noise is one of the effects mentioned, and in all but one, numerical standards limiting noise are given. In three of the ordinances, the unit of measurement is the sone. In all of the others, the unit used is the decibel.

The sone is a unit of loudness, an explanation of which is beyond the scope of this paper. It does give a reasonably accurate measurement of the annoyance created by various sounds but it does not have general acceptance among acoustical scientists yet. Also, it cannot be measured directly by any instrument so that it does not lend itself to the establishment of a standard easily administered. However, I believe that the ordinances using sones to measure noise limits are not too unreasonable.

The decibel is a measure of sound pressure. Low-pitched sounds are considerably less annoying than those of high pitch. Therefore, greater intensity of sound can be permitted in the low end of the noise spectrum than in the high end. There is no instrument available which takes into account this subjective psychological characteristic of noise. The practical way to handle it at present is through the establishment of decibel limits for the sound levels at each of several frequencies.

With the definite exception of the Chicago and Clarkstown ordinances and the possible exception of the three ordinances using sones as units of measurement, all of the other ordinances are improperly and inadequately written. For example, one states that sound levels should be measured by a method "approved by the U.S. Bureau of Standards." The U.S. Bureau of Standards does not approve anything along this line. The American Standards Association does set standards for certain sound level meters, including frequency weighting networks to be incorporated in those meters. However, the frequency weighting networks are not adequate to judge the annoyance created by sounds.

Smoke. All of the ordinances examined except one established numerical standards governing the emission of smoke. In each case the Ringelman chart is specified as the measuring instrument and in one ordinance the umbrascope is listed as an optional measuring device. The limitations on smoke vary from the requirement that only smokeless fuel be used to a limitation which permits Ringelman No. 3 (60 percent density).

Standards for limiting smoke emission have probably been the easiest of all to determine because of the extensive experience with smoke abatement ordinances. A simple measuring device has been developed and is readily available.

An important consideration in establishing smoke standards is whether the control is consistent with overall municipal smoke control. One ordinance omitted any mention of smoke, undoubtedly because of the excellent smoke abatement ordinance and administration in the particular county. (My analysis did not attempt to determine how zoning standards fitted with the general smoke control ordinance, or even whether there was general smoke control in the municipality.)

Dust and Dirt. Each of the 11 ordinances introduced a provision to limit dirt and dust emission. In three of them such emission is flatly prohibited.

The provisions on smoke and particulate matter in the Chicago ordinance, however, are quite detailed, running to several pages. The ordinance sets up a rather complicated method of calculating emission including tables allowing for different heights, velocities, and temperatures of the emission. Then the limitation is stated in pounds of particulate matter per acre of lot area during any one hour.

It is quite probable that the provisions on particulate matter in the Chicago ordinance are the most equitable. Again, however, measurement will not be an easy matter, especially for small cities. The simple provisions from the other ordinances have much to recommend them. There is evidence that the writers of some of the other provisions may have copied something about which they knew little; because of this lack of knowledge, the result is garbled. The provisions that refer to standardized methods of measurement are likely to be the most satisfactory to administer.

Odor. The control of odor is provided for in each ordinance. None of them give objective standards against which to measure the odor nuisance. The provision in the Anne Arundel County ordinance is typical: Any use shall "emit no objectionable odors outside the lot lines of the tract."

While the complete prohibition of the emission of substances with unpleasant odors may have been the purpose of some of these ordinances, at least some of the provisions were included as temporary controls. The lack of simple scientific methods for odor measurement and the lack of data on the threshold of smell are still such as not to give the planner confidence. Obviously, even a substance of unpleasant odor is harmless in an olfactory sense until it reaches the concentration necesary to pass the threshold of smell. For this reason, complete prohibition is not too logical. Satisfactory odor standards are yet to come.

Toxic Gases. Most of the ordinances contain provisions on toxic gases. As with odors, the provision merely is a prohibition against emission, with one exception. The Penn Township provision is typical of the prohibiting clause: "All industrial uses shall . . . emit no noxious, toxic or corrosive fumes or gases." The Center Line ordinance establishes definite standards for certain dangerous gases.

The emission of poisonous gases is one of those matters in which there should be only one standard. With odor, it is possible that for many years it will not be economic to clean up certain processes such as brewing, baking and petroleum refining. Since these are legitimate industries, they must have a district in which they are permitted—as far downwind from residential districts as possible. But there can be no district in which a gas such as hydrogen sulfide in a toxic concentration can be permitted. It may be that standards for toxic gases are more properly located in general health or air pollution ordinances. If not located in such general ordinances, it may be necessary to use the zoning ordinance as a trailblazer.

The provisions for the control of toxic gases leave much to be desired. The Center Line ordinance, while it does use numerical standards for a few of the most prevalent industrial gases, omits others such as the by-products of lead smelting.

Glare and Heat. Provisions on glare and heat are contained in seven ordinances but in none of them are there any numerical standards. A typical provision is that for Warren Township: "Glare and heat from arc welding, acetylene torch cutting or similar processes shall be performed so as not to be seen from any point beyond the outside of the property."

There are available adequate units for the measurement of heat (degrees of temperature, calories, B.T.U.) and glare (footcandles). At the same time, it would seem unnecessary to complicate the zoning ordinance with standards expressed in such units. Prohibition in the simple terms of the quoted provisions is probably entirely satisfactory.

Industrial Sewage Waste. In four ordinances, numerical standards governing industrial wastes are established. In two others, Anne Arundel County and Penn Township, industrial sewage standards are incorporated by reference to the state department of health. Analysis indicates that the standards were primarily directed toward the prevention of stream pollution, perhaps with the idea of establishing higher standards than those of the state department of health, or of giving the local government the power to act quickly and directly to avoid prolonged abuse.

The standards are those commonly used in sanitary engineering and stream pollution control. One different provision is introduced in the Parsippany-Troy Hills ordinance, which provides that the maximum quantity of effluent shall not exceed 10 percent of the minimum daily stream flow. The zoning study commission in Chicago used the approach of studying the capacity of the municipal sewerage system to handle wastes in different parts of the system.

Several of the ordinances have been written presumably for areas as yet undeveloped industrially. (For example, Anne Arundel County: the sewerage system is also relatively undeveloped. Probably the writer of this zoning text assumed that there is not yet any limit to the capacity of a system that might be built—it is not yet necessary to make rules to limit sewage discharge on a density basis.)

Provisions relating the capacity of an existing sewer system to a specific area within a community have yet to be written.

Vibration. "Excessive vibration" is more often than not one of the manifestations forbidden in industrial districts. It appears in only three of the ordinances reviewed.

The proposed Chicago ordinance does not establish objective measurements, but it does provide differentiation. The only ordinance to contain a numerical limit on vibration is that for Center Line.

Fire and Safety. Standards to reduce fire and safety hazards, while considerably short of the idea of objective measurement, are improved over the provisions in pre-World War II ordinances. They are customarily tied in with building or fire safety codes.

Several of the ordinances include detailed standards regarding the storage of materials, particularly of flammable materials. These are directed for the most part to fire and safety protection. By far the most complete provision against fire and safety hazard is found in the Chicago ordinance.

Electromagnetic Interference. One reason for the technical education and research district in Southfield Township was to establish a district in which electronic laboratories could locate with assurance that they would be free from outside electromagnetic interference. These standards are quite complex and must be completely incomprehensible to anyone who is not an electronic engineer. In the ordinary industrial district, standards such as these may be superfluous. With the increase in importance of the field of electronics, and the increase in number of laboratories, there may be a wider need for such protection. The equity of these electromagnetic standards and the problems of measurement and enforcement are subjects on which only electronics experts are qualified to speak.

Radioactive Emissions. The imminence of general use of nuclear fission as a source of electric power raises the problem of protection from dangerous emissions. These first ordinances using performance standards have not attempted to set up numerical standards for such emissions, however, a few show recognition of the possibility of dangerous radioactive emissions.

Density and Yard Controls. Each of the 11 ordinances contains at least one of the forms of density and open-space control: minimum lot area, 5 ordinances; front yard, 10 ordinances; side yard, 9 ordinances; maximum height, 9 ordinances; lot coverage, 3 ordinances; and floor area ratio, 6 ordinances.

Perhaps most noteworthy is the fact that controls of this type are

used at all in industrial districts. In most older ordinances, regulations
for industrical districts were confined almost entirely to listing of permitted or prohibited uses. Except where a lot might adjoin a residential district, it was customary to allow construction up to any property line, unlimited height, 100 percent ground coverage, and to
specify no minimum lot area.

Bulk and density controls are not performance standards but are
specification standards. Their object, however, is to regulate several
aspects of industrial development for which we do not now have (and
perhaps never will have) suitable objective measurements. These include in particular aesthetics and traffic generation.

Several court decisions, and in particular the U.S. Supreme Court
decision in *Berman* v. *Parker*, show that aesthetics is being recognized
as a proper municipal concern. Most industrialists also recognize the
importance to themselves of attractive plants, both their own and that
of their neighbors.

Probably the most disliked effect of industry is the traffic it creates.
The only method now known to decrease traffic is to decrease the density of development. If it were possible to set a limit to traffic generation (for example, "no use or density of development which generates
in excess of 100 vehicle trips per acre per day will be permitted"), then
specification controls such as these would not be needed—at least for
the control of traffic. Control of traffic generation by lot area and
floor area ratio is far from satisfactory, but it can bring a decrease in
traffic generation, particularly where a floor area ratio of 0.50 or less
is established.

Industrial noise limits are applied to the noise from processes and
operations of the factory itself. Sometimes these are required only to
be kept below the normal street traffic noise, a perfectly logical requirement. If a reduction of density serves to decrease traffic noise,
then industrial noise must also be lessened. More important than traffic noise as the criteria with which you compare industrial noise, is the
effect of traffic noise itself on neighboring property. Several studies
have shown that industrial process noise is a relatively minor offender. All studies have shown traffic noise to be a major offender.

Many of the industrial annoyances for which performance standards
are used are the same effects that traffic produces, and for which, when
they are caused by traffic, no limits are set. Besides noise, these
would include dust and dirt, vibration, carbon monoxide gas, safety,
odors, and glare. For this reason, density controls, insofar as

they are effective in reducing traffic, may be the most important of all industrial zoning controls.

Use Lists. The goal of performance standards was the complete elimination of all lists of uses. Any use which met the standards for a district was automatically permitted to locate in that district. But there were several questions that were left unanswered and it was recognized that the goal would probably never be reached. Most of the ordinances studied list some uses that require special review procedures, for example, or that are prohibited.

There are two quite different methods of applying performance standards. The more common method is to apply the standards to the *zoning district* regulation. In the second method, the performance standards are applied to the description of the *uses*. There is little doubt that performance standards properly used should be applied to districts rather than to uses.

My general conclusion is that there is no reason to believe that the theory behind the use of performance standards in industrial zoning is not just as correct as it ever was. Some major steps have been made toward putting that theory into practice. At the same time, the first handful of ordinances using performance standards exhibits some serious weaknesses.

Probably the most serious weakness is that the planners have rushed into highly technical fields to adopt standards and measurements about which they know very little. This is particularly well illustrated in the standards for noise. (For example, one ordinance permits in the industrial district a noise of "85 decibels." This is a rather high level for frequencies under 150 cycles per second, but it is probably bearable. However, in the higher ranges, especially above 4,000 cycles, an 85 decibel sound level would be practically insufferable.)

Even the typographical errors that go unnoticed and get enacted into law are illustrations of the fact that planners may be getting out of their depth. In one ordinance the particulate matter was limited to "0.3 *grams* per cubic foot" rather than "0.3 *grains* per cubic foot." A gram is equal to about 15.4 grains. This means that this particular ordinance would permit the emission of dust in some 15 times as great a quantity as normally is considered acceptable.

We still know practically nothing about how to administer performance standards. This is something that we are only going to learn by experience. Somebody has to take the first steps and it would not be surprising if many of the steps were false. The only persons who never make any errors are the persons who never do anything. For that reason, much as I might criticize some of the zoning ordinances written thus far, I would also extend compliments and bouquets to the men who have had nerve enough to venture out in this field. If we are ever to come up with fair, equitable, and rational zoning for industry, somebody has to stick his neck out first.

Zoning May Not Be Planning, But . . .

**Extracted from the ASPO Newsletter
editorial, February 1965.**

An awful lot of planners and an awful lot of planning commissions spend an awful lot of time working with and worrying about zoning problems.

ASPO has tabulated information for 270 city planning agencies. The average city planning commission spends 48 percent of its time on zoning. It spends 16 percent of its time in subdivision review, and 36 percent of its time on all other planning matters. Eighty planning commissions reported spending 75 percent or more of their time on zoning.

These, then, are the facts of life out in the bush, among the natives.

How well are the schools preparing our youth for the great adventure? In the course of ASPO's annual survey of planning graduates, we assembled the curricula of the universities that are educating our young to be planners, fitting them for their careers in the real world. We did not find a single course that used "zoning" in its title (although we did not have curricula from all planning schools and there still may be one school that is not ashamed to clearly label a course in zoning). We were usually able to locate some mention of zoning, however, under a course in "land-use regulation" or "planning law" or some euphemism such as "implementation techniques." In one catalog, zoning was listed only as one of about a dozen subheadings describing a course in urban land economics.

Although there is some variation, the typical planning school curriculum will have 20 to 40 courses of which one will touch on zoning. If we were to assume that these single courses were always required of the student, and that the full time of the course was given over to a study of zoning techniques, zoning law, and zoning administration (which it quite evidently is not), then the average young planner coming out with a master's degree would have devoted about 5 percent of his two graduate years to an understanding of zoning.

What about the literature in planning? In the United States, the periodical literature of planning—in the academic interpretation of the word—is pretty well confined to the *Journal of the American Institute of Planners*. In a quick check over the past two years, I counted a total of 54 articles or quasi-articles (but not book reviews), of which there were two: Norman Williams' annual reviews of judicial decisions—which were principally on zoning; and one—Michael Heyman's review of legislation—which was partially on zoning. None of the regular articles, the pieces published by professors to prevent perishing, will have any truck with zoning. In pages, this ratio would also figure out to be about 5 percent of the printed material.

There can be no questioning it: Graduates now being tagged by the universities as "planners" turn up their noses at zoning. To be concerned with zoning is *infra dig*. To be asked to work in the sordid details of zoning is a mortal insult. Part of this attitude is a result of fear—fear of the unknown. They don't know anything about zoning, really. We have met young graduates with an MCP who had never even seen a zoning ordinance. But part of the attitude is a preciousness that is afflicting planning, now that it has gone academic. A zoning ordinance does not administer itself. It requires patience not preciousness, infinite patience with people. You cannot do zoning with a felt tip pen and a broad sweeping movement of the arm.

Once before, in its very early days, planners became precious, with vistas, Greek temples, and ornamental curlicues. At that time the lawyers stepped in, invented zoning, and made it possible to actually improve the lot of cities, instead of just to talk about it. History seems to be repeating itself. While planning thought soars in ever-mounting helical hop-dreams, the legal profession has started to scratch around in the dirt of zoning. Sooner or later the lawyers will figure out ways of doing the things that planners should long ago have figured out how to do—if they had not been so scared of getting their hands soiled.

The Zoning Game

Condensed from the foreword to "The Zoning Game, Municipal Practices and Policies," by Richard F. Babcock, 1966.

Persons who have had experience with zoning are rarely neutral about it. Ordinary citizens become rabid partisans, either pro or con. The planner for whom the zoning game is, more often than not, a primary occupation, if not a preoccupation, usually detests it. This is especially true if the planner is one of the younger, or simulation-model, social-milieu, spatial-manipulation brand. How can you possibly get steamed up about whether a beauty shop is a customary home occupation when there is so much to be talked about on the choice theory as related to intergroup dynamics and calculated human intervention in normative social processes?

But for its devotees, the fascination of the zoning game never ends. The fascination of bridge as a game lies in the enormous number of possible permutations of the cards, so that although the number of different hands is finite, each new deal seems difficult and is quite unlikely to be exactly repeated during the player's lifetime.

The number of permutations in zoning problems may also be finite, but it is a number of a much greater magnitude than can be obtained with 52 playing cards dealt among four hands. Bridge or chess or any other such game is played everywhere with the same set of rules. The rules may change slightly over the years, but basically they remain constant and at any given time they are universally uniform. Not so with the zoning game. And this adds the extra fillip of interest that conventional games lack. Zoning may be likened to a great national bridge tournament, with 3,000 games going on at the same time, and with each foursome playing under its own set of rules. In fact, the opposing pairs at each table might use different rules.

The literature of zoning is not very extensive. After all, it is quite young, as human institutions go. In 1966, comprehensive zoning celebrates only its 50th anniversary. To be sure, many words are written on zoning problems, but these are mostly found in the opinions of appellate courts, or in rehash and reinterpretation of those opinions. The really good and thoughtful and valuable books on zoning can be counted on the fingers of one hand.

The trouble is—aside from the boredom of the younger players of the zoning game—that the stuff being written, including the great bulk of the opinions from the bench, is almost wholly library research. Most zoning literature could be compared with the sort of passionate love stories that might be written by a cloistered celibate. This book has been written by an enthusiastic participant in the zoning game.

Perhaps because it is still so young, or perhaps because it is a rather violent disruption of man's pseudo-sacred rights in property, zoning is an institution that largely reflects the ideas of certain strong men: Bassett, the father of zoning; Bettman, the brilliant apologist; Pomeroy, the flamboyant prophet. Babcock, the combatant, bids to be another of those whose name will be long remembered by players in the zoning game.

9

About Planners

Editor's Commentary

Dennis O'Harrow believed that planning "will remain fundamentally an art . . . the personal skill of the planner—the artist—is paramount." He said that "any accomplishments that planning can boast of in the past, or can hope for in the future, are the accomplishments of individual persons and not of a system, a science, or a discipline."

His views on what makes a good planner permeate his writing. The materials in this chapter state specific abilities and traits, as in the editorial on "A Good Planner."

About education for planning, only hints of his total concern and total attention—only some strong biases—appear in speeches and editorials. His deep interest and range of attention emerged primarily in the enormous amount of time he spent talking with students; in the priority he gave whenever possible to requests from planning schools for a visit as consultant or lecturer; in his decade of serving, with special pride, as a member of the Selection Committee of the Sears-Roebuck Foundation City Planning Fellowship Program, whose commitment and leadership were influential in improving financial assistance and standards in planning education; and in the allocation of ASPO staff time and budget to the situation that was building up in the '50s: the lagging supply of trained planners for the increasing demand.

To emphasize the signs of trouble, to warn the profession, to focus attention on needs and provide factual data for action, ASPO instituted in 1956 a comprehensive annual survey of planning school enrollments and degrees supplemented by pertinent information on school budgets, faculty, tuition, research funds, scholarships, student backgrounds, starting salaries, and other special aspects of planning education. This widely used and quoted survey became a joint publication of ASPO and AIP in 1966, as did ASPO's annual listing of degree programs in planning and urban studies.

DOH's biases on education and planning as inferred from his discussions of planning problems and procedures, as typified in the handful of statements in this chapter, boil down to:

- A new species of planner is required for successful planning in the real world, for planning that considers and adapts to the actual economic and social situations.
- When planning education has either an other worldly approach to these realities or an orientation that merely produces "an ever-normal plannery" for plan making, it is not preparing planners who can plan, who can operate in actual situations, who can meet the needs and demands for planning that will be carried out.

The 1964 "widget factory" speech became a pamphlet: *The Production of Planners*, published by the University of Pittsburgh Institute of Local Government. The review for the ASPO Newsletter, written by the Institute's director of urban affairs, George S. Duggar, says that the publication "reports Dennis O'Harrow's pertinent and impertinent comments on planning education . . . the Schuster report comes out relatively unscathed, but the reader need not worry that anything else does."

The "Fish or Cut Bait" editorial two years later was equally scatheful on the M.A. to Ph.D. to research-teaching progression. It included a suggestion, however, a DOH thesis: The Ph.D. who has actually done some planning is a better researcher and a better teacher; we should introduce experience as a prerequisite for the planning Ph.D. Some of the reaction was scatheful also—both pro and con; the editorial evoked voluminous arguments and comments, some of which were published in the *ASPO Newsletter* (June–July 1966 and January 1967); some of which continued for months when educators and practitioners got together.

The "Passing Grade" editorial reflects numerous discussions with planning directors who brought to him their worries about the inability of some planning graduates to meet the standards of professional work expected of them on the job: "C or B is no longer a passing mark in an office that demands A-grade work," as he put it.

About jobs in planning he could be equally critical—and particularly helpful. Anyone who has ever known ASPO knows that ASPO was the prime source of information and contacts on jobs: publications of job ads, semimonthly since 1957; innovation of a conference job market in 1952. Less widely known are ASPO's battles to eliminate residence requirements for planning jobs and written examinations for planning directors, and the campaigns to improve salaries for planners—with constant use of inquiry-answers, consultations, and committee work as well as surveys, articles, and speeches. On fair play by employees and employers, DOH used editorials to prescribe some famous do's and don'ts.

And on the need for more, and more effective use of, professional planners, he prescribed a new remedy: the training and utilization of paraprofessionals. His October 1966 editorial, giving a "logical analysis with a leavening of illogic," used the feedback from planners and community college administrators following a meeting of a small group of ASPO members and presidents of community colleges that had been held at his suggestion and funded by the Sears-Roebuck Foundation. The premises, and hence the conclusions, of this editorial might be disputed: beginning in 1970, the shortage situation began to reverse. But the predictions may prove valid: numerous jobs created by the planning prerequisites written into federal programs; a development explosion when the money situation eases; the need to extend the effectiveness of professional planners; the logical use of trained paraprofessionals. Support for this approach to better utilization of professional planning personnel and improved administration of planning programs became ASPO policy: an official statement (recommended by the ASPO Education Committee and debated and adopted by the ASPO Board and membership at the 1967 ASPO Conference) of a policy of "active encouragement, liaison, and professional assistance toward" further development of junior and community college curricula in community services and public affairs—not only to train technicians for specialized work in planning and related agencies, but also to open the field to those barred because of the time and cost of obtaining professional education, and to educate people generally for more knowledgeable citizenship.

This chapter touches on some of his worries—and optimism—concerning planners and planning. It ends with a statement from his last paper, his presidential address to the International Conference of the International Federation for Housing and Planning, in West Berlin, Germany, a few hours before his death—one of those messages so pervasive and powerful in his writings that in valedictory to Dennis O'Harrow, his peers proclaimed him the "conscience of the planning profession."

What Makes a Good Planner

**An Advocate of the People, quoted from
the ASPO Newsletter editorial "The Peoples'
Problems Are Planners' Problems,"
March 1955.**

So long as we live in a democracy the people must be heard. Their case is entitled to the best presentation we can give it. We, as planners, must act as their advocates.

**Understanding People, quoted from "The
Need for Local Planning Assistance," a
speech to the Southern Association of State
Planning and Development Agencies,
Memphis, October 15, 1952.**

We must plan for people as they *are*, not as we might wish them to be.

"We must plan for people" has been the battle cry of enthusiastic young planners for some years now. Too often, the young planner's idea of "people" was based on his intimate knowledge of the likes and dislikes of one person—himself. Personally, he preferred Bach to bebop, therefore, people should have more and better access to Bach.

Planning is beginning to try to understand people as they are, and to plan for them on that basis. Psychology and sociology are being consulted. And the two sciences promise to bring some decided changes in our thinking.

**An Endless Curiosity, extracted from the
ASPO Newsletter editorial "People,"
May 1957.**

Planning calls for an endless curiousity about people—how many, where they are, what they are, what they do.

Some of the information we gather can be used in a quantitative fashion. Information used quantitatively helps us judge the magnitude of any proposal we make, the size of a sewage treatment plant, the area to be reserved for residential building, the width of a highway. We can devise tables and graphs to illustrate quantitative information—and we do, to document the reports we make.

However, planners cannot afford to stop with only that knowledge of people which can immediately be arranged in a table and used to back up a project proposal. We have to squirrel up all sorts of information on people which we may never use directly. This is a qualitative sort of information and we get it from many sources— some reliable and some questionable.

While we don't talk about it, a lot of what we know about people comes from a dangerously small sample: ourselves, our own family, our circle of friends, our fellow-employees. We must always keep looking for new information that will help us discount the bias in our personal sample. We must be alert to what characteristics of people are different from our own, what people do now that they didn't do when we were children, or what has changed in the past few years.

It would be wonderful if all our information about people came to us with chi-squares and correlations and 95 or 99 percent confidence determinations. But it does not, although some data will eventually be rigorously demonstrated. By that time people will be changing again, and we shall need to prepare to serve those changes.

Much of the effectiveness of planning depends on our skill at foretelling what people will do before they do it. It behooves us to be alive to all signs and omens.

Idealism and Realism, extracted from the ASPO Newsletter editorial "Idealism, Realism and Moderate Sin," July 1957.

We ought to get it out of our heads—and out of the heads of our critics—that idealism and realism are opposites. Actually, they complement each other, go hand in hand. Realism is an objective appraisal of the present, idealism is an objective plan for the future.

A big trouble is some of the stuff that tries to parade as realism. Take "political realism," for example, a phrase that is frequently thrown up to planners. You must give here, ease up there, we are told, because of political reality. Don't insist on decent subdivision standards, park and playground reservations—it isn't realistic politically. Don't try to enforce a housing code—it doesn't make political sense.

But political realism is not giving in to the pressure of a self-seeking minority, it is trying to act in accord with the way the majority would vote if they were given a fair statement of the case and a chance to vote. There isn't much doubt how the people would vote if you put it up to them: Do you want parks, or don't you? Do you think housing should be safe and sanitary, or should you let a guy get away with whatever he can? This is true political realism, because sooner or later the people will vote on all these questions—if not directly then indirectly by voting in the candidates who answer the questions the way people want them answered, and voting out the others.

The so-called practical people prefer to spend $10 of their children's money for cure, rather than $1 of their own money for prevention. Slums, crowded and overbuilt cities, traffic jams and traffic deaths, air pollution, stream pollution, and land pollution—the idealists want to stop these things before they happen. You will do well to throw in with the idealists, for in the end they turn out to be the most practical people.

The Right Qualities, extracted from the ASPO Newsletter editorial "A Good Planner," December 1958.

What makes a good planner? How do you spot one? How do you spot a not-so-good one? What does the one have that the other lacks? How did they both get that way?

It would help personnel examiners and mayors and plan commissioners a lot if we could give straight-out answers to those questions. In fact, it would help even to know for sure how we differentiate between good and bad planning, just in the abstract. But you can't hang around this business for long without picking up some ideas, some prejudiced answers to the questions.

One of the first good signs that comes to mind is the sense of responsibility to the community. The planner has a moral contract with himself to finish what he starts, to stay with a job until the planning operation is running smoothly or is over the next hump. If he is a consultant, he doesn't sign off the minute a report is delivered. If he is a consultant and has underestimated the cost of a job, he skips the profit or takes a loss rather than turn in shoddy work.

A good planner is intellectually honest. This is important. If he is a hypocrite or weaseler, people find him out eventually and he loses his effectiveness.

Closely related to intellectual honesty is the ability to see oneself and one's actions in the proper scale. Any planner who is worth his salt recognizes his own ignorance of the processes of urbanization. He is not weak or apologetic, neither is he cocksure nor arrogant. He has a sense of humor. If he pontificates, if he is self-important—shun him!

A good planner has courage without being pigheaded. This is a most difficult trait to define and to acquire. It could be the same as maturity. It includes the ability to compromise but not to surrender; it includes the strength to acknowledge mistakes.

Of these criteria of a good planner, not one is taught in planning schools. Probably some of them are learned in planning schools. A student gets older while he is in school, which aging process theoretically has some relation to his acquiring maturity. Perhaps the planner gets more lift towards acquiring these virtues through experience. The art of successful compromise is learned through compromising successfully—aided occasionally by the lessons learned from unsuccessful compromise.

But there remains a suspicion that the good planner is born so or is developed so by a lot of things that we don't understand. He is the type of person who would have been good in a number of callings, which is one reason why civil service examinations are futile exercises. They just don't get at the right qualities.

The Real Pro, quoted from the ASPO Newsletter editorial "Odds and Ends," January 1964.

A planner sent me a clipping from a newspaper column whose writer stated that he had once longed to be a "real pro," which he defined as someone going about his familiar routine with efficiency and dispatch. But he no longer feels that way, the columnist says, because a real pro "never takes a chance, the great deeds are done by dreamers."

The planner who sent the quotation felt that this described an ailment of planners, too many "real pros." My correspondent to the contrary notwithstanding, I believe there is not enough professionalism in planning. And I am not referring to the qualifications that are being debated in connection with registration. I refer to the efficiency and dispatch that the columnist wrote about. The ability to deliver what is ordered, the ability to meet deadlines, yea even the definition of a politician, the man who deals with the art of the possible.

The opposite of the "real pro" is not the "dreamer," it is the dilettante.

The Paramount Skill, quoted from the preface to *Principles and Practice of Urban Planning,* **edited by William I. Goodman.**

Planning strives hard to be a science, but it will always remain fundamentally an art. Which is to say that while techniques are important and constant improvement is desirable, the personal skill of the planner—of the artist—is paramount. What he does is not nearly as crucial as how he does it.

About Education for Planning

The Required Background, quoted from "The Relation of Health and Welfare Planning to City Planning," a speech to the National Council on Social Work, Chicago, May 30, 1952.

An area of confusion I should like to clear up is the term "physical planner." Fewer and fewer city planners are true physical planners. In fact, I would go so far as to say that no person in responsible charge of a successful city planning operation is truly a physical planner. If you wish honestly to understand and to improve cities today, you must have a background, either through education or acquisition, of sociology, economics, public administration, law and the arts of communication, as well as a background in design and engineering.

A Long and Difficult Process, quoted from the ASPO Newsletter editorial "Planning in the United States: Strength Through Diversity," May 1955.

The professional city planner operates in a world somewhere between the topmost planes of pure science and the bottom-most practical application and politics. He must be able to see over the tops of the tallest trees without ever taking his feet off the ground.

The strength of any science or profession or branch of knowledge will be found in the ability of its servants to practice self-criticism. This probably explains the growth of planning beyond the civic design stage. The planners looked and found themselves wanting—wanting in knowledge of people, of economics, of politics. The more they required of themselves the more difficult it became to live up to their own requirements.

As a result of these difficult requirements, good planners are scarce. The education of a planner is a long and difficult process and there is very little agreement on what his education should be.

The New Species, extracted from "The Capture and Training of Planners," a speech to the Chicago Chapter, American Institute of Planners, June 9, 1955.

The general method of selecting a graduate course for a would-be planner is to look at his background—his prior college record, that is—match this against a predetermined standard, then inject into him all those courses by which he falls short of your standard. This sounds like a foolproof scheme. You find out what the fellow lacks of being a trained planner, then you fill in the gaps by teaching him the rest. But there are two major chances for error.

The first comes in sizing up what the student already has. You can't tell a Christmas present by looking at the wrapping paper.

The second source of error in the fill-in-the-missing-part scheme is, of course, the standard picture of a planner that you are trying to match.

What are some of the things that you are concerned with in urban renewal, for example? Well, it's politics—two kinds, clean and dirty.

It is irate housewives and the weird workings of citizens organizations. It is red tape—federal, state, and local versions. It is race relations.

It is juvenile delinquency. It is contracts, mortgages, assessments, builders, real estate developers. It is how to get things done with a staff that is inadequate both in number and experience.

I have a feeling that in most schools there is a great deal of other worldly approach to the problems of operating in the realities of the urban milieu. The breed of persons I describe is a new species that has been spawned as a result of the hyperurbanization that now afflicts the world. It's a group that has to be equally at home in municipal finance, the sociology of mass housing, the law of eminent domain and the economics of industrial location. We frequently call them "generalists" because they have to move about freely in so many different fields.

But are they planners in the L'Enfant-Burnham-Olmstead meaning of the word? We can say that the planning profession has changed and evolved with a changing world. But that leaves out the designer, or at least says to him "You're an anachronism—out of date—not a true city planner!"

While the planners I speak about may have to be all things to all people—an economist to economists, a sociologist to sociologists, an engineer to engineers—there is one theme to all their operations. That theme is interest in the *city*, the development of the city, the operation of the city, the problems of the city. Maybe we should stop calling them planners and start called them "urbanists."

What Is a Widget?, condensed from "The Production of Planners," a speech to the jubilee year tour group of the Town Planning Institute of Great Britain, Pittsburgh, September 28, 1964.

At times I get the feeling that planning education in this country is very much like the owner of a factory going out and saying to his workers on the production line, "Well, boys, today we will start making widgets." Then the dialogue starts:

"What is a widget?"

"I don't know."

"Well, don't you think that we ought to send somebody out to find
out what widgets are supposed to do?"

"Certainly not! That would interfere with our creativity, with our
individual initiative, with free enterprise."

We had in the United States (as of June 1964) 33 universities offering
degrees in planning. When you get 33 factories making widgets, all
designed by the same nonobjective process, you get quite a variety of
widgets. You go out to buy one, and you are never quite sure what
you will come home with. I will assume that the purpose in granting a
planning degree is to indicate that the grantee has achieved a measur-
able and satisfactory competence in planning.

Now what is a planner? Perhaps we are not quite ready for that
question. What takes place in the office of a public planning agency, a
city planning department, a county planning commission?

Based on some 16 years in the office of the American Society of
Planning Officials, listening to stories, reading reports, answering
questions, visiting planning agencies all over the United States, I have
become firmly convinced (as I am sure everyone in my position would
be) that the most important single operation in planning in the United
States from the standpoint of personnel, money, brain power,
troubles, politics, public acceptance or damnation, and almost every
other measure that you can name—the most important single activity—is the administration of land-use control ordinances, principally
the zoning ordinance. The ordinary public planning office in the
United States will spend from one-third to nine-tenths of all its energy,
time, and money on administration of the zoning ordinance.

So, under my widget theory, zoning is likely to get short shrift in
the planning curriculum. And it does. In fact, in the ASPO office we
have hired young planners from prominent planning schools who had
never even seen a zoning ordinance or zoning bylaw before they came
to work for us. This neglect of zoning has another effect. Not only is
the fledgling planner ignorant of zoning, he avoids it wherever possible. He often resigns a post in which he is required to spend time
working with zoning. It doesn't fit in with his plans for "career advancement."

I would guess that something over 99 percent of our planning efforts
are directed toward planning for urban areas. Therefore, it would
seem reasonable that a young man being trained to enter the planning
field should know something about the problems and mechanics of urban government, the nuts and bolts skills of public administration and

operating a city. So naturally, under the widget theory of production, our young men come out into the world completely illiterate in this subject.

I am, for the sake of emphasis, unfair to the universities of America when I indicate that they are turning out a product that does not meet the market demand. Actually, a very large proportion of the planners in the United States are busily occupied in making plans, and for this the universities do prepare their students.

I illustrate this situation by drawing an analogy with another governmental activity. Our government buys a great amount of corn, wheat, oats, rye, and so on in order to stabilize the market price of the grain. The government then stores it in hundreds of clusters of storage bins for two or three years, after which they take it out into the Pacific Ocean and dump it overboard. When this system was first invented it was christened "the ever-normal granary."

For the past several years now, the federal government has financed the making of city plans. This activity has reached a federal expenditure of some $30 million a year, which is theoretically matched by an additional $10 to $15 million furnished by the local community. As a result, of course, we must make enormous numbers of plans, and we must have ever-increasing numbers of planners to make these plans. This undertaking I now call "the ever-normal plannery."

However, the U.S. Department of Agriculture, although it still buys surplus grains, has also another scheme in which it pays the farmers for *not* growing certain crops. In view of the surfeit of plans in the United States, I feel quite sure that someday we must also adopt this same philosophy and pay planners for *not making plans*.

There is an old saying that there are ways to kill a cat other than by choking it to death on butter. There are other ways to kill planning besides spending too much money on it. Nevertheless, it is still, it seems to me, a most effective method of murder. I am not just being facetious about this. It is my belief that there is a basic orientation in American planning (which is naturally reflected in university curricula) that looks upon the *plan* as the end-product, the ultimate good, the *raison d'etre*. We cannot be bothered with the sordid details of accomplishment, of carrying out the plan. This is why we hate the details of zoning administration. This is why we prefer to view the city from a high theoretical level, rather than to see it as a sprawling, complex machine whose streets you must sweep, whose garbage you must haul, whose buildings you must protect from fire, whose people you must protect from crime, and whose exchequer you must guard carefully. And it is this preciosity, in fact, that leads us so much of the time to the preparation of plans that can never be carried out.

Since the invitation to me to make this address delicately hinted that I would be expected to produce a kind of Schuster report, it behooved me to look at the report again, something I have not done for many years (*Report of the Committee on Qualifications of Planners*, Sir George Schuster, Chairman, Cmd. 8059, His Majesty's Stationery Office, London, 1950). I fail to find anything that has happened in the 14 years since it was issued that would make it out of date. For example, take the following:

> [Our] analysis indicates that there is a two-fold planning function to be performed: (1) The determination of policies—social, economic and strategic; and (2)The preparation and carrying through of a plan for the use and development of land in conformity with these policies (Par. 53).

The determination of policies—what we call a policy plan—has only since the '60s been recognized in the U.S. as the indispensable foundation for planning development. And note the words "carrying through of a plan." We still avoid recognizing this as a part of the planning process.

The Schuster committee goes on to say:

> Cost . . . must dominate positive planning, since there is no end to the improvements in environment which are ideally desirable (Par. 65).
>
> . . . An essential qualification which must be represented in the staff of any planning department is ability to appreciate the relation of cost to planning . . . (Par. 176).

The report stresses the differentiation between the two kinds persons needed on a planning staff:

> Our appreciation of the relations between the chief planning officer and the experts, and again between the overall function of "planning" and the ancillary function of "design," points to the need for two broadly distinguishable classes:
>
> (a) persons with qualities of judgment and administrative ability who have experience and understanding of the specialist skills required without necessarily being fully qualified in any particular lines; and
>
> (b) persons with technical qualifications who do not necessarily require skill in handling the general problems of administration (Par. 185).

It is important to remember, even if the point is an elementary one,
that no system of pre-entry (university or college) education can produce a qualified "planner" in the sense of a man qualified to hold a
responsible post in a planning organization. For this, practical experience must be added. What pre-entry education can do is to produce
people who are good "potential planners," that is to say, people with
an educational foundation which will enable them to profit by experience and thereby to acquire the qualifications for a key planning officer as we have defined them . . . (Par. 189).

And, finally, the principal qualification for a chief planner is stated in
this sentence:

. . . the overriding need is to secure for town and country planning
what we have called the "wisdom of good minds" (Par. 167).

There were two points in the Schuster report which, however, do indicate that the report is now 14 years old. One of these is quite minor. In
many places throughout the report, the committee points out that the
basic training for a planner can be in any one of many fields: "There
are . . . subjects which have a special affinity to planning—such as
economics, sociology, geography, estate management, architecture,
engineering, etc. . . . ."

But there was also this statement: "There are, no doubt, certain subjects, such as modern languages or higher mathematics, which are so
entirely disconnected from the work involved in town and country
planning that the graduate in them is unlikely to want to qualify for
such work" (Par. 191). Since that was written, we have seen two revolutions in the world. One is the enormous increase of national foreign
aid flowing from the Western nations to the underdeveloped nations. I
can conceive that a young man who first specialized in Swahili as a
modern language might be particularly interested in town planning in
Africa, and one who specialized in Spanish could become easily convinced of the need for town planning in Latin America. Furthermore,
because of the second revolution, that of electronic data processing, I
can see how a student of mathematics could become interested in
problems of town planning—in fact there are a number of such people
in the United States. So, if I were really preparing another Schuster
report for the future, I would make no exceptions as to the basic
disciplines which would lead one into town and country planning.

The second and really more significant point about the Schuster
report is not one that can be precisely illustrated with a quotation.

Throughout the report there is mention of the social and economic issues involved with planning. This is emphasized time and time again, and although it was not an original idea with the committee, it is used to batter away at the bastion of infallibility that certain of the technical professions were inclined to build up.

This idea was the basis on which the report recommended the widening of the so-called planning profession.

The change in this that I see since 1950 is one of emphasis. The Schuster report—and most of our thinking, writing, talking, and teaching—emphasize the primacy of land-use planning, noting that it has effects on the economic and social conditions and problems of the area. Therefore, our planning should consider and adapt to the economic and social situation in the community. Nowadays, however, we are clearly heading for a troika, in which, on an equal basis with land-use planning (or physical planning), we shall have social *planning* and economic *planning*.

There is quite a ferment around the world on this problem of who are planners, what is planning, and how do you educate them for it. The American Institute of Planners is searching its soul in meeting after meeting. There is ferment in Britain on the same subject. The *Economist* (June 27, 1964) echoes the Schuster report:

> [Town planners] consider the complexity of the task of engineering land, people, and investment into a livable, workable whole is so great and the special skills involved so numerous, that it is useless to pretend that any sort of training can turn out an individual fit to describe himself as a town planner. Planning must instead be done by teams of experts, each contributing to the common task.

The article points its finger right at the Institute:

> The Town Planning Institute cannot bring itself to decide whether to accept the recommendation of its own special committee to admit the membership of the people with a general planning training (which means a smattering of all the branches of knowledge involved) and also specialists in any of these branches.

The article also quotes statistics which I feel quite sure could be matched on this side of the Atlantic:

> Even among the chief planning officers of counties and county boroughs, there are still 40 percent not trained in planning at all (often the job goes to an engineer). In the urban and rural districts of over 20,000 population, only one in nine planning officers is so qualified.

However, I disagree violently with the gratuitous observation with which the *Economist* ends this particular paragraph: "The dismal consequences are all too visible everywhere." I do not find England dismal, nor will my planning blood calmly accept all the blame for dismalness in England or anywhere else it is found.

As the text for my concluding observations on this subject, I take one final sentence from the *Economist* article: "The town planning profession is probably unique in that there are dedicated members of it who maintain it should not exist at all." This is, of course, an extreme case of schizophrenia. (The *Economist* described us as "a notoriously fissiparous lot," which sent me to the dictionary.) It is, nevertheless, an embodiment of the key problem. Is there actually a separate *profession* of planning? Or is this qualification for so-called planning really a skill in synthesis? A multilinguistic ability in the several jargons spoken by architects, engineers, sociologists, economists, and so on? A special understanding of the intricacies and interrelationships of the forces that operate in an urban area? A dedicated, but objective and practical attitude toward promoting the public interest? Is planning, perhaps, an "overlay" skill? The Schuster "wisdom of good minds" that could appear anywhere?

If we finally decide that there is no such thing as a planning *profession*, I see in this no threat at all to us as individuals working in the fields that we work in, nor do I see in this any reason to abandon our national institutes. Certainly there is no end of subjects to which we can address ourselves in our meetings, no visible end to the problems of urban development that stretch ahead of us over the years, the decades, the centuries. No matter who we are, how we are trained, what we call ourselves—we know and our governments know and the citizens in our community know that our skills are needed and that a lot more people like us with our abilities are needed, and that as the world continues to spin and the number of human beings increase and crowd closer and closer together, the colleges and universities are going to have to turn out more and more people to do exactly the things we are doing or trying to do.

I said that planners are persons who make plans. I am, therefore, inclined to believe that the converse is also true: planning is whatever planners do. This might sound circular and not a very tight definition. However, there is a limit to the accomplishment of planning. As my authority here I quote from the poet laureate of planning, Sir Frederic Osborn:

Plan Man Can;
But no man, be he never so tyrannic or Panjandrian,
Neronian, Titonian or vainly Ozymandian,
Arabian or Fabian, enchanted Kubla-Khanian,
or Pan-Humanitarian, or Franc'Hispan-Falangian,
Can Plan Man.

"Fish or Cut Bait," extracted from the ASPO Newsletter editorial, April 1966.

Really, I like Ph.D.'s; they are normal human beings when they are not actively being Ph.D.'s. Although one should never make cracks about a minority group, I am getting alarmed at the prospect of an increasing attrition in the ranks of potentially useful planners, young people who propose to desert the tinsel and fleshpots of the world for the Groves of Academia. The basic requirement for admission to those groves is a sheet of paper labeled "Doctor of Philosophy."

As I see it, the planning schools themselves are responsible for the upsurge in Ph.D.'s, and all because they are becoming increasingly schizophrenic about their mission. They want to continue to train planners, but they have been bitten by the research bug and they also want to become research institutions.

If your object is to have your teaching done by research-type Ph.D.'s, you need a lot more manpower than otherwise. A research-type Ph.D. should spend at least two hours on research for each hour he spends on teaching and, ideally, the ratio should be higher. Even at the two-for-one figure, it will take three research-type Ph.D.'s to make one full-time instructor. Couple this to the planning school explosion and you can appreciate what a great demand for Ph.D.'s is building up. Also, of course, we must recognize the rigid caste system in universities that insists that all the help have a Ph.D., a system that makes the castes of India look like the Brotherhood of Man. We certainly do not want the members of the planning school faculty to be second-class citizens.

What really worries me is not so much the loss of good people to public service, nor the quantity taken by the three-to-one ratio. There is still an ample supply of intelligent and well-motivated kids who could become first-rate planners. We are an affluent country, we can afford the ineffiency of the lush university customs. And I do not want to downgrade research. But I am concerned about what sort of teaching this system is going to give us.

I believe that in order to teach something you should have had some practical experience with it. I have never heard of a reading teacher who could not read, nor of an arithmetic teacher who could not add. I grant that the pupil may someday surpass the instructor. The swimming coach who turns out a champion does not need to be a champion himself, but he sure has to be able to swim before he starts telling others how to do it.

I am convinced that in order to teach planning, the instructors should be able to plan, should first have done some planning. So when a child dives into nursery school at the age of four and does not surface again until about 23 years later as a Ph.D., it will be hard to prove to me that he really has what it takes to teach planning—even one-third of the time.

Planning has always seemed to me to be a very practical field. This makes planning a *profession*—not a *discipline*. It is more like medicine than it is like sociology. In both medicine and planning there is a world of room for research, but what we really hope to produce are doctors who can heal, planners who can plan. We don't leave the teaching of surgery to a man who has never made an incision or tied a suture. So . . .

While I am not averse to pointing out a problem without offering a solution, I do have a suggestion. There are even a couple of precedents. The first precedent is the customary requirement for registration as an architect (another rather practical profession). The general rule is that an architect may not be registered as a professional until he has practiced architecture under the supervision of a registered architect for three years. The second precedent is the award of professional degrees by some engineering schools. This takes place only after the graduate has had five years of field experience in engineering and submits an approved thesis on a subject in which he has had experience during the five years.

There is a bit of ferment in the academic world right now about the growing number of almost-but-not-quite Ph.D.'s. These are the ones who have done all of their course work, passed all their exams, but have not finished their dissertations. They have gone out in the world beyond the cloisters and are apparently doing pretty well. The more realistic members of the establishment, who believe that such people have something to offer, would like to bring some of them back. But it cannot be done, they do not have the papers. These renegades are known unofficially as ABD's—All But Dissertation. Even if the ABD were a real degree, those who held it would be below the salt and could not be accepted.

I know that you cannot fight Academic Snobbery, not even as effectively as you can fight City Hall. But I propose that we simply introduce experience as a prerequisite for the degree of Ph.D. in planning. When the student finishes his academic stint, he becomes an ABE—All But Experience. He is shoved out of the nest and told to go to work. After three years of satisfactory planning experience, he gets his Ph.D. and can hold up his head among his fellow academicians. And he is better able to teach professionals because he is a professional himself. I believe the Ph.D. who had actually done some planning to qualify for his degree would also thereby be a better researcher.

As I said, I like Ph.D.'s, several of my best friends are Ph.D.'s. That is, they still *were* my friends before they read this editorial.

"Passing Grades," extracted from the ASPO Newsletter editorial, July 1967.

Each time a child crosses the threshold from one school level to the next—kindergarten to grade school to high school to university—he receives a shock. He finds that the new school demands more of him: more reading, more homework, more accuracy, and, especially, more responsibility on his part—less handholding by his teachers.

To some extent the student is prepared for the increased demand because he has experienced it already, the second grade was more difficult than the first, the third more difficult than the second. Still the transition before was easier and the change less abrupt. The step to a higher level is so great that many never make it, although they may appear to have done so, attending classes until they have exhausted their instructors' patience or have reached the legal age-minimum for dropouts. Most young people, however, are able to survive the change. The principal tool in the survival kit is the passing grade. The passing grade tells nothing of substance, only that in the judgment of an unknown teacher, the student met unidentified local standards in his work.

Very few students, at least among those who are not premeditated high school dropouts, pace themselves to achieve no more than a passing grade in all subjects, although many will hold their efforts to the minimum in subjects in which they have no interest. Nevertheless, some students, trying their best, end their educational career, be it high school, college or university, with a level of accomplishment that is labeled "passing," i.e., considerably short of perfection, even of competence.

Educators attempt to convince the students that at each successive stage there will be less tolerance of mistakes and sloppy work. The passing grade gets higher as the education gets higher, from the E just above failing F in grade school to the C in college and the minimum B in graduate school. But, even though the student is accustomed to stricter grading and higher standards as he progresses, he is rarely prepared for the standards he is expected to meet in his first job, if that job is in a first-rate organization. In such an organization, after a reasonable shakedown, mistakes cannot be tolerated. C or B is no longer a passing mark in an office that demands A-grade work.

Of course, there are second-rate and third-rate organizations, just as there are second-rate and third-rate schools; and in these, B and C work is acceptable. But it is a traumatic experience for both employer and employee when the *magna cum laude* graduate of Podunk U. discovers how completely unprepared he is for work in an organization that demands professional quality in his performance. Many students who come out with the mistaken idea that their passing grades—and even their better-than-passing grades—are genuine hallmarks of their sterling ability, do learn to adjust to the stiffer demands of professional performance. This is possible if, along the way, the student has acquired skill in self-appraisal and self-criticism. If he lacks these skills, he is in for a rough time.

The employer who has had to accept the school's certificate at face value must discover for himself the flaws that are glossed over. After a reasonable trial, he should be able to appraise the worth of the certificate as 50 or 60 or some other percentage of par. If the employer also has a position that requires only a 50 or 60 percent ability, the new graduate can be fitted in. But if there is no such position, or the employer cannot afford to pay for a certificate worth considerably less than face value, he must encourage the new graduate to transfer to another organization.

There is some hope of a better day to come. In an article describing the new method of teaching by computer, *Changing Times* predicted the elimination of grades in education, both grades as measures of competence and as years of school. The computer will not be satisfied until the student has really learned the subject. He is permitted to leave the subject when, and not until, he knows it. The bright student will finish sooner than the less bright, but their mastery of the subject will be the same at the end. In the long run, the quick learner will complete his education with competence in more and more difficult areas than will the slow learner. This should make possible a more accurate assessment of the student's ability than is now possible with diplomas and grade transcripts.

About Jobs and Planning

**"The Battle for Brains," quoted from
the ASPO Newsletter editorial,
September 1955.**

I don't hold much for security in the usual sense because I think the planner wants a different kind of security. I think what he wants is a reasonable assurance that his work will be taken seriously. The most frequent question I get about specific jobs is "What is the 'climate' for planning?" It does not necessarily correspond to the meteorological climate. But honestly, how often can we assure anyone of security in the acceptance of planning?

We can't buy glowing advertisements, we can't write off big salaries as a cost of doing business. We can't offer lush scholarships, big expense accounts, stock bonuses, Christmas melons. Usually we can't even offer a normal opportunity for advancement. It almost looks like we are going into the battle for brains with a popgun and a wooden sword. But maybe we do have another weapon—a secret weapon.

It's so secret that I don't think even planners know what it is. I have a hunch that planning offers something that is considered naive in this practical, pecuniary world of ours. Maybe we should ask the planning commissioners what induced them to get on a planning commission where they could be targets for every self-seeking operator that they happen to thwart. If they can tell us this, then maybe we'll know why several thousand of our 164 million people chose planning as a full-time job.

When we learn what our secret weapon is, let's bring it out in the open and start using it. We're going to need it badly in the battle for brains.

Facing the Competition, quoted from "When to Promote and When to Recruit," an article written for Public Personnel Review, **June 1955.**

Except for reasons of political expediency, there seems to be no excuse for residence requirements. These reasons have no place in recruiting for public administration employees at a professional level.

One of the most serious dangers in government service is stagnation. Even though an employee may eventually rise from the lowest position to the top spot in a department, I believe that he should know that sooner or later he must be able to meet unrestricted competition for the next job up the ladder. The other side of the picture is that the city should also know that it faces unrestricted competition for the services of its best men.

"Lady, Please Don't Pinch the Melons!" extracted from the ASPO Newsletter editorial, July 1953.

Human beings are not cantaloupes on a fruit stand, to be picked up, pinched, and smelled, finally to be discarded because you didn't want a melon for breakfast anyway. If there is a job to be filled, we at ASPO want to help locate the right man for the job. We feel that through this activity we make one of our greatest contributions to our primary objective: the improvement of city planning. That is why we sometimes have pretty strong reactions when we find that a job is not all that it is painted to be.

It is considered good personnel administration (and we agree) to promote persons from lower into higher positions. We applaud this practice. But we do not like to be asked to advertise a job when it is cut and dried that a staff member already on the scene will be promoted into that job. Even less do we like to be asked to advertise an examination that is merely to legitimatize the status quo. The ground rules in some cities provide that after six months or so a temporary appointee has only to make a passing grade to become permanent. If this is the rule, so be it. But it is dishonest to say that a vacancy exists for which other persons may apply.

I often wonder why this callous attitude toward human beings? It seems to me that the best explanation is lack of experience in those persons responsible for recruiting. I cannot see how anyone who has ever hunted for a job can behave in this manner. Perhaps the war, when men were commodities, the same as trucks and airplanes and barrels of powdered eggs, had something to do with it.

We do not pretend to be personnel experts. But during the course of a year we read several hundred letters from human beings looking for planning jobs, and we personally interview many others. We know that we speak for these men and women when we ask that those responsible for filling new positions observe a few simple rules of honesty and courtesy:

> Don't offer a job when you don't have one and all you want to do is to pinch the melons.
>
> Don't say that you have a job at one salary, then offer the applicant a lower salary.
>
> Don't say you have a job if you plan to promote a staff member or to legitimatize a temporary appointee.
>
> Don't ask an applicant for a personal interview unless you are willing to pay his expenses.
>
> Acknowledge every application promptly.
>
> Make your decision promptly and inform *all* applicants that the decision has been made.

Actually, this whole article was summarized many centuries ago better than I could hope to do it: Therefore, all things whatsoever ye would that men should do to you, do ye even so to them.

"Queen for a Day," extracted from the ASPO Newsletter editorial, May 1954.

Shortly after "Lady, Please Don't Pinch the Melons!" appeared, I received a phone call: "N'yaa! Please don't pinch the *lemons!*"

I listened to the caller's experiences. Some months ago he had several jobs to fill, and we had given him the names of some persons interested in changing jobs—or so they had told us. The prospective employer had written to them, describing the openings and asking whether or not they were interested. He had received acknowledgment of this communication from less than one-fifth of the persons he had written. One of the few who did answer was a planner whose record and references looked good. Since the man lived a great distance away and the position was a junior one, the employer decided to offer the position without a personal interview. He wrote, offering the man the job. He has yet (a year later) to receive any acknowledgment of his offer. One young man was brought in for a personal interview (expenses paid). The employer was satisfied with what he saw. The applicant was satisfied with what he was offered and agreed to report for work in about three weeks. On the day he was to begin his new job, he wired the employer saying that he had decided to take another position, one paying a little more money.

Although most of the reaction to the melon-pinching editorial was favorable, there were enough of these quite graphic descriptions and stories from the other side of the fence to show that the sins are not committed only by the employers. Perhaps the most frequent complaint from the employers was against the butterfly type. This is the man who stays not quite long enough to become completely trained— or just short of the time when he is beginning to pay his own way— then moves on to another job.

In spite of what we might like to think about scientific testing and examination, the final selection in many jobs is frequently based on some mighty insignificant items—seemingly. These would include such things as promptness in answering correspondence, neatness in completing an application form, courtesy during the personal interview and—don't ever forget—the slightest comments of previous employers. I ended the melon-pinching editorial by quoting the Golden Rule. It applies just as much on the other side of the fence. I can't imagine anyone who does not know how *he* would like to be treated if *he* were applying for a job. But there are many people who have never been in the position of having to employ someone. So it is in order to make a few suggestions to the applicant for a job on how the employer likes to be treated:

Answer all correspondence promptly.

A letter of application should be typed and should be short. *All* written material submitted should be as neat as possible.

Make your employment history brief. State your experience, but *don't* try to magnify it by puffing up each individual task you did on every job. This misguided dropsy will do just the opposite of what you intended.

If you go to a city for an expense-paid personal interview, you should honestly and seriously be considering the job. That's what you are there for; you haven't been made queen for a day.

A personal interview is a two-way proposition: it gives the prospective employer and employee a chance to size up each other and to ask relevant questions. It is not an appropriate time for the would-be employee to tell his prospective boss how to organize and run the office.

Don't accept a job, intending to stay less then two years, unless the employer knows your intentions.

Don't accept a job until you are sure that you want to take it. Then keep your word.

When you take a job, notify any other employer who you feel reasonably sure is still considering you. (This takes a little judgment— not everyone to whom you have written a letter of inquiry wants to hire you.)

"Imagine Your Surprise!" extracted from the ASPO Newsletter editorial, May 1958.

A number of planners have spoken and written to me about unexpected discoveries they have made when they took over new jobs. On one day I had a visit from one newly appointed director and a long distance phone call from another one, each reciting with an air of surprise uncomfortable facts that they had discovered. Each man had been on his job about two weeks, each man was an experienced and technically competent planner, each job was comfortably over the average salary. It is easy to say, "Well, you should have looked into that before you took the job!" But there is no feeling quite so desperate as the one you have when you find out on your first day that you should better have stood in bed.

There are a number of reasons why people take a new job, many of them not related to the new job itself. Sometimes they are fleeing because of dislike for the present boss. Sometimes, after serving as low man on the totem pole for so long, they need to escape. Sometimes their debts nag them, or the climate nags them. And, of course, sometimes they are broke, out of work, and have five or six children to feed. Most of the time, they aren't seeking to get *into* a new job, they are seeking to get *out of* an old job.

There is nothing really sinful about this approach to changing jobs. The desire to ditch the old job, to see new landscapes, to start with a clean slate—this is part of the attitude of everyone who moves. The urge to leave, however, leads you to overlook, underestimate, or forget conditions of the new job that make it less attractive than you first thought. Because I can still recall that sinking feeling, I have made a little checklist for people considering a new job. In the first place, if there is something particularly and specifically unpleasant about your present job, you will check on this point in the new job. And you are almost certain to approve the new job if it is free from your *bete noir*, you won't stop to consider that there might be even worse *betes* of another color. So the first rule is be particularly careful if you know that some specific aspect of your present job is the most compelling reason for moving.

The next warning concerns brand new jobs and directors of brand new planning agencies. When a community first achieves grace through Recognition of the Value of Planning, it may be filled with the glory of Salvation, but it has little appreciation of how much it costs to operate the Church. To be less metaphorical, many well-meaning chairmen of fresh-hatched plan commissions hire directors on the strength of legislative promise of funds. When the director arrives, he finds that there is enough money for his salary but not a penny more for such frills as furniture, travel, office rent, maps, draftsmen, and secretaries. The word to the inquiring would-be director is: make them show you the bank deposit slip or its public finance equivalent for the *entire* budget. When it comes to public appropriations, don't trade in futures.

There is a variation of the foreshortened budget that seems almost a law of the land. This is where a brand new planning operation is to be financed by two or more governmental bodies. It is a safe bet that at least one of the sponsors will welsh on the promise to help support planning. Eventually you *may* get them all in, but it won't be easy. If you enjoy fund raising, then maybe you will like this.

Of course, a lot of new planning operations get established, solvent, and respected. So you can't automatically turn away from a new agency. Just try to avoid having them do a financial experiment with you as a laboratory animal.

I must point out to those about to take a new job, and who might forget it, that planning is quite a waste of time in poor government. The question is whether you want to plan, or you want to reform and reorganize government. Poor governmental organization where planning is just starting is slightly more hopeful than the same situation in a city or county that has long had a semblance of planning. In the latter case, the maladjustments will be firmly entrenched. The word here is to find out all you can about the total governmental organization before you decide. In particular, check the present method of handling basic planning controls: subdivision regulation, zoning administration, zoning variances, capital budgeting, renewal planning, building permits and inspection, traffic engineering, architectural control, air pollution abatement.

There are other aspects of government that you should check. What is the reputation of the government for honesty and efficiency? Try to get an unbiased judgment on this. If you are to replace a man on the job, find out why he left. Don't forget that most county governments are fundamentally rural governments and many are suspicious of city slickerisms such as planning, even though they may give lip service to it.

Probably most planners going into a new job have a pretty clear idea of what the new salary means. Don't forget that a 10 or 20 percent increase quickly disappears because of moving expenses, greater rent, higher cost of living. If you leave a subordinate position in one city to take the top job in another city, don't overlook the costs accompanying your increased social status.

No new job will be perfect. You cannot afford to dodge all problems or you just will not go anywhere. But try to be realistic and see whether a new job is actually worth taking. Or are you just running away from something you don't like about your present job?

Imagine your surprise *before* you change jobs, not after.

**Rules for Public Service, extracted from the
ASPO Newsletter editorial "The Payroller,"
April 1960.**

Too much security for the public planning employee may induce laziness, but that trait was probably latent in him before he ever started to work for a government. The public planner's knowledge of his own security, however, may lead to a characteristic that bothers people, and rightfully so. It may produce in the planner an inflated idea of the infallibility of himself or his calling.

Nearly everyone believes that the organization for which he works is pretty important in the grand scheme. This is especially true of one who works for a government, with justification. Government is particularly important in the area in which a planner works, in the building and rebuilding of public facilities and in the development and redevelopment of land. So, armed with the knowledge of governmental power and protected by the comfort of his personal security, the planner can easily slip into arbitrary dealings with the public. He is so familiar with the rules of the game that he forgets their complexity, forgets that an outsider may not understand or may have legitimate reason to question.

In a great part of his work, the public planner uses the police power. Zoning, platting control, building and housing codes are all authorized under the police power. And the police power can be by far the most arbitrary of all governmental powers. Actions carried out under it need only the justification of the general welfare of the public. It is very easy, when you do so many things clothed with this authority, to feel that anything you wish to do for the welfare of the public may also be done with the same authority. This leads to such proposals as using the zoning ordinance for questionable objectives: for getting additional right-of-way for streets, for example; or in using subdivision control to avoid the legitimate cost of expanding park facilities.

What with inflation, the low scale of government salaries, and the enormous amount of planning help sought, the public planner is also tempted to take outside work. Whenever a man works for two persons, there is always a chance for conflict of interest between his two employers. If he serves one well, he may serve the other ill. It would be miraculous if this had not occurred more than once, in view of the number of public planners who are consulting on the side.

In spite of the foregoing list of failings, I would pick the public planners and their honesty, intellectual integrity, common sense, and ethics over any group in *any* profession. However, there are some suggestions that may help them to be an even better group:

1.   The top employee in any planning agency should not be under civil service. He should be employed by and subject to dismissal by the chief executive of the government for which he works. This is subject only to the qualification that his status should be

the same as the legal, budget, and personnel officers. He should not be singled out for special treatment.

2. There should be definite rules on outside consulting work. In general, a public planner should undertake no work in the county in which his city is located. If he works for a county, he should not consult anywhere in his own county or in adjacent counties; for a metropolitan agency, nowhere in the region or a buffering tier of counties. Where his city has a boundary on a county line, that adjacent county, too, should be off limits.

3. Probably all work for private developers should be banned. Of course, it is plainly wrong to work for a developer on anything that is to come before the city for action. And even though the work is not with something that will need municipal approval, the public planner must know that he will be suspected of bias if that developer has appeared before the city in the past or will in the future.

4. *All* outside work should be cleared with the executive authority before accepting it. This protects both the planner and the city. If the rules prohibit outside work by government employees, the planner should obey the rules or get another job.

5. *All* outside work should be done on the planner's own time and away from his governmental office.

These five suggestions can be translated into rules that the planner should understand and agree to when he takes a public job, and rules that the governmental agency should put into effect for the current staff, whether it is hiring now or not. Two more suggestions to the public planner himself.

6. The planner should get a true picture of the extent of sovereignty of government, and of his place in it. He must not forget that democratic government, is *by* and *for* the people, as well as *of* the people. Government is a servant of the public, not its master. It follows then that the planner cannot be more than the agency for which he works; he, too, is a public servant.

7. A planner should not take a job with a governmental planning agency unless he has decided to be loyal to governmental policy. This relates to his freedom for independent action, particularly for independent speech. Planning—which is determining what to do and when to do it—is part and parcel with administration, with the executive phase of the operation. If the

executive is impotent, divided, torn from within, neither the planner's planning nor any other planning worth a damn will be carried out. This does not mean that, prior to the final decision, the planner should not advance his ideas, even though they might not be accepted. It is his function to bring originality and independent thought to bear on the problems. But before acceptance, his original thought should be aired circumspectly, perhaps only within the walls. After the decision is made, he must abide by that decision, even though it is not what he would have done. To paraphrase: If you can't join them, beat it!

The Paraprofessional, extracted from the ASPO Newsletter editorial "The Market for Planners: A Logical Analysis with a Leavening of Illogic," October 1966.

Currently, there are more jobs for planners in the United States than there are planners to undertake the jobs. There are two conclusions: either the jobs go unfilled or the jobs are filled by nonplanners.

Tight money is slowing down development and the apparent immediate local need for planners, but this will be more than offset by the planning prerequisites that are being written into federal grant programs, to say nothing about the inevitable development explosion when the money situation eases.

If we assume that planning is important, even necessary, we cannot accept the first conclusion. Therefore, we should look at the second conclusion: planning jobs filled by nonplanners. Is this as bad as it appears?

There are three types of nonplanners in planning positions. The first type is the person trained in some other field who has become interested in planning and has chosen planning as a career rather than staying with his original training. This includes all of the real pioneers, and a large proportion of the senior planners today. They have come from architecture, engineering, law, geography, and any number of other fields. This group would also include a small, but significant flow of young persons into the field today. By any objective standard, the quality of planning by this group of nonplanners is equal to that done by the formally trained planners.

There is a second group of persons who may be called "planners" because that is the only title available, but who are pursuing their own calling of architect, lawyer, engineer, public administrator, journalist, illustrator, economist, sociologist—within the planning department. They do not pretend to be planners, but they are members, important members, of the planning team. The team is an assembly of the bundle of skills that is necessary for a comprehensive attack on urban problems. To fill vacancies in these positions is nearly as difficult as to recruit additional planners.

The third type of nonplanner is the person with no formal training in one of the related professions and frequently, with no training beyond high school. He is not often in a position of great authority, rarely in the top job. He is a zoning inspector; he may even be the chief zoning administrator. He works on brushfire projects. He meets the public and explains the intricacies of the planning process. He makes needed surveys. He does statistical research. He frees the trained and experienced professional planner with special expertise from routine jobs that do not require special expertise. But there is a long and painful training process before most of these people are worth their salt. I propose introducing planning into junior colleges, picking up these people immediately after high school or retreading older persons, so that we can begin to build up a supply of paraprofessionals.

A good idea, logicially arrived at. At this point, we begin to learn about some of the problems that, although they may not be insuperable, are not necessarily going to be solved by logic.

Junior college training for planning technicians has been tried in a few schools, but the exposition of planning was so well done (or so poorly done, if you are trying to produce paraprofessionals), that most students opted for going on to work for a bachelor's degree.

The most difficult problem in junior college occupational training is the name given to the training and the trainees when they graduate. (Note even the word "occupational"; this has been necessary to set the junior college apart from high school, or perhaps even from reform school, training.) "Subprofessionals" is not good, it is too much like "sub-normal." Medicine, where the most experience has been, happily uses the term "paramedical" for the training in medical laboratory technology. Retail selling is now the "distributive" profession. "Technician" is not good, but "technology" is acceptable.

Civil service also presents problems: If you insisted on a bachelor's or master's degree in city planning before, how can you accept a two-year junior college degree now?

The quantity of paraprofessional planners needed presents a problem. While planners have what seems to them a shortage, in absolute terms the need is small. No occupational training program can be successful unless there is assurance of employment. Since junior college occupational training is geared to the local market, there may be no more than a dozen of the largest metropolitan communities that can offer reasonable prospects of employment to a reasonable size graduating class of planning technicians.

And, of course, there are all the problems of curriculum, text, teachers, internships, and financing for both students and the college.

One of the most successful planning departments in the country operated with two planning degrees on a staff of 60 persons. The problems are difficult, but they can be solved if we are willing to tackle them.

Public Service Technicians, condensed from "Junior College Training for Public Service," a speech at the Annual Meeting of the American Association of Junior Colleges, St. Louis, March 3, 1966.

The lead article in the February 1966 issue of *Changing Times* is titled "Tomorrow's Jobs—Where the Best Will Be." The very last paragraph of the article states:

> **Government.** Growingest growth industry of all, with big expansion in education, health services, hospitals, sanitation and police. Local governments, cities, counties, states, school districts—will account for most of the job increase; no appreciable expansion seen in federal manpower requirements.

Whether it is actually the *growingest industry* I haven't tried to verify, but government certainly is large and is growing. The present civilian employment in government is between 10 and 11 million—about 14 percent of the total employment in the United States. This is approximately the same number as work in all durable goods manufacture; it is more than work in all retail trade, and more than work in the combined fields of agriculture, mining, and contract construction. And government employment is growing more rapidly than total national employment.

I propose that the administrators of junior and community colleges look at the opportunities for occupational training in public service. I will narrow the field to public service with state and local (especially local) agencies, and to those jobs not connected with teaching. This brings the total public service employment figure down to about 4 million, but still considerably more persons than are employed in wholesale trade; or in the manufacture of both electrical and transportation equipment, including automobiles; or in the manufacture of both food products and apparel. In the medical field, state and local noneducational public service is nearly three times as great as the employment in hospitals in the United States.

The second important fact is that professionalization in public service has increased rapidly since the end of World War II. It would be difficult to document this completely, but two figures indicate the trend. In 1940, 6 universities in the United States were offering professional training in city and regional planning and graduating about 40 students each year; in 1966, 46 universities confered nearly 500 degrees in professional planning. The best general indication of professional public administration in the city is its adoption of the city manager form of government. In 1940 there were 302 city manager cities over 5,000 population, by 1966, there were 2,007 such cities, and the number increases by about 100 each year.

Professionalization (I shall not try to define the term) has taken place all through the public service. Besides city managers and city planners, there are professionals in public finance, public personnel, public health, police, fire, welfare, public housing, urban renewal, public works, traffic control, assessment. In some of these occupations there are, of course, analogous private professions, yet each one differs markedly from its private counterpart. In spite of the occasional pronouncement to the contrary, operating a government is not the same as operating a private business, and a public service professional is not the same as a private enterprise professional.

The next point is that there are not enough public service professionals being created to handle the work we have now. The shortage in the future, with the prospect of 100 million new urban residents before the end of the century, is overwhelming. There are four options: (1) you can overwork the professional and thereby reduce his effectiveness; (2) you can underutilize him by requiring him to do work that can be done by a less highly trained technician; (3) you can have the subprofessional jobs done improperly by inadequately trained persons; or (4) you can just forget having the work done at all.

The problem is the same that has faced the medical profession, the problem that the community colleges are already trying to solve.

A couple of months ago a small committee of members of the American Society of Planning Officials met for a day and a half with an American Association of Junior Colleges committee of community college presidents. Our original idea was to encourage community colleges to undertake the training of technicians for planning, renewal, and code enforcment agencies, where the shortage of personnel is probably relatively more acute than in any of the public service occupations. However, as the meeting progressed it was obvious that the total needs were much greater than we had thought, so the discussion developed into a coverage of the whole range of public service—except education. We had included on the ASPO committee a city manager, an urban renewal director, and a transportation and highway consultant, who were able to document the needs in these other branches of public service.

We know from the detailed management studies ASPO has made in cities throughout the United States that there are dozens of job classifications and thousands of positions that could be filled by public service technicians trained in properly designed two-year courses of study at the junior college level. I have prepared a list of these jobs—which I am certain is incomplete:

Public management
  administrative aides
Zoning and subdivision
  technicians
Statistical technicians
Computer technicians
Building inspectors
Assessors
Traffic engineering aides
Urban renewal technicians
Housing code enforcement
  officers
Public housing managers
Community organization
  workers
Welfare and family
  assistance workers

Recreation supervisors
Park operation technicians
Public finance technicians
Public personnel technicians
Public records technicians
Protective services; police and
  fire
Public health personnel, admin-
  istration and technical
Environmental health
  technicians:
    Water supply
    Sewage treatment
    Solid waste disposal
    Air pollution abatement
Library assistants
Engineering aides

Draftsmen	Surveyors
Cartographers	Photogrammetric technicians

I believe the following four types of training and curricula in public service are appropriate for the community college:

1. A new two-year program for specific public service technicians, such as the zoning technician, the building inspector, the assessor, the recreation supervisor.

2. An orientation toward public service in some of the current terminal occupational training programs, such as engineering aide, draftsman, computer technician.

3. In-service training programs in practically every aspect of public service.

4. The introduction of new courses, and a new orientation in some of the existing courses, for study of urban affairs and urban problems in the two-year transfer programs.

Even in my own mind there are many unanswered questions. But no doubts. I know the need, I believe in the importance, and I have confidence in the ability and facilities of the community college to contribute. And I believe there is no better way to earn the title of *community* college, than to serve the community by helping to train for those skills that every community so badly needs.

About the Planning Profession

**Measuring Success, extracted from the
annual report of the executive director,
March 19, 1957, at the ASPO National
Planning Conference, San Francisco.**

I attribute much of the current acceptance of planning to the fortunate fact it was *not* accepted too well years ago. It has much resemblance to good professional fortune telling. If you can predict a nice unpleasant disaster that will happen unless your advice is followed, and your listeners *don't* take you advice, and the disaster *does* happen—boy, you've got it made! Now we are popular, we are well paid, we are appreciated and respected, we are the subjects of flattery by imitation (and by a certain amount of muscling-in).

If these be the criteria of success, we have achieved it. But if success be measured by the steady progress upward of our cities, then I question seriously whether we have gone very far.

We have a big bold program for urban renewal. But what progress is there in tearing down a slum in the city while we build one with new green lumber in the suburb? Is success achieved by the construction of 3,000 miles of new superhighways each year while you add 3 million new autos each year to use it? Is progress measured by new dwelling units, or new double-shift schools?

It seems to me that we are becoming quite skilled in cleaning up some of the past mistakes in urban development. This is necessary and it is good. But I feel we are awfully shy of any real facility for guiding urban growth into the future.

It is probably a most inappropriate analogy, but I think of the development of physics. I do not have any sense of the growth of urbanistics to compare with the progress from the corpuscular theory of light through the wave theory to the quantum theory. I do not look on new towns that we have built and new shopping centers that we design as having the basic solidity of conception that we have in the controlled release of atomic energy.

It seems to me that most of what we are doing is pouring the same old dead wine into new bottles. It is still flat and sour and filled with unpleasant particles of sediment. But I am not really pessimistic. I think that on the horizon I see some glimmer of dawn. I believe that slowly and painfully we are beginning to understand what we are trying to do. It is slow, but it is certain.

The State of Planning, extracted from the annual report of the executive director, May 20, 1958, at the ASPO National Planning Conference, Washington, D.C.

I feel some discontent with the word "planning" to describe what we are interested in and what we do. A literal definition covers only a part of our activity, falls far short of what are plainly our goals. "Planning" as a name for our activity is like "medicine" as a name for the activity that word designates. While the dictionary definition is now wider, medicine once meant the healing pills, powders, and pul-vules, the lotions, salves, and ointments, the calomel, castor oil, and cascara of our childhood—of my childhood at least.

This activity we call planning also has gone far beyond the prepara-tion of maps and schemes into an activity, a technology, that calls on and receives support from a host of sciences and arts. It gets more dif-fuse, more difficult to pin down—yet at the same time it gets stronger, more useful, and gathers more unquestioning adherents.

The reason for this is pretty clear. We've got the job now of building and operating an urban environment for 2 million more people each year—first 2 million more, then 3 million more. Of the making of peo-ple there is no end! We have to house them, feed them, clothe them, employ them, give them a social, economic, and physical milieu that keeps them healthy and happy. This is a broad problem, a problem of infinite variety—but nevertheless it is clear-cut and well defined. We call it "planning," although the field is more than any dictionary yet includes in its definition of that term.

We do not know how to solve this problem—hence we turn to re-search. That is why, in my opinion, the field of planning becomes stronger. We have recognized there are no eternal verities. We are learning to question pronouncements, to question authoritarian type precepts.

It is clear that planning will never solve completely all the problems of providing a perfect living environment—no more than medicine will ever completely conquer all illness and disease. But this is good. We have in planning a field, activity, science, art—whatever we choose to call it—that will always be new, fresh, and exciting because it is always renewing itself, always examining itself, always improving itself.

The state of planning, I can report, is excellent. It is moving into an era of prosperity, a boom. Our biggest danger is inflation—inflation of our egos and of our authority and of our position. We must be careful not to let inflation get out of hand.

"The Planning Present," extracted from a speech, May 11, 1959, at the 25th ASPO National Planning Conference, Minneapolis.

The "present" is a thin knife edge, with the past on one side and the future on the other, a separation having zero dimension in time. If you wish to talk about the present, you are forced to talk about a period which really starts somewhere in the past and ends somewhere in the future—terminal points that each must determine for himself. I see the present as beginning three or four years ago and ending three, four, five years in the future—the stretch of six to ten years that we are now in the middle of!

I think the key to planning in the present is that the idea of planning is widely accepted. This does not mean that we are beyond the need for explaining any particular plan that we prepare—explaining in a persuasive manner, perhaps. But the people who quarrel with the basic premises of planning, which are (a) we've got some mighty difficult urban problems, and (b) we should use the best brains and talents and methods we can scare up to solve these problems—people who object to those premises are getting scarcer and scarcer.

As a cause or result of this acceptance—it makes no difference—we have planning by a host of agencies that were undreamt of years ago. There is an endless number of activities in planning. Some will have beneficial effects in the future, some will be found to be boondoggling of the most useless kind.

This diversity of activities obscures two of the most significant aspects of planning today. The first of these is the adoption of planning, its philosophy, and its techniques by nongovernmental groups. We in planning were certainly a minority group at one time. Now there is an ever-growing number of the old line trades, professions, and businesses who accept and use planning: banking, real estate, department stores, public utilities, the construction industry, the transportation industry, architecture—yea, even the engineers.

I took a quick census of the ASPO Board of Directors to see what fields they represent. Only four of the 12 members of the board are professional planners. Each of these can be said to have another important calling: two are engineers, one is a lawyer and engineer, and one is an alderman. Of the others—three are lawyers; one is a banker; one is an industrial realtor; one is a clothing manufacturer; one is a chief municipal executive officer; one is a newspaper publisher and banker. But, of course, every single one of them is a planner, as I define a planner—which is a person who believes in using the best available information and talent to attack the problems of urbanism.

What does this mean? It means that the planning idea is no longer the sole possession of a chosen few persons, but that it belongs to anyone and everyone who wants to use it. And there are a lot of people who do want to use it. The planning idea is like democracy—it just doesn't work if it is in the hands of a few. In fact, it is not democracy until it is part of the basic attitude of the people. Actually more than just being *like* democracy, planning is *part* of democracy!

The second aspect of great significance is the proliferation of research, the dissatisfaction with pat answers, the disbelief that *old* is necessarily *good*—or that old is necessarily *bad*—the spirit of inquiry and questioning. This spirit of inquiry was missing from the past. It is no criticism of the early planners to say that their bump of skepticism was underdeveloped. In the protective armory of a minority group it is necessary that the members have definite ideas and a high opinion of the value of those ideas. Otherwise the chances for survival are slim. This is why minority groups frequently have strong traditions and immutable rituals—such as master plans and pyramided zoning ordinances. As long as there was a suspicion that the planning idea was less than respectable, then so long were the guardians of that idea zealous in preserving it in its pristine form. But now we can afford the luxury of self-examination and self-criticism. None of us can tell what revelations introspection may bring, but I believe that we can antici-pate great changes in our methods of meeting urban prob-lems—startling changes!

You must either live and grow in step with the times, or the world leaves you behind. The planning idea will live and grow with the world and at the world's speed. Even if we wished, there is nothing any of us can do to prevent its development. Nevertheless, we should recognize this and be prepared to hear ideas the likes of which we never heard before. We should be prepared for economic and social and physcial analyses on a scale with a boldness that we cannot now imagine.

In any situation, the seeds of its future are here—now—today—in the present. I believe that the most important seeds of the planning future will be found not in the techniques, the tools, the ordi-nances—in zoning, subdivision control, capital budgeting, master plans—but, instead, will be found in the *people* now planning, the *spirit* in which they are now questioning, and the *courage* with which they hear the answers.

**The Contribution of Lawyers, extracted
from the ASPO Newsletter editorial "Planning and the Lawyers," April 1967.**

It is conventional to say that we draw on many fields—engineering, architecture, economic, sociology—and synthesize the wisdom of these arts and sciences into an art of planning. We include law as a major contributor to planning.

I would question the contribution of *law* to planning and would substitute the contribution of *lawyers*. We are inclined to think of planning as a science, although we know that it is not, and uncon- sciously to draw a parallel with the contribution of mathematics, a hard science, to physics, another hard science. But arts advance not so much by the contribution of techniques as by the contribution of men. The electronic organ has not produced a composer for the organ who is superior to Bach.

This, then, is a brief note—as the lawyer would say—and acknowl- edgment of the debt planning owes to lawyers. I will omit footnotes, *supras, infras, ibids,* and case citations but can supply them if necessary.

The most obvious contribution of lawyers has been to the problem of translating plans into reality. To start with the early recorded history of modern planning in United States: I do not have a list of delegates to the first national conference on city planning in 1909, but a major participant was Andrew Wright Crawford, assistant city solicitor for Philadelphia, who remained active in the field for many years. At the second conference in 1910, a young lawyer was serving as secretary of the conference, a man with undoubtedly the longest continued service to planning of anyone in the United States: Flavel Shurtleff. In 1911, the names of two other illustrious lawyers were on the list of conference delegates: Lawson Purdy and Frank Backus Williams.

Probably the most important series of events in American planning was the appointment and report of the New York Heights of Building Commission, the appointment and report of the successor Commis- sion on Building Districts and Restrictions, and the adoption of the New York zoning resolution—all taking place from 1912 to 1916. Here, again, were Mr. Williams and Mr. Purdy and, as chairman of both commissions, the lawyer who was often, with justification, called the "father of zoning": Edward M. Bassett.

So that this will remain a note and not a volume, I jump to 1926: *Euclid* v. *Ambler* and Alfred Bettman, Esq. Mr. Bettman's name had first appeared in the 1913 National Conference on City Planning Proceedings as a member of the conference committee. In the first hearing before the U.S. Supreme Court, the zoning ordinance of the village of Euclid, Ohio, had been declared unconstitutional. A rehearing was granted and Mr. Bettman was permitted to file a brief *amicus curiae* on behalf of the National Conference on City Planning, the National Housing Association, and two state associations of planning boards. The Supreme Court reversed itself and upheld the constitutionality of zoning. Mr. Bettman's brief undoubtedly preserved zoning for us.

Alfred Bettman was a charter member and the first president of the American Society of Planning Officials. A simple tabulation of his contribution to planning would take many columns, as would the contributions of the other lawyers named. And I add to the list Walter Blucher, lawyer, planner, and charter member and first executive director of ASPO. Several lawyers have served as president of ASPO since Mr. Bettman: Morton Wallerstein, Benjamin Kizer, Harold Shefelman, David Craig—all distinguished contributors to planning. I will not try to name all of the persons trained in law who have contributed and are contributing to planning. There really are not great numbers of them, but their influence far outweighs their numbers.

One interesting subfield, however, is worth commenting on. This is education for planning: Charles Abrams, Esq. (Columbia University); Paul Davidoff, Esq. (Hunter College); Burnham Kelly, Esq. (Cornell); William Doebele, Esq. (Harvard); Jacob Beuscher, Esq. (University of Wisconsin); Daniel Mandelker, Esq. (Washington University School of Law).

This note could be expanded to a full monograph, and I hope that someone does it someday. I would also hope that it would expand to include some quasi-lawyers among planners, lawyers without portfolio who have in turn contributed to the law profession, men such as Hugh Pomeroy, Gordon Whitnall, John Reps.

But the monograph, if and when it is written, must concentrate on the men, not the profession. Because any accomplishments that planning can boast of in the past, or can hope for in the future, are, in my opinion, the accomplishments of individual persons and not of a system, a science, or a discipline.

"Professional Registration of Planners,"
condensed from a speech at the American
Society of Civil Engineers Annual Conference, New York City, October 14, 1958.

I am confused by registration for planners. I am confused by the problems presented; I am confused by my own attitude toward it.

Members of the American Society of Planning Officials are a
motley crew. We have students, we have housewives. We have garden
club ladies and League of Women Voter ladies. We have ministers,
lawyers, mayors, city managers, councilmen, county supervisors. We
have young people, we have old people. We have members of plan
commissions, of boards of appeals, of boards of zoning adjustment, of
planning departments, of citizens' planning councils, of housing
authorities, of city councils. We have college professors, and we have
persons who are practically illiterate (to judge by the letters they write
us). And, if you won't pin me down on the definition of a planner, we
have city planners, county planners, metropolitan planners, regional
planners, state planners, national planners, civil servants, political appointees, private consultants. We have on our rolls about 90 percent
of the members of the American Institute of Planners.

While I cannot state that the official position of the American Society of Planning Officials on the subject of registration and certification
of planners is thus and so, I can speak with a great deal of freedom and
frankness because I can tell you what my experience has shown me is
the attitude of ASPO members on some of these things—the attitude
of persons who are definitely interested in planning and interested in
the things that planning can do. My confusion is primarily in answering the question on how or if you register, and the efficacy of registration and certification. I am not the least bit confused about the ideas,
the needs, the desires of those members of my organization who represent the public—the plan commissioners, the city councilmen, the city
managers, the mayors, the leaders of civic organizations.

What do these persons want? They want the best possible advice,
the best possible guide, the best possible plans for the future development of the city or county or region in which they live or in which
they serve. They would like to have some method by which they
could prejudge the quality of service they might get from the person
they hire as an employee, as a planning director, as a consultant, as an
advisor. They really don't care what this person calls himself, whether

he calls himself a planner, an engineer, an architect, a geographer, a butcher, a baker, or a candlestick maker. In general, however, because the type of work they want done, or the advice they want to receive on their problems of urban development, falls generally in a field that is called city planning, they may be inclined to turn first to a person who call himself a city planner or who claims to be able to do city planning. Some do, but others think of what they want done as only an architectural design problem (such as a civic center or a new library or a revitalization of a central business district) or as an engineering problem (streets, expressways, sewerage systems, water supply) and they turn first to (and hire) architects and engineers. And these persons frequently have no experience with, background for, nor interest in the relationship of the individual project to the whole community, city, or metropolitan area.

If there is any single idea that is characteristic of the planning approach to a problem, it is this: that any project, change, improvement in an urban area is properly designed only when it is designed in the context of the entire urban environment of the area, when it is designed in the light of its relationships with all facets of the urban operation. This distinguishes *city planning* from *project design.* So how can the person who will give the *gestalt* approach be identified?

In many states, the city officials will turn to the advertisements (called professional cards) in the magazine published by the state league of municipalities. I checked one of these listings. From firm names and, in some cases, the names of principals of the firms, I was able to list 18 persons who claimed proficiency in city planning.

I checked our own membership list, and I checked the roster of the American Institute of Planners. Not a single one of these persons listed was a member of either organization. I certainly do not claim that such membership is a criterion of a man's ability to do urban planning. But if a person claims that he can keep abreast of the rapidly changing field of urban planning without following the literature, the research publications, the meetings of either of these organizations—then I am suspicious. When 18 of them, all from one state, seem to be able to do this—well, the term "feather merchant" seems to be most appropriate. It is probably not quite so slanderous as fraud, fake, or quack. If these words seem unusually strong, I can assure you it is purely intentional.

The federal government has done much to encourage city and metropolitan planning through a system of matching grants-in-aid. At the same time, the smell of fresh federal money has brought out one of the most doubtful collections of urban specialists you could imagine. And I hasten to add that some of them are members of the American Society of Planning Officials.

While working on these remarks, I received a call from the chairman of a newly formed regional planning commission that was in the process of interviewing consulting firms regarding a comprehensive plan for the region. They had received proposals from several firms, and the price quoted varied from $150,000 to $200,000. But a proposal had been received the night before from a firm located in Chicago. What could I tell him about this organization? For obvious reasons, I am not too happy about being pinned down on any particular consulting firm, although I am willing to get violent anonymously, as I have here. But this firm that I was asked about had a very impressive sounding name, had proposed to do the job for $49,000, and was an organization that I had never heard of, nor had I ever heard of the principals in the firm. And while I do not claim to know every planner in the United States, I certainly am reasonably familiar with the names of the competent planning consultant firms in the city of Chicago. I still haven't been able to locate *anybody* who ever heard of either the firm or its two principals. You know without my saying it that the commission would be throwing its money away if it hired this outfit for $49,000.

I am not prepared to say exactly what a planner is, but I will say that if you *are* a planner, you *know* it and you are able to recognize a fake. It isn't quite like the old question about hippopotami: "How can you tell a boy hippopotamus from a girl hippopotamus?" And the answer was, "Who cares about it but another hippopotamus?" A lot of people care about who is a planner and who isn't a planner. The kind of future this nation and other nations all over the world will have is going to depend quite directly on how well planners perform this particular art, how well we know and practice the particular profession that is called city planning. We cannot afford to be led up blind alleys by self-styled urban experts who are simply out to make a killing.

I don't know whether registration will help the members of the American Society of Planning Officials to achieve the ends they seek. I don't know whether local registration, or state registration, or national registration—or any of these—would be worthwhile. I don't know whether registration or certification will work. When it comes to deciding whether or not registration is better handled by the government or through the auspices of a professional society, I am also confused. I think this is a problem that has to be faced in any professional organization and in any form of registration—whether you can actually measure and certify competence.

There are a number of different views on registration. Naturally enough, some of these will revolve around the security, protection, recognition, prestige, and status of the persons who are hired as planners or who call themselves planners, or the persons who want to do planning, or the persons who think they can do planning, or the persons who think nobody else can do planning but themselves. These attitudes are natural and they have their place, I assume, in the growth of professions or skills or arts.

Nevertheless, for me the most valid approach to the problem is one with the object to determine how we can get the best job of guiding urban development and urbanization, how we can assure ourselves as citizens and public officials that we are not being shortchanged or flimflammed, either with malice aforethought, or in all innocence. Other considerations must necessarily be secondary.

Claim-Jumping: A Questionable Practice, condensed from the annual report of the executive director, April 3, 1967, at the ASPO National Planning Conference, Houston.

We who work in planning or are interested in planning bear a great semantic burden. We have a field or an art or a science that we call capital P Planning, but when we speak of it, the capital P is not audible, and the word sounds the same as small p planning, which is a generic term that encompasses many, many activities. In fact, we are not averse—when we speak to the unanointed—to illustrating our specialty by pointing out that planning is a ubiquitous exercise of the human intellect, that we *plan* family picnics and vacations, that an insurance agent *plans* our life insurance program, that a sales manager *plans* his next sales campaign, etc. So why should we not *plan* our cities? To plan is only doing what comes naturally.

The problem is that we may have convinced ourselves that because we can demonstrate the universal presence of, or at least the universal need for, small p planning, we must try to rise to the occasion and prove our ability to foresee the future and plan every aspect of the human comedy. Which is quite a load, even for our broad shoulders.

It is not important to find the precise date at which a new idea gets started, but it does help us to be objective about a chameleon trade like ours if we can arrange the changes in some order. We started out at the turn of the century hoping to produce the City Beautiful. By the early '30s we had shifted our emphasis, spurred primarily by the increasing fallout from the Detroit auto factories, to building the City Efficient. Then came the Great Depression of the '30s, and we became aware of Social Problems. Certainly, one reason for our awareness was that many of us were actively participating in a Social Problem by being members of the disadvantaged majority.

It was at this time that we discovered the social problem of slums, which could be solved by clearing the slums and building public housing, a kind of urban development with which we seemed to be familiar. There was a split in our ranks at that time, with some of us going into the infant field of public housing and some staying with conventional planning, albeit a modified planning, now with a mission and a social conscience.

The Great Depression also made us aware of economic problems, not only because of our miserable personal economic situation, but also because economics was forcefully pointed out to us by the National Resources Planning Board. However, our planning publications and our plans did little to reflect our concern with the economy until after the war. By then our communities were succumbing to industrial promotion fever and each hopeful town and village was insisting that we demonstrate its superb qualifications to be the site of the next General Motors assembly plant. You had to be careful in those days— if you told the truth you might get fired.

Sometime early in the '60s, social planning began to take over. We saw it in the literature and heard it in the orations and smelled it in the politics. Two groups were involved in this takeover.

The first group was from among our own fellows. They argued that planning made no sense unless it was directed toward improvement of the human condition—an argument that is hard to refute. They believed that they detected no such improvement resulting from our previous operations; ergo, we should attack the problem directly by shifting to social planning. The second group came from outside the planning fraternity. These were the militant sociologist types, people who understood perfectly how society functions, who were about as objective in their scientific approach to urban problems as an old-fashioned Dodger fan was in his theories about baseball umpires.

The socially conscious planners beat their breasts and cried "Mea culpa! How poorly we have planned!" The planning conscious sociologists agreed: "You certainly are at fault, you have done a lousy job," and proceeded to give a bill of particulars, reciting all the social ills that planning had failed to correct. "Failed to correct" is too mild, the social types would argue; planners should be held responsible for *creating* a passel of social problems, not the least of which were slums and discrimination against minority groups. The two groups disagreed, however, on which was the proper one to carry on in the future. The social types felt that they were the qualified ones because only they understood society. On the other hand, the planning types believed *they* should do social planning because capital P Planning is an esoteric theology understood only by the initiated—which they were, by their own admission.

It also became apparent during all this brouhaha that the two groups agreed on another point—physical planning was a pejorative term. There are few greater insults you can offer a man than to call him a physical planner. Physical planning—our traditional concern with rational prearrangement for transportation, public facilities and the use of land, air and water—is kitchen work, grubby details fit only for the scullion mentality.

What we are really seeing here is reciprocal claim-jumping. The militant social scientists—instinctively recognizing the fatuity of their multiple-correlation exercises and envious of the status and financial triumphs of their hard-science brethren, the physicists, chemists, and mathematicians—have decided to move into planning where the prospects seem better for striking it rich. Those planners who are hell-bent to solve all mankind's problems seem to feel that they have completely worked out their own diggings, and they now want to work the other fellow's claim because he has obviously spent all of his time assaying samples and none of his time panning gold.

We all probably agree basically with each group's assessment of the other's accomplishments: planning has not been nearly as effective as we hoped it would be; and social science has been the most dilettante of all fields of study. But I, for one, take exception to the idea that either the planners or the social scientists are omniscient and, therefore, uniquely qualified to lay claim to everything in sight.

No one would dispute that our planning has been improved because we are becoming aware of people and social problems. To the list of outside experts who have given us better understanding of what we are or should be doing, we can add the economists, the systems analysts, the ecologists, and several other groups. We should never let up in our enthusiasm for absorbing any new ideas that can help us do better what we have set out to do.

That is just the point. We must recognize that we do have a job to do, which is to plan for the human habitat. We must be honest, at least with ourselves, and admit that we are not yet doing it very well. But just because we have not been able to do the job to our own satisfaction, this is no reason to spread ourselves even thinner and to take on all the other jobs in this world. It seem to me that what has moved some of our own planners to grandiose ideas may not be so much a belief that they have all the answers, but more that we are not doing so well here, so maybe we will do better elsewhere.

I think we should stick to working our own patch of ground. Maybe we should even consider erecting a fence around our claim. Not so much to keep others out, but to keep ourselves in—to keep us from jumping to another claim where we have no business to be, before we have fully worked out our own.

Valedictory, August 28, 1967

Quoted from the president's address to the International Federation for Housing and Planning International Conference, West Berlin, Germany, August 28, 1967.

The truth is that in spite of the miracles of radio and television and communications satellites and high-speed printing and mass production of books, magazines and newspapers, we still learn best by the very, very primitive method of talking face-to-face with people and seeing things with our own eyes.

One of the most dangerous diseases in the world today is xenophobia—the fear of strangers, of foreigners, of persons who differ from you in language, in clothing, in religion, in food, in race. Xenophobia is a disease that can be fatal for the entire world.

The only lasting cure is for us to meet and see and talk to each other, to understand that we, as human beings, have the same hopes and desires, and the same questions and problems—we are more alike than we are different.

Bibliography

The Dennis O'Harrow papers include both published editorials, speeches, and articles and various unpublished materials. The bibliography is chronological with publications listed alphabetically, except for a separate listing of research studies undertaken for specific clients.

Unpublished sources are not available to the public. However, the American Planning Association may allow material from this book or from original published sources to be reprinted if requests are made in writing to: Publications Departments, American Planning Association, 1313 E. 60th St., Chicago, IL 60637.

Sources are given for articles written for various journals and speeches published by other organizations.

The abbreviation *ASPO* is used for the American Society of Planning Officials. (This organization, together with the American Institute of Planners, formed the American Planning Association in 1978.) *ASPDA* is the Association of State Planning and Development Agencies, for which O'Harrow was assistant director and newsletter editor during the period 1948–53, when ASPO served as the secretariat; this organization is now defunct.

The bibliography was compiled with the assistance of the Merriam Center Library, which houses the archives of ASPO, ASPDA, and the American Planning Association.

1948
Editorials—*ASPDA Newsletter*, Vol. 3
  "British Industrial Estates." (December, p.1)
  "Greener Pastures." (September, p.1)

1949
Editorials—*ASPDA Newsletter*, Vol. 4
  "Form and Content: Or You Don't Have to Eat the Whole Egg." (November, p.1)
  "These Tax Claims." (Feburary, p.1)
  "What Chains?" (July, p.1)

Speeches and Papers

"Patterns and Progress of Development in the Nation and in the Mid-Continent Area," delivered to the Mid-Continent Council of Development Agencies, Denver, Colorado, October 18.

"Planning," delivered to the League of Women Voters, Evanston, Illinois, September 22.

"Planning—"Why?" delivered to city planners by Mayor Thomas A. Burke in Cleveland, Ohio, October 11. (Ghost written.)

"The Suburbs' Stake in the City," delivered to the Women's Joint Committee on Adequate Housing, Chicago, Illinois, June 2.

"What Is City Planning?" delivered at Northwestern University, Evanston, Illinois, November 11.

Articles

"The Economic Improvement of Depressed Areas." *Public Aid in Illinois* 16 (January): 2–3.

"State Planning and Development: Review of the Planning Year (1958)." *APSO Newsletter* 15 (January): 1.

1950
Editorial—*ASPDA Newsletter*, Vol. 5

"The Smell of Soap." (April, p.1)

Speeches and Papers

"Planning and Zoning," delivered to the North Dakota League of Municipalities, Valley City, North Dakota, September 11.

"What Is City Planning in the United States," delivered to the German Personnel Delegation, Public Administration Center, Chicago, Illinois, April 13.

"What They Didn't Teach," delivered at the University of Chicago, June 5.

Articles

"Growing Pains of a Village Government: Problems of Developing a New Town With Private Capital." *American City* 65 (January): 80–81.

"How to Recruit a City Manager." *Public Management* 32 (November): 242–44.

"State Planning and Development." *Book of the States 1950–1951.*

Research Report

"Cemeteries in the City Plan." ASPO Planning Advisory Service Report No. 16 (July).

1951
Speeches

"Performance Standards in Industrial Zoning," delivered at the ASPO National Planning Conference, Pittsburgh, Pennsylvania, October 15. Also ASPO Planning Advisory Service Report No. 32 (November). Also published in Jersey Plans 12 (Winter): 14–28.

1952
Speeches and Papers

"Civic Planning Advocated for the Area's Future," delivered at Marietta College, Marietta, Ohio, April 10.

"Nearly Everyone Lives in a City," delivered at Columbia College, Chicago, Illinois, April 3.

"The Need for Local Planning Assistance," delivered at the Southern Association of State Planning and Development Agencies Conference, Memphis, Tennessee, October 14.

"The Place of Mass Transportation in the City," delivered to the Citizen's Public Utility Committee for the Metropolitan Area of Chicago, Illinois, May 24.

"Planning Expedites Intergovernmental Relations," delivered at the First Tennessee Conference on Intergovernmental Cooperation, Nashville, Tennessee, April 30.

"Planning Procedure for Small Towns," delivered at the Seventh Annual Town and Community Planning Conference at Iowa State College, Ames, Iowa, May 9.

"The Relation of Health and Welfare Planning to City Planning," delivered to the National Council of Social Work, Chicago, Illinois, May 30.

Articles

"Planning Gets More of Cities' Budget." Florida Municipal Record 25 (June): 8.

State Planning and Development." Book of the States, 1952–1953.

"Why This Interest in City Planning?" *Public Management*
34 (May): 88–101.

1953
Editorials—*ASPO Newsletter*, Vol. 19

"Lady, *Please* Don't Pinch the Melons!" (July, p. 49) Reprinted in *Public Personnel Review* 15 (January): 2.

"A Law Can Be No Better Than Its Enforcement." (January,
p.1)

"So You Are Going to Solve the Traffic Problem." (February, p. 9).

Speeches and Papers

"City Planning and Air Pollution," delivered to the Midwestern Air Pollution Prevention Association, Gary, Indiana,
October 16.

"City Planning for Reduced Noise," delivered at Fourth
Annual National Noise Abatement Symposium at the Armour
Research Foundation, Chicago, Illinois, October 23.

"Overall Planning," delivered to the Municipal Association
of South Carolina, Greenville, South Carolina, February 16.

"Solving Metropolitan Area Problems," delivered to the St.
Louis Metropolitan Plan Association, St. Louis, Missouri,
December 2.

"Subdivision and Fringe Area Control," delivered to the
American Public Health Association, New York, New York,
November 11. Also delivered to the Middle States Public Health
Association, St. Paul, Minnesota, June 2, 1954 and published in
American Journal of Public Health 44 (April): 473–77.

"What Kind of Training Do Public Agencies Require of the
Planners They Hire?" delivered to the Conference on
Education of Planners at Wayne State University, Detroit,
Michigan, October 15.

Research Report

"Criteria and Standards for Shopping Center Stores." ASPO Planning Advisory Service Report No. 47 (February).

1954

Editorials—*ASPO Newsletter*, Vol. 20

"Dog Days." (August, p. 65–66)

"The Function of the Public in a Variance Hearing." (December, p. 115–16)

"Homeostasis." (July, p. 57–58)

"Member of the Board of Appeals." (January, p .1)

"The Middle Future." (February, p. 9–10)

"Planners Must Try Their Zoning Cases." (March, p. 19)

"Planning for Planners." (November, p. 103)

"Public Transportation Axioms." (April p. 27–28)

"Queen for a Day." (May p. 39–40)

Speeches and Papers

"City Problems of Today and Tomorrow," delivered to the Scientific Research Society of America at Argonne National Laboratory, Argonne, Illinois, June 23.

"Local Planning in a Metropolitan Region," delivered to the Detroit Regional Planning Commission, Detroit, Michigan, May 1.

"Making the Modern City Livable," delivered at the annual meeting of the Ohio Planning Conference, Akron, Ohio, February 25.

"Planning and Public Economics," delivered at the annual conference of the Pennsylvania Planning Association, Pittsburgh, Pennsylvania, November 11.

"State Planning," delivered at Harvard University, Cambridge, Massachusetts, May 22.

"Town Planning and Public Transit," delivered to the Canadian Transit Association, St. Andrews, New Brunswick, Canada, June 15.

Articles

"Every Man His Own Prophet." *Better Roads* 24 (December): 3–4.

"Planning and Zoning—Developments in 1953." *The Municipal Yearbook 1954*, International City Managers' Association.

"Three Basic Levels in Planning." *Michigan Municipal Review* 27 (May): 86–87.

1955

Editorials—*ASPO Newsletter*, Vol. 21

'The Battle for Brains." (September, p. 69)

"Cooperation with the Inevitable." (October, p. 77–78)

"Entropy." (July, p. 49–50)

"Louisburg Square and Others." (December, p. 97)

'Nineteen Hundred Fifty-Four." (January, p.1)

'The Peoples' Problems Are Planners' Problems." (March, p. 17–18)

"Planning in the United States: Strength Through Diversity." (May, p. 33–34)

"Small Talk or Prejudices." (August, p. 61–62)

"Urban Renewal—The Whole Job." (February, p. 9)

Speeches and Papers

'The Capture and Training of Planners," delivered to the Chicago Chapter, American Institute of Planners, Chicago, Illinois, June 9.

'The Church and City Planning," delivered at Park Forest Unitarian Church, Park Forest, Illinois, May 31.

"Our Expanding Cities," delivered to the Conference of National Organizations, Atlantic City, New Jersey, June 20.

"Planning Put to Work," delivered at the Development Conference, Connecticut Federation of Planning and Zoning, Hartford, Connecticut, March 24.

"Steps to Secure Sound Zoning," delivered to the Great Lakes States Industrial Development Council at Notre Dame University, South Bend, Indiana, January 7.

'Trends in Planning," delivered at 41st annual conference of the International City Managers' Association, Bretton Woods, New Hampshire, October 5. Also published in *Public Management* 37 (November): 252–254.

"Zoning for Industry," delivered at the annual conference of the American Society of Civil Engineers, New York City, October 27.Also published with the title *Industrial Zoning Standards*, ASPO Planning Advisory Service Report No. 78 (September).

Articles

"Planning and Zoning—Developments in 1954." *The Municipal Yearbook 1955*, International City Managers' Association.

"When to Promote and When to Recruit." *Public Personnel Review* 16 (June: 176–77.

1956

Editorials—*ASPO Newsletter*, Vol. 22

"By Whose Thumb?" (June, p. 41)

"Cities of Distinction." (May, p. 33)

"Clearings in Prefab Jungles." (September, p. 65–66)

"Consulting Fees—Part One." (March, p. 17–18)

"Consulting Fees—Part Two." (April, p. 25–26)

"The Dilemma of the Nonconforming Use." (January, p. 1)

"Divine Rights and Civil Rights." (December, p. 89–90)

"Notes for Budgeters." (October, p. 73–74)

"The Personnel Situation." (February, p. 9–10)

"Telephones and Challenges." (July, p. 49)

Speeches and Papers

"Are Fringe Areas 'Free Riders?' " delivered at the annual meeting of the Municipal Finance Officers Association, Washington, D.C., June 5. Also published in *Municipal Finance* 29 (November): 100–4.

"Meeting the Planning Needs of Metropolitan Areas," delivered to the Pittsburgh Chapter, American Society for Public Administration, Pittsburgh, Pennsylvania, May 22.

"Physical Aspects of the Problem: What Can be Done in New York City?" delivered at the New York University Conference on New York City's Traffic Problems, New York City, January 19.

"Planning Your Community for Tomorrow," delivered at the annual meeting of the Warren Chamber of Commerce, Warren, Ohio, November 27.

"Roads to Renewal," television program, WTTW Chicago, September 5.

"Special Districts and Authorities," delivered at the annual conference of the American Public Works Association, Forth Worth, Texas, September 26. Also published in *Public Works Engineers' Yearbook 1956*, American Public Works Association.

Articles

"Planning and Zoning—Developments in 1955." *The Municipal Yearbook 1956,* International City Managers' Association.

"Town and City Planning." *Encyclopaedia Britannica,* 14th ed.

1957

Editorials—*ASPO Newsletter,* Vol. 23

"The Form of Growth." (October, p. 81–82)

"Hours of Leisure." (February, 9–10). Reprinted in *The American Recreation Society Bulletin* 9 (July): 10–11.

"Idealism, Realism, and Moderate Sin." (July, p. 57)

"On Waking in the Middle of the Night." (January, p. 1–2)

"On Walking." (August, p. 65)

"People." (May, p. 41–42)

"Planning: In or Out?" (March, p. 17–18)

"The Quantity of Government." (September, p. 73–74)

"A Time to Be Mellow." (December, p. 97–98)

"The Zoning Breakthrough." (November, p. 89)

"Zoning for Sale." (June, p. 49)

Speeches and Papers

"Chicago Grows—By Plan or By Chance?" delivered to the South Side Planning Board, Chicago, Illinois, May 2.

"City Planning and Traffic Engineering," delivered to the Institute of Traffic Engineers, Detroit, Michigan, September 26.

"The Community and the Family," delivered to the National Congress of Parents and Teachers, Cincinnati, Ohio, May 20.

"The Coordination of Governmental Action in a Metropolitan Area," delivered at the Symposium "The New Highways: Challenge to the Metropolitan Region," sponsored by Connecticut General Life Insurance Company, Hartford, Connecticut, September 9–12.

"Memorandum on Urban Renewal," delivered to the Council of State Governments, Chicago, Illinois, September 5.

"Planning for a Workable Program for Community Development," delivered to the New Jersey League of Municipalities, Atlantic City, New Jersey, November 21. Also published in *New Jersey Municipalities* 35 (January): 25–27, 29–31.

"Simplicity in Planning," delivered to the Stark County Regional Planning Commission, Canton, Ohio, January 14.

Articles

"The Churches and Urban Redevelopment." *The City Church* 8 (May-June): 18–21.

"Comment on Paul J. Mishkin's 'A Critical Look at Zoning Law' " *Municipal Law Service Letter* 10 (January): 5–7.

"Moving Too Slow or Too Fast?" *Journal of Housing* 14 (October):
312.

1958

Editorials   *ASPO Newsletter*, Vol. 24

"Anyone for Planning?" (November, p. 93–94)

"Community Contribution and Community Control." (March, p. 17–18)

"Etcetera." (July, p. 57–58)

"A Good Planer." (December, p. 105)

"Ideas-Ahead-of-Their Times." (April, p. 25–26)

"Imagine Your Surprise." (May, p. 33–34)

"Let's Get the Record Straight." (September, p. 77)

"The Next Ninety-Nine Years." (January, p. 12)

"The Next Step." (October, p. 85)

"Words, Words, Words . . . ." (August, p. 65–66)

Speeches and Papers

"Impact of Air Pollution on Our Economics and Society: Industrial and Community Development and Property Values," delivered at National Conference on Air Pollution, Washington, D.C., November 19.

"Plan Talk and Plain Talk," delivered at the Southern California Planning Commissioners' Congress, Pasadena, California, January 9.

"Planning and the Future," delivered at the University of North Carolina, Chapel Hill, North Carolina, May 2. Also delivered to the Southeast Chapter of the American Institute of Planners, Nashville, Tennessee, December 3–6.

"The Principles of Zoning," delivered to the Women's City Club of New York, New York City, January 15.

"Professional Registration of Planners," delivered at the annual conference of the American Society of Civil Engineers, New York City, October 14.

"The Role of Planning in Modern Local Government," delivered to the Colorado Association of Planners, Boulder, Colorado, February 15.

"Urban Sprawl: Patterns, Implications, and Prospects—Principles of Metropolitan Regional Planning," delivered at the National Health Forum, Philadelphia, Pennsylvania, March 18.

Articles

"Cities Don't Need to be Ugly." *Kiwanis Magazine* 43 (June): 11.

"Comprehensive Planning and Major Federal-City Programs." *City Problems of 1958*, U.S. Conference of Mayors.

Research Report

"Churches and Planning Controls." ASPO Planning Advisory Service Report No. 106 (January).

1959

Editorials—*ASPO Newsletter*, Vol. 25

"Buffer Zones." (July, p. 61–62)

"Explanation and Prediction." (October, p. 85–86)

"The Future Belongs to Those Who Plan for the Future." (April, p. 29–30)

"Jobs in Planning." (August, p. 69–70)

"Magic and Master Plans." (February, p. 9)

"Observations on Air Polluting." (January, p. 1–2). Reprinted in *Minnesota Municipalities* 44 (June): 175, 184, 186.

"An Open Letter to a Businessman Just Appointed to the Planning Board." (March, p. 17–18). Reprinted in *Texas Town and City*, 45 (June): 22.

"A Prayer for Perspective." (November, p. 97)

"Virtue Begets Its Own Punishment; or the Bigger They Are, the Harder They Fall." (December, p. 105)

"Why Plan? Why Not!" (May, p. 37–38)

Speeches and Papers

"Commentary on Paul J. Mishkin's paper 'Are the Established Legal Principles of Zoning Valid and Adequate for Current Conditions of Rapid Metropolitan Growth and Urban Development?' " delivered at the Local Government Law Round Table of the Association of American Law Schools, St. Louis, Missouri, December 28. Also published in *Municipal Law Service Letter* 10 (January): 5–7.

"Flexibility in Planning—the Present Problem," delivered at the annual.meeting of the International City Managers' Association, St. Louis, Missouri, October 28.

"Getting the Job Done," delivered at the Arizona City-County Planning and Zoning Conference, Tucson, Arizona, October 2.

"Metropolitan Problems—How Do You Solve Them?" delivered at the Local Government Conference on Planning, Pennsylvania Planning Association, Pittsburgh, Pennsylvania, November 12.

"The Planning Present," delivered at the ASPO Annual National Planning Conference, Minneapolis, Minnesota, May 11.

"Public Planning and Private Plans," delivered at Company Planning Conference, sponsored by Roosevelt University, Chicago, Illinois, June 11.

"Shape of Plans to Come," delivered at the annual meeting of the Ohio Planning Conference, Columbus, Ohio, February 16.

"Simplicity in Planning," delivered at the annual meeting, Stark County Regional Planning Commission, Canton, Ohio, February 16.

Articles

"Annexation: Good or Bad? *Changing Times* 13 (November): 15–17.

"Letter to the Editor" (on Swimming Pools). *Recreation* 52 (January): 4–5.

1960

Editorials—*ASPO Newsletter*, Vol. 26

"Can a Man Serve Two Masters?" (March, p. 17–18)

"The First Rotten Apple." (February, p. 9–10)

"Government Is Different from People." (May, p. 33–34)

"Indeterminancy and Planning." (June, p. 41–42)

"Like Concessions, Man!" (August, p. 69–70)

"The New Millionaires." (October, p. 89–90)

"The Payroller." (April, p. 25–26)

"The Petty Trader." (November, p. 97–98)

"Planning—The Next Ten Years." (January, p. 1–2). Reprinted in Bureau of Community Planning, University of Illinois *Newsletter* 1 (June): 1–2.

"This Is Your City." (September, p. 81)

"Who Should Plan?" (December, p. 105–6)

Speeches and Papers

"Nature and Functions of Urban Areas," delivered to staff engineers at the Taft Sanitary Engineering Center, Cincinnati, Ohio, March 28.

"Realism in Community Development," delivered at the Second Annual Community Development Conference, Ohio State University, Columbus, Ohio, November 4. Also published in *The Tennessee Planner* 21 (September): 1–8.

Article

"County Planning—What Is It?" *County Officer* 25 (April): 104, 127.

Book Review

The San Francisco Bay Area: A Metropolis in Perspective by Mel Scott. *Land Economics* 36(August):311–12.

1961

Editorials—*ASPO Newsletter*, Vol. 27

"ASPO: 1950–1960–1970." (January, p. 1–2)

"Dear Sir: Our Ninth-Grade Civics Class . . . ." (September, p. 85–86)

"A Department of Urban Development." (February, p. 13–14)

"Federal, State and Local." (April, p. 29–30)

"Hugh Reynolds Pomeroy." (August, p. 69)

"Information Theory." (October, p. 93–94)

"Onions *in Onions* 95¢." (December, p. 113–14)

"The Planning Commission." (July, p. 61–62). Reprinted as "Save Planning Commissions," *St. Louis Post Dispatch,* July 29.

"Reprise: A Department of Urban Development." (May p. 37–38)

"Smoke Means Work." (March, p. 21–22)

"Tools for Planning." (November, p. 101–2)

Speeches and Papers

"Civic Psychology," delivered to the Canadian Federation of Mayors and Municipalities, Halifax, Nova Scotia, Canada, June 2.

"Planning Criteria for Metropolitan Areas," delivered at the Conference on Environmental Engineering and Metropolitan Planning, Northwestern University, Evanston, Illinois, March 21.

"Things to Come in Land-Use Control," delivered at the Annual Convention of Society of Industrial Realtors, Miami Beach, Florida, November 14.

"Why Are We Going Where?" delivered to the Southwestern Legal Foundation, Dallas, Texas, October 26.

"Why Planning and Financing Must Be Related," delivered to the Railway Systems and Management Association, Chicago, Illinois, April 14.

Book Review

"And on the Eighth Day . . . ." by Richard Hedman and Fred Bair, Jr. *ASPO Newsletter* 27 (September): 87.

1962

Editorials—*ASPO Newsletter*, Vol. 28

"Design for Research." (July, p. 69–70)

"A Few Figures from Thistles." (April, p. 33)

"For Planning and Development: A New Technique." (May, p. 41–42). Reprinted in *Virginia Planning News.* (November, p. 1–3)

"Jacobin Revival." (February, p. 13–14)

"The Keys to the Kingdom." (March, p. 25)

"Many Tongues." (October, p. 97–98)

"A New Contest." (August, p. 77–78)

"Newcomers to Planning." (January, p. 1)

"The Public Defense." (November, p. 105)

"Salaries in Scale." (September, p. 89–90)

"Scylla and Charybdis." (December, p. 121)

Speeches and Papers

"Interprofessional Relations," delivered at the annual conference of the American Institute of Planners, Los Angeles, California, October 15.

"Land-Use Controls and Comprehensive Planning," delivered at the annual meeting of the Michigan Society of Planning Officials, Bay City, Michigan, May 17–18.

"New Techniques for Shaping Urban Expansion," delivered at the Housing and Home Finance Agency Conference on the Problems and Needs of Urban Expansion, Washington, D.C., June 7–9. Also condensed and published as ASPO Planning Advisory Service Report No. 160 (July).

"The Planning Agency's Role and Asthetics," delivered to the Twenty-Seventh Annual Institute of Government, "Urban Amenity—Goal for Municipal Policy," at the University of Washington, Seattle, Washington, July 11.

"The Urban Future," delivered before the Joint Conference, National Sand and Gravel Association and National Ready-Mixed Concrete Association, Chicago, Illinois, February 6.

Article

"Strength Through Diversity." *The Town-Planning and Local Government Guide* (Melbourne, Australia) 6 (January): 145–146.

1963

Editorials—*ASPO Newsletter*, Vol. 29

"Competitive Exclusion." (October, p. 101–2). Reprinted in *Forward* 1:9–10.

"The Critics." (November, p. 109)

"The Expert Witness." (December, p. 121–22)

"Faster, Faster." (January, p. 1)

"Hang Together or Hang Separately." (March, p. 25)

"The Numbers Game." (September, p. 93–94)

"Publish or Perish." (February, p. 9)

"A Rose by Another Name." (May, p. 41–42)

"Shades at the Banquet Table." (June, p. 65-67)

"Sharon Biedelmaier's Grandmother." (April, p. 33)

"Wherefore by Their Fruits . . . ." (July-August, p. 81–82). Reprinted in *Area Digest* 2 (Winter): 16–18)

Speeches and Papers

"The American City—Can It Be Saved?" delivered at the University of Cincinnati under the Sperry Hutchinson Lectureship Program, Cincinnati, Ohio, April 9.

"The Four Horsemen of Planning," delivered at the annual conference of the Florida Planning and Zoning Association, Sarasota, Florida, December 4–7.

"Land Use Planning—The Role of State Government," delivered at the Annual Southern Governors' Conference, White Sulphur Springs, West Virginia, August 19.

"Public Service: The Puissant Minority," delivered at the University of Cincinnati under the Sperry Hutchinson Lectureship Program, Cincinnati, Ohio, April 9.

"The Roles of Engineering and Urban Planning in the Urban Highway System," a paper delivered at the Ninth Pan American Highway Congress, Washington, D.C., May 6–18. Published in the OAS Official Records OEA/Set.K/1.9.1.

"The Organization of the Local Planning Function." Urban Planning for Public Officials. Session 2. Chicago: University of Chicago Industrial Relations Center.

1964

Editorials—*ASPO Newsletter*, Vol. 30

"License for Bearbaiting." (November, p. 117)

"Member of the Wedding." (March, p. 25)

"The Mink-Trimmed Beer Wrench: A Sort of Christmas Fable." (December, p. 125)

"The Moving Target." (September, p. 93)

"New Towns or New Sprawl." (October, p. 105–6)

"Odds and Ends." (January, p. 1)

"Progress Is People." (May, p. 57–59)

"Semantic Suicide?" (June, p. 69)

"Too Much and Too Soon." (April, p. 33)

"Who Shot the Albatross?" (February, p. 17)

"Zoning: What's the Good of It?" (July-August, p. 77–78)

Speeches and Papers

"The Future of the Central Business District," delivered at the annual convention of the National Retail Merchants Association, New York City, January 8.

"Organization of Intergovernmental Relations," delivered at the annual meeting of the Highway Research Board, Washington, D.C., January 16.

"The Production of Planners," delivered to the Jubilee Year Tour Group of the Town Planning Institute of Great Britain, Pittsburgh, Pennsylvania, September 28.

"Who Plans?" delivered at the annual conference of the Texas Municipal League, Dallas, Texas, October 4–6.

1965
Editorials—*ASPO Newsletter*, Vol. 31

"ADP and the Planning Agency." (October, p. 105–6). Paper delivered at the Annual Conference on Urban Planning Information Systems and Programs, sponsored by Northwestern University and ASPO, Chicago, Illinois, September 15–17.

"Begin at the Beginning." (November, p. 113–14)

"Chop Suey and Other Matters." (August, p. 81)

" . . . Except in Areas Used for Business or Industry." (July, p. 65–66)

"No Time for Softness." (January, p. 1–3)

"Out of Little Acorns." (April, p. 29–30)

"Plans and Anti-Plans." (December, p. 121–22)

"The Shape of World War III." (September, p. 89–90)

"What Price Half-Life?" (March, p. 21–22)

"Zoning May Not Be Planning, But—." (February, p. 9)

Speeches and Papers

Dallas 1985—What It Takes," delivered at Southern Methodist University, Dallas, Texas, September 29.

"The Issues of the Day and the Emerging Urban Society," delivered at the annual conference of the American Institute of Planners, October 17.

"Planning: A New Look," delivered to the Citizens Council on City Planning, Philadelphia, Pennsylvania, June 1.

"Some Thoughts on Evolution," delivered at the dedication of the new headquarters of the International Federation for Housing and Planning, The Hague, Netherlands, December 13.

Article

"Urban Planning." *Grolier Encyclopedia.*

1966

Editorials—*ASPO Newsletter,* Vol. 32

"Expressways and Parks: A Suggestion." (January, p. 1–2)

"Fish or Cut Bait." (April, p. 37–38)

"From the Backs of Old Envelopes." (December, p. 125–26)

"The Lord Gave and the Lord Hath Taken Away." (November, p. 117)

"The Market for Planners: A Logical Analysis with a Leavening of Illogic." (October, p. 109–10)

"A New Tune for the Piper." (March, p. 21–22)

"Replication; or Double the Trouble." (February, p. 9–10)

"Strategy Is the Way You Make a Big Buck." (September, p. 97–98)

"What This Country Needs Is a Good . . ." (September, p. 97–98)

Speeches and Papers

"Junior College Training for Public Service," delivered to the American Association of Junior Colleges, St. Louis, Missouri, March 3.

"My Brother: My Friend," delivered at the annual congress, American Public Works Association, Chicago, Illinois, September 15.

"A Place for Everything," delivered at a symposium on "The Maine Coast: Its Prospects and Perspectives," Bowdoin College, Brunswick, Maine, October 20.

"Planning for Messopolis: A Neglected Problem," delivered at the ASPO National Planning Conference, Philadelphia, Pennsylvania, April 18. Also published in *Planning* 1966, p. 266–75.

"President's address," delivered at the 28th World Congress of the International Federation for Housing and Planning, Tokyo, Japan, May 14.

Other Publication

"Foreword" to *The Zoning Game; Municipal Practices and Politics*, by Richard F. Babcock. Madison, Wisconsin: University of Wisconsin Press.

1967

Editorials—*ASPO Newsletter*, Vol. 33

"A Broad Brush with a Sharp Edge." (June, p. 69–70)

"Claim-Jumping: A Questionable Practice." (May, p. 57–58). Reprinted from paper delivered at the ASPO National Planning Conference, Houston, Texas, April 3.

"The Living End: the City and Its Critics." (January, p. 1–2)

"Metropolitan Planning—Now and Later." (February-March, p. 13–14.

"Passing Grades." (July, p. 85–86)

"Planning and the Lawyers." (April, p. 37–38)

"The Plan's the Thing." (August, p. 97–98)

"Zoning: What's New?" (September, p. 105–7)

Speeches and Papers

"The Future of Planning in Puerto Rico," delivered in San Juan, Puerto Rico, August 10.

"Planning, Zoning and Aesthetic Control," delivered at the American Bar Association seminar on aesthetics and the law. Chicago, Illinois, June 3.

"President's Address," delivered at the International Federation for Housing and Planning International Conference, West Berlin, Germany, August 28.

"Regulation of Land Use for Urban Growth," delivered at the University of Chicago, March 21.

"Urbanization in Developing Nations," delivered at the ASPO National Planning Conference, Houston, Texas, April 5.

Articles

"Fighting the Urban Problem," guest editorial in *Public Management* 49 (May): 105–6.

"A Place for Everything." *Maine Digest* 2 (Winter): 13–18.

"Preface," *Principles and Practice of Urban Planning*. 4th Edition. International City Managers' Association, 1968.

Sponsored Research Projects

The APSO program of research services for specific clients was initiated by Dennis O'Harrow and began with the following studies, which he prepared, in some cases with the assistance of members of the research staff. Only those marked with an asterisk were released by the sponsor for distribution. However, many of the basic findings and the practical expertise gained by the ASPO research staff were incorporated in ASPO's Planning Advisory Service and in research reports for general distribution. The dates given indicate when the project was started; many continued over a period of one or two years.

Administrative Studies for Planning Agencies

1960 Northeastern Illinois Metropolitan Planning Commission

1961 Pittsburgh City Planning Commission

City of Des Moines, Iowa

City of Denver, Colorado

Indianapolis-Marion County Planning Department

City of Norfolk, Virginia

Baltimore County, Maryland

1962 Broome County, New York

1963 Tucson-Pima County, Arizona

San Jose, California, Planning Department

1964 Phoenix, Arizona, City Planning Department

1966 Atlanta, Georgia, Metropolitan Planning Commission

Kanawha County, West Virginia, Planning and Zoning Commission

Special Research Services and Studies

1952 "Economic Analysis of Proposed Neighborhood Shopping Center," Bismarck, North Dakota.

"Planning Problems in the Vicinity of the Atomic Energy Commission Savannah Power Plant." United Community Defense Services.

1957 "Report on Zoning." Wauwatosa, Wisconsin.

1961 "State Responsibility in Urban Regional Development." Council of State Governments.*

1962 "Urban Trends: The City of the Future." American Public Works Association.*

1963 "Bibliography on Regional Planning." American Society for Public Administration.*

"Metropolitan Planning Survey 1963." U.S. Housing and Home Finance Agency.

1964 "Citizens Manual: Planning for Minnesota Communities." Minnesota Department of Business and Development.

"Metropolitan Planning Survey 1964." U.S. Housing and Home Finance Agency.

1966 "The Urban Planner in Health Planning: Problems and Possibilities." U.S. Public Health Service.

"New Directions in Connecticut Planning Legislation." Connecticut Development Commission.

"Problems of Zoning and Land-Use Regulation." National Commission on Urban Problems. (Published 1968)

"Zoning Study: Proposed System for Regulating Land Use in Urbanizing Counties." Anne Arundel County, Maryland and Marcou, O'Leary & Associates.*

1967 "New Communities and Land-Use Control." Advisory Commission on Intergovernmental Relations and National Commission on Urban Problems.

"A Planning System for Puerto Rico." Puerto Rico Planning Board.

Zoning Ordinance Review
1961 Sioux City, Iowa

Fairbanks, Alaska

1962 Wauwatosa, Wisconsin

1963 Denver, Colorado

Glenview, Illinois

1964 North Las Vegas, Arizona

1967 Atlanta, Georgia

Biographical Note on Dennis O'Harrow

Dennis O'Harrow served on the ASPO staff for nearly 20 years, from January 1948 to 1952, as assistant director, as associate director in 1953, and as executive director from January 1954 until his death on August 29, 1967. Until July 1953, his responsibilities also included the positions of assistant director and newsletter editor for the Association of State Planning and Development Agencies, a period during which ASPO served as the ASPDA secretariat. In 1951, he was the director of the Youngstown Comprehensive Plan, on leave of absence from ASPO.

Throughout these years he served on more than 30 boards and committees as a representative of the planning profession or as a representative of ASPO. Among them, in chronological order: he was a member of the National Industrial Zoning Committee from its founding in 1948, and chairman 1959–66. In 1954, he was named a member of the Bureau (Board of Governors) of the International Federation for Housing and Planning, headquartered in The Hague, Netherlands; he served as deputy president 1962–66, and was elected IFHP president at the Tokyo World Congress in 1966—the only American to be so honored since 1935, and only the second in the 50-year history of the organization.

During the '50s, Dennis O'Harrow began his service on committees such as the Housing and Home Finance Agency Advisory Committee on Urban Renewal, Highway Research Board Advisory Committee on the Study of Parking, National Urban Transportation Committee, Conference on Metropolitan Area Problems, National Association of Housing and Redevelopment Officials' International Committee, and the Interamerican Planning Society Advisory Council.

His official role in the 1313 Public Administration Center began in 1954, and he was chairman of the Public Administration Service Board of Trustees, 1955–60. He also served as visiting lecturer in planning at the University of Chicago.

He was a member of the Selection Committee for the Sears Foundation City Planning Fellowship Program since its establishment in 1958.

He was elected the first president of the village of Park Forest in 1949 and later served on the Park Forest Plan Commission and Zoning Board of Appeals.

For the city of Chicago, during the '60s he served on the Committee on Urban Progress and the Commission on Human Relations' Advisory Housing Committee.

In 1961, Dennis O'Harrow was appointed by Illinois Governor Otto Kerner as Commissioner of the Northeastern Illinois Planning Commission.

On the national scene, he was a member of the U.S. Public Health Service National Advisory Committee on Community Air Pollution, the Federal Power Commission Industry Advisory Committee on Underground Transmission, the U.S. National Committee of the International Council for Building Research Studies and Documentation, and the National Association of Home Builders–Urban Land Institute Advisory Committee on Residential Land Use.

He was a member of the Alfred Bettman Foundation Board of Trustees, Roosevelt University's Advisory Council for the Graduate Program in Urban Studies, and the URBANDOC Project National Advisory Council.

Dennis O'Harrow became a member of the American Institute of Planners in 1952 and served on several AIP committees. He was given the AIP Distinguished Service Award in 1965. In 1964 he was named an Honorary Member of the Town Planning Institute of Great Britain, becoming the second American to hold this honor. The ASPO Medal, the Society's highest honor, was awarded to Dennis O'Harrow, posthumously, at the 1968 ASPO National Planning Conference.

He was a member of Chi Epsilon (honorary civil engineering), Tau Beta Pi (honorary engineering), and Sigma Xi (honorary science).

He was the author of innumerable technical articles for journals and encyclopedias, prepared several ASPO administrative studies, and wrote major reports published by various agencies as well as by ASPO. He prepared several zoning ordinances and subdivision control ordinances. He also served on various editorial advisory boards.

Dennis O'Harrow was born in 1908. He graduated in civil engineering from Purdue University in 1931 and was employed by the Indiana State Highway Commission, 1931–33; as director of research, Indiana State Planning Board, 1934–38; and as planning technician, National Resources Planning Board, 1939–42. He was a Lieutenant Commander, U.S. Naval Reserve, 1942–46. He then worked as a private planning consultant until joining the staff of ASPO in January 1948.

Biographical Note on
Marjorie S. Berger, Editor

Marjorie Berger was associated with Dennis O'Harrow throughout his years at ASPO, serving as ASPO assistant and associate director, as writer/editor of the *Newsletter* and other publications, and as organizer of the annual conferences. During her ASPO career, 1947–76, she also was author, editor, and advisor for a variety of books and reports concerned with careers in planning, and was involved with ASPO's international activities. She became an affiliate member of AIP in 1963 and served on several AIP committees. She was elected to the Council of the International Federation for Housing and Planning in 1970 and became an honorary vice-president of IFHP in 1980.

Marjorie Berger was graduated from the University of Chicago, having majored in public administration, and did graduate work in economics at the American University in Washington, D.C. From 1942 to 1946, she served in the Foreign Information Branch of the U.S. Office of Price Administration as Assistant Chief of the United Kingdom Section and as an economist on the Advisory Staff of OPA's Economic Advisor's Office, writing research reports and providing information requested by government officials, members of Congress, and journalists.